Voting and Eligibility Age in Sweden, 1866–1921

"Bengt Sandin's excellent study is the first to argue that age is fundamental to uncovering the reasoning behind shifts in voting rights as Sweden moved toward a more democratic, urban, and industrialized society. This thoroughly researched history skilfully integrates age as the key to the reasons behind voting rights shifts in Sweden's changing cultural, demographic, class, gender, and economic landscape over more than five decades. Politicians grounded their arguments in traditional values favouring perceived "stable groups in society" namely, "those who were married and settled." The democratic reforms denied the growing population of unmarried, working-class young men and women the right to vote. Changing voting age requirements curbed the political power of cities with a growing population of young working-class people. Voting age shifts generally maintained that political power would continue to be held by those traditionally defined as "mature" enough to guarantee the stability of the existing power structure. Sandin shows that this complex history is fundamental to understanding continuing debates over voting rights in modern democracies."

—Kriste Lindenmeyer, Ph.D.
University Emerita, Rutgers University—Camden.

"In *Voting and Eligibility Age in Sweden,* 1866–1921*: Democracy with Guarantees* Bengt Sandin offers the first comprehensive treatment of the politics of the voting rights age at the time when parliamentary democracy was introduced in Sweden. The book shows how perceptions on the democratic rights of young people (and sometimes not so young people) among members of parliament and government reflected conflicting ideas about class, family, rural interests, and demographic change – an issue that remains controversial also in democracies today."

—Ludvig Beckman,
Department of Political Science, Stockholm University.

"Bengt Sandin's Voting and Eligibility Age in Sweden, 1866–1921: Democracy with Guarantees is a book for our own historical moment. The book addresses a missing subject in historical social and political studies. With today's concerns about the maturation of Gen Z combined with threats to democracy, an original investigation of the historical relationships between "coming of age" and political participation over a critical one-half century could not be more timely. Sandin

creatively integrates his long-standing expertise as a historian of children and youth, with political history both of Sweden in particular and the Western democracies in particular. Voting and Eligibility Age in Sweden merits a wide readership."
—Harvey J. Graff, Professor Emeritus of English and History, Ohio Eminent Scholar in Literacy Studies, and Academy Professor, *Ohio State University*

"In this book, the historian Bengt Sandin lays bare the intricate connections between class, gender, perceived moral standing, and other crucial dimensions of the social order as they have informed the debates over suffrage reforms in late 19th and early 20th century Sweden. While previous studies in general have stressed the struggle to extend voting rights to women and the working class, Sandin's important contribution to this field of study is to focus on age as a less controversial delimiting principle even as it nonetheless indirectly achieved aims close to the heart of those seeking to conserve a more traditional and conservative order. Limiting voting rights in terms of age thus operated as a nominally universal logic even as it de facto functioned as a proxy for more openly discriminatory principles."
—Lars Trägårdh, Professor of History at the *Institute for Housing and Urban Research (IBF), Uppsala University.*

"Bengt Sandin's impressive volume makes a compelling argument to consider the political importance age limits have played (and still play) for electoral reform. His insights from the case of Sweden, especially concerning the socioeconomic and cultural narratives of age and gender reformists employed to defend their interests, show us how to regard the significance of the minimum voting age for the history of democracy in new ways."
—Birgitta Bader-Zaar, *Department of History, University of Vienna.*

Bengt Sandin

Voting and Eligibility Age in Sweden, 1866–1921

Democracy with Guarantees

palgrave
macmillan

Bengt Sandin
University of Linköping
Linköping, Sweden

ISBN 978-3-031-95275-3 ISBN 978-3-031-95276-0 (eBook)
https://doi.org/10.1007/978-3-031-95276-0

This work was supported by Magnus Bergvalls stiftelse Olle Engkvist stiftelse Steve Jones Dagmar Saléns Stiftelse Åke Wibergs stiftelse

"Politikens Åldersgränser; Rösträtt och valbarhet i Sverige från 1840-tal till 1920-tal" by Bengt Sandin, 2024. Published by Makadam förlag

This Palgrave Macmillan imprint is published by the registered company Springer Nature Switzerland AG.
The registered company address is: Gewerbestrasse 11, 6330 Cham, Switzerland

Maria

Preface

This book has its origin in a project that sought to illuminate the obstacles to voting that remained after 1921, when "universal and equal" suffrage was introduced in Sweden. Creative, enthusiastic meetings and discussions led to new knowledge about the meanings of democracy and its limits after 1921. For my part, new questions about the period before 1921 were also raised. The project was led by the economic historian Fia Sundevall, associate professor at the Department of Economic History and International Relations, Stockholm University. The project also involved, besides myself, the historian Martin Ericsson, the historians of ideas Annika Berg and Julia Nordblad, the economic historian Mattias Lindgren, and the political scientist and childhood researcher Jonathan Josefsson.

This book is about how the period before 1921 had a decisive impact on the design of voting regulations after the reforms of 1918–1921. I am very grateful to all those who have provided feedback in different ways during the work. It has been an exciting journey. It started with the seminars in the research group, where I could present my material for discussion on several occasions. As I have subsequently tried to formulate my thoughts, many people have listened patiently and suggested new angles, and others have read and commented on drafts at different stages. Above all, Jonathan Josefsson and Fia Sundevall have listened, read, and commented. I am very grateful for having had the chance to work with you and for everything I have learned. Jonathan and I have cooperated in gathering material and writing articles that in different ways touch on what is discussed in this book. Ludvig Beckman's useful responses have also been incorporated in this book.

Johanna Sköld, Eirinn Larsen, Silke Neunsinger, Christina Florin, Ingemar Norrlid, and Kjell Östberg have also asked important questions as the text began to take shape, which led to further clarifications and digressions. Maija Runcis, Malin Arvidsson, and Jonathan Josefsson then read the manuscript. Finally, Ingrid Söderlind, Lars Berggren, Fia Sundevall, Alf Sjöblom, Kriste Lindenmeyer, and Maria Sundkvist read all or part of the text. The many wise, critical, and constructive comments led me to rearrange parts of the text and further explore some matters. I hope I have made good use of your contributions.

I am also very grateful that Viveka Adelswärd let me into the Barony of Adelsnäs estate archive. The physical proximity to the mill environment in Åtvidaberg and the letters and actions of the proprietor Theodor Adelswärd as a person have made me aware of the fascinating complexity of the social position of the elites and the significance of social development for the growth of democracy in Sweden.

I have also had the opportunity to discuss the project with economic historians and political scientists at Gothenburg University and the political science seminar at Linköping University. Various drafts of the work have been presented at the annual meeting of the Swedish Political Science Association, the Nordic Historians' Meeting, and the European Social Science History Association in 2021.

I am also extremely grateful to the staff at the City Archives in Norrköping, the National Library, the Labour Movement Archive and Library, and the university libraries at Uppsala and Linköping for helping me navigate the archives and libraries' recesses.

During the work on this study I was employed as a researcher at the Labour Movement Archive and Library. It was a pleasant and instructive time of learning for me, even though COVID-19 made it difficult for me to be physically present.

The Swedish text has been translated in English by Alan Crozier.

Linköping, Sweden Bengt Sandin

Contents

List of Figures

List of Tables

CHAPTER 1

Introduction

In the early twentieth century the right to vote was a key issue in Swedish political debate. In November 1918 the Liberal Party under Nils Edén's leadership and the Social Democrats under Hjalmar Branting resolved to propose a suffrage reform. The Social Democrats accepted the Liberals' demand that the right to vote be reserved for tax-paying citizens, and it turned out that they were prepared to give up their demand for voting from the age of 21, for which they had been campaigning since the beginning of the suffrage struggle in the late nineteenth century. A note in the draft document by the Social Democratic minister of ecclesiastical affairs, Värner Rydén, stating that "the age limit for universal suffrage should be lowered from 24 to 21" was deleted in the final text of the communiqué.[1] This was a significant stance to adopt. The Social Democrats showed their willingness to implement a suffrage reform, but did it mean that they simultaneously abandoned an important principle?

In Rydén's draft, we can follow how the joint communiqué evolved. The two parties described the reform they spoke of as universal and equal suffrage, but they did not agree on everything. Women's suffrage was one premise that they shared, but the issue of tax payment and tax liability as a basis for the right to vote was a matter for discussion. Nor was the voting age self-evident. The Liberals and the Social Democrats who formed a government in 1918 could not agree on the age limits. The Social Democrats had long taken the line that the voting age should be the same as the age of majority. But this was one point at which Liberals[2] and

B. Sandin, *Voting and Eligibility Age in Sweden, 1866–1921*,
https://doi.org/10.1007/978-3-031-95276-0_1

leading representatives of the Right[3] took a different view. The high age limit for male suffrage that the leader of the conservative Farmer´s Party, Arvid Lindman, had established in 1909 resonated with the Liberals' proposals from the last decade of the nineteenth century. The negotiations about a suffrage reform between the governing parties and the leaders of the Right in the autumn of 1918 had resulted in proposals for further inquiries, leaving the issue to be considered during the ordinary session of Parliament in the spring of 1919. The Right was left out when the Edén government published its declaration of intent.

The political crisis in Sweden and the food shortage at the end of the First World War, together with the revolution in Russia, the civil war in Finland, and the political unrest in Germany, meant that the question of allowing the people to exert an influence through the ballot box could no longer wait. Värner Rydén's diary gives a dramatic and graphic description of the atmosphere—the threat of revolution. The suffrage issue had not been resolved by extending male suffrage in elections to the Second Chamber in 1909. Women and a large share of men still lacked the right to vote. And in the cities, people were hungry and angry.

Although Arvid Lindman had given more men the right to vote in elections to the Second Chamber, this was limited by the requirement to have an income or property and to have paid taxes. Also, no one could vote if they were dependent on poor relief or had been declared bankrupt, and men also had to have completed their military training. At Lindman's suggestion, Parliament had also introduced a higher age limit for voting in elections to the Second Chamber. Men had to have reached the age of 24 in the year prior to the election. Before that, the voting age for men in both municipal and Second Chamber elections had been the same as the age of majority, that is, 21. That was a requirement the Social Democrats had demanded and on which they had campaigned. Women could not vote in elections to the Second Chamber, but unmarried women could vote from the age of 21 in municipal elections if they had declared income and paid taxes. After a change in tax legislation in 1908, this also applied to married women. It was clear that they were dependent on their husbands' civic status. The husband had to be registered for tax and not subject to any of the other voting restrictions. An income-graded voting scale also limited municipal suffrage. The barriers to participating in political institutions were consequently limited in a number of ways and remained partly after the 1919–1921 reforms, as the following tables from a study over economic restrictions by Fia Sundevall demonstrate in the following table for the lower chamber and the municipal councils.[4] The limitations for the municipal councils also affected the regional government and the First Chamber, as we shall see in the following discussion. However, age became a central parameter as other comprehensive limitations to political participation were abolished (Tables 1.1 and 1.2).

In the negotiations that followed in late November and early December 1918, involving all the parliamentary parties, the issue of age limits was crucial as regards both the right to vote and the age of eligibility. The agreement on universal and equal suffrage ended with men and women being allowed to vote in municipal elections from the year after they turned 23; for elections to county councils (and thus to the First Chamber, appointed indirectly through the county councils and the municipalities), a voter was required to be at least 27 years of age. The age limit for voting in Second Chamber elections was also 23, which meant that the voting age for men was one year lower than between 1909 and 1921. However—and this must be underlined—in the year when all married women became legally competent at 21 (unmarried women were already legally competent), the voting age became 23. In 1921, women and men were not considered politically competent—entitled to vote—at the age of 21, the year they came of age and became legally competent. The 40-graded

Table 1.1 Suffrage requirements for the Swedish Parliament, 1866–1970 (Lower chamber)

Gender	*Age*	*Basic requirements besides age, national citizenship, and census registration*	*Grounds of disenfranchisement*[a]
1866: Men only 1921: Men and women.	1866: 21+ 1909: 24+ 1921: 23+	1866–1909: Minimum income and property value thresholds: yearly income of minimum 800 Swedish riksdaler (SR) *or* owner or tenant of property with a tax assessment value of min. 1000 SR (for owner) or 6000 SR (for tenant).	1866–1920: Tax debts 1866–1937: Loss of civil rights (from 1909: felony) 1909–1922: Incomplete military service training 1909–1945: Poor relief 1909–1945: Bankruptcy 1909–1989: Guardianship

[a]It should be noted that each disenfranchisement criterion encompassed a complex set of rules, the intricacies of which cannot be conveyed in tabular representation. Sundevall tables include reforms initiated after 1922

Table 1.2 Suffrage requirements for Swedish Municipal Councils, since 1862

Gender	*Age*	*Basic requirements besides gender and age*	*Grounds of disenfranchisement*[a]
1862: Women[b] and men.	1862: 21+ 1919: 23+	1862–1919: Registration in the municipality census (as an individual or private company) + income, property, or other capital taxed over 700 rds. 1919: Swedish citizenship.	1866–1937: Loss of civil rights (from 1909: felony) 1866–1945: Tax debts 1909–1945: Bankruptcy 1909–1989: Guardianship 1918–1945: Poor relief

[a]It should be noted that each disenfranchisement criterion encompassed a complex set of rules, the intricacies of which cannot be conveyed in tabular representation. Sundevall tables include reforms initiated after 1922

[b]Until the 1910s: only unmarried or widowed women

voting scale, a scale that allowed up to 40 votes per individual or legal entity as businesses, depending on the level of income, for municipal elections, was completely abolished. Equal suffrage was in effect from now on but not for those below these age limits. Before 1921, men who satisfied the other voting requirements could, through their municipal suffrage, influence the composition of the First Chamber from the age of 21 until 1909, and between 1909 and 1921 from the age of 24. At the same time, after 1921, there was still a remnant of the requirement to pay taxes (local elections). No one could vote if they had been declared legally incapacitated or had been punished for certain crimes, had declared bankruptcy, were in receipt of poor relief for long-term subsistence, or (in the case of men) if they had neglected or refused to participate in military training. The struggle for democracy would continue. The age of eligibility was set at 23 for elections to municipal councils and the Second Chamber, 27 for elections to county councils, and 35 for the First Chamber (Table 1.3).[5]

These changes put the search light on the role age limits play in suffrage politics and the processes that led to raising and lowering the voting age. There is a paradox that needs to be understood: while some actors fought for or accepted an extension of suffrage, the same people also tried to exclude certain age groups.

I shall discuss the negotiations about the right to vote in connection with the decisions taken between 1909 and 1921, while also considering the social and political processes that made the voting age such a central

Table 1.3 The ages for voting, eligibility, and legal competence in Sweden 1860–1921

Year	*Voting age*				*Eligibility age*				*Age of legal competence*	
	Municipality	*County council*	*First Chamber*	*Second Chamber*	*Municipality*	*County council*	*First Chamber*	*Second Chamber*	*Men*	*Women*
1866	21	21	21	21	25/25		35	25	21	25 (unmarried)
1884										21 (unmarried)
1909		21	24	24	25/25	25	35	21		
1921	23	27	27	23	27	27	35	23		21 (also married)

Source: Bengt Sandin and Jonathan Josefsson, "Age as a Yardstick for Political Citizenship: Voting Age and Eligibility Age in Sweden during the Twentieth Century", Continuity and Change 2022:2, pp. 257–280

Note: The years stated are the years when a reform came into effect, not when it was decided issue as early as the opening years of the twentieth century. This book is about political age limits and how democracy was hedged by guarantees to preserve the status quo. Age limits are an example of how reforms were designed as safeguards against change. In this respect, the politics clearly reflected dramatic social developments, with new class relations and social conditions in the growing towns and industrial communities. It is a story about the struggle for democratic reforms in a nation which would, only a couple of decades later, be noted for its ambition to build a welfare state, an egalitarian and democratic society. Why, then, was the young generation excluded from the reforms of the electoral system? That is the overall aim of this study.

My study thus examines the cultural charge of age limits, the political negotiations about suffrage reforms, and the social and demographic development. The issues that were discussed then are still topical. Age remains a crucial dividing line in the right to vote. And the voting age has been a subject of political debate and change. It was greatly influenced by other political debates about the development of society. The changes reflected who the ruling elites wanted to invite into the democratic conversation, how the struggle from below was waged, and where it derived its power. That, in turn, was also dependent on which other political issues were on the political agenda. At the beginning of the twentieth century, for example, the debates concerned the organisation of poor relief and the pension issue, women's night work and marriage legislation, child welfare in the family and institutions for children, the temperance issue, and legislation on working hours; the eight-hour day. The organisation of schools was always a matter of debate and subject to major changes. Sweden's role in the growing conflicts between the great powers and the question of how the armed forces should be organised were other important matters. The decision to introduce compulsory military training concerned who should bear the financial costs of the defence forces, but also the meaning of citizenship for men. Defence became a burning issue as a result of the internal national debate, the direction of foreign policy, and the conflicts raging in the surrounding world.

All these questions also concerned, in different ways, the ability of people to influence their own lives and represent the larger context of voting rights. The question of women's suffrage reflected the conditions for women's work and their right to education, political rights and the view of the family, and it was thus also a class issue. The parliamentary debates on industrial relations and economy, working hours, pensions, and poor relief excluded many young workers who were affected by the decisions. Military training for men, which was introduced around 1900 in order to secure the national defence, was, of course, based on an age categorisation that was also reflected in the suffrage debate. Should young men supposed to defend the country not be eligible to vote and have a say in the big political issues of the day?

A change in the outlook on children and young people also played a role, one can assume. The social and political transformation of Swedish society during the early twentieth century greatly affected the living conditions of children and adolescents and how the relationship between the state and the family was perceived. There was also the question of the role and responsibility of the state in relation to what we today call civil society. Children and young people, school and upbringing, were at the centre of a broad debate about family, gender relations, and social norms. Adolescence became an issue of debate in Sweden, as in many other countries. The parenting given by young working-class parents, married and unmarried, was critically scrutinised and questioned, and society devised support measures of various kinds. Age categorisations were central to the political system and to the political debate. They formed the basis for social reforms during these years and substantiated a critique of the shortcomings of the political system.[6]

The book begins with a chapter on previous research and the study's premises. It also presents the theoretical foundation and specifies the questions in greater detail. The following chapters examine the implications of age limits for the political process. Social and demographic developments between the 1860s and 1921 are discussed in a separate concluding chapter before the concluding discussion.

The content is chronologically arranged. The study ends with the reforms of 1918–1921 but begins with the decision to establish a bicameral parliament and the municipal reform in the mid-nineteenth century. The design of these reforms created the conditions for the process that is studied in this book. Together with Jonathan Josefsson, I have written about the period after 1921 and therefore omit that here.[7] The processes studied created the conditions for the democracy established after 1921 and also shaped its limitations and shortcomings. This book examines how it happened.

Previous Research on Age, Democracy, and Voting Restrictions

The question of age is not prominent in studies of the so-called democratic breakthrough or later constitutional changes. A common feature of recent research in Sweden about the expansion of voting rights, concentrating on the period up to the 1920s, is the focus on processes and basic structural conditions. The emphasis is not on individual actors and their significance. The suffrage issue is instead highlighted as part of a fundamental long-term process of economic, social, and political change. However, a renewed interest in women's organisations at the national and local levels has also made significant contributions to the understanding of the grassroots of the suffrage movement.[8] At the same time, there is a focus on the right to vote in elections to the Second Chamber, what is called the *political suffrage issue*. Suffrage in elections to municipal councils and the First Chamber serves more as a backdrop to the discussion.[9] Some researchers also emphasise that the parliamentary game was played against a background of increasing social conflicts in Sweden, which were exacerbated during the last years of the First World War. The social unrest in countries like Finland, Germany, and Russia also played a major role.[10] Changing age limits and relations between the generations can of course be viewed as one such long-term change, but not much importance has been ascribed to these changes. Age is noted as one factor among others, but its cultural and social significance has not been examined closely.

While older research took an interest in parliamentary debates, forms of governance, and political negotiations, this has been replaced over time by an interest in the broader political movements and the mobilisation of the people. Research initially focused mainly on the extension of male suffrage and on the working classes. It later moved towards a greater emphasis on women's political rights and national and local suffragettes. We may also note studies about the demands of the labour movement or what made the ruling elites accept the extension of suffrage and the broadening of democracy.

The historians Lars Berggren and Kjell Östberg point out that the voting age was part of the compromise on suffrage in 1917/1918 intended to guarantee social stability. Still, they do not discuss in detail how raising the age limits for eligibility and voting could be perceived as guaranteeing social stability.[11] In Carl Göran Andrae's broad historical analysis and meticulous description of "Sweden in the face of the revolutions of

1917–1918", great attention is devoted to the politics surrounding the decisions of 1917 and 1918 in the light of threats of revolution and the stance of the left. However, he does not examine the significance of voting restrictions on the basis of age.[12] Nor is age an important aspect in Christina Carlsson Wetterberg's examination of the Social Democratic view of women and women's politics in the early twentieth century, or in Staffan Runestam's and Niclas Stenlås's studies of the First Chamber Right and the suffrage issue. In Stefan Olssons's book about the conservatives and their accommodation to democracy, it does not attribute voting age any importance.[13] Sven Anders Söderpalm has shown how industrial and banking interests understood the inevitability of democracy, which probably affected the negotiations by undermining some of the rigid opposition put up by conservatives in Parliament. Nevertheless, he does not go into the details of the compromise.[14] Historian Pasi Ihalainen analyses national and transnational debates on constitutional reforms 1917–1918 in British, German, Swedish, and Finnish parliaments. It is a very ambitious presentation that gives important insights into the different characteristics and their background. The voting age is mentioned about the debates in Britain, Sweden and Finland, but is not analysed in any detail.[15]

The historian Sverker Oredsson, in his biography of the Liberal Party leader Nils Edén, has focused on his central role in the struggle for universal and equal suffrage. He emphasises Edén's importance in implementing female, universal, and equal suffrage, but does not pay any close attention to the significance of age in connection with the negotiations.[16] The journalist Per T. Ohlsson also touches on this period in the book *1918*. Here the emphasis is on the political process and how Swedish political culture created the conditions for a compromise that laid the foundation for today's political culture.[17] The political scientist Leif Lewin also provides an interesting account of the mechanisms of the political game in which the question of the voting age was a subset. Unlike Ohlsson and Oredsson, Lewin emphasises that the Right also achieved some success in the final outcome of the processes.[18]

One scholar who has examined age limits is the historian Ebba Berling Åselius. In her book, she pointed out how the age limits introduced in connection with the suffrage reforms of 1902–1909, together with other voting restrictions, reflected the desire of conservative and liberal political forces to create guarantees of stable social development.[19] The extension of the right to vote, what was called universal suffrage, thus meant at the same time that political influence was regulated through exclusion by means of various dividing lines for suffrage—the thresholds and criteria known in Swedish as ***streck*** or "lines"), mainly the gender line, the age threshold, and the criteria concerning taxes, migration, and poor relief.[20] Registration as a taxpayer was a basic prerequisite. The voting age for men was now separated from the age of majority for men. According to Berling Åselius, raising the age from 21 to 24 meant that voting was delayed for several annual cohorts, "although this did not target any particular social class".[21] In other words, Berling Åselius does not perceive that the exclusion of four annual cohorts disfavored any particular social group of potential voters, unlike the other criteria. As we shall see, this was also an argument used by those who wanted to raise the voting age. She emphasises, however, that the age threshold was also an argument in the discussion about women's suffrage, following a proposal from conservative women, but she does not closely examine the discussion in connection with the compromises of 1917/1918 from these perspectives. Berling Åselius also shows that the voting restrictions reflected in various ways, not only gender and class but also the outlook on marriage.[22]

Sten Carlsson and other historians and political scientists have pointed out that the question of changes to the voting age was raised in suffrage discussions as early as the 1890s.[23] In their analyses, one may note a great interest in the political relationship between the municipalities and the state, in how municipal self-government reflects local and regional power relations, and in the democratic significance of local self-government. These are important elements in studies by the historians Ingemar Norrlid and Göran B. Nilsson. Their research forms an important basis for my analysis of the suffrage debates. It goes well together with later research by economic historians Carolina Uppenberg, Mats Olsson, and Erik Bengtsson, who show a renewed interest in local power elites or suffrage from the perspective of economic history and politics. In his book "The World's Most Equal Country?", Erik Bengtsson addresses the problem of how this politically and economically unequal country could develop into a modern welfare state.[24] The political scientist Nils Stjernquist's thorough book on the bicameral era also points out that the raised age limits were part of the compromises and guarantees that, together with factors such as voting for electors to the county councils, were granted to the conservatives in connection with the compromise in 1918.[25] Previous researchers have thus pointed out that a rise in age limits was part of the compromise of 1918–1921 and that changes in age limits after 1921 have been up for political discussion.

Another couple of works may be worth mentioning. In his article on the voting age and the delimitation problem of democracy, political scientist Ludvig Beckman shows how changes in the voting age in Sweden during the twentieth century can be understood in principle. He notes that the changes can best be explained in terms of the parties' self-interest; the voting age was lowered to achieve success in elections. In the article, he thus explores the interests and arguments that motivated the actors; he points out that the increase in the voting age in Sweden deviated from the general pattern (see Fig. 1.1 below).[26] The historians Ingrid Söderlind and Kristina Engvall have also taken an interest in age limits as an expression of a changed view of children and young people, while the political scientist Gunnel Gustavsson has discussed age limits as a question of the forms and scope of democracy. As part of a research project about the period after

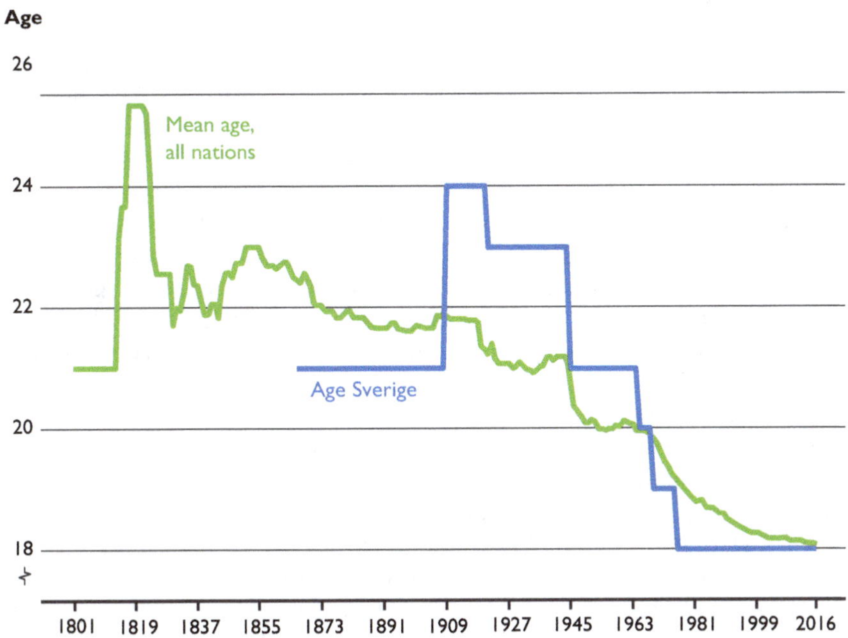

Fig. 1.1 Average voting age in all independent countries with general elections. (Source: Ludvig Beckman, "Rösträttsåldern och demokratins avgränsningsproblem", i Katarina Barrling och Sören Holmberg (red.), Demokratins framtid (Stockholm: Sveriges riksdag, 2018))

1921, Jonathan Josefsson and Bengt Sandin have drawn attention to the arguments about age limits and the political processes and how the arguments relate to structural and demographic changes.[27]

The discussion in these articles is important and highly relevant from a broader perspective. In the dominant theoretical discussions of democracy, the rights of suffrage, eligibility, and political participation have been regarded as something to which only adults and full-fledged citizens are entitled. These ideas have also influenced contemporary and historical studies of democratisation. Electoral laws, electoral institutions, and voter behaviour have often been studied from a comparative perspective, using quantitative methods based on the assumption that those who are underage are not political citizens.[28] Research on democratisation by political scientists has nevertheless drawn attention to the need for historical perspectives. A historical approach would question whether the population above the age of majority has always meant the same thing in different places and different periods. Political scientists Giovanni Capoccia and Daniel Ziblatt have argued for what they call the need for a "historical turn", advocating more rigorous empirical research into the breakthrough and development of democracy. They also point to the need for more research on voting rights and gender, education, economic resources, and minority status. Scholars are thus encouraged to be more attentive to history and context.[29] In broad comparative analyses, scholars such as political scientists Richard Katz and Adam Przeworski have discussed, for example, gender and ethnicity. Although they have mentioned age limits, they do not undertake any further analyses that include the dynamics behind voting restrictions on the basis of age. Unfortunately, Katz's important survey has some inaccuracies regarding Sweden in particular. He states, for example, that the voting age in elections to the Second Chamber in 1866 was 25 when it was actually 21. This makes it difficult to interpret the Swedish development and demands for a raise in the voting age during the subsequent period. The large comparative and quantitative research programme Varieties of Democracy (V-Dem) does not take into account various voting restrictions, which means that Sweden after 1921 is considered to have 100 per cent suffrage, despite the fact that significant restrictions on voting rights remained.[30] When coding the voting rules in different countries, the researchers did not consider

> restrictions based on age, residence, having been convicted for crime or being legally incompetent. It covers legal de jure restrictions, not restrictions

> that may be operative in practice de facto. The adult population as defined by statute is defined by citizens in the case of independent countries or the people living in the territorial entity in the case of colonies. Universal suffrage is coded as 100%.[31]

In addition, the emphasis is on the Second Chamber or equivalent lower house, which neglects the dynamics between the different chambers in the national parliaments. Nor do Katz and Przeworski include local and regional elections, which means that the interaction between this level and the national level is ignored.[32]

Katz and Przeworski also emphasise the right to vote in Second Chamber elections, which also complicates a reasonable interpretation of Swedish development compared with other countries.[33] The relationship between the different political levels is likely to have a decisive impact on the nature and outcome of the suffrage struggle. Political scientists Staffan Lindberg and Jan Teorell observe that the lengthy process in Sweden can to a large extent be explained by the special position of the First Chamber in the Swedish constitution, which is also a point that Nils Stjernquist makes in his study.[34] At the same time, the international surveys in Katz and Przeworski are of great value, opening for discussions about both what is uniquely Swedish and what Sweden shares with other countries.

The Swedish Voting Age in Comparison—the Uniqueness of the Swedish Experience

The raising of the voting age in Sweden stands out by international standards. At roughly the same time many European countries were gradually lowering the voting age from the age that had been established—around 25—through constitutional reforms in the early and mid-nineteenth century. Sweden had a lower voting age from 1866, set at 21, combined with economic voting barriers. The economic barriers were set high, resulting in a highly elitist electoral system. The limited electoral participation in Sweden mainly resulted from the economic barriers being more elitist than in nations such as Germany, France, Norway, and Finland. The historical data about changed age limits in different countries mostly concern lower houses, equivalent to Sweden's Second Chamber. It is striking that countries such as Australia, the United States, Canada, New Zealand, and countries in South America, from the beginning of their liberation process, had lower voting ages than their respective colonial masters, with the occasional exception.[35] Countries such as Denmark, Finland, Iceland, France, Greece, and Italy lowered the voting age in the late nineteenth and early twentieth centuries. The pattern in Sweden was the reverse.[36]

The Swedish debate at the end of the nineteenth century consequently took place against a different background than other European countries because the voting age had been set at 21 with the introduction of the bicameral parliament in 1866. As we shall see, the voting ages for the old Diet of the four estates played a major role in that decision, but it was the economic requirements that dramatically limited the number of people who could vote and could be elected. These restrictions were also very effective, creating a particularly elitist political system compared to other European countries. Sweden, which would become one of the world's most equal countries during the twentieth century, was one of Europe's least equal countries around 1900 in economic and also political terms.[37] In the 1890s, for example, 24 per cent of the male population over the age of 21 in Sweden had the right to vote, while in Norway, which was in union with the same monarch with Sweden, 77 per cent of the male population over 21 could vote. In Germany the corresponding figure was 82 per cent and in France 84.5 per cent. In addition, voter turnout in Sweden was among the lowest in Europe (Table 1.4).[38]

Regarding the right to vote in municipal elections, the Swedish system that developed during the nineteenth century was likewise elitist compared to countries such as the United States, Britain, Switzerland, Denmark, Norway, the Netherlands, and Belgium. The historian Einar Mellqvist summarises his review of the municipal voting rules somewhat laconically as follows:

> What the Swedish voting rules resembled most were the Finnish and English rules, but nowhere was the inequality greater than in Sweden. This was true already at the beginning of the nineteenth century, and the continued development in our country increased the differences vis-à-vis other countries apart from Finland, which followed the Swedish pattern. In making such a comparison, however, it should be recalled that the municipalities in Sweden had greater powers and greater independence than was the rule in other countries. The right to taxation enjoyed by Swedish municipalities should be especially emphasised.[39]

Table 1.4 The right to vote in elections to the lower house in European countries in 1896

	Percentage of the population entitled to vote	*Percentage of men over 21 entitled to vote*	*Voter turnout as a percentage of those entitled to vote*
Sweden 1896	6.3	24	45.3
Norway 1898	18.7	77.2	70.4
Denmark 1898	17	65.7	59.7
Great Britain and Ireland 1897	13.2	64,7	60.9
Netherlands 1897	11.8	45.1	76.7
Belgium 1898	21.9	79.4	–
Austria 1897	21.2	82.2	68.1
Hungary 1898	5.2	19.5	–
Switzerland 1890	22.6	83.5	58.9
France 1893	27.2	84.9	71.1
Italy 1897	6.8	24.2	58.5
Spain 1891	22.4	82	73.7
Portugal 1890	19	74.6	–
Serbia 1890	16.6	68	–
Greece 1881	23	83.7	66.7

Source: SOS i sammandrag 1912. Statistisk tidskrift H 157. (Stockholm: P. A. Norstedt & Söner, 1912)

Municipal suffrage was of great importance as a basis for elections to county councils and to the First Chamber. Moreover, municipalities had the right to taxation and a degree of self-government.

The Swedish development took place within the framework of the general European democratisation process, but it also had its distinctive features. Sweden was not at the forefront of the process and as other nations marked by the paths set by governmental institutions and political traditions.[40] Political scientist Daniel Ziblatt presents the historiography of democracy in Europe as a path to democracy that "was difficult but exceptional and achieved under nearly inescapable 'forces' of history";[41] a unique story of modernisation and development—a narrative that does not take into account that the growth of democracy was accompanied by or gave rise to anti-democratic processes or was based on exclusion intended to achieve a limited appropriate electorate.

Not only Daniel Ziblatt, but also scholars such as historian Charles Tilly, political scientists Daron Acemogly, and Ruth and David Collier have questioned this linear success story. Capoccia and Ziblatt propose an alternative research strategy with a historical focus. They seek to apply a historical perspective showing that history also contains setbacks. The usual history of progress is based on today's democratic values. Capoccia and Ziblatt not only highlight the different waves of democratisation and their differing character and dependence on previous political institutions, but also point out that democratic institutions risked counteracting each other.

> the different elements of democracy (civil liberties, responsible executives, and universal suffrage) do not always travel together. But [...] one can argue that democracy emerged historically as an amalgam of discrete institutional reforms that at times undercut each other.[42]

An analysis of the emergence of democracy must, therefore, also consider the fact that the processes of change can be contradictory, as Capoccia and Ziblatt demonstrate. Different political motives and social changes cannot be assumed to be synchronised or even to follow the same temporal logic. The development was composed of many different processes based on changing social groupings and conflicting institutional changes.[43] Last but not least, as I will show, it was affected by the age composition of the population and the age threshold chosen for the right to vote.

The Quest of This Study

In previous research about the parliamentary interaction concerning the compromises on suffrage in 1917–1918, the age of the electorate and the voting thresholds have been touched upon but not examined in detail. Scholars have focused on certain aspects of the long-term processes, such as the transformation of class society and women's changing social and political conditions. There is good reason to undertake a more profound examination, for example, by supplementing the gender and class perspectives with the factors of age and generation. Consequently, we must consider the social and economic background to the reforms and the geographical (spatial) aspects of the suffrage debate. The overall aim of this study is thus to investigate what role age limits played in suffrage politics and how this can be understood in relation to social change.

As noted above, research in recent years has tended to focus on the right to vote in elections to the Second Chamber of the Riksdag, with an emphasis on the suffrage struggle outside the Riksdag. Perhaps this explains why little attention has been paid to the complicated relationship between municipal suffrage and voting in elections to the Second Chamber, despite its importance in the public debate and specifically the issue of the voting and eligibility ages. The relationship between municipal suffrage and parliamentary elections was deemed more important in earlier research as local self-government was the backdrop to the critique on the voting rights.[44] In the present study, municipal suffrage will therefore also be considered. The relationship between Parliament, county councils, and municipalities has significant consequences for the discussion of the role of central government and the regulations concerning suffrage. In addition, municipal suffrage had a decisive influence on the composition of the First Chamber, which further underlines the importance of also considering the voting age in local elections.

In this context, previous research provides different possible interpretive frameworks for understanding what has been called "the democratic breakthrough". Was the right of the male working class to vote the crucial issue, or was it female suffrage? Or should we place the emphasis on the fact that the decisions simultaneously guaranteed the preservation of the First Chamber and the persistence of the monarchy, while large groups were excluded from this extended democracy? Was it important that Social Democrats and Liberals agreed that women should be given the right to vote or that the Liberals and the various groupings constituting the Right agreed that paying tax and being at least 24 years of age should be the basis for the right to vote?

It is also justified to ask other critical questions. Was it a victory for a shared Social Democratic and Liberal vision of a better and more democratic society, or was it also an expression of a Liberal and Conservative defence of established social structures? Is it beneficial to analyse the process in terms of conflicts between town and country that were also brought to the fore in the debate? Do the conflicts have a geographical dimension that simultaneously reflects unequal economic and social development? A close reading of previous research undoubtedly allows for these different interpretations.[45]

In addition to the normative questions of who should be included or excluded on the basis of age, the discussions about the voting and eligibility age in the twentieth century also reflect changes in how the roles and tasks of the central state, Parliament, county councils, and municipalities, and their relationship to the citizens, have been assessed and perceived. That is why we should consider how the issue of voting and eligibility age relates to other political issues and major societal changes, as well as which arguments were put forward and which actors took part in the debates. These changes concerned the political institutions and the systems that regulated relations between different political bodies, a sluggish system influenced by decisions in the past. "It is what researchers have described" as "path dependence": the actors were dependent on already established solutions.[46]

In many cases these solutions were perfectly sufficient, but they were also challenged by the contemporary social and political situation. In other words, the premise for my study involves several aspects that concern the room for manoeuvre and the political will of the elites but which are also dependent on prior political decisions and solutions. Previous international research has explained the development with reference to the way the elites responded to the demands for increased democracy and participation in political institutions. Adam Przeworski captures the problem well in his title "Conquered or Granted?" but for Sweden he barely touches on the complex relationship between different political levels and the ability of different elites to exert influence.[47] A large share of Swedish research yesterday and today has drawn attention to the question of the willingness of the governing class to compromise during the process in the late 1910s. There is, therefore, also reason to reflect on the social changes in the light of the political discussions about age limits and electoral systems, and regarding which elites were involved, and the stance they adopted on the demands for increased influence.

Moreover, it is important to note that the electoral system was based on local elections and elections to two different chambers with partly different rules, thus representing different elites and different parts of society's political interests. Those who ruled were hardly socially homogeneous. The path dependence that may be envisaged as having affected Swedish development also has to do with the way the regulatory systems evolved. Sweden's development is partly unique by international standards, since the voting age was raised in connection with democratisation, as pointed out above. We can observe how the removal of certain voting restrictions played a significant role even after the introduction of universal and equal suffrage for men and women.[48] As Fig. 1.2 shows, the removal of economic and gender barriers was combined with an increase in age restrictions and the retention of obstacles such as proof of tax payment and military training.[49]

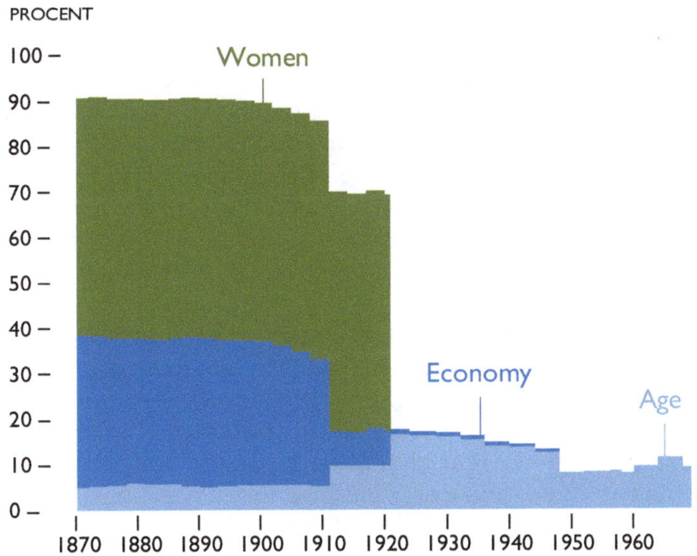

Fig. 1.2 Groups excluded from voting in elections to the Second Chamber (1870–1969). (Source: Mattias Lindgren, "Hur många drabbades? Kvantitativa effekter av rösträttsbegränsningarna" in Berg and Ericsson (eds.) 2021. Note: The original chart continues after 1969, because Lindgren's analysis has a time span that differs partly from mine. The proportion of the population over 18 years of age. Age includes all over 18 but has not reached the age limit at the time. Economic lines include various limitations; bankruptcies, dependence on poor relief, outstanding taxes etc)

The figure should be understood against the background that, when the bicameral parliament was established in 1866, the number of eligible voters and eligible candidates was limited in different ways.[50] In this respect, Sweden represents a political experiment that deviates from the general European pattern. Interestingly, Sweden after the 1860s is more comparable to, say, the United States, where the voting age was established around 21 but where the right to vote was consistently limited by other means based on residence, economic status and class, ethnicity, or race.[51] This design of the new political system during the mid-nineteenth century and its institutions was challenged by economic and social development during the latter part of the nineteenth century.

I want to formulate the starting points for this study around issues like these. The voting age and the eligibility age were included in the agreements that led to the suffrage reform of 1909; having thus become part of the existing regulations, the age issue was also important in the final discussions between 1918 and 1921. I insist on returning to the question of what role the voting age and the age of eligibility to stand for office as a member of parliament play.

The analyses will focus on the barriers to voting—the restrictions on universal suffrage—and how these reflect different social and political interests, sometimes with the same goal but sometimes in conflict. The increasing demands for extended suffrage and constitutional reform were countered with proposals for various measures and reforms put forward by different political interests and economic elites, with the intention of creating a "democracy with guarantees". In this study, I will examine what these guarantees were, how they were presented and what supporting arguments were used, by whom, and how they were culturally charged—given meaning and translated into political decisions.

My analysis concerns both long-term changes and short-term political events. I am interested both in causal relationships and in how demands for specific voting barriers were related to each other. Who were the actors and the groups that demanded higher age limits during what has been called the democratic breakthrough? What social and cultural implications did age restrictions have? How did the discourses relate to social and demographic developments? How did the discussion of age limits interact with the view of working-class participation in the emerging democracy? Did higher voting ages have different meanings in different contexts and for different social classes and for men and women?

Methodological Considerations

The study is based on an analysis of arguments, motives, and contexts as they appear in the public debate, mainly in parliamentary and press material but also in memoirs and private notes, along with investigations in previous research of the broader political and social history after 1900.[52] I will describe and scrutinise how the arguments and proposals for changing the voting and eligibility ages were justified. It is also important to consider which actors argued for change, and also what arguments were adduced for the status quo. In the analysis, the emphasis is on the social values, judgements, and behaviours associated with different ages while also taking into account the spatial dimensions: the geographical locations and social roles that were thought to represent different ages. This gives me the tools to clarify the logics on which the different lines of political argument were based and to explore the motives that may have formed the grounds for political positions.

The analysis is also based on the fact that cultural meanings are not unambiguous and one-dimensional; they are influenced by spatial aspects, by gender and by class. In the investigation I will pay attention not only to the issue of voting rights and eligibility in relation to class and gender, but also to the relation between town and country and between large and small urban environments.[53] The emphasis is not on the broader political context and the suffrage struggle outside Parliament to which changes in the voting age can be linked; instead I focus on the discussions in and around Parliament and how these can be understood. In that sense, this study comes closer to older research which concentrated on the actors in Parliament and the national arena, although my approach is different. Since the political parties and party loyalties in the period after 1900 were exceptionally changeable, my aim is to paint a picture of the debate with broad brushstrokes. But the leading party representatives are also given some space. The diversity of voices can give us knowledge of the depth, breadth, and meanings of the process of cultural change. And unlike in earlier research, the parliamentary debates and politics will be related to social developments.

The long-term course of change is an important starting point for understanding the discussions of age and the age structure of society. This concerns both the long-term economic and social processes that affected the suffrage issue and the dependence on previous decisions and institutions that characterised politics. It is thus a question of path dependence, but also of the sluggish social changes that social historians describe as "la longue durée". Such processes concern, for example, demographic regimes but may also include basic cultural structures. In concrete terms, this entails examining the demographic development and the cultural meaning of various arguments and how these are expressed in substantive political negotiations.[54] The political processes examined in this study can best be described as *critical junctures* when conflicts were negotiated and politicised, and when alternative political solutions were opposed to each other and created the conditions for changing politics and institutions. This is a perspective that highlights the actions of different people, with each actor understanding only parts of the ongoing processes and not the long-term consequences. Accordingly, the result could be different from what was intended. Therefore, the stated intentions of the proposed amendments cannot be understood in terms of the effects of the changes. It cannot be taken for granted that the proposals were well-designed or achieved the desired objectives. Even the historical actors involved must have thought that the process was highly fragmented and did not lead forward in any clear and coherent way. It is not mere chance that, in retrospect, some of the decisions seem random, contradictory, and inconsistent.[55] All in all, this means that the present study considers both short-term changes and the effect of long-term structural processes, limitations, and possibilities.

For that reason, I have also sought to ask whether it is possible to link the discussions in the Riksdag and the culturally conditioned arguments to long-term economic and social changes in Sweden. My ambition has been to get behind general assessments that industrialisation and the transformation of class society created the conditions for a critical debate about voting rights and democracy in the late nineteenth and early twentieth centuries. I am concerned with what it was in industrialisation and the transformation of society that created the conditions for the critical debate about democracy. That is why I am also interested in demographic changes, crime, marriage patterns, and urbanisation with the help of published statistics and government reports. This is part of my analysis of social and demographic changes that may have influenced the historical actors but also of the type of information they mobilised in their reasoning about voting restrictions. The public statistics thus fulfil different tasks in my analysis. It is both an analysis of the cultural concepts and the type of information used by contemporary actors and an expression of my ambitions to come to grips with what aspects of the social change impacted the debates and the practice of voting restrictions.

Outline

Chapter 2 discusses the design of suffrage in the period 1840–1900. This serves as a background and an institutional framework for developments around the turn of the century. Here I present the starting points for the reforms in the middle of the century with regard to age limits and how they were connected to other voting restrictions. The chapter also considers how the rules were challenged during the course of the century. This provides the necessary backdrop to the ensuing discussion. Chapter 3 then looks at the formative period from 1900 to 1909, when the social and political conflicts over the right to vote, along with a host of other political issues, created the cultural framework for the form that suffrage should and could take. Here I also relate the age limits for voting to other voting restrictions and to the political process of extending male suffrage. The politics surrounding the right to vote in the post-1909 period are discussed in Chap. 4. The years from 1909 to 1917 saw the establishment of political alliances that would set their stamp on the debates leading to the resolution of the suffrage issue. Special attention is paid here to the complicated relationship between the Liberals and the Social Democrats and the matters on which the Right and the Liberals shared fundamental values. Chapter 5 discusses the final battle over the suffrage issue in the context of the 1918 decisions on municipal suffrage and the agreements about the subsequent reforms of 1919 and 1921. Here the discussion concerns age limits and how they had different meanings in relation to suffrage in elections to municipal councils, county councils, and the two chambers of the Riksdag, depending on what other voting restrictions applied. The last part of the chapter analyses the negotiations in the Riksdag's joint committee, with the aim of clarifying how the issue of age limits enabled a compromise between the different political blocs. Here I follow the dynamics of the meetings and the crystallisation of the values that were at stake for the main actors. Chapter 6 examines the actual reforms and the subsequent political evaluation of the decisions taken in 1918, through an analysis of how the members of parliament afterwards explained their position on the compromise reached in the joint communiqué of the special committee in December 1918. Chapter 7 sets the study of the debates and the political processes in relation to social and demographic developments. There I pay particular attention to the situation of the younger urban population, to criminality, to the family and marriage in the debate at the turn of the century, and to demographic developments. The chapter concludes with a section about the people affected by the new voting rules. Who was excluded when democracy was extended? Chapter 8 summarises the study: the social and cultural meanings of age limits, the relationship between age, gender, and class, family and youth as sources of conflict, and the long-term and short-term processes of change

Notes

1. See Chap. 5 of this work.
2. The Liberal Party grew out of the Swedish Universal Suffrage League (Sveriges allmänna rösträttsförbund), founded in 1890. In 1897 a liberal parliamentary party was established, called the People's Party (Folkpartiet), which in 1900 became the Liberal Coalition Party (Liberala samlingspartiet), which then also included several other liberal parliamentary groups. In 1902 a national liberal party was formed, the National Free-minded Association (Frisinnade landsföreningen).
3. The Right (Högern) was a relatively fragmented and changeable group. Through the formation of the General Electoral League (Allmänna valmansförbundet) in 1904 the parliamentary parties began to cooperate before elections to counter the radical mobilisation. In the First Chamber between 1888 and 1909 there was the Protectionist Party (Protektionistiska partiet), In 1910 this became the United Right Party (Förenade högerpartiet). The Minority Party (Minoritetspartiet) was another conservative group that existed between 1888 and 1904. From 1905 until 1909 the group acted under the name of the Moderate Party (Moderata partiet). In 1912 these parties combined to form the National Party of the First Chamber (Första kammarens nationella parti, often called the First Chamber Right), which lasted until the 1934 parliament. The Farmers' Party (Lantmannapartiet) was in the Second Chamber from 1867. The group of the Moderate Reformers (De moderata reformvännerna) was founded in 1903 but became the National Progressive Party (Nationella framstegspartiet) in 1903, which merged in 1912 with the Farmers' Party to become the Farmer and Bourgeois Party (Lantmanna- och Borgarepartiet) until 1934 (known as the Second Chamber Right). A more radical Farmers Party (Bondeförbundets riksorganisation) was founded in 1913. A National organisation of Farmers (Jordsbrukarnas riksförbund) was organised in 1915 based on earlier civil society organisations that had emerged around the defence issue in 1914. Both these latter organisations were represented in the parliament after the 1917 election and established a parliamentary group called the Farmers free group (Jordbrukarnas fria grupp) and merged in 1921 under the name Bondeförbundet (Farmer's Party) that during the 1920 distanced themselves both from the conservative parties (urban middle class, bank and industrial interests) and the Social Democrats plans for ambitious and expensive social reforms. In this book the Farmer's Party I refer to is Lantmannapartiet that was a central political actor in the Right up to the late 1910s.
4. Fia Cottrell-Sundevall, "Money and the Vote: Economic Suffrage Restrictions in Sweden, Before and After the Introduction of 'Universal Suffrage' in 1921", Suffrage, Capital and Welfare: Conditional Citizenship

in Historical Perspective, Eds. Fia Cottrell-Sundevall, and Ragnheiður Kristjánsdóttir (Palgrave, 2024).

5. Annika Berg and Martin Ericsson (eds.), *Allmän rösträtt? Rösträttens begränsningar i Sverige efter 1921* (Göteborg & Stockholm: Makadam, 2021).
6. Lars Berggren and Kjell Östberg, "Reformism eller revolution: Arbetarrörelsen inför rösträttsbeslutet 1918–19", in Ulrika Holgersson and Lena Wängnerud (eds.), *Rösträttens århundrade: Kampen, utvecklingen och framtiden för demokratin i Sverige* (Göteborg & Stockholm: Makadam, 2018), pp. 196–198; Hans-Erik Olson, *Från hemgård till ungdomsgård: En studie i den svenska hemgårdsrörelsens historia* (Stockholm: Riksförb. Sveriges fritids- och hemgårdar (RSFH), 1982); Bengt Sandin, "Children and the Swedish Welfare State: From Different to Similar", in Paula S. Fass and Michael Grossberg (eds.), *Reinventing Childhood after World War II* (Philadelphia: University of Pennsylvania Press, 2012), pp. 110–138; Fia Sundevall, "Military Education for Non-Military Purposes", *History of Education Review* 2017:1, pp. 58–71; Bengt Sandin, "The Parent – A Cultural Invention: The Politics of Parenting", *European Journal of Developmental Psychology* 14:6, 2017, pp. 733–746; Bengt Sandin, Johanna Sköld, and Johanna Schiratzki, "Var går gränserna för statens ansvar?", *Statsvetenskaplig tidskrift* 2022:2, pp. 349–378.
7. Jonathan Josefsson and Bengt Sandin, "Ålder som måttstock för politiskt medborgarskap: Rösträtts- och valbarhetsålder i Sverige under 1900-talet", in Annika Berg and Martin Ericsson (eds.), *Allmän rösträtt? Rösträttens begränsningar i Sverige efter 1921* (Göteborg & Stockholm: Makadam, 2021), pp. 157–189; Bengt Sandin and Jonathan Josefsson, "Age as a Yardstick for Political Citizenship: Voting Age and Eligibility Age in Sweden during the Twentieth Century", *Continuity and Change* 2022:2, pp. 257–280.
8. Berggren and Östberg 2019. Malin Arvidsson, 'Malmös Förening för Kvinnans Politiska Rösträtt', *Ale.*, 2022:3, pp 1–18. Arvidsson, Malin, 'Samarbete med förhinder: socialdemokratiska kvinnors relation till LKPR 1907–1921', *Arbetarhistoria.*, 2022:3–4, pp 60–69, Malin, Arvidsson, *Nelly Thüring: teosof, feminist, socialist*, (Makadam förlag 2024, Gunnela, Björk, *Att förhandla sitt medborgarskap: kvinnor som kollektiva politiska aktörer i Örebro 1900–1950*, (Arkiv, Diss. Stockholm: Univ., 2000 Lund, 1999), Gunnela, Björk, *Kata Dalström: agitatorn som gick sin egen väg*, (Historiska Media, Lund, 2017).
9. Christina Florin, *Kvinnor får röst: Kön, känslor och politisk kultur i kvinnornas rösträttsrörelse* (Stockholm: Atlas, 2006); Staffan Lindberg and Jan Teorell, "Demokratins utveckling i världen: Tendenser under och efter rösträttens århundrade", in Ulrika Holgersson and Lena Wängnerud

(eds.), *Rösträttens århundrade: Kampen, utvecklingen och framtiden för demokratin i Sverige* (Göteborg & Stockholm: Makadam i samarbete med Riksbankens jubileumsfond, 2018); Josefin Rönnbäck, *Politikens genusgränser: Den kvinnliga rösträttsrörelsen och kampen för kvinnors politiska medborgarskap 1902–1921* (Stockholm: Atlas, 2004); Josefin Rönnbäck, "För förändringarnas skull: Om kvinnor, politik och kampen för medbestämmande", in Maria Sjöberg and Yvonne Svanström (eds.), *Att göra historia: Vänbok till Christina Florin* (Stockholm: Institutet för framtidsstudier, 2008). For the period up to the mid-nineteenth century see Åsa Karlsson Sjögren, *Männen, kvinnorna och rösträtten: Medborgarskap och representation 1723–1866* (Stockholm: Carlsson, 2006); Åsa Karlsson Sjögren, "Kvinnors röst i sekelskiftets städer: Kommunalt valdeltagande före den allmänna rösträtten", in Maria Sjöberg and Yvonne Svanström (eds.), *Att göra historia: Vänbok till Christina Florin* (Stockholm: Institutet för framtidsstudier, 2008); Arvidsson 2022a, 2022b, 2024; Björk 1999, 2017.

10. Berggren and Östberg (2019).
11. Ibid., p. 170.
12. Carl Göran Andræ, *Revolt eller reform: Sverige inför revolutionerna i Europa 1917–1918* (Stockholm: Carlsson, 1998).
13. Christina Carlsson Wetterberg, *Kvinnosyn och kvinnopolitik: En studie av svensk socialdemokrati 1880–1910*, diss. (Lund: Arkiv, 1986); Staffan Runestam, *Förstakammarhögern och rösträttsfrågan 1900–1907* (Uppsala: Acta Universitatis Upsaliensis, 1966). Niclas Stenlås, "Demokratins vedersakare? Högerns kamp för och emot demokratin", in Christer Jönsson (ed.), *Rösträtten 80 år: Forskarantologi* (Stockholm: Justitiedepartementet, 2001). Stefan Olsson, *Den svenska högerns anpassning till demokratin* (Enskede: TPB 2003).
14. Sven Anders Söderpalm, *Storföretagarna och det demokratiska genombrottet: Ett perspektiv på första världskrigets svenska historia* (Lund: Gleerup, 1969).
15. Pasi Ihalainen, *Springs of Democracy*, (Finnish Literature Society / SKS 2017).
16. Sverker Oredsson, *Nils Edén: Demokratins statsminister* (Stockholm: Ekerlid, 2017).
17. Per T. Ohlsson, *1918: Året då Sverige blev Sverige* (Stockholm: Albert Bonniers förlag, 2017).
18. Leif Lewin, *Det politiska spelet: En simulering av beslutsfattandet i svensk inrikespolitik* (Stockholm, 1978); Leif Lewin, *Ideologi och strategi: Svensk politik under 100 år* (Stockholm: Carlsson Bokförlag, 2017); Leif Lewin, *Konsten att bilda regering när ingen har majoritet* (Göteborg: Daidalos, 2020).

19. Ebba Berling Åselius, *Rösträtt med förhinder: Rösträttsstrecken i svensk politik 1900–1920* (Stockholm: Acta Universitatis Stockholmiensis, 2005), pp. 77–80, 87–89, 59–103.
20. The term *streck* or "line" denoted both the dividing line set for what was required for the right to vote and the line that was drawn to cross out names on the electoral rolls if they had not paid tax or were disqualified for other reasons.
21. Berling Åselius, pp. 196–199, quotation p. 198.
22. Ibid., pp. 188–191. This also means that when Berling Åselius examines who was excluded by the different dividing lines in elections after 1909, she does not consider the "age line"; ibid., pp. 124–164. Men aged under 24 or over were not formally entitled to vote. The term *streck* was used both for those who were excluded even though they were formally entitled to vote and for those who were not entitled to vote on account of gender or age.
23. Sten Carlsson, *Lantmannapolitiken och industrialismen: Partigruppering och opinionsförskjutningar i svensk politik 1890–1902* (Stockholm: Lantbruksförbundets Tidskrifts AB, 1953); Erik Thyselius, *Kampen för allmän rösträtt: En fullständig historik och förklaring öfver rösträttsfrågan från början till närvarande tid* (Stockholm: Fröléen, 1902); Torbjörn Vallinder, *I kamp för demokratin: Rösträttsrörelsen i Sverige 1866–1900* (Stockholm: Natur & Kultur, 1962).
24. Göran B. Nilsson, "Den samhällsbevarande representationsreformen", *Scandia* 35:2, 1969; Göran B. Nilsson, *Självstyrelsens problematik: Undersökningar i svensk landstingshistoria 1839–1928* (Uppsala: Acta Universitatis Upsaliensis, 1967); Ingemar Norrlid, "Kommunen som bolag? En studie i liberal rösträttspolitik före första världskriget", *Scandia* 36:1, 1970; Ingemar Norrlid, *Demokrati, skatterättvisa och ideologisk förändring: Den kommunala självstyrelsen och demokratins genombrott i Sverige* (Lund: Liber/Gleerup, 1983); Carolina Uppenberg and Mats Olsson, "Under the Landlord's Thumb: Municipalities and Local Elites in Sweden 1862–1900", *Social History* 47:3, 2022, pp. 265–289; Peter Aronsson, *Bönder gör politik: Det lokala självstyret som social arena i tre Smålandssocknar, 1680–1850*, diss. (Lund: Lund University Press, 1992); Erik Bengtsson, *Världens jämlikaste land?* (Lund: Arkiv förlag, 2020).
25. Nils Stjernquist, *Tvåkammartiden: Sveriges riksdag 1867–1970* (Stockholm: Sveriges riksdag, 1996), pp. 85–90.
26. Ludvig Beckman, "Rösträttsåldern och demokratins avgränsningsproblem", in Katarina Barrling and Sören Holmberg (eds.), *Demokratins framtid* (Stockholm: Sveriges riksdag, 2018).
27. Sandin 2022; Kristina Engwall and Ingrid Söderlind, "Barn och demokrati i ett historiskt perspektiv", in Christer Jönsson (ed.), *Rösträtten 80 år:*

Forskarantologi (Stockholm: Justitiedepartementet, 2001); Kristina Engwall and Ingrid Söderlind, "Barns röst och rätt", in Maria Sjöberg and Yvonne Svanström (eds.), *Att göra historia: Vänbok till Christina Florin* (Stockholm: Institutet för framtidsstudier, 2008); Gunnel Gustavsson, "Rösträtten och barnen", in Christer Jönsson (ed.), *Rösträtten 80 år: Forskarantologi* (Stockholm: Justitiedepartementet, 2001); Gunnel Gustavsson, *Rösträtt för barn: En demokratisk framtidsfråga?* (Umeå: Statsvetenskapliga institutionen, 2009).

28. Robert Dahl, *Democracy and Its Critics* (New Haven: Yale University Press, 1989), p. 233; Nancy Fraser and Axel Honneth, *Redistribution or Recognition? A Political-Philosophical Exchange* (London: Verso Books, 2003); Francis Schrag, "The Child's Status in the Democratic State", *Political Theory* 3:4, 1975, pp. 441–57; J. Wall, "Can Democracy Represent Children? Towards a Politics of Difference", *Childhood* 19:1, 2012, pp. 86–100.
29. Richard S. Katz, *Democracy and Elections* (New York: Oxford University Press, 1997) p. 217 Table 13.1; Giovanni Capoccia and Daniel Ziblatt, "The Historical Turn in Democratization Studies: A New Research Agenda for Europe and Beyond", *Comparative Political Studies* 43:8–9, 2010, pp. 931–968.
30. Berg and Ericsson (eds.) (2021).
31. *V-Dem: Varieties of Democracy, Codebook,* version 11.1 (March 2021), p. 47. Jan Teorell et al., "Measuring Polyarchy across the Globe, 1900–2017", *Studies in Comparative International Development* 54:1, 2019, pp. 71–95; Carl Henrik Knutsen et al., "Introducing the Historical Varieties of Democracy Dataset: Political Institutions in the Long 19th Century", *Journal of Peace Research* 2019:3, pp. 440–451.
32. Teorell et al. (2019).
33. Adam Przeworski, "Conquered or Granted? A History of Suffrage Extensions", *British Journal of Political Science* 39:2, 2009, pp. 291–321; Katz (1997, pp. 216–230 Table 13.1). It is in this context that Sweden becomes a particularly important object of study as regards democratisation and age. The decidedly elitist electoral system, ironically, also led to a relatively uncorrupt electoral system after the breakthrough of democracy. Unlike other countries such as the United States, the system was so elitist that the elites did not need to manipulate it in order to retain power. This is the tentative opinion of Erik Bengtsson (2020, pp. 95–102).
34. Lindberg and Teorell (2018), Stjernquist (1996, pp. 75–100).
35. Alexander Keyssar, *The Right to Vote: The Contested History of Democracy in the United States* (New York: Basic Books, 2000); Katz 1997, pp. 216–238.
36. Katz 1997, p. 218; Ruth Berins Collier and David Collier, *Shaping the Political Arena: Critical Junctures, the Labor Movement, and Regime*

Dynamics in Latin America (Notre Dame, IN.: University of Notre Dame Press, 2002); Leonora Lottrup Rasmussen, "Constitutional rights in conflict. The evolution of political and social rights in Denmark, 1849–1961", *Suffrage, Capital and Welfare: Conditional Citizenship in Historical Perspective,* Eds. Fia Cottrell-Sundevall, and Ragnheiður Kristjánsdóttir (Palgrave, 2024); Ragnheiður, Kristjánsdóttir, The Politics, Practices, and Emotions of Suffrage Exclusion in Iceland, 1915–1934 (2024). *Suffrage, Capital and Welfare: Conditional Citizenship in Historical Perspective*, Eds. Fia Cottrell-Sundevall, and Ragnheiður Kristjánsdóttir (Palgrave, 2024); Minna, Harjula, "The Poor and Deservingness for Political and Social Citizenship: 'Universal suffrage' in Finland Since 1906", *Suffrage, Capital and Welfare: Conditional Citizenship in Historical Perspective*, Eds. Fia Cottrell-Sundevall, and Ragnheiður Kristjánsdóttir (Palgrave, 2024).

37. Bengtsson (2020, pp. 76–77).
38. Ibid., pp. 78–82, from *Statistisk tidskrift* 1898, 114–115, table 20.
39. Einar D. Mellquist, *Rösträtt efter förtjänst? Riksdagsdebatten om den kommunala rösträtten i Sverige 1862–1900* (Stockholm: Stadshistoriska institutet, 1974), pp. 24–36, quotation p. 36.
40. Bengtsson (2020, pp. 95–101), Ihalainen (2017).
41. Daniel Ziblatt, "How Did Europe Democratize?", *World Politics* 2006:2, pp. 311–338, quotation p. 311.
42. Ibid., pp. 337–338; Capoccia and Ziblatt (2010).
43. Capoccia and Ziblatt 2010; Ruth Berins Collier, *Paths toward Democracy: The Working Class and Elites in Western Europe and South America* (Cambridge: Cambridge University Press, 1999); Collier and Collier (2002).
44. Norrlid (1970, 1983), Göran B. Nilsson (1967); see however Bengtsson (2020, pp. 50–53), who does consider these perspectives.
45. Cf., e.g., Ohlsson (2017), Oredsson (2017), Lewin (2020)
46. Douglass C. North, *Institutions, Institutional Change and Economic Performance* (Cambridge: Cambridge University Press, 1990); Stanley L. Engerman and Kenneth L. Sokoloff, "The Evolution of Suffrage Institutions in the New World", *Journal of Economic History* 65:4, 2005, pp. 891–921.
47. Przeworski (2009).
48. Berg and Ericsson (eds.), 2021. The study is based on the research project funded by the Swedish Research Council (Vr 2017–00778), as noted in the Preface.
49. Mattias Lindgren, "Hur många drabbades? Kvantitativa effekter av rösträttsbegränsningarna", in Annika Berg and Martin Ericsson (eds.), *Allmän rösträtt? Rösträttens begränsningar i Sverige efter 1921* (Göteborg & Stockholm: Makadam, 2021), pp. 249–260, figure p. 255.

50. Georg Andrén, *De ekonomiska valbarhetsvillkoren till första kammaren i 1866 RO: Deras tillkomst och motivering* (Göteborg: Wettergren och Kerbers förlag, 1933); Georg Andrén, *Sveriges riksdag: Historisk och statsvetenskaplig framställning*, vol. 9, *Tvåkammarsystemets tillkomst och utveckling* (Stockholm, 1937).
51. Keyssar (2000).
52. The basic data come from printed parliamentary papers (Riksdagstrycket). These have been retrieved from the digitised Riksdag archives, https://www.riksdagen.se/sv/dokument-lagar/. In addition, I have used newspaper articles. The articles have been retrieved through the National Library of Sweden's digital search service, https://tidningar.kb.se/. Important keywords in searching the newspaper material and parliamentary records have been the Swedish words for "age", "voting age", "suffrage", "line", "eligibility". I have used published memoirs and diaries, as well as documents from personal archives in Arbetarrörelsens arkiv och bibliotek (ARBARK), Baroniet Adelsnäs Gårdsarkiv, Riksarkivet (the National Archives), and Uppsala University Library. I have consulted Social Democratic papers in ARBARK. Gunnar Gerdner's papers in Uppsala University Library contain excerpts from various personal archives and from different archives of the Liberal Party and the Social Democrats.
53. The analysis does not aim to examine the sustainability and legitimacy of the arguments from a normative perspective, but instead to specify the content of arguments, the roles of the actors and their historically defined and changing conceptual meanings. See for example Isabela Fairclough and Norman Fairclough, *Political Discourse Analysis: A Method for Advanced Students* (Abingdon: Taylor & Francis, 2013); Henri Lefebvre, *The Production of Space* (Oxford: Basil Blackwell, 1991); Santa Arias, "Rethinking Space: An Outsider's View of the Spatial Turn", *GeoJournal,* 2010:75; Helena Tolvhed, "Intersektionalitet och historievetenskap", *Scandia* 76:1, 2010, pp. 59–72; Clary Krekula, Anna-Liisa Närvänen, and Elisabet Näsman, "Ålder i intersektionell analys", *Kvinnovetenskaplig tidskrift* 26:2, 2005, pp. 81–94.
54. Fernand Braudel, *Civilization and Capitalism: 15th–18th Century*, vol. 1, *The Structures of Everyday Life* (London: Collins, 1981).
55. I have been inspired by the following scholars who have considered this from various angles: Capoccia and Ziblatt 2010; Collier 1999; Collier and Collier 2002; North 1990; Przeworski 2009; Fernand Braudel and Siân Reynolds, *The Structures of Everyday Life: The Limits of the Possible* (London: Fontana, 1985).

CHAPTER 2

Age, Voting, and Eligibility Restrictions 1840–1900

The voting rules that were created to appoint members to the two chambers of the Riksdag after the reforms of the mid-nineteenth century guaranteed that those who contributed more to the state, through their personal competence or status, or in material terms, also had greater rights. It was also on this basis that the right to vote in municipal elections was determined, thus influencing the appointment of members to the First Chamber of the Riksdag. It was thus the contribution to the municipality—the ***kommun*** or community—that was considered to be the basis for the citizens' influence. Other criteria were representing a public interest, corporation, or property holding in the community and not being a burden on other citizens, for example, by dependence on poor relief. The municipality was perceived almost as a joint-stock company. Influence was supposed to be commensurate with the individual's contribution. At the same time, contrary to these arguments it was argued that suffrage should be an individual right for every person regardless of income and property. According to this "personality principle", the right to vote was ultimately understood as a civil right.[1]

To vote in elections to the Second Chamber, men were required to have the right to vote in the municipality and a property with a ratable value of at least 1000 kronor (or a lease valued at 6000 kronor) or a taxable income of at least 800 kronor per year. These levels remained unchanged throughout the period leading up to the reforms of 1907–1909, although they were eroded by inflation and wage increases.[2] There were

B. Sandin, *Voting and Eligibility Age in Sweden, 1866–1921*,
https://doi.org/10.1007/978-3-031-95276-0_2

also requirements of property and income for eligibility to the two chambers of the Riksdag (Fig. 2.1).

Municipal suffrage followed a scale graded according to income and property, which, from the 1860s, was based on the sum of tax units (*fyrk*) at which a person was assessed or the amount of tax paid in kronor. One person could hold the overwhelming majority of the votes in a municipality. Companies, legal entities, the estates of deceased persons could also vote. One individual could thus, for example, vote both as a high-income earner and as the owner of a company. In 1909, the maximum number of votes was limited to 40, which restricted the influence of the owners of the largest fortunes who could previously have an absolute majority in a municipality. The First Chamber was appointed indirectly through the county councils, which were appointed by the municipalities. In this way, municipal suffrage was also the basis for elections to the county councils and the First Chamber. Additionally, the right to vote for the Second Chamber was based on individuals having municipal suffrage.[3]

Let us look more closely at the arguments about the voting restrictions that were introduced in the mid-nineteenth century in connection with the new Riksdag and the reform of the municipalities. The main outlines of this development are well-known from previous research. The reforms in the mid-nineteenth century benefitted the middle class, but also strengthened the interests of well-to-do farmers and landowners. In the following section I supplement that picture with a discussion of how this was also based in various ways on firm notions about how political influence should be limited. It was a matter of economic and social limitations on who could be admitted to the democratic institutions. It was against that background that the suffrage struggle in the late nineteenth century also came to concern the age limits for voting and eligibility. The following section first examines how the low voting age was institutionalised with the constitutional changes of the mid-nineteenth century. The extensive economic restrictions on the right to vote and the age limits for eligibility played a major role here in establishing a parliamentary order that favoured established, social classes. I then look at how this order was challenged at the end of the nineteenth century.

The economic and social development of the mid-nineteenth century—the numerical development and economic conditions of the working class, industrialisation, and urbanisation—led many politicians and debaters to question the legitimacy of the established voting restrictions. What were the alternatives? And who would those with power dare to

Fig. 2.1 Karbasen on 13 December 1902. Inequality of municipal voting rights was a central issue from the late nineteenth century, and this cartoon describes it as manufactured and patented in Sweden; 856 individual workers votes were outweighed by 165 votes based on income superiority. Source: Karbasen, 13/12 1902. Kungliga biblioteket (KB)

accept as partakers in political institutions? This was when the idea of raising the age limit for voting began to spread. In the following section I put the age limits in a broader political context.

The New Parliamentary Order

The composition and form of the Diet of the four estates was a topic of discussion from the late eighteenth century and throughout the first half of the nineteenth century. The peasant estate was expanded to include also tenants of the nobility and other categories of peasants, and the burgher estate was modified to include certain industrial interests. Other adjustments in representation were made to adapt the composition of the Diet to the changes in class society. The selection of those eligible to vote was questioned on various social and legal grounds but not with reference to age, although the age of majority was a crucial criterion. The discussion could concern topics such as adjustments to the requirement of franchise of a town in order to belong to the burgher estate, or the forms of tenure for peasants' land holdings, or broader representation in the houses of the nobility and the clergy. Until the mid-eighteenth century, legally competent women could also vote in elections to the Diet if they met other requirements such as franchise of a town. Since 1721 the age of majority had been 21.[4] However, the representation of the nobility was based on the oldest male member of the various families acting for the family in the house of the nobility. The oldest members represented a family and kin constellation, provided they had reached the age of majority.

Both economic and social status were cited as justification for the political influence of different groups in the Diet and influence over the financial undertakings and governance of local communities (the parishes and later the municipalities).[5] By tradition, the right to vote had "been perceived as accompanying the homestead or property", as the Law Committee pointed out in connection with the discussion in the Diet in 1817–1818. This was probably why women sometimes occurred among the voters in various local assemblies. A change could be perceived as an interference with ownership itself.[6]

Liberal proposals for reform of the Diet during the early nineteenth century were met with sustained opposition and numerous counterproposals. As early as the 1840s, however, the basic features of a bicameral system were formulated, and the then minister of justice, Louis De Geer, specified the details and pushed the reform through during the 1860s.

The nobility and the clergy remained firmly opposed for a long time.[7] Discussion about the form of the new Parliament reached a positive juncture when the church was given its own political body in the synod (Kyrkomötet), which partially constituted a separate sphere of political legislation. Similarly, the transformation of the parishes into secular municipalities and the establishment of county councils meant that the peasants and local economic interests gained considerable influence. It is therefore natural that the reform of local governance—the municipal assembly—also led to strict requirements for municipal suffrage; taxes had to be paid and the value of a person's vote was in proportion to the value of his property and income. Ownership and tax power were linked to property rather than to the individual. Perhaps this was why it did not seem controversial that the age limit for municipal suffrage should be set low at 21 for men, provided that they were registered in the municipality and had property and income. The requirements also excluded those with no property of their own, such as adult offspring still living with their parents. Eligibility was set at 25, and only men could be elected, which was a restriction on the gender-neutral wording in the previous parish ordinances.[8] From 1858, unmarried women could apply for legal competence at the age of 25, and from 1865 they automatically became legally competent at the age of 25, lowered in 1884 to 21. In that sense, more social groups than just propertied male farmers became eligible to vote in the municipality, but the voting scale dramatically curtailed the selection of eligible voters. In addition, property gave more votes than ordinary wage incomes, which favoured farmers, while legal entities could exert significant influence in the "joint-stock company" that was the municipality.[9] This was the beginning of a recurring discussion about how this system should be designed, but also of a debate about the connection between municipal representation and representation in the Riksdag.

After the failure of a number of more limited proposals for a reform of the Diet, the outlook for reform improved. The establishment of a special synod for the clergy and the reform of parish government through the establishment of municipalities and county councils in 1863 ended the opposition in several quarters. The design of elections to municipalities and county councils also guaranteed the influence of the nobility. This influence was further strengthened by the fact that the two chambers in De Geer's proposal were politically equal; the First Chamber did not become purely an upper house with a limited mandate. The risks in the reform of the Second Chamber were thus not so great because the First

Chamber, with its limited selection of eligible members and, as a consequence, its extreme upper-class character, could block any changes that it deemed too far-reaching. However, this did not necessarily mean that the First Chamber was always more conservative than the Second Chamber. The outcome depended on the political and economic issues involved, as historian Torbjörn Nilsson has shown.[10]

The idea of a bicameral parliament that is broadly similar to De Geer's proposal was firmly rooted in the discussions as early as the 1840s and was referenced when the decisions were taken in the 1860s. The same is true of the idea of different economic thresholds, a relatively low voting age of 21 but with a higher eligibility age of 25 for the Second Chamber and 35 for the First Chamber.[11] The reforms in Sweden corresponded to the wave of elite-driven democratisation processes that swept over Europe's monarchies at this time. It was propelled by the middle class and liberal economic interests within different social groups. The effect was that political influence became securely entrenched among economically well-off groups.[12] What differed was that the voting age in Sweden was set uniquely low in comparison with other countries in Europe.[13]

The direction that was pointed out in the early nineteenth century, with the reform of parish assemblies, with a low voting age but extensive economic restrictions on voting, shaped the conditions for the Riksdag and the debate that we will follow in this work. There can be no clearer illustration of path dependence. It was not through the innovation of a high voting age that the right to vote was restricted but through other measures rooted in the previous political system. However, there is also reason to reflect on the significance of these measures. From Louis De Geer's statements it is clear that economic suffrage requirements had cultural meanings that could be partially translated into age terms.

In an important piece published in the *Post- och Inrikes Tidningar* in 1865 Louis De Geer declared that the economic voting restrictions were an appropriate way of sifting out groups in the population that ought not to have any political rights. Among other things, he considered an ongoing discussion about literacy as a requirement for suffrage, and economic selection criteria that make one suspect the influence of John Stuart Mill. He did not agree entirely with the English philosopher. Like Mill, he emphasised that the economic selection criteria were really a tool for distinguishing educated and independent individuals. Yet he rejected literacy as an appropriate criterion, on the grounds that a majority of the Swedish population was already able to meet this requirement (besides which it would be difficult to administer). Since the education of the people was so far advanced in Sweden, other tools were required to distinguish suitable voters. In that respect, money was a better tool, albeit not ideal.

> Money is enlisted to help here only in the same way that one uses a substance in chemistry to separate a useless sediment. For a person who wholly lacks both property and income, it is almost impossible to acquire and maintain the education and independence required for political competence; and what is intended [...] as a condition for exercising political rights, is to exclude, in the interests of education, the utterly uneducated, but not at all to exclude the poor because they are poor.[14]

However, he did acknowledge that the system had its defects. It could lead to the exclusion of the educated poor and the inclusion of uneducated but better-off people, yet it would be a better system than the selection criteria for the various estates in the Diet. Nor did he think that the municipal and county council elections, of which the country now had some experience, showed that representatives were elected for what they "have" rather than what they "are".[15] However, the shortcomings of the selection system could have negative consequences in the future, he admitted. The old Diet and the proposed new Riksdag shared the "future error of wholly excluding the actual worker who, without any capital of his own or any higher intelligence in the product of his work, is essentially confined to his physical strength". This could become a problem if the representatives did not enjoy the trust of the people or had "precisely this trust to thank for their election".[16] It was a balancing act:

> Now while it is true that intelligence is the greatest force in society, one must not leave the numerical preponderance out of the equation either; and there is always some insecurity hovering over a society in which a great force is left outside the circle within which rights exist. However, this danger can rarely be remedied without simultaneously remedying an even greater one. Yet the danger that may arise from the exclusion of the actual working class from political rights still seems more distant among us than in most other countries, partly as a result of our comparatively small urban population.[17]

De Geer thought that the farmers were the group that acted as mediators between physical labour, capital, and intelligence. Therefore, he did not believe that this would become such a big problem in Sweden, but he emphasised that it was important that not too many people felt excluded.

And on this point he hoped that others, in more developed countries, could find a solution before the problems became acute in Sweden. It was all about power, compromise, and change.

> But in order not to hasten pressure from below, and to be able to control its movements when it does come – and it will come some time – it is necessary to give the right of representation to people in such numbers as can be done without peril, and to do so in such a way that at least whole categories of the represented, dissatisfied with an unfair distribution, do not feel compelled to forge alliances with the excluded mass.[18]

De Geer also underscored how important it was that the reform should grant influence on the educated middle class. The farmers and the middle class were the stable foundation on which the future Second Chamber should build. Nor was the intention behind the high suffrage requirements that excessively large groups should be excluded, but the goal was nevertheless to marginalise the working class as a political force.[19]

The way to guarantee the influence of the elites largely depended on the eligibility criteria, and here the age of eligibility played a major role. The proposal outlined by De Geer placed great emphasis on property and income, as well as considerable maturity, following models in the proposals discussed during the preceding decades. The age of eligibility for the First Chamber was 35 and for the Second Chamber, as for municipal offices, 25. These age requirements for eligibility were justified in the same way as the economic requirements (income and property) by the fact that they were accompanied by better education and greater experience. That is what De Geer calls the conservatism of property, thus including an implicit age norm.[20] The demands for education resulting from the economic requirements meant that the lower social classes would also be excluded from influence in the Second Chamber, even if it became more democratic. That these rules also influenced which age groups could and should be allowed to vote will be clear from the continued political discussion.

Louis De Geer, who was the central political motor of the proposal during the 1860s, claimed in his memoirs that it was fundamentally pragmatic. It was only in retrospect that he read up on the great theoretical works of the time. In any case, he did not want the proposal to be viewed as an expression of any specific doctrine. Later scholars have questioned his self-presentation and have been able to identify the sources of his inspiration. Nils Stjernquist points out that he must at least have been well acquainted with various contemporary bicameral systems, but Stjernquist emphasises that the new parliamentary order also shows great continuity with the old Diet, with its equal chambers and the rules that applied to cooperation between them.[21] It is in this light—the retention of the age limits that applied in the old Diet—that we can understand the age limits that came to apply in the new bicameral parliament. The Diet may have served as a model for determining the relationship between the chambers. They enjoyed equal authority in the new constitution, as they had before.

Both in the *Post- och Inrikes Tidningar* article and his memoirs, De Geer argued that the voting rules for Lower House elections should not be made more democratic. While he argued that more democratic rules would not entail any great risk, he stressed that: "if one wanted to combat democracy, it was here that one had to 'fight inch by inch against concessions'."[22] De Geer regarded his construction with the two chambers as sufficiently stable, in the short term at least, and with sufficient resilience for a sustained battle against democratising tendencies. That would come, as it turned out.

His concerns about the growth of the urban and working-class population and the potential for alliances between the middle class and the working class were justified. Göran B. Nilsson points out that an increasing interest in voting among the poorer electorate in the late nineteenth century led to an increasing democratisation of the Second Chamber. In contrast, the proportional *fyrk*-based voting scale in municipal elections, which affected the county councils and the First Chamber, became a guarantee of influence for wealthier economic interests. The farmers were strong in many of Sweden's rural municipalities, but their influence in places with large estates and industrialised rural municipalities was limited both by the large agricultural enterprises and by the emerging industries. These also gradually increased their influence in the county councils, at the same time as the democratisation of the Second Chamber progressed. The influence of mill communities and urban areas increased as a result of population development. The growing population paid dividends in the form of more members of parliament. The growth and increasing influence of the towns and cities was also reflected in the political discussion.[23] The static system of rules created by De Geer and the Riksdag in the mid-nineteenth century was challenged by social and economic development just a few decades later, with consequences both for the content of politics and for the political system. Two questions came to the fore: curtailing the influence of towns, and the need to create guarantees in the face of the looming democratic development. Both of these processes were related to the issue of a higher voting age.

A Challenge to the New Order—the Voting Age

The economic cycles of the last decades of the nineteenth century showed that more and more male income earners met the formal qualifications to vote in elections to the Second Chamber. A large share of the male population had risen above the limit of 800 kronor in income (or property valued at 1000 kronor) for the right to vote in Second Chamber elections, just 40 years after the decision on the new parliamentary order, and they also met the income requirement of 500 kronor to vote in municipal elections. The number of men with the formal right to vote in Second Chamber elections thus became quite large, but in reality it was limited by the fact that it was based on municipal suffrage. This was subject to a number of restrictions such as nationality, registration, income, and, perhaps above all, certified payment of tax (*utskylder*). This significantly limited the number of possible voters.

Towards the end of the nineteenth century, many men from the industrial working class had met the economic criteria for suffrage but were excluded by the requirement to have paid tax. This meant that many were entered into the voting lists but were disqualified for not paying taxes. In addition, the voting scale for municipal elections rewarded income and property in a way that meant that the influence of the vast majority of the population with small incomes was marginal. Although the number of votes an individual could hold in the towns had been reduced back in 1869, from one twentieth of the total votes to one fiftieth, this had a rather limited effect.

In the towns the number of people formally entitled to vote increased dramatically both as a percentage of the population and in absolute terms.[24] In the Stockholm city council elections in 1892, however, 58 per cent were deprived of their right to vote, mainly for failure to pay tax, and in 1900 the figure was 62 per cent. In all urban municipalities, 71 per cent of those with the lowest tax rate had not paid tax and thus were excluded from exercising their right to vote.[25] Difficulty in paying taxes, of course, mainly affected those with low and irregular incomes. Since 1884, unmarried women over the age of 21 had been able to vote in municipal elections if they were registered to pay state tax and could show that they had actually paid it.[26] However, tax liability could be adjusted through a decision at the municipal level, meaning that the criteria for suffrage could vary from one municipality to the next.[27]

The suffrage issue became a matter of serious concern in the 1870s, but there was no clear division according to party lines. Party constellations were generally loose, shaped as they were around concrete issues and therefore also changeable in character. For the parliamentary parties, the important issues were initially the tax system, free trade, and the system for maintaining a trained army. Instead, the suffrage issue was pursued by social movements. The Swedish Universal Suffrage Association, which was politically liberal, was founded in 1890 for this purpose. The association organised its own "People's Parliament" (Folkriksdag) in 1893 and 1896, together with Social Democrats. These were elected with universal and equal suffrage for women and men from the age of 21. Cooperation between the two parties faltered because the Social Democrats also pursued the issue under their own auspices. The People's Parliaments challenged those in power through their mere existence, but they had difficulty agreeing internally on ends and means. Differing opinions as to the meaning of democracy clashed here.[28] The hegemonic position of the Riksdag in representing the people was challenged by the mere establishment of an alternative institution. The People's Parliaments appealed to the government and the king for universal and equal suffrage from the age of 21. The public was mobilised, and a petition for universal suffrage was signed in 1899 by 364,000 men and women. Both the king and the prime minister explicitly disapproved of this attempt to create an alternative democratic platform.[29] The success of the demands for suffrage reform was limited.

It was in this context that the question of the voting age came to the fore. It was as a result of the discussion about how to ensure that extended suffrage would not undermine the status quo, how to achieve what was then termed "suffrage with guarantees".[30] The Social Democrats' motions in the People's Parliaments give a hint of the burgeoning importance of age limits in the discussion. In his motion to the People's Parliament in 1893, Hjalmar Branting opposed the suggestions that had been put forward to lower the income limits for suffrage to the Second Chamber, with a suggested figure of 500 kronor, and to investigate various possible "so-called guarantees" for voting reform. Branting argued that the suffrage issue could not be resolved by lowering the qualification amounts for income; it was the requirement of paid taxes that had to be abolished. He maintained the demand for equal and universal suffrage for men from the age of 21. He also objected to any talk of raising the voting age—another one of the guarantees that had been proposed. Society, he argued, needed the force of youth and there was no reason why young adults should be excluded from their place in civic life. "The adult youth of the working classes who have reached the age of majority certainly do not come straight out of the nursery at 21; they have already experienced life from different sides during the struggle to earn their bread." Moreover, given the current life expectancy, it would be a serious disadvantage if the age of political competence was constricted for "the stepchildren of society". Guarantees were a reactionary political trap, Branting argued emphatically.[31] The main obstacle for the working class was precisely the requirement to have paid municipal and state taxes, what was called the "tax line" in the debate. In the towns in particular, this tax threshold had major consequences for a large share of the eligible voters from the working-class population.[32]

A reform of the income amounts was also completely misguided, according to Branting, since the tax-free deduction was different in different municipalities and could also be changed by one session of Parliament. In this way, Parliament could include or exclude people from the right to vote, at a political whim.[33] He demagogically called this "rubber legislation, under the mask of liberalism and progress that is so favourable to the interests of the ruling classes".[34] Branting also noted that the reform would benefit rural freeholders while the governance of the towns would remain firmly in the hands of the gentry.[35]

The difference between the formal right to vote in elections to the Second Chamber and the exceptions that accompanied the dependence on prevailing rules for municipal suffrage was perceived as a fundamental injustice in several different respects. Influence over the towns was the focus of Branting's interest and argumentation. He also perceived the raising of the voting age as an attempt to exclude young workers. A higher age limit would thus further exacerbate the exclusion of the working class.

Mobilisation for a change in voting rules engaged both Liberals and Social Democrats. It also led to sharp conflicts between the parties. Among other things, the Social Democrats wanted support for a proposal for a general strike demanding the right to vote, but they failed to get Liberal interests to back this. The People's Parliament of 1892 had decided to support a proposal for the right to vote from the age of 21, while there were motions in the People's Parliament at the same time calling for voting from the age of 25. In the People's Parliament, there was thus an opinion in favour of a different stance from the one represented by Branting. The Social Democrats withdrew from the People's Parliament before it met in 1899. It was now the voting age became important in the discussion of suffrage with guarantees. Sixten von Friesen, a leading Liberal, proposed a motion in the Riksdag the same year that the voting age should be raised to the age of 25.[36]

The proposal to raise the voting age, what these proposals meant, is the focus of the discussion in the next chapter. But first a few words about the broader political context. The issue of "democracy with guarantees" that had now arisen was ultimately also a matter of demarcation between different groups that were excluded for various reasons. This concerned not only the working class but also the small people of the towns: craftsmen, merchants, and homeowners, as well as rural labourers, crofters, tenant farmers, and also, as we have seen, adult offspring living at home with no income or property of their own.

Path Dependence and Change. Clipping the Wings of the Urban Interests and Guarantees for the Establishment

When political citizenship—which at the time meant the right to vote in elections to the Second Chamber—was thus formally expanded around the turn of the century, it was simultaneously limited in practice, to a remarkable extent. The increasing demands for more democratic voting rules also led to a discussion, and a specification, of those who should be judged eligible to vote, who should be eligible for election, and how the electoral system should be designed. It was in this context, in the public debate about suffrage with guarantees, that people began to question the age limits established as part of the reforms of 1863–1866. However, the age limits cannot be understood unless we simultaneously consider the broader context and the structure that was created. The question of the voting age was formulated both as a separate issue with slightly different meanings, as we shall see in the following chapters, and as an aspect of the requirements to have performed military training. It also permeated the discussion of female suffrage and, of course, the reasons cited for retaining economic thresholds for the right to vote, as is evident from De Geer's writings.

The connection between the rules for voting in municipal elections and First Chamber elections was questioned immediately after the reforms of the 1860s, leading to restrictions on how many votes a single person in the towns could have. But the interest in making the voting rules in cities more democratic was dampened after the Paris Commune of 1871 in France. The uprising illustrated the dangers of excessive popular influence, at a time when other political issues were becoming more important, such as tariffs and defence. Another question was the design of the electoral system; the number of members depended on the size of the population, which led to a strong increase in the influence of towns and cities as a result of urbanisation. This triggered a debate about how the influence of towns and urban municipalities could be limited. Curtailing the power of the towns ("clipping their wings" as it was called) was deemed necessary because population growth threatened to upset the balance of power between town and country.[37] There is reason to reflect on whether this fear also concerned the age composition of the urban population. I will come back to that.

The demands of the Social Democrats and the suffrage movement for electoral reforms in the last decades of the nineteenth century made the suffrage issue acute. The struggle for the right to vote was also waged in large public demonstrations, which were sometimes countered with harsh measures by the state. The general strike of 1902 for the right to vote underscored the demands and determination of the labour movement. The Liberals' interest in a suffrage reform did not only involve a commitment to the working class but also concerned the influence in the municipalities of farmers and unmarried men living at home, as well as merchants and craftsmen in the towns.[38] And this was when the bourgeois female suffrage movement largely took the form of a critique of the lack of commitment from the established suffrage advocates in Parliament. Both Liberals and Social Democrats moved in the Riksdag for a change in voting rights but with an emphasis on male suffrage.[39] In 1904, however, at the urging of the women's suffrage movement, the Liberals proposed a motion for a tax reform that could give married women with their own income and property the right to vote in municipal elections.[40]

The legitimacy of the static economic restrictions on voting rights was gradually undermined according to the model on which the reforms of the 1860s were based, as a barrier against the influence of the broader strata of society. The dissatisfaction was heightened by the fact that the constituencies appointed members after majority elections, which meant that, for example, worker majorities could lead to real shifts in power. In the long run, this could also have the effect that political minorities in the power-holding strata of the population were left without representation.[41] There was an acceptance of a gradation of the right to vote according to economic status and contribution to the local community by wealthy groups, but the graduated right to municipal suffrage was also perceived as unfavourable to the local agrarian elites, partly as a consequence of the industrialisation of rural areas.[42]

The Conservatives therefore tackled the suffrage issue as well. The introduction of proportional representation became a political demand early on, to ensure influence, and this was one of the proposals put forward when the Farmer's Party became involved in the campaign for "universal suffrage with guarantees" around 1900. Other issues that provoked criticism from established rural interests were the relationship between the influence of towns and rural areas in Parliament and the influence of companies (legal entities) in the emerging industrial communities in rural areas.[43]

It was the relationship between the two chambers of Parliament and the link with the municipal level that became a key issue making the suffrage question rather difficult to resolve. There was a basic structure that limited the political manoeuvring space on the issue. The proposals for reform would consider different voting and eligibility ages for the different levels depending on what other rules could be applied. However, the elites who set the agenda did not agree on how the guarantees should be designed. By all accounts, the numerically limited elites had different but partly overlapping backgrounds—public officials, landowners, farmers, and capitalists—with divergent and sometimes opposing interests to protect. There could also be differences between different parts of the country depending on social structure and economic development.[44] The political stances do not always lend themselves easily to positioning on a left-right scale: members of parliament changed their positions on substantive issues, switched parties, or simply established themselves as independents, but their views ended up influencing the development of the modern party system. It was the conflicts over the suffrage issue that led to the formation of the modern political parties that would dominate in the twentieth century. At the same time, the electorate also changed with the emergence of new communities, economic interests, and social strata.[45]

Concluding Reflections

Social and economic developments thus challenged the political order created in the 1860s. The complexity of the suffrage issue was exposed in the attempts to limit the electorate in different ways. It was far from obvious how the guarantees for the status quo should be designed. The growth of the urban population and the improved economic position of the working class were reflected in the debate, as was the complex relationship between municipal suffrage and the right to vote in elections to the Second Chamber. The Social Democrats' solution was to give all men equal and universal suffrage from the age of 21, in local elections and in elections to the Riksdag, with certain exceptions, while the Liberals and the Right tested different ways to modify the voting rules and the relatively extensive restrictions on the future electorate by means of voting thresholds. Their ambition was to establish a higher voting and eligibility age. It is in this context that the issue of the voting age became an explicit feature of political discussions.[46]

Let us therefore examine the arguments invoked during the last decade of the nineteenth century and in the years just after 1900. This was when an interpretive framework was created that makes it possible to understand how culturally charged the issue of the voting and eligibility age was. It was a question of whom those with power could trust in the society that was emerging, and who could thus be granted a voice in the transformation of society. It therefore affected both local politics and national politics and the interaction between them.

Notes

1. Ebba Berling Åselius, *Rösträtt med förhinder: Rösträttsstrecken i svensk politik 1900–1920* (Stockholm: Acta Universitatis Stockholmiensis, 2005), p. 26; Jonas Hultin Rosenberg and Fia Sundevall, "Contributivist Views on Democratic Inclusion: On Economic Contribution as a Condition for the Right to Vote", *Critical Review of International Social and Political Philosophy* 2022, pp. 1–25.
2. A calculation reveals the following development: 800 kronor in 1866 corresponded to payment for the same working hours to the tune of 1,425,658 kronor in 2020 measured by the wage index for male industrial workers (wage earners from 2005); 800 kronor in 1900 corresponded to 623,725 kronor in 2020; 800 kronor in 1910 corresponded to 463,600 kronor in 2020; 800 kronor in 1918 corresponded to 197,250 kronor in 2020.

Source: http://historicalstatistics.org/Jamforelse-pris.htm (hämtad 17/10 2022). (retrieved 17 October 2022).

3. Einar D. Mellquist, *Rösträtt efter förtjänst? Riksdagsdebatten om den kommunala rösträtten i Sverige 1862–1900* (Stockholm: Stadshistoriska institutet, 1974); Ingemar Norrlid, "Kommunen som bolag? En studie i liberal rösträttspolitik före första världskriget", *Scandia 36:1*, 1970; Göran B. Nilsson, "Folkval och fyrkval 1863–1909", Scandia 30:1, 1964, pp. 89–137; Erik Bengtsson, Världens jämlikaste land? (Lund: Arkiv förlag, 2020).; Carolina Uppenberg and Mats Olsson, "Under the Landlord's Thumb: Municipalities and Local Elites in Sweden 1862–1900", *Social History 47:3, 2022.*
4. *Bihang till Riksdagens Protokoll 1862–1863*, 3 Saml. *Konstitutionsutskottets Memorial* no. 7; Staffan Förhammar, *Reformvilja eller riksdagstaktik: Junkrarna och representationsfrågan 1847–54* (Stockholm: Almqvist & Wiksell, 1975); Georg Andrén, Sveriges riksdag: Historisk och statsvetenskaplig framställning, vol. 9, Tvåkammarsystemets tillkomst och utveckling (Stockholm, 1937), pp. 7–20.
5. Andrén (1937, pp. 156–182); Nils Stjernquist, *Tvåkammartiden: Sveriges riksdag 1867–1970* (Stockholm: Sveriges riksdag, 1996); Åsa Karlsson Sjögren, *Männen, kvinnorna och rösträtten: Medborgarskap och representation 1723–1866* (Stockholm: Carlsson, 2006); Åsa Karlsson Sjögren, "Kvinnors röst i sekelskiftets städer: Kommunalt valdeltagande före den allmänna rösträtten", in Maria Sjöberg and Yvonne Svanström (eds.), *Att göra historia: Vänbok till Christina Florin* (Stockholm: Institutet för framtidsstudier, 2008).
6. Mellquist (1974, p. 24) and Karlsson Sjögren (2006, pp. 155–182). For a comparison see how under-age children could vote in certain Austrian municipalities if they owned property: Gerald Kohl, "Alter und Wahlrecht: Zum Verhältnis bürgerlicher und politischer Rechts- und Handlungsfähigkeit seit der Mitte des 19. Jahrhunderts", *Parliaments, Estates and Representation* 28:1, 2008, pp. 151–163.
7. Andrén (1937, pp. 20–46) and Förhammar (1975).
8. Karlsson Sjögren (2006, pp. 171–179).
9. Mellquist (1974, pp. 58–61, passim); A. O. Winroth, "Myndighetsålder", in *Nordisk Familjebok* (Stockholm: Nordisk Familjeboks förlag, 1913); Elin Hinnemo, *Inför högsta instans: Samspelet mellan kvinnors handlingsutrymme och rättslig reglering i Justitierevisionen 1760–1860* (Uppsala: Acta Universitatis Upsaliensis, 2016). Married women also had some bargaining power in terms of authority over property, businesses, and household operations.
10. Andrén (1937, pp. 46–76); Torbjörn Nilsson, *Elitens svängrum: Första kammaren, staten och moderniseringen 1867–1886* (Stockholm: Almqvist

& Wiksell International, 1994); Stig Ekman, *Slutstriden om representationsreformen*, diss. (Uppsala: Appelberg, 1966).

11. *Bihang till Riksdagens Protokoll, 1862–1863*, Tredje Saml. Konstitutionsutskottets Memorial no. 7; Andrén (1937, pp. 20–46) and Karlsson Sjögren (2006, p. 175, passim).
12. Ruth Berins Collier, Paths toward Democracy: *The Working Class and Elites in Western Europe and South America* (Cambridge: Cambridge University Press, 1999), pp. 33–76. However, she does not discuss Sweden in this context, but only in connection with the development of socialist parties. Ekman (1966, pp. 26–185, 375–380).
13. Richard S. Katz, *Democracy and Elections* (New York: Oxford University Press, 1997) p. 217 Table 13.1. According to Katz, as noted above, Sweden also had a voting age of 25, which is obviously incorrect.
14. Louis De Geer, "Ännu ett ord om representationsförslaget", *Post- och Inrikes Tidningar* 23 September 1865; Ekman (1966, pp. 219–230).
15. De Geer (1865).
16. Ibid.
17. Ibid.
18. Ibid.
19. Louis De Geer, *Minnen* (Stockholm: P. A. Nordstedt & Söner, 1906), vol. 2, pp. 8–19.
20. Georg Andrén, *De ekonomiska valbarhetsvillkoren till första kammaren i 1866 RO: Deras tillkomst och motivering* (Göteborg: Wettergren och Kerbers förlag, 1933),p. 34; Andrén (1937, pp. 65–75); Göran B. Nilsson, Självstyrelsens problematik: Undersökningar i svensk landstingshistoria 1839–1928 (Uppsala: Acta Universitatis Upsaliensis, 1967), pp. 38–42.
21. De Geer (1906, vol. 1, p. 238), Andrén (1933, pp. 28–36, 1937, pp. 131–145), Stjernquist (1996, pp. 34–35).
22. De Geer (1906, vol. 2, p. 4) and De Geer, 23 September 1865.
23. Göran B. Nilsson (1967, pp. 38–42).
24. Mellquist (1974, pp. 112–116, 122).
25. Ibid., pp. 116–124.
26. The previous age limit, valid since 1863, was 25. The right to vote thus followed the age of majority.
27. Mellquist (1974, pp. 63, 116–130).
28. *Folkriksdagen 1893, 1896: Samling Tryckta handlingar* (n.p., n.d.); Rolf Fridholm, "Folkriksdagarna 1893 och 1896", *Statsvetenskaplig tidskrift* 30:5, 1927, pp. 411–440; Victor Lundberg, *Folket, yxan och orättvisans rot: Betydelsebildning kring demokrati i den svenska rösträttsrörelsens diskursgemenskap 1887–1902* (Umeå: h:ström – Text & kultur, 2007).
29. Fridholm (1927, pp. 422–424) and Bengtsson (2020, pp. 117–122).
30. Berling Åselius (2005, pp. 37–59).

31. Hjalmar Branting, "Motion nr 32 Hj. Branting, med förslag till principuttalanden dels emot planerna inom första kammaren om ny utredning av rösträttsfrågan och af rösträttens s. k. garantier, dels emot andra kammarens förslag om 500-kr streck", *Folkriksdagen: Tryckta handlingar vid 1893 års folkriksdag* (Uppsala, 1893), p. 54.
32. Ibid., pp. 54–60.
33. Ibid., pp. 60–62.
34. Ibid., p. 62.
35. Ibid.
36. Stjernquist (1996, p. 60) and Fridholm (1927, pp. 434–440).
37. Stjernquist (1996, pp. 58–61), Mellquist (1974, pp. 124–138, 156–159); Berling Åselius (2005, pp. 36–58).
38. Stjernquist (1996) and Berling Åselius (2005, pp. 36–58).
39. Rönnbäck (2004, pp. 27–38, 58–61).
40. Ibid., p. 115. This proposal then reappeared in 1908 in a motion from the Conservative government. Here we can identify a certain openness from Liberals and Conservatives to give influence in local elections to women from the more prosperous classes. The Social Democrats were critical of the proposal because it entailed raising taxes for poor families. In 1908 it was also a matter of enabling married women to participate in municipal administration; Riksdagstrycket, *Motion AK 1904:168*, pp. 8–11, *Protokoll FK 1904:36*, pp. 58–61, *Protokoll AK 1904:39*, pp. 63–69, *Bevilјningsutskottets betänkande 1908:22*, pp. 6–10, *Protokoll AK 1908:53*, Branting's statement, pp. 67–69.
41. Berling Åselius (2005, pp. 15–18).
42. Norrlid (1970) and Mellquist (1974, pp. 124–138).
43. Mellquist (1974, pp. 139–154).
44. Berling Åselius (2005, p. 19); Torbjörn Nilsson, "Högern 1900–1940: En historisk vandring mot demokrati", in Christer Jönsson (ed.), *Rösträtten 80 år: Forskarantologi*, Stockholm: Justitiedepartementet, 2001, p. 75; Runestam (1966, pp. 71, 89). Ingemar Norrlid, "Kommunen som bolag? En studie i liberal rösträttspolitik före för- sta världskriget", Scandia 36:1, 1970), pp. 234–245; Mellquist (1974) and Uppenberg and Olsson (2022).
45. Pirjo Markkola, Seija-Leena Nevala-Nurmi, and Irma Sulkunen, *Suffrage, Gender and Citizenship: International Perspectives on Parliamentary Reforms* (Newcastle: Cambridge Scholars Publishing, 2009); Stjernquist (1996, pp. 57–67).
46. Berling Åselius (2005, pp. 87–88).

CHAPTER 3

Who on Earth Can Be Trusted?

The suffrage issue, as we shall see, was raised with increasing intensity in parliamentary debates during the 1890s, with various concrete proposals put forward. The proposers brought up what they viewed as unfair aspects and suggested partial reforms. These could concern, for example, the exclusion from suffrage of crofters, tenant farmers, or adult offspring living at home,[1] or more general issues such as the fact that population development in the towns and cities had a negative effect on rural representation in Parliament, or the risks of the increasing influence of the working class. Craftsmen, tenants, and low-wage earners were also mentioned among those who were disadvantaged by the suffrage rules. The criticism was sometimes harsh and there was little agreement among members. The arguments had completely different social premises. The reforms of the 1860s had been favourable to broad groups of the propertied rural population. Around 1900 they found themselves squeezed between the demands for increased influence from political interests that spoke for those without property and the dominant influence of the companies and legal entities that resulted from the industrialisation of the Swedish countryside. Rural municipalities simultaneously became increasingly dependent on initiatives from the state to solve issues of poor relief and schooling. Municipal self-government was influenced by regulations and decisions at the state level.[2]

It was also around 1900 that voting age limits were debated in the Riksdag after having been discussed in the People's Parliament. In the first

B. Sandin, *Voting and Eligibility Age in Sweden, 1866–1921*,
https://doi.org/10.1007/978-3-031-95276-0_3

part of this chapter I analyse how the age limits relate to other voting restrictions. In the second part I examine how the age limit was established as a central figure of thought in parliamentary debates. Then, in the last part of this chapter, I follow how these ideas were expressed in the political process and established through the decisions of 1907–1909. There is good reason to start with a discussion of the changing conditions of the municipalities because the political dynamic between the state and the citizens was based on far-reaching municipal self-government. In the last section, I return to the question of why the age limits for voting in municipal elections were not affected by the reform of male suffrage in elections to the Second Chamber.

Reformed Voting Rights with Guarantees

The historian Ingemar Norrlid, in his study of the municipality as an economic entity with influence for the participants in relationship to their wealth (sometimes expressed as a joint-stock company), discusses how this idea was undermined towards the end of the nineteenth century. Two processes were significant in this: first, the unreasonable size of companies' voting shares, which allowed them to dominate certain municipalities, and second, the increasing economic pressures on poor relief and the establishment of a mass-educational system (folkskola) that increasingly required national regulation and support from the central government. The work of the municipalities in these areas was not just a local, private, individual, affair; these activities required central oversight, national coordination and joint initiatives, far beyond the scope of any one municipality. Farmers' interests demanded a reduction in the number of votes for industries and corporations, and this was combined with a demand to favour the influence of those who owned agricultural properties; it was the relationship between the municipality and the stable and stationary rural population, with long historical ties to their native district, that had to take priority.[3]

These were arguments that could be based on the idea of the municipality as a company with property owners and taxpayers, but the arguments also expressed criticism of the way the system favoured large enterprises. Over time, this led to a wider discussion of whether municipal suffrage should be based on income and property or solely based on individuals having paid taxes.[4] It is worth emphasising the argument that it was the stability of the farming population and its permanent ties to the local community that specifically legitimated their demands for influence in both the local and national politics in this time of dramatic social development and change.[5] Given this way of thinking, it is easy to understand that municipal politicians all over Sweden were doubtful not only about the influence of capital on rural industries but also about the influence of unpropertied groups. The growth of the towns with their mobile working population also threatened rural interests in Parliament. Shortly after the reforms of the mid-nineteenth century, demands to limit the influence of legal entities soon led to restrictions on the number of votes that an individual could have in the towns. As for rural areas, it was not until 1900 that a moderate restriction was introduced. This continued to be a burning issue.[6]

The political establishment eventually felt compelled to act when it came to the right to vote in elections to the Second Chamber. The first bill in 1896 by the Gustav Boström government was particularly reticent about proposing any significant changes. The bill stressed the importance of ensuring that the reforms would not risk the peaceful development of society. The number of workers entitled to vote had already increased dramatically as a result of higher wages. Therefore, according to the bill, there was no justification for any further extension of suffrage. The bill confined itself to proposing a modest reduction in the levels of the income threshold and the value of a leased property, and that state taxes (*bevillning*) had been paid. To some extent, the government met the demands. A further proposal to introduce proportional representation instead of majority voting was intended to limit the future dominant influence of popular majorities. The voices of the minorities had to be protected.[7]

The proposal thus did not represent any dramatic change in the system established by the reforms of the 1860s. And that was what the critics immediately seized on. David Persson of Tällberg pointed out in his motion that the proposal was designed to have as little impact as possible on the composition of the Second Chamber, and he wondered whether the proposers did not consider that the owners of “small plots of land or properties” deserved the right to vote, given their patriotism and the fact that they paid the same state tax as others. In addition, he wanted to see some information about how many people would lose their right to vote because of the proposal to raise the age limit for voting and retain the requirement to pay state taxes.[8] However, it is unclear what increase in the age limit David Persson was referring to, since the bill does not mention any age limits for voting and eligibility to the Second Chamber; it was instead based on the voting age for municipal elections, which was 21.

There is no comment on this in any other motions. At the same time, it is certainly the case that the idea of a higher voting age, around 25, had been repeatedly mentioned in various party discussions at the end of the nineteenth century.[9]

Other motions called for restrictions on the influence of the wealthy and protection for those with less financial muscle. Lars Eriksson of Bäck proposed that municipal suffrage should be granted to every citizen from the age of 21, but that voting should be graded when electing members of parliament and electors to the First Chamber. Everyone eligible to vote in the municipality would receive two votes in those elections and then a greater number of votes depending on income or property, up to four votes. At the same time, Eriksson proposed a reform of municipal suffrage through a new scale that could reduce the impact of those with most votes.[10] Two Liberal members of parliament who were early advocates of a suffrage reform, Julius Mankell and David Bergström, stated that the bill should have been limited to proposing a threshold of 500 kronor (i.e. a reduction from 800 kronor) and the rules that applied to the municipal threshold (i.e. having paid municipal tax and having no outstanding taxes), without the other restrictions that had now been proposed. They declared themselves unable to support the government's "illusory reform" and proposed suffrage from the age of 21 for Swedish citizens who were entered in the municipal electoral rolls.[11] Jöns Bromée and Erik Eriksson proposed voting rights to the Second Chamber on the basis of municipal suffrage, with the following argument:

> To exclude from political suffrage the now very numerous class of settled, law-abiding, politically interested, and politically "mature" citizens, who consist of tenants or owners of homes on someone else's land, seems to us to be neither fair nor politically prudent.[12]

Nor did they mention any other possible restrictions or any other voting age than that which applied to municipal suffrage.[13]

The government's bill was innovative in that it proposed the introduction of proportional representation, but it did not contribute anything new in other respects. The requirement to hold a tax certificate (*debetsedel*), i.e. to be registered as a taxpayer and to have actually paid tax, was already one of the regulations. The reductions in income levels were not particularly dramatic, nor did they address the fundamental problems relating to the influence of the rural population. It is also clear that the debate was about how broader suffrage could be combined with guarantees for social groups that already had power and influence.[14]

The issue thus came to concern who could be considered a patriot (and thus eligible to vote) and which groups in society the authorities and those in power could trust. The changed tax system, with the transition from basic taxes (tax on real estate/agricultural property) to individual income taxes, along with the transition of the national defence from the allotment system (a parish maintaining one or more soldiers) to mandatory general conscription, made it reasonable that such contributions to society should earn a person the right to vote, that is, to have an influence in politics. Payment of taxes and fulfilled military training could also be perceived as criteria for responsible behaviour and patriotism, as previously pointed out.[15]

The political interest in extending suffrage did not only reflect the influence of the working class. A crucial point in the debate was, of course, that alongside the influence traditionally exerted by propertied people in the countryside and by capital, there was now the factor of "the very large class of settled, law-abiding, politically interested, and politically 'mature' citizens" mentioned in the debates.[16]

These issues have also been discussed in previous research. In her study, Ebba Berling Åselius distinguished three different basic positions on the suffrage question. The first position emphasised that the right to vote in parliamentary elections should be based on municipal suffrage, meaning that those liable to pay municipal taxes were entitled to vote. By lowering the minimum income level for municipal suffrage, the proportion of voters could be increased. This proposal was included in the government bill of 1896. The second line (embraced by the Liberals Julius Mankell and David Bergström) argued for universal suffrage for "respectable" men (those who had not gone bankrupt or been declared legally incapacitated) who paid municipal taxes, but without any other restrictions. That was the platform on which the Social Democrats would stand. Moderate conservatives with a progressive outlook adopted a third position, advocating for extended voting rights with more comprehensive "guarantees".[17]

At the same time, it was clear that an extension of suffrage in Second Chamber elections, combined with guarantees, had become a fundamental feature in the discussion around the turn of the century. Let us delve a little deeper into the different ideas as to how the right to vote should be expanded and limited. The gradation of the right to vote and eligibility in economic terms, as introduced with the decisions of 1862–1866, was, as we saw earlier, already loaded with normative implications. The economic gradation of suffrage and eligibility was supposed to ensure that the selected voters and candidates were sufficiently informed, independent, experienced, and educated. In context, it was unquestionable that the electorate should be demarcated in this way, not only by gender, but also in terms of which social classes and age groups were included.[18]

The demands for a change in voting rules challenged these, partly implicit, ideas about guarantees that well-informed and independent male citizens of the right age should have an influence that could guarantee the stability of society. There were numerous and diverse solutions which did not follow clear and obvious party lines but were generally based on a discussion of male suffrage. Ideas about class elections (i.e. elections to represent specific groups as in the old Diet) were put forward, but also how different restrictions could be designed to enable broader suffrage reform. The Social Democrats' first programme from 1897 called for universal and equal suffrage in municipal and political elections, with all adult citizens entitled to vote from the age of 21 and without gender differences.[19] These demands formed the background to the discussion about suffrage that Liberals and the Right initiated in Parliament around the turn of the century. It was not the Social Democrats who set the agenda; they had no members of parliament as a party until 1902, but the party leader, Hjalmar Branting, was elected on a liberal party ticket in 1896.[20] The discussion focused on the right to vote in elections to the Second Chamber (what was called "political suffrage") and the restrictions on voting rights in municipal elections, and on the relationship between the voting regulations for municipal and parliamentary elections. As we have seen above, these issues were closely linked and had consequences for the proposed solutions. Now, the age of the electorate has become a central point of reference also in the discussion and the political interactions (Fig. 3.1).

The Age Threshold Is Established as a Figure of Thought

In 1899 the Liberal member of parliament Sixten von Friesen proposed a dramatic raise of the voting age to 25 in elections to the Second Chamber. During 1898 and the spring of 1899, a series of motions had been proposed in Parliament about the right to vote for the Second Chamber. We note, among others, motions by Gullbrand Elowsson, Johan Nydahl, David Bergström with the support of Hjalmar Branting, Carl Lindhagen,

Fig. 3.1 Karbasen 1 March 1902. Karl Staaff's and the Liberals' balancing act between voting rights limitations and universal suffrage, as was presented in the social democratic joke newspaper. Source: Karbasen 1/3 1902. KB

and others.[21] The demand for universal and equal suffrage for every man from the age of 21 was rejected by the Constitutional Committee in May 1899, citing the fears expressed in the 1880s by De Geer, the architect of the constitution, that this was "not compatible with the calm and sound development of society":

> If the demand for universal and equal suffrage proposed by Mr Bergström and others and by Mr Lindhagen were granted, the whole of the present electorate would be turned into a minority, and all power in elections would accrue to the social class that are now below the so-called line, a system of suffrage which, in the opinion of the Committee, would not be compatible with the calm and sound development of society, and the implementation of which would thus not bring any lasting benefits even to that social class.[22]

The right to vote was not the right of the individual, the Committee argued. Nor was it a right associated with the obligation to pay taxes; it had to be subordinated to the good of the state so that influence accrued to the experienced, mature, and independent members of society.[23] This perspective on utility for the state was based on a limitation of how far individuals' demands for influence could be extended in relation to their individual contributions. What was good for the state was a more important factor.

Sixten von Friesen's motion for a higher voting age was signed by no fewer than 70 members of parliament, but not by the Social Democratic leader Hjalmar Branting. The so-called People's Parliament of 1898 had ended in disagreement between Liberals and Social Democrats over how to pursue the suffrage issue. The Liberals, for example, did not support the idea of a general strike over the right to vote. The People's Parliament was reconstituted in 1899 into a liberal coalition party, under the leadership of von Friesen, and the initiative was transferred to the Riksdag. Von Friesen's letter to the Constitutional Committee was referenced in a motion in 1900, which had over 80 signatories at the time. Among these we find the proposers noted above as well as Karl Staaff and several well-known Liberals. Branting, however, who was voted in on a Liberal list, was not among the signatories.[24]

Two years later, Branting described the Liberals' transformation in the 1890s in critical terms. They had abandoned the idea of universal suffrage; they had moved to the Right and embraced the idea of "the 25-year guarantee" and other criteria of exclusion.[25] The proposal to introduce a new higher age limit clearly demonstrates the conflict between Liberals and Social Democrats. On this issue, Liberals and Conservatives shared fundamental values.

The Liberal motion began with a quotation from the architect of the 1860s reforms Louis De Geer's memoirs from 1892, in which he endorsed the idea of extending the right to vote because "the education that is necessary for political judgement has in recent years penetrated down to deeper strata of society [...] among them chiefly a large proportion of manual workers."[26] However, it was reasonable that the right to vote in parliamentary elections should be limited to those entitled to vote in their municipalities, according to De Geer.[27] Citing De Geer was useful for advancing various lines of political argument. Against this background, the motion then describes the government bill of 1896, the mass petition to the King in Council in 1898, and all the various proposals during the Riksdag in 1899. According to the motion, many people had understood that suffrage should be reformed, but the various proposals had either demanded too much or too little in relation to the current laws and the requirements of the time.[28] However, a common goal had become increasingly clear for the men behind the motion: that a bill for suffrage reform for the Second Chamber should be designed "with the basic idea of political suffrage for men entitled to vote in municipal elections who have reached the age of 25".[29]

Such a reform would decisively ensure sound development without undermining the "worthy representatives" who already had seats in the Second Chamber. It would moreover give a legitimate influence to a large number of people with sufficient education and an independent livelihood, "for example, the large number of manual workers, craftsmen, low-wage earners, small property owners, small tenant farmers and crofters, who currently lack any political authority".[30]

An extension of the suffrage would be both a question of social justice and a measure that would "truly help to preserve society" and underpin a national sense of solidarity, not least in view of the extended conscription. Basing political suffrage on municipal suffrage was not entirely without problems, according to von Friesen, since municipal suffrage could be changed with a single decision by Parliament (while a change of the voting rights for the Second Chamber required a second parliamentary decision after an election). The advantage was that the right to vote was based on good insights of conditions in the constituency.

Broader suffrage would be a matter of social justice and simultaneously a measure that would really help to "conserve society" and sustain an organic sense of national solidarity. The solution proposed by von Friesen was to replace the property threshold and income requirements with a new general rule:

> The condition of having reached the age of 25 for exercising political suffrage is admittedly new for us, but it is consistent with the requirements in the electoral orders of many European countries and, far better than the current property threshold, it is surely suitable as a guarantee against abuse of suffrage. First of all, because greater maturity in judgement is to be expected in a man at the age of 25, at a time in life when members of the manual class have often started a family, than at the age of 21, and, secondly, a voter of the said age has already had a few years to become used to exercising the right to vote in the municipality, which, as is well known, comes with the age of majority. Finally, a voter at the age of 25, when he has generally, in so far as he is able, discharged such an important duty to the state as military service, may also be said to have a greater demand to participate in the conduct of public affairs. This age limit is already established for eligibility – in addition to other positions of trust – to the Second Chamber, which means that the proposed provision would mean only that the conditions for voting and eligibility for the Second Chamber will coincide.[31]

It was a simple and, in the long term, as we shall see, successful move to emphasise the higher age limit as a substitute for the complex discussion about income and property levels, which moreover excluded many of the groups to whom the Liberals wanted to appeal. The initiative was also successful in the short term, in that it led to a joint letter from both chambers to the King in Council about the need to investigate more closely how suffrage could be designed. However, the higher age limit was linked to a series of supplementary criteria that are recognisable from previous motions. In addition to the raised voting age, the proposal required "permanent residence within the constituency, having fulfilled obligations to society through proper payment of taxes over a certain period of time", and also having completed "ordinary military training in peacetime, unless postponement or exemption has been granted", and the letter from the Riksdag left it open whether the right to vote "should build on the principle of equal suffrage, or else with some gradation of the right to vote".[32] The letter also stated that the differences in representation in parliament between town (*stad* or borough) and country, as well as between market town (*köping*) and country, should be included in the review of the rules.[33] The letter thus bears the imprint of a compromise between different reform proposals. The basic suggestion was expanded with a range of additional possible criteria, from "responsible behaviour to the fundamental raise in the voting age". With this proposal, older people (men) with the right to vote were still subject to these norms of "responsible behaviour". Voting was still to be conditioned.

In this letter the Riksdag had not committed itself absolutely to any specific solution, but the raising of the voting age to 25, which was initiated by von Friesen and had found support among the Liberal suffrage reformers, had found its place in the reform package of the time. It would turn out that this also became the common foundation for the continued discussion between Liberals and Conservatives up until the important decisions in 1918–1921.

The "Age Line" from a Figure of Thought to a Concrete Proposal

The Liberals' tentative initiative gained a hearing. In 1902, a mainly Conservative cabinet led by Fredrik von Otter presented a proposal that the voting age for the Riksdag should be raised. Von Otter led the government between 1900–1902, dealing with two major issues—the conscription reform and the suffrage issue.[34] The suffrage proposal did not lead to a decision, but nevertheless had consequences for the later development. The proposal had a mobilising effect on the women's suffrage movement and was an expression of the process in which the Liberal proposals were united with the Conservatives' ambitions to achieve a suffrage reform with guarantees. As we shall see, the politicians did not entirely agree, but the figure of thought of the "age line" now took on a more concrete form.

The law scholar Hjalmar Hammarskjöld drafted the government's memorandum on a future suffrage reform. He later took office as minister of justice in a government dominated by the Farmer's Party. The memorandum states that the right to vote in elections to the Second Chamber should roughly correspond to the criterion for municipal suffrage, that the requirement to pay taxes should be tightened in accordance with the 1896 bill (i.e. include proof of having paid state and municipal taxes), that the voting age should be raised to 25, and that a graduated voting scale should be introduced to the effect that "marriage or a certain age of maturity should be established as the main or sole grounds for the granting of extra votes".[35] In addition, the differences between urban and rural representation would be evened out. Constituencies would also be distributed so that the interests of minorities could be taken into account, and proportional representation could possibly be introduced in some constituencies. In addition, the memorandum stated that: "Completion of military training should, if possible, be ascribed some significance for the right to vote." It also included a comment that the criterion of paid taxes was of minor importance and that the item about military training "is likely to be dropped due to practical difficulties".[36] Here we see that the idea of a higher voting age became fundamental in the proposal of the Farmer´s Party. In the bill that followed we also see how Hammarskjöld specifies and justifies the age limits. Here, the age limits are made concrete in social and economic terms. Age takes on a social and political meaning there. Let us follow the lines of thought in the bill that followed.

In the bill that was later presented in the Riksdag, it was suggested that the new voting age should be 25 and that married men who had reached the age of 40 should have double votes. It thus meant a significant increase in the voting age from 21, the age limit that applied in municipal elections, but the proposal also contained a number of other possible requirements. In addition, the bill pointed out that a change in voting rights required a thorough investigation of all possible consequences. Given the significance of municipal suffrage for elections to the First Chamber, this opened the possibility that municipal suffrage would also be constitutionally enshrined and that

> several guarantees besides higher age, such as permanent residence within the constituency, the fulfilment of obligations to society through the proper payment of taxes over a certain period of time, completion of ordinary military training in peacetime, unless postponement or exemption has been granted, [...] as well as whether, in the event of extended suffrage, the electoral system should still be based on the principle of equal suffrage, or whether any gradation of the vote should be adopted.[37]

The higher age limit was thus not quite sufficient, as stated in von Friesen's letter above; other guarantees were required, possibly including extra votes for married men. The bill cites examples from various European countries showing that universal suffrage was not without restrictions: citizenship, having reached a certain age, being a permanent resident in the constituency, "not being disqualified on some specific grounds – such as criminality, bankruptcy, incapacity, being in receipt of poor relief, having unpaid taxes, failure to do military training".[38] These concrete restrictions were not perceived as being contrary to the idea of ***universal*** suffrage. Suffrage required guarantees, it was pointed out, either through the division of voters into classes or through a gradation of the vote.[39] Universal suffrage therefore tended to be a concept with a relatively fluid meaning—universal voting rights for those not excluded from voting rights.

There were many examples of how other comparable countries had restricted suffrage to prevent the most numerous classes from gaining too much influence: voting according to one's estate, constituency divisions, extended voting rights for certain cooperatives (occupational groups). The ability to pay taxes could also differentiate voting rights.[40]

Particular interest was devoted to the relationship between urban and rural areas as regards the consequences of extended suffrage. More guarantees were needed if the towns' privileged right of representation were to be "left unaltered". It was in this context that the demand for a higher voting age became significant. This could also be detached from the age of majority. The bill refers to Riksdag's letter and states that a higher age should be "tied" to the right to vote, since:

> It is surely also irrefutable that a more mature age is a prerequisite for independence and sound judgement, and that it is therefore fully justified to set a slightly higher age than the normal age of majority as a prerequisite for political suffrage.[41]

Various possible criteria were then presented as being consistent with the idea of universal suffrage, the need for proportional representation to guarantee the rights of political minorities, as well as the introduction of a graduated voting scale.[42] In the bill the government also explicitly discusses the relationship between income gradation and the right to vote.

> Whether and in what way a gradation of one kind or another should be implemented obviously depends to a considerable degree on the extension of suffrage. In this regard, there is an interaction between the extension of suffrage and gradation. The more suffrage is extended, the greater is the need for gradation and, conversely, extended suffrage may be introduced if it is combined with gradation.[43]

The government also noted that, if political suffrage were extended, the electorate would also become larger. This was a worry since the proposed raise in the voting age and the criteria of tax payment and military training did not sufficiently limit the electorate. Additional qualifications were required. This was where the role of male breadwinner stood out as a crucial factor in the extension of the right to vote.

> [It is] a legitimate demand that certain additional special qualifications should be established, not as conditions for suffrage in general, but as requirements for suffrage that is strengthened in a particular manner. In this respect, the criteria that may be considered are mainly a somewhat higher age and the capacity of family breadwinner. It is as undeniable as it is consistent with general thinking that an older man usually possesses greater experience, judgement, and independence than a younger man. If greater influence is granted to older men than to younger ones who are more susceptible to changing trends, this should ensure greater security against abrupt reversals, [...] the stability thus increased may benefit one political orientation as much as the other. A gradation on the basis of age is thus advantageous to all parties in the long run, in so far as they do not intend or desire hasty upheavals. It seems appropriate to set the age that entitles a person to a vote at the age when the obligation to undergo military training ceases.[44]

It was considered important both to strengthen voting power at the age of 40 and to set the minimum age at 25. Here the argument clearly declares the social value of a higher age. Greater experience, judgement, and independence guaranteed against the propensity for abrupt upheavals that characterised the younger generation. It was portrayed as beneficial to all parties except those implied to desire "hasty upheavals". Further arguments were also cited in support of a higher age:

> What has now been said about a higher age as a condition for strengthened voting rights also applies in essence to the role of family breadwinner. To this it may be added that the family breadwinner has more interests to safeguard than an unmarried man, and in some way can be said to represent also his family and especially his wife, that he bears a heavier tax burden, and that in rearing the next generation he is particularly deserving of the public good. The family is the foundation of society, and the family breadwinner should be highly esteemed as a valuable contributor to the welfare of society.[45]

The role of head of the family was emphasised. A father also had broader interests to safeguard and represent the whole family, particularly his wife; this important task for society ought to be the foundation for political influence. Marriage was thus the institution on which the right to vote should be based.

The proposal would also bring other advantages because, as with the way the Dutch and British systems were designed, it could guarantee that political influence was "vested in people with an independent and stable position in life", if political suffrage was equated with municipal suffrage and "if a vote of higher value is granted to a voter who either is or has been married or has reached a certain higher age". Older men and married men generally had better financial standing, which could also justify increasing the influence "of those now entitled to vote and of agrarian interests".[46] However, it was noted that a gradation in terms of property or income might also be necessary.[47] Summing up, the bill proposed that men should be entitled to vote in the year after they turned 25 and would have an extra vote after the age of 40 if they were married or had been married. The bill also introduced the requirement of military training.[48] Military training was assumed to have been completed at the age of 25 and therefore also constituted an age limit.[49]

The discussion in the bill of a high voting and eligibility age concerned the need for stability which could be achieved by ensuring that voters had sound judgement, independence, and the responsibility that was believed to come with being in charge of a family. There was also a shift in emphasis from a generally higher voting age to an extra vote in certain cases. Influence was to be given to the family as represented by the male breadwinner. Age serves as a foundation that is accompanied by other specified thresholds. Age normally brought family responsibilities, stability, better finances, and so on. Failure to satisfy the other criteria was thus described as an indication of something anomalous, abnormal, and also symbolic of a lack of civic competence in those who have reached the age at which they should be mature and competent.

What concerned politicians was the increasing political impact of the towns in Parliament due to the growing urban population.[50] In this way, the bill also implicitly sought to counter the potentially increasing influence of the urban working class. The other voting restrictions were, of course, only relevant to the population group with the right to vote by virtue of higher age. In addition, a link was made to the fact that the right to vote in elections to the Second Chamber was also based on municipal suffrage. From 1904 a minimum annual income of 500 kronor or property with a taxable value of 100 kronor was required, which meant that suffrage was restricted to 19 per cent of the adult population.[51]

The bill thus emphasises the family as the basic corporation on which the state rested. In this way it is the corporation that determines the right to vote and trumps the individual vote, i.e. the personality principle. Also important in this context is that the man's political role depended on his status as head of the family and representing a wife who was not legally competent (even widowers would nevertheless have the right to vote). This was explicitly tied to a notion of age and the role of breadwinner, which was dependent on social stability. Responsibility and presence in the local community were other prerequisites. Younger and unmarried men, and women in general, were also denied a role as independent individuals with this emphasis on the male breadwinner. Regardless of whether the discussion concerned age limits or other restrictions, it rested on the idea that socially stable and locally based population groups should take priority.

At the same time, the bill reflects a broader discussion of the relationship between the interests of the state and those of the individual, on the one hand, a personality principle grounded in the Enlightenment and natural law, on the other hand, a principle that put the interests of the state before the right of the individual. The latter view has its roots in a view of the state as an organism in which individuals are subsumed into a greater whole. Here, the right to vote becomes a function "that could only be assigned to those citizens who were judged to be sufficiently qualified" and was linked to an idea of duty and responsibility in the larger societal whole.[52] In this sense, the right to vote also concerned the public interest that individuals represented, i.e. the corporation or group to which they belonged.[53]

The issue of class voting and corporation was also relevant in connection with the fact that the bill cited examples from other countries.[54] It was in this perspective that female suffrage was controversial because it could be thought to undermine the patriarchal family and the relationship between the sexes. The fact that men represented the family as a corporation in this conceptual framework was also used as justification for an extension of male suffrage in the discussion of the 1902 bill. Belgium was among the international examples, where the number of votes an individual could have depended on age, starting at the age of 25, and it was also suggested that certain occupational categories should receive more votes. In addition, a married breadwinner would have double votes.[55]

The 1902 bill had been drawn up by the minister of justice, Hammarskjöld, but turned out to have very weak support in Parliament and was also questioned by other ministers in the government. The political consequences of the bill's failure were also obvious from the fact that it energised the women's suffrage movement. The explicitly negative view of female suffrage in the 1902 bill was provocative, leading to the formation of local women's suffrage associations in different parts of Sweden. The membership and the number of associations increased gradually and led in 1903 to the formation of a national organisation, the National Association for Women's Suffrage (Landsföreningen för kvinnans politiska rösträtt, LKPR), when Parliament and government were perceived as misogynistic. The reaction of women was also manifested in increased agitation—they wrote letters to newspapers, published their own newspapers and books, travelled around Sweden to deliver speeches, and so on.[56]

Another feature of this was the initiative of the female suffragists in Stockholm to investigate the legal conditions by which married women with property at their disposal could also obtain a tax certificate and the right to vote.[57] The government bill of 1902, as Berling Åselius points out, rejected women as political actors.[58] What may seem odd is that supporters of the personality principle in parliament did not understand all women as "persons", citizens with individual rights. At the same time, as we saw above, the personality principle was not applied strictly, but also included aspects of corporatist thinking that reflected preconceptions about which groups and which individuals contributed to society.

The National Association for Women's Suffrage wanted to highlight the rights of married women who were in charge of their own property. According to Anna Wicksell, who cited this discussion a few years later, the bill was defeated in Parliament mainly because it would have served as a precedent for the personality principle at the expense of the property principle.[59] However, their argument was based on the view that married women's own property ought to give them a voice in public matters, which also was a contributivist argument of similar nature claiming the property principle, although they also questioned that a man's vote should be the family's sole vote. In parallel to this, in the political debate there was also a discussion of marriage legislation, which paved the way for a more individualistic outlook on the family as well.[60]

It is interesting to touch briefly on how the age question was raised in the parliamentary debate. Staaff, who would become the leader of the Liberals and later accept and argue for some of the guarantees, was ironic about the secrecy surrounding the process of drafting the bill and its far-reaching demands for guarantees.

> As is well known, the bill includes a principle of extending the suffrage and six guarantees against this principle. One guarantee is the 25-year threshold; guarantee no. 2 is the conscription threshold, guarantee no. 3 is a stricter taxation threshold; guarantee no. 4 is qualified suffrage; guarantee no. 5 is single-member constituencies; and guarantee no. 6 enshrines the municipal voting rules in the basic laws. This means many guarantees, Mr Deputy Speaker. What is distinctive about these guarantees is that one cannot assess their effects: one cannot judge the extent of their impact.[61]

He made it clear that he could accept an age threshold, but not the age thresholds that were now proposed; above all it was unreasonable to introduce the so-called qualified right to vote, that is, that some citizens had more than one vote. This meant that the votes of other people were devalued, but it was also illogical: if younger men under the age of 25 were excluded, this should, according to Staaff, reasonably mean that there should be a corresponding upper age limit of 55 for voting. Older people were already overrepresented in the First Chamber: "But to create a special, greater vote for old men in our country, that seems like a rather peculiar guarantee for us with our well-circumscribed senate – that is to say, a chamber of old fogeys [*gubbkammare*]".[62]

It is important to underline that Staaff's attitude and rhetoric were consistent with his negative view of the First Chamber and his ambition to develop Second Chamber parliamentarianism that would greatly limit the role of the First Chamber of "old fogeys". He also objected to the fact that the guarantees as outlined could not be applied in a legally secure and uniform manner either.[63] As we shall see in the next section, however, he too put forward a proposal for suffrage reform four years later that was based on the idea of raising the voting age. His criticism of the bill was thus no deeper than that.

Consistently positive opinions were expressed in the debate about the idea of raising the voting age, and concrete proposals for even higher age limits were aired, for example, by Baron Lieutenant General Carl Wilhelm Ericson. He said that a higher age ought to be considered. Any guarantees should be designed so that they were the same for everyone, "rich and poor, but not so that they are different for different social classes". Here he mentions military training, but particularly the requirement to pay taxes as a crucial proof that

> the person concerned has so much interest in exercising universal suffrage that he at least wishes to observe the order, care, and sense of duty entailed by the due fulfilment of tax liability. In a word, this is nothing more than one can ask of every worker who wishes to act in an orderly fashion. This cannot be too much to ask.[64]

He also argued for levelling out between town and country, along with proportional representation. He would have preferred an age limit over 30 for both candidates and voters, as this was a significant turning point in men's lives. It was at that age that they married or became socially stable, based on a sense of gravity and responsibility for home and family.

> This age limit of 30 is a highly significant turning point in a man's life. It is clear from statistics – and we have been given a brief statistical summary – that it is precisely at the age of 30–31 that marriages are generally contracted in our country. No one can dispute that one has a significantly different view of things than earlier in life when one founds a home of one's own home and starts a family. Those who are not married live with other people, and their feelings, perceptions, and outlooks go in the same direction. In a word, when it comes to a person's outlook, sense of gravity, and view of things, men in our country undergo a very substantial change at the age of approximately 30.[65]

In the subsequent speeches, the Liberal Julius Centerwall emphasised that he, unlike Baron Ericsson, was not afraid of universal suffrage without guarantees. His wording is graphic:

> Such are the sail ropes that break as soon as a storm comes. The only guarantees I am willing to accept would be a slightly higher age limit, for example, 25, completed military training, if necessary – for nowadays the lads probably fulfil their military training whether they want to or not – and having paid taxes at the time of the election.[66]

Although he appreciated Branting's statement in the debate, Centerwall nevertheless shared the view of the need for guarantees of completed military training, paid taxes, and a higher voting age.[67] Branting's proposal was a voting age of 21.

The issue of guarantees and their significance is also a consistent leitmotif in the debate. It was not easy to agree on the long-term consequences of the guarantees.[68] The architect of the suffrage proposal, the minister of justice Hjalmar Hammarskjöld, also took the floor to defend his proposal. He elaborated his arguments for the higher age limit and additional votes for older married men, proportional representation, and measures to balance the influence of town and country. Family breadwinners represented their family and thus a large part of the population, and were considered to be a better-quality electorate by being settled, reliable, law-abiding, responsible members of society, who discharged their duties to the state and the municipality. In these respects married men and older men were clearly better than younger or unmarried men. He demonstrates this with statistical references:

> as to the marriage criterion, it has been possible to invoke the point of view of representation to some extent, in so far as one could say that the head of the family represents not only himself but also his family; and what one might call the point of view of capacity has also made itself felt, in that both higher age and marriage would provide guarantees of a better-quality voter, so to speak, thus constituting an equivalent to the settled status that is required in several countries and is a testimony to a more intimate relationship to the community [...] a constituency whose voters are composed exclusively of heads of families, probably representing a population five times that of the men themselves, ought to have more to say than a constituency consisting exclusively of single persons, equal in number to the heads of families. Moreover, the basic idea of gradation is surely confirmed by day-to-day experience. In particular, I appeal to the major employers in industry and agriculture in this regard, as to which elements are the most reliable, stable, and best, the married and older men on the one hand or the unmarried and younger men on the other.[69]

In this argumentation, responsibility for a family was one of the main justifications for raising the voting age. This social status was accompanied by reliability and stability. It also separated married from unmarried workers. A family breadwinner also represented many more people than one unmarried voter. Here Hammarskjöld also implies that the men in such constituencies had a larger representative mandate. He then substantiated his argument with evidence from public statistics and from his own survey. It was younger men who committed crimes and they were also the ones who did not pay their taxes to the state and the municipality.

> In 1899, out of 100,000 men between the ages of 25 and 40, there were 145 who were guilty of crimes of the kind that are now in question, that is to say, more serious crimes, while of those aged between 40 and 70 there were only 40; the crime rate was thus more than 3.5 times higher among the younger than the older men. A comparison between unmarried men over the age of 21 and married men shows an even more favourable ratio, for the crime rate among the unmarried is more than six times greater than among the married men, including widowers and divorced. And as for being guilty of not paying taxes, one might be inclined to believe that married men might be more likely to fail to pay taxes, because they might find it harder to afford to pay, but it turns out that the situation is quite the reverse. Again, I shall only cite a couple of figures so as not to tire you with too many, and I shall content myself with stating that in rural Östergötland County, out of municipal voters between the ages of 25 and 40, some 12.9 per cent have failed to pay municipal taxes, whereas among men aged over 40 the figure is only 6.5 per cent. The ratio is roughly the same if one compares unmarried with married men.[70]

Hammarskjöld then stated that a higher age limit would have many advantages. The quality of the electorate would be better and the conditions would be the same for all classes of society; from that point of view it could not be accused of being anti-democratic and "out of keeping with the times".[71] Moreover, the reform would have a positive effect on those currently entitled to vote in relation to those without suffrage, and on agricultural interests in relation to other (i.e. urban) interests. It was a small but important shift because it would have the effect of conserving society, especially in rural environments with a large population employed in industry.[72]

> In constituencies with a mixed population, i.e. in rural constituencies with a fairly large industrial population, it is most pronounced, and that is where it would have its greatest value. As I have said, it places the greatest emphasis on this as a symptom. The effect of gradation is not large, but it is nevertheless the case that gradation according to age and marital status works in the right direction, for the conservation of society.[73]

The arguments recur in a number of other speeches in the debate.[74] At the same time, it can be noted that the arguments about crime and good behaviour could be turned against the demands for an extension of male suffrage. Statistics on crime and morality clearly indicated that women were much more responsible and law-abiding members of society, as pointed out by the member of parliament Sigfrid Wieselgren. He noted that the establishment of the First Chamber was in itself a guarantee of stability but he also referred with approval to Carl Lindhagen's motion on women's suffrage. The family as a unit depended on the women's contributions, and they were a force for social stability.[75]

Hammarskjöld's motion failed to gain a majority and the government resigned. Many other solutions were proposed in the Riksdag. At the same time, these motions testify that the idea of voting restrictions was accepted in broad political circles as a way forward. The Liberal Party's motion was largely a repeat of Sixten von Friesen's proposal from 1900. This motion was also defeated.[76] However, in 1903 the King in Council commissioned a statistical inquiry into the consequences of raising the voting age, to ascertain the number of men aged over 25 and how many of them had not paid their taxes.[77]

The Social Democrats maintained the demand for suffrage from the age of 21 but accepted certain restrictions. Their demands for suffrage concerned men who had reached the age of majority and were respectable, and they seriously questioned the ambition to introduce far-reaching "guarantees". The proposal to limit the influence of the towns, what was called "clipping the wings", was sufficient in their view. The Social Democrats opposed the taxation thresholds and the raising of the voting age. Proportional representation could be accepted but only if it was combined with the introduction of a unicameral parliament.[78] In 1899 Branting had moved for the introduction of proportional representation in the light of the situation in the towns, where the graduated scale made it difficult for working-class minorities to be represented.[79] Later, in connection with the debates in 1902 and the parliamentary motion on universal suffrage, he was more in favour of the principle of proportional representation for all assemblies, but he stressed the importance of abolishing the First Chamber. He also acknowledged that industrial workers benefitted from the electoral system as this favoured the towns. This was not reasonable, he admitted. Universal and equal suffrage should be introduced for men, while constituencies should be made equal and a proportional representation system should be introduced, with a simultaneous limitation of the power of the First Chamber. However, he questioned whether women had hitherto been so committed to the suffrage issue, even though he supported the demand for female suffrage in principle.[80]

The tone of the motion was restrained. In an article in the newspaper *Social-Demokraten*, however, Branting did not mince words. The government's suffrage bill was a declaration of political bankruptcy, anything but honest and forward-looking, and a blow to the working class. The quasi-statesmen took back with one hand what they had given with the other, by adding one guarantee after the other.

> The 25-year line is not enough. The wiseacre quasi-statesmen, who botch everything they touch and will drive us to national destruction, if they get their way, have additionally come up with the idea of an extra three-year taxation harassment line, a conscription line, double votes for married men and for bachelors over 40, single-member constituencies in the big towns (to ensure seats for the right), a municipal 500-kronor line that cannot be lowered but can easily be raised to get rid of bothersome working-class voters – we believe the list is long enough.[81]

The difference between the Social Democrats' position and the 1902 bill could not be expressed with greater clarity. The guarantees, including a higher voting age, for which the Liberals and Conservatives sought support, were in stark contrast to the demands for universal and equal suffrage for men. In this context, the Social Democratic congress also put its foot down and made it clear that it did not prioritise women's suffrage. The party's political will to fight for women's suffrage took second place to tactical considerations. The congress simultaneously resolved to intensify the struggle for political suffrage through demonstrations and a three-day general strike in mid-May 1902.

The gender threshold for the right to vote became fundamental in the following years, albeit contested by occasional motions from Liberals and Social Democrats.[82] At the same time, the differences in the positions of the Social Democrats and the other parties are also obvious. The conflict would set its stamp on the discussion until the decisions of 1918–1921 and beyond.

On the Right, there was disagreement but a shared interest in the question of how a change in suffrage could be combined with guarantees. In a speech in the First Chamber, Bishop Gottfrid Billing spoke of the need for an inquiry into the electoral method, but in his opinion, there was widespread agreement about a higher age limit combined with military training requirements and tax payment.[83]

In both chambers, there was agreement between the majority in the First Chamber and the agrarian parties in the Second Chamber on the need for voting restrictions. Billing's proposal for an inquiry was also ultimately adopted jointly by both chambers without further arguments being cited. According to the political scientist Nils Stjernquist, the principle of municipal tax payment as a basis for voting rights to the Second Chamber was now called in question: "in the long run, the graduated scale in municipal elections was also threatened."[84]

The incoming government under Boström declared early on that it wanted to work for suffrage with guarantees. According to *Stockholms Dagblad* of 6 July 1902, "every Swedish man above the age of 25 who had fulfilled his duties of military training and tax payment to the state and municipality" would have the right to vote.[85] The government's suffrage bill of 1904 also established this idea explicitly. According to the bill, the right to vote would be based on having reached the age of 25 in the year before the election, but the link to the rules for municipal suffrage would be removed. In its place would come a number of other restrictions, among them bankruptcy, poor relief, double tax payment (both state and municipal taxes fully paid in the last three years), and military training. The tax restriction was presented as a criterion of "orderly behaviour". In addition, proportional representation would be introduced.[86]

These changes were an obvious consequence of the fact that the rules drawn up for elections to the Second Chamber would no longer be based on municipal suffrage. Municipal suffrage was not constitutionally protected and could be changed by a sitting parliament and thereby also influence elections to the Second Chamber. Thus, the voting restrictions in municipal elections did not have sufficiently powerful legal protection. Bostrom's proposal was thus very much a development of the 1902 bill in terms of the voting restrictions. Still, now a restriction on the grounds of receiving poor relief was also suggested, with the justification that similar restrictions were also found in neighbouring countries, founded on the understanding that poor relief was a loan to be repaid.[87]

The bill had a mixed reception among the Liberals, who could not agree on a common stance or any counterproposal. Nor could the chambers agree, and so the bill was defeated, but it was clear that, for example, the tax criterion had strong support even among the Liberals. The Riksdag now had a majority in favour of limiting voting rights with the help of certain dividing lines, as Ebba Berling Åselius emphasises in her careful review of the voting restrictions. These thresholds were now established to solve the issue of voting rights with guarantees.[88] Higher age limits thus became established as a crucial foundation for limiting voting rights to the Second Chamber in subsequent parliaments.

It is worth recalling the cultural significance of age limits. In a pamphlet from 1902 by the historian Sam Clason, written before he began his political career as a Conservative member of parliament, he discusses the proposals for suffrage reform. His support for Hammarskjöld's proposal was explicit. He argued that raising the age limit to 25, as von Friesen suggested, did not entail any major reduction of the electorate because the number of municipal voters under 25 was limited. It was chiefly in Stockholm that it could affect the number of persons entitled to vote.[89] At the same time, he stressed that the right to vote should be based on a "family gradation":

> the very step of getting married represents a separation of the upright men who marry from the less upright men who, instead of marriage, choose casual relationships. In many other cases, entry into marriage sorts out, within the various classes, the strongest and most able-bodied elements from the less able-bodied, those who do not reach the average level within the class. The endurance of marriage has a further educative effect and gives richer experience; in equal social conditions, a married man is, as a rule, more settled and thoughtful than an unmarried man. The head of the family, who breeds and raises a future generation in the home, thereby performing an essential social task for the state, thoroughly deserves the special recognition of the state, and this recognition can rightly be granted in the form of increased political influence.[90]

In the last chapter of this book we shall return to the question of how many people were affected by a restriction on voting rights for those under the age of 25.

In conclusion, we may note that the issue of the voting age was part of a broader effort to establish "guarantees" that those in power would not be marginalised. Other important parts of the package of guarantees were proportional representation and the proposals for the reform of the voting scale for municipal suffrage. A tangible concern, for Clason as for other members of parliament, was that the right to vote in municipal elections could be changed by one session of Parliament. By separating voting rights for municipal councils and Parliament, it would be more difficult to implement changes that affected the right to vote in elections to the Second Chamber. This highlighted the importance of the voting restrictions being introduced for the Second Chamber when this right would no longer be based on municipal restrictions. Now it was also time to introduce new restrictions such as those concerning poor relief and military training.

In the conflicts over the right to vote there was also debate about the role of the Riksdag and the King, a matter on which Liberals and Conservatives had different views, while the Social Democrats demanded the abolition of the monarchy and the First Chamber. The Social Democrats and the Liberals collaborated on several issues, but as we have seen, there was also agreement between the right-wing parties and the Liberals about the question of guarantees and voting restrictions. This developed somewhat in the shadows behind the conflicts over the design of parliamentarism.

In the following sections I shall examine in more detail how the political process concerning proportional representation, the conditions for municipal suffrage, and the right to vote in elections to the Second Chamber influenced the rules on age limits. In other words, the question is how the age limits were affected by these two different models for stronger parliamentary influence. Here the conflict concerned the Second Chamber parliamentarism espoused by the Liberals and the preservation of the strong position of the First Chamber, which was the policy of Lindman and the Farmer's Party. The age limit was a central element of this process of change, but it meant different things depending on how the other voting rules were designed and whether or not the right to vote in elections to the Second Chamber was based on municipal suffrage.

In the conflicts over the design of parliamentarism, the Right, under the leadership of Arvid Lindman, drew the longest straw. The Liberals' vision had to be given up when the proposal by the Right for universal suffrage for men (limited by age and other criteria) also preserved the equal status of both chambers of Parliament. This also ensured that the Right would still be able to block any move towards more democratic suffrage.

Parliamentarism, Proportionalism, and Age Limits

The Liberals thus accepted the extension of male suffrage to the Second Chamber, with limitations according to certain criteria, and with a gradation of municipal suffrage. The Liberals gave priority to male suffrage with a series of grounds for disqualification that were largely the same as those advocated by the Right. However, they were open to reviewing municipal suffrage for married women who had property of their own; this could be done by changing the tax legislation. Yet the Liberal proposal drafted by Staaff in 1906 had the same premises as the government bill of 1904 with regard to voting restrictions. The Liberals' proposal for the extension of suffrage in 1905 suggested a voting age of 25 at the time of the election, which was then adjusted in the 1906 proposal to the year after reaching the age of 24 (Fig. 3.2).[91]

The Social Democrats wanted voting from the age of 21 and refused to accept the tax threshold or the design of the poor relief threshold. Temporary dependence on poor relief should not be grounds for losing the right to vote, they argued. Their emphasis on the age limit of 21 was partly a matter of principle. In their view, there were no weighty reasons why it should be different from the age of majority. Their stance was also strategic: a voting age of 21 would mean a larger number of younger voters, which could benefit them and balance the influence of the older population. They argued, as we saw earlier, that young workers actually lived an independent life and supported themselves. The Social Democratic parliamentary group emphasised in its report on political work 1906–1908 that their priority, like that of the Liberals, was the right to vote in elections to the Second Chamber, and it was for tactical reasons they supported the Liberal proposal. They objected to the proposal being limited by "rigorous guarantees"—the age limit and the tax criterion.[92] The Social Democratic parliamentary group and the executive committee of the party board also discussed this at a meeting on Sunday 25 February 1906, where several members objected to "the deterioration that has occurred as a result of the higher age limit" and, of course, the tax criterion. Others pointed out that the proposal did not benefit urban industrial workers but only agricultural workers.[93] "The raising of the age limits would be the most unpleasant" of the consequences, as Fredrik Thorsson pointed out, which may explain the negative attitude. The Social Democrats would lose potential voters. "The three excluded age cohorts would remove 150,000 and the other guarantees 250,000, altogether 400,000 votes, and we would thus have an electorate of one million. Now we will not be able to rally the people in opposition to this proposal."[94] It was difficult for Social Democratic agitation that the proposal did actually benefit working-class men to a large extent. That the age limits together with the tax criterion were the most troublesome is shown in another statement by Albin Weidenhaijn. He said that the party should carve out a profile for itself by also campaigning for female suffrage, declaring that:

Fig. 3.2 Karbasen 12 March 1904. Balzazar's Feast, an omen that power was about to slip from the rulers' hands, illustrates the balance between voting rights and guarantees. Participants from the elites feast on the goodies of the voting restrictions, including the age line, while the threat of major strike clouds the party. The scales of universal suffrage outweigh the guarantees. Source: Karbasen 12/3 1904. KB

> the Stockholmers were now also acting for payment of taxes, but considered it dangerous that these tax criteria were included. What seemed most dangerous to him, however, was that the age limit had been raised. The reduction in urban representation would have a reactionary effect, and both the poor relief criterion and the bankruptcy criterion would have a highly disadvantageous effect. The proposal that was now to be submitted to the parliamentary group should not be as before, but must also include women if we are able to count on sympathy for it within our party.[95]

Branting also criticised the Liberals' proposal. It was too little to satisfy the Social Democrats but too much for them to oppose it. In short, there was no solution to the issue of equal male and female suffrage: three annual cohorts of young men were quarantined (admittedly for one year less than in the 1902 bill), and the suffrage bill was limited by the poor relief criterion and the double tax criterion (i.e. the requirement to have paid both paid municipal and state taxes). "Nothing but remnants of these hateful 'guarantees'" that the Liberals shared with the Right. However, he was pleased that it benefitted the rural working class.[96] The Social Democrats supported the Liberal proposal in 1906, but in the party's parliamentary motions in 1905 and 1906 they argued for male suffrage from the age of 21 and only limited restrictions. However, a draft of the party board's proposal for a reform of the constitution included a call for both male and female suffrage from the age of 21, with eligibility from the age of 25 and 30, respectively, for the two chambers.[97] Carl Lindhagen proposed a motion for women's suffrage to the party congress in 1904, but in 1905 the congress decided to prioritise male suffrage for tactical reasons.[98] We can thus say that the Social Democrats chose to support the Liberal proposal, despite their objections, because they deemed it impossible to win over public opinion given the political situation (Figs. 3.3 and 3.4).

When he was in government in 1906, Staaff had failed to convince Parliament of the bill aimed at reforming the Second Chamber. He did not propose women's suffrage but proposed the raising of the voting age. He was heavily influenced by British parliamentarism, envisioning a parliament of the British type in which the First Chamber would be marginalised by the majority elections of the Second Chamber. He feared that a proportional system would lead to party divisions and weaken the Second Chamber. The First Chamber would have only a suspensive veto.[99] This idea had some support among Social Democrats, although they also

Karbasen.

Skamrers rufva valrer dumberens lass!

4:DE ÅRGÅNGEN.
LÖRDAGEN DEN
3 DECEMBER 1904.

SITUATIONEN.

Damen: Nej tack, det är ingenting som passar!
Expediterna: Så oanständigt att låta oss plocka fram hela lagret.

N:o 49. 10 ÖRE.

GRUMMES PRIMA TVÄTT-TVÅL erkändt den bästa.

Fig. 3.3 Karbasen on 3 December 1904. Social Democratic leader Branting is evaluating the situation on the lookout for reasonable offers. He did not appreciate the shop's offers of various voting rights restrictions, including age restrictions, much to the irritation of the shopkeepers, who had shown all they had to offer. Source: Karbasen 3/12 1904. KB

Fig. 3.4 Karbasen on 3 March 1906. Will he walk or fall? The Liberals are walking a tightrope, trying to balance guarantees and universal suffrage. Source: Karbasen 3/3 1906. KB

wanted to abolish the First Chamber. The First Chamber rejected the proposal. This meant that the two chambers disagreed, and the bill was defeated. Staaff had misjudged the state of opinion. Until around 1904, liberal parliamentarians were open to discussing a proportional electoral system before tying their agenda to the model of British parliamentarism. Theodor Adelswärd, who later served as a minister in the liberal cabinet, favoured in 1907 a proportional electoral system, combined with a higher voting age.[100] The idea of a higher voting age was compatible with both proposals of majority and proportional electoral constituencies.

In 1907 the Conservative government led by Lindman proposed a solution with double proportional elections (i.e. for both chambers) and universal male suffrage with guarantees in the form of a variety of dividing lines. The suggested voting age for men was the year after reaching the age of 24 (i.e. suffrage from the age of 25), in other words, the same as the Liberals' proposal, the consequences of which had been investigated by the Central Bureau of Statistics in 1900.[101] The bill was passed by Parliament. It went further than Staaff's proposal, which had been limited to a reform of the Second Chamber. Lindman based his proposal on a proportional electoral system at all levels. He thus tackled the issue of municipal suffrage, the First Chamber, and the right to vote in elections to the Second Chamber all at the same time, winning over those Liberals and Conservatives who were dissatisfied with the span in the number of votes an individual could have. The result was a slimmed-down version of the voting system decided in 1862/66. The 40-grade voting scale replaced the 100-grade scale and partially reduced the influence of companies and corporations in small municipalities. Rural Conservatives and Liberals were not prepared to abandon the power that the retention of a graded scale gave to wealthy farmers in the municipalities. However, the local power of the companies could be broken, which favoured the farmers' interests. The loss of rural influence in the Second Chamber could be offset by a greater influence in the First Chamber. Moreover, the lowering of income thresholds and the remuneration and travel expenses now offered to members of parliament meant that parliamentary service was not solely reserved for those with the highest incomes.[102]

After the Riksdag supported the Lindman bill, first in 1907 and then in 1909, the Social Democrats changed their policy. In 1907 they tabled a motion demanding universal and equal suffrage for men and women, and in 1909 they presented the same demands.[103] In the minutes of the Social Democratic parliamentary group the comments on Lindman's proposal included criticism of the "serious shortcomings: women excluded, young people restrained, the remnants of a minimum income and property threshold [...] the 40-grade municipal voting scale, the retention of an excessively high income limit for eligibility, the equal status of the chambers still unchanged". But it was noted simultaneously that it was a step in the right direction, and these defects could be rectified later.[104] The same criticism was repeated in the deliberations of the parliamentary group, but a number of voices in the discussion declared that the proposal was nevertheless better than Staaff's bill. It should be noted, however, that the suffrage thresholds did not figure prominently in the discussion, although Branting emphasised that the tax criterion was the one that entailed the greatest risk of limiting working-class influence. In the Social Democratic press, on the other hand, the criticism concerned the age limits and the power of old upper-class men (Fig. 3.5).[105]

In his speeches in the debate Branting also protested against the fundamentally conservative character of the reform. Although power relations in the Riksdag would benefit the male working class, so that in this respect the government bill was as good as Staaff's proposal, women and the younger generation were still excluded, and although the First Chamber was "moderately" democratised, its power was actually strengthened, with "the representation of wealth" for the "so-called leading classes in our society". Branting also expressed his disappointment with the Liberals for dismissing or disregarding the problems of the First Chamber. He also criticised the 40-grade municipal suffrage scale.[106]

As regards elections to the Second Chamber, Lindman's solution included raising the voting age and significantly expanding the male electorate. This was viewed by many as a step in the right direction. But the reform had other meanings. The position of the First Chamber was defended, and the higher voting age, together with the various thresholds, had a negative impact on the influence of the working class and the towns. The reform upheld rural interests that were not necessarily positive for the Social Democrats, as rural workers were resistant to the left wing. That worried Gustav Möller who also noted about ten years later that:

> the question of industrial workers' suffrage has never been resolved. The so-called universal suffrage of 1907 was essentially a reform in the interests of agricultural workers, while industrial workers, who had been the real bearers of the suffrage demands and the suffrage struggle, were themselves left behind as the main group among those without rights.[107]

Fig. 3.5 Karbasen on 2 June 1906. Staaff hands over to Lindman a bureau full of failed suffrage proposals and repressive political decisions against, for example, freedom of speech and the right to strike. Source: Karbasen 2/6 1906. KB

The shared opinions of the Liberals and the Farmers' Party were sufficient to steer the bill through the Riksdag. The Right also obtained the guarantees of minority influence that a proportional electoral system could entail. The proposal for proportional representation in both chambers enabled Lindman's proposal to win support in the Second Chamber, but also within the parliamentary Right in the First Chamber, who had previously been hesitant about proportional elections for the Second Chamber. Lindman's proposal took a clear stand to preserve the First Chamber and provide protection for political minorities through proportional representation. Moreover, by setting the voting age for elections to the Second Chamber in the year after turning 24, the Right was given the guarantee that came with a higher voting age, as well as the suffrage thresholds concerning tax payment, poor relief, and bankruptcy, thus balancing the broadening of the male voting base. However, the suffrage restrictions in municipalities that came as a consequence of the 40-grade voting scale acted against the interests of capital, reducing the influence of companies and legal entities while strengthening agrarian interests in the First Chamber.[108]

The result of all the debates was thus a higher voting age in elections to the Second Chamber, suffrage thresholds, a 40-grade municipal voting scale, and a proportional election system. From 1909 onwards, when the reform came into force through a second decision of Parliament, the right to vote in Second Chamber elections was no longer based on municipal suffrage. Why, then, had Lindman not proposed a higher age limit for municipal suffrage?

The 40-Grade Scale as a Dividing Line by Age

The reform of 1909 meant that different voting ages were set, 21 for municipal elections (which also affected elections to county councils and the First Chamber) and 24 for Second Chamber elections. The initiatives to raise the voting age for Second Chamber elections from the 1890s did not affect the debates about municipal suffrage and the question of age limits. In the argumentation about the economic gradation of suffrage at the municipal level, the explanation was quite obvious: the 40-grade scale gave power to those who were established and economically independent, that is, generally speaking, the older segments of the population. Lindman returned to this in the debates in the late 1910s. The 40-grade scale was equivalent to raising the voting age, and it had the same outcome, which made it possible to retain an age limit of 21.[109]

A couple of circumstances deserve to be highlighted. First, it was not until the Lindman bill was tabled that municipal suffrage really became part of the discussion about suffrage reform and, consequently, also the reform of elections to the First Chamber. The Liberal government's bill had focused on the Second Chamber in order to strengthen it at the expense of the First Chamber. The power of the First Chamber would be reduced to a suspensive veto. The Liberal bill included no suggestions for the reform of municipal suffrage. Secondly, the exchange of views from the 1890s onwards concerned how an extension of the right to vote in Second Chamber elections also risked strengthening the representation of the towns and cities in Parliament and thus increasing the political influence of the working-class population. This could be counteracted by raising the voting age, thus favouring Liberal and Conservative forces and maintaining the influence of rural areas in Parliament. The question of the unreasonable political consequences of the municipal suffrage scale, with the dominant influence of big mill owners, was a more important issue for rural areas. Raising the voting age would have had no corresponding effect because the cohorts of young workers were so much smaller in the countryside. This made it much more important to limit the multiple votes of mill owners and industrialists in favour of the propertied farmers in the municipalities.[110]

The Liberals were not prepared to abolish the municipal voting scales, and agrarian interests prioritised income and property and payment of taxes as guarantees concerning those who were allowed to participate in municipal elections, as Ingemar Norrlid notes in his study of "the municipality as a company". That struggle, as already mentioned, was waged both against the unpropertied/low-paid and against the influence of local capital. It was a struggle by the local elite, waged on two fronts.[111] It was not until as late as 1915 that Staaff's successor Edén stood in the same corner as the Social Democrats on this point and demanded the abolition of the 40-grade scale. We shall also have reason to return to this matter later on. There was a palpable community of political values among right-wing interests and the Liberals when it came to municipal suffrage.

In the discussions about reform in 1866, the income and property thresholds had already been perceived as an alternative to a higher voting age. This obvious and fundamental stance was not so controversial, and it recurs in the parliamentary debates.[112] The Liberal member of parliament

Theodor Adelswärd argued in several speeches in 1907, both inside and outside the Riksdag, for double proportionalism, that is, proportional elections to both chambers, and a higher voting age. He did, however, want to abolish the income thresholds and introduce women's suffrage.[113] He argued that a proportional electoral system should not be perceived as a conservative guarantee but as a fair means to allow the representation of the people to reflect different views and interests.[114] But let us look more closely at the role that age limits played in his argumentation.

In a speech on 13 January 1907 to his constituency in Östergötland, Adelswärd declared himself in favour of introducing a proportional electoral system since it would guarantee influence for minorities. He also objected here to the idea that this would be a conservative guarantee, addressing the claim from the Social Democrats. A voting scale based on income or property was therefore, in his opinion, also incompatible with the idea of proportional representation, and therefore, "if voters are divided according to property limits, the result will be a kind of class election, for which proportional elections would be a substitute and therefore should not in fairness be used concurrently with these".[115] If property does not constitute the foundation for the right to vote, a different principle must be used:

> I think I can find it in an age limit [...] I have envisaged this age limit for suffrage to the First Chamber as being set at age 30, but since elections will be held only every six years, the average age at the time of first voting would be 32½ years. [...] the electorate for the First Chamber would amount to 83% of that for the Second Chamber, thus not quite one-fifth less than that, but this one-fifth would winnow out the elements that are least suitable as voters for this chamber and the remainder – constituting over 80 per cent of those who have started a family and are settled, and of whom, it may be hoped, a large share will have "homes of their own" in the not too distant future – should overwhelmingly consist of voters who are not inclined to elect subversives to the First Chamber.[116]

He also objected to the issue of municipal suffrage now being raised at all. That was an unfortunate confusion of parliamentary and municipal suffrage that was caused by the fact that appointments to the First Chamber depended on municipal suffrage:

> If that dependence between these matters is maintained, irrespective of whatever restrictions on municipal suffrage are introduced in connection with a changed electoral method, [...] the same difficulties will persist. For

> one should not believe that the question of municipal suffrage, used as a payoff in the political compromise, can be definitively resolved by this means. The limits of the graded scale, determined with regard to elections to the First Chamber, must be purely arbitrary, because it is not ~~logically~~ directly connected with it.[117]

In this context he also noted that graded suffrage could be justified in the municipalities, but that this was not an appropriate basis for elections to the First Chamber. The proportional representation system, in his view, should be based on an age limit and a minimum income and property requirement for eligibility to the First Chamber. The age limit would mean that it was settled, stable people who would have the right to vote.[118] In a speech to students in Stockholm on 28 April 1907 he argued that it was the incomplete application of the idea of proportional elections to the First Chamber that had led to this confusion of municipal and parliamentary suffrage issues. Moreover, "this confusion has led to the illogical and unnatural circumstance that the age limits for voting in elections to the First Chamber (21) would be lower than for elections to the Second Chamber (24)".[119] He also expressed his concern that the First Chamber would become too much of a "farmer's chamber and that this will underline the class conflicts in society rather than eliminating the ills of bourgeois society, against which there has been justified criticism".[120]

In the parliamentary motion that he presented on 20 March of the same year, 1907, he also contended that Lindman's proposed reform was full of contradictions and not sufficiently elaborated. Proportionalism was incompatible with tax and income thresholds but compatible with an age limit. The other thresholds were in fact more likely to counteract this and would introduce an electoral system based on different categories of people—a system based on class. The proposal was designed to satisfy Parliament. As for the guarantee that was established by the obligation to have paid tax, with its intention "to weed out the disorderly, those who lack a sense of responsibility to the state and the public good", he perceived it as wrong, partly because it led to corruption and "buying votes".[121] By the latter, he probably meant that tax could be paid on an individual's behalf to enable him to vote.

> There are unquestionably other and better means available to the state to demand tax from those who, out of indifference and lack of a civic sense of duty, seek to evade fulfilment of the same unless compelled. The same

> applies to the fulfilment of military training. Stricter legislative measures may perhaps be required to ensure that the duties of tax payment and military training are satisfactorily fulfilled, but such measures are likely to fall within areas other than legislation on political suffrage.[122]

In arguing for women's suffrage, he emphasised the equality of women with men in knowledge and upbringing, but also that women were morally superior. It was also as homemakers in working-class homes that women were of far greater importance than men.[123] Here Adelswärd returned to the strange circumstance that the consequence of the government's suffrage bill was that Second Chamber elections had an age limit of 24 while the age limit in elections to the First Chamber was 21. This had hitherto been of secondary importance in First Chamber elections because the individual's influence was limited by the voting scale and the *fyrk*-based scale.

> But to the same extent that the grading of votes is curtailed and the individual's influence becomes greater, the age restriction must take on a completely different meaning. Moreover, since in many societies the ordinary income is so high, with few exceptions, that it generally exceeds the minimum income requirement for municipal suffrage, the right to vote in such municipalities may be regarded as universal, and since municipal suffrage is also granted to women, the strange circumstance arises that, according to the government bill, the electorate to the First Chamber will include elements who are not entitled to vote in elections to the Second Chamber, namely, some age groups of younger citizens and women!
>
> The gradation of voting rights according to the amount of property is nothing more than a basis for calculation in a kind of class election. The application of proportional representation to a graded voting scale is thus tantamount to the simultaneous use of proportional elections and class elections, i.e., two different means to achieve the same thing, one of which can substitute for the other, but, if used simultaneously, cannot fail to distort the result which one is tasked with achieving.[124]

Theodor Adelswärd's conclusion and proposal for bringing about differences between the chambers was, therefore, that the First Chamber should be appointed by electors and that the age limit for voting in elections to the First Chamber should be 30. Such a restriction would affect everyone equally but could have the effect of:

> "winnowing out!" of the electorate those elements whose way of life and way of thinking are least stable and responsible and thus least suitable for appointing members of the First Chamber. I am assuming here that the task of this chamber is to be the restraining element in the representation of the people and to safeguard against abrupt upheavals and the excessive influence of passing opinions.[125]

Theodor Adelswärd's arguments are explicit in the criticism of the Conservatives' proposals and perhaps the strategy behind the suffrage bill, but also because age is a key argument for him. A higher voting age is associated with social stability, family formation, and a measure of prosperity (owning property). It was also in these terms that he justified his view of women's suffrage. The issue of gender equality was not only a matter of the rights of individuals, but also a question of ensuring influence for values that could be linked to the family. In holding this opinion, he was probably close to the women's suffrage movement.[126]

It was not only in Parliament that the discussion was carried on. The Social Democratic newspaper *Fram* severely questioned the decision by Parliament to deny three age cohorts the right to vote. An article in 1908 blamed the Liberals who had initiated an increase in age limits, thus "striking young people from the roll of citizens" and then throwing this right to the "reactionary beast". "The Liberals [then] threw the other pieces of meat – the tax lines, the conscription line, etc. – to the same reactionary beast to satisfy it."[127] The newspaper also noted that when all men of age were to be granted civil rights, this was swept away on the grounds of the immaturity of youth, their lack of mature judgement. Different criteria were used to evaluate the contributions of younger and older people to society, and different age criteria applied to maturity: being of age in the eyes of God and the government, in economic and political terms. In 1909, the paper predicted, Lindman will "handle the bell-ringing at the burial of the corpse of young people's civil rights, while the Liberal and Conservative legislators [...] will heave a sigh of relief when the funeral is over".[128]

The contrast with the Liberal stance is dramatic. Theodor Adelswärd, like other Liberals and Conservatives, saw the value of a high voting age since it allowed greater influence to the older and more stable population. It was precisely this evaluation of the population that the Social Democrats protested against in the party's internal discussions, in Parliament and in the press. At the same time, Adelswärd's analysis suggests and confirms that the complicated relationship between elections to the municipalities and to the First Chamber was of crucial significance for the design of the political compromises. In the municipalities, the 40-grade suffrage scale was necessary to ensure the influence of the farming class in rural areas, according to the Conservatives and Liberals. This excluded or limited the influence of groups with little or no property, and also the influence of companies and legal entities. The younger generation was clearly not numerous enough in rural areas to pose a problem, and the graded voting scale in any case ensured the influence of more stable and older strata of the population. It was also important that those who were granted the right to vote in the municipalities paid taxes in proportion to their income and property, and discharged their tax payments (Fig. 3.6).

Female Suffrage, Age, Tax Payment, and Class

The idea of guarantees was nevertheless retained in the Liberal and Conservative proposals. Tax regulations were also significant, and on that point to the Liberals and Conservatives were close to each other in their political assessments. But the issue of women's suffrage was not removed from the decision-making processes in Parliament. Staaff had proposed a motion in 1904 to grant municipal suffrage to married women who had an income and could pay tax. In 1906, following a decision by Parliament in May under the Staaff government, the Central Bureau of Statistics was commissioned to inquire into the possibility of women's suffrage from the age of 24. The decision to set up an inquiry was made before the Lindman government took office in June 1907, and the report was published in 1908. In other words, the Bureau's report was not presented until after the first decision in 1907 on male suffrage from the age of 24. The report followed the model used in 1903 when the Bureau had also inquired into the consequences of a higher voting age for men. When women's suffrage was discussed, age was important both explicitly, with the age limit of 24, and implicitly in the focus on married women in tax law. The debate, as we shall see, was based on the framework for evaluating the voting regulations established after 1900.

The question of whether married women could receive a tax certificate and thus the right to vote had been raised by the women's suffrage association in Stockholm, as the historian Josefin Rönnbäck has shown. In 1902, the National Association for Women's Suffrage distributed a questionnaire to legal experts to investigate whether married women with a tax

Fig. 3.6 Karbasen on 3 October 1908. When the wind blows from the left, the First Chamber softens the fall. In the opinions of the political left, Lindman was also the saviour of the First Chamber, a bastion of conservatism. Source: Karbasen 3/10 1908. KB

certificate could be granted municipal suffrage, as unmarried women could. That was the case, as it turned out, but it required women to apply specifically to be registered on the electoral roll. This then formed the basis for the National Association's propaganda for increased female participation in elections. The discussions about tax regulations created an opening for an extension of married women's suffrage, even though they were not legally competent, which had an impact on the subsequent debate.[129]

The preparation of the amendment to the tax legislation was thus under way at the same time as the inquiry into women's suffrage.[130] Lindman's suffrage bill of 1907, as noted above, would not allow women to vote on the same terms as men. The bill explicitly dismissed the issue, citing the forthcoming inquiry which Parliament had commissioned and which was not yet completed. This position was harshly criticised in the parliamentary debate by the former prime minister Staaff, among others.[131] However, it is possible to examine the differences between these two issues, the question of women voting on the same terms as men and the matter of tax legislation. As before, the focus is on the age limits.

In 1904 Karl Staaff moved that the tax rules be amended to make it clear that married women with property under their own administration could be given municipal voting rights (and as a consequence were also eligible for municipal office), provided that their husbands paid taxes. They were required to declare their property and file their own tax return. The proposal had a mixed reception; among other things, the obligation to file a tax return was questioned. It was defeated because the First Chamber rejected it as recommended by the relevant standing committee. The issue was nevertheless raised again in 1908 as a proposal by the Lindman government and was accepted by both chambers. The bill was challenged by Branting, however, who objected to the way it favoured a minority of married women rather than all women regardless of income and property. It would also lead to higher taxes for those with lower incomes. Branting argued that it would be a more reasonable reform if married women in general were given the right to vote.[132]

When the decision was then implemented, it required that both the wife and the husband separately declare their income and property, but the tax was calculated on the combined income of the wife and the husband. The government's stated reason in 1908 for this was to avoid differences in taxation between families in which the wife earned money and families in which she did not.[133] In that respect, the design of the bill was in line with Branting's criticism, although the idea was still that a wife's right to vote depended on whether or nor her husband paid tax. It is not possible to determine whether this was a deliberate adaptation to criticism. The overall rationale for the reform, according to the bill, was to enable more women to be active in civic life. The new municipal law allowed married women to hold municipal positions provided they had the right to vote, and with the new tax legislation more women had this opportunity. The reform was necessary, according to the bill, if the provisions in the municipal law about women's participation in society were to be meaningful.[134] The decision in Parliament meant that even women with a small income could be registered for tax and entitled to municipal suffrage, which Anna Wicksell described as an unintended consequence of the work on the bill. A discovery of a lapse in the legislative process that the women's movement could take advantage of and exploit in their propaganda.[135]

The inquiry into suffrage for women from the age of 24 did not lead to any concrete proposal. Nor was that the intention. The inquiry was set up as a comprehensive investigation into women's suffrage, and as a result the inquiry focused both on municipal suffrage and on Second Chamber elections under the conditions that applied, after the bill of 1907, to the proposal concerning male suffrage. The report devotes most space to a description of the surplus of women in the population, the large proportion of unmarried women and widows, and the proportion of workers in the female population. In addition, it presents data on how many self-supporting women over 24 could be assumed to lose their right to vote because they did not pay tax or were dependent on poor relief. The inquiry noted, however, that women were more conscientious in paying their taxes than men of comparable economic status, but about 20 per cent were dependent on poor relief, mainly older women. Generally, however, women were in a weaker economic position. Throughout the report a distinction is made between urban and rural data. In the towns and cities, working-class women predominated and the proportion of unmarried women was high, and in some constituencies dominant. In rural areas, about 50 per cent of women belonged to the working class and would gain the right to vote. It was estimated that the female electorate over the age of 25 would amount to about 480,000 women, or one third of the entire electorate, if they were granted suffrage.[136] The requirements of income and tax payment thus reduced the number of women who could vote if such a reform was passed. The right of married women to vote depended on the husband's right to vote and the extent to which he did not fall short of the various thresholds. A wife's suffrage was not autonomous from their spouses. The conclusions of the inquiry were that an extended suffrage reform would strengthen the lower social classes but that the higher age shifted the balance towards the married population. A large share of the unmarried population over 24 would however fail to meet the suffrage criteria.

The inquiry did not serve as a foundation for any bill to extend the right of women to vote in elections to the Second Chamber. It is nevertheless important that the inquiry was actually effected, and that the government chose a different path to extend women's suffrage, namely, through tax legislation, which limited the impact on municipal suffrage. There was thus a clear alternative: women could be entitled to vote in parliamentary elections on the same terms as men from the age of 24. This would have benefitted working-class women even though many failed to meet all the suffrage criteria. In their original form, the revisions of the tax legislation, on the other hand, would, as we saw above, mainly benefit better-off married women. With the decision of 1908, the circle of married women was broadened to include those with smaller incomes, but it also included bourgeois families where the women had incomes of varying sizes and the men managed to pay their taxes.

The willingness and ability to pay tax was greater among women, according to the official statistics. But among the working class, the requirement of paid taxes meant that large groups would be disqualified.[137] Moreover, in the large cities, the tax legislation meant that the authorities decided on local rules for adjusting the income levels for taxation.[138] Those with low incomes were thus excluded, with reference to the expenditure situation in some municipalities. Such support for those on low incomes meant that their civil rights were curtailed concurrently and furthermore the conditions for suffrage could vary from one town to another.

When it came to women's suffrage, class was another factor to consider, besides gender and marital status. The decision made in 1908 comprised women with lower incomes, but it also made them subordinate to the family principle.[139] At the same time, married women with their own income or property who had municipal suffrage were given priority over the entire group of women over the age of 25, and municipal suffrage took priority over the right to vote in elections to the Second Chamber. In numerical terms it was probably a small group that gained the right to vote through this reform, but most likely these women were also generally over the age of 25.[140] The class probably played a part as well when it came to the limited interest in an extension of women's suffrage. The inquiry had after all shown that it would have favoured the urban working class also when limited to women over the age of 25.

Concluding Reflections

The decisions to introduce a low voting age in connection with the reform of Parliament and the municipalities in 1862/1865 were a consequence of how the rules of the old Diet were designed. Age was not an important selection instrument when members of the four estates were appointed, as long as they had reached the age of majority. Affiliation to an estate of the realm, and thus the right to vote, was regulated by having the franchise of a town, having attained a certain social position, belonging to a noble family, or owning property. The age of majority defined basic social adulthood. Yet it was not enough; it was subordinate to other aspects of belonging to an estate. The same premises governed the new parliamentary order. However, the economic requirements for the right to vote also involved ideas about age. It was especially through the rules of eligibility that the economic requirements were implicitly also envisaged as corresponding to age, maturity, independence, and experience. The economic criteria for suffrage to the Second Chamber were not as exacting as for municipal elections, where the voting scale excluded a majority from any real influence. In that sense, it was more democratic and rather soon became less important as a clearly demarcating criterion when wages rose towards the end of the nineteenth century. Sweden's unique position in comparison with other countries, with a low voting age to the Second Chamber and with economic requirements stated as fixed amounts, meant that, when demands for more democratic representation were increasingly heard in the late nineteenth century, the question of the voting age as a selection instrument also came to the fore. The right to vote in elections to the Second Chamber was also de facto limited in that it obliged the voter to have municipal suffrage. The minimum requirements for this were lower (500 kronor) but were based on criteria such as proof of payment of taxes. The calls for extended male suffrage had implications for the discussion of both municipal suffrage and the right to vote in elections to the Second Chamber.

The realisation that the design of suffrage was unfair also concerned rural groups and the lower middle class, not just the working class. The demands for more democratic suffrage quickly led to the question of how this could be achieved while guaranteeing that power would not be transferred from those who exercised it. A higher voting age in parliamentary elections corresponding to what was practised in other countries, such as Belgium, Denmark, Germany, and Austria, together with other restrictions, seemed like an idea worth trying. In Finland, the early passing of a universal suffrage legislation for both men and women in 1906 included economic restrictions but also a high voting age to exclude young voters, particularly women.[141]

The calls for an extension of the right to vote by lowering the economic requirements led to a discussion about the social and cultural foundations of suffrage. Liberal representatives who had initially been in favour of universal and equal suffrage from the age of 21 changed their positions around the turn of the century. They had new thoughts about suffrage and its limitations. They put forward the idea of a higher voting age (together with guarantees) that was quickly adopted by parties on the Right in Parliament as well. A shared position was established here among the Liberal and Conservative groups that concerned age and maturity, and which basically reflected the stance that the right to vote should be limited to represent the stable strata of society. Closer examination shows that it was ultimately the family as a unit or corporation that had to be represented. The age limits for voting simultaneously appear as a class issue that concerned the young male working class in the towns and the role of the family in society. As Berling Åselius has pointed out, this dual focus also affected the proposals for female suffrage and would leave its mark on the debate for a long time.[142] The well-behaved family as the foundation stone of society became a central topic in the parliamentary debates. The low marriage rate and the late marriage age, as we shall see later, are reflected in the proposals for a voting age above 25 and in the idea that married men could have two votes. Suffrage as the individual's vote, which Liberals also demanded, could also accommodate corporatist elements: the patriarchal family as a corporation.

The 1907–1909 reform established so-called universal male suffrage from the age of 24, with a number of restrictions concerning economic status and responsible behaviour, and only for elections to the Second Chamber. The voting thresholds also reflected the fact that the right to vote in Second Chamber elections would no longer be based on municipal suffrage and the limitations applying to that. The restrictions imposed for elections to the Second Chamber were now given constitutional protection. The voting system meant that seats in the chambers would be distributed proportionally. This protected minority interests, as one of the measures to establish guarantees for the people in power.

Judging by the debate, the question of the extension of the right to vote therefore had dramatically different meanings depending on economic development and the growth of the towns. The design of the electoral system from the 1860s favoured the influence of towns at the expense of the countryside. Age restrictions on voting could be assumed to limit voting rights effectively in towns but did not have the same effect in rural areas, where the number of young unmarried adults was much lower. On these issues, Liberals and the Right were largely in agreement, and also on the issue of tax payment and other criteria of responsible behaviour. They could also see eye to eye on ways to curtail voting rights in rural areas (given a low voting age), through various economic restrictions, while simultaneously limiting the power of the big companies. The impact of financial restrictions on the voting age was indirect, but it had the desired effect. The 40-grade voting scale for municipal suffrage gave power to the older, more stable population. Both Liberal and Conservative voter groups in rural industrial communities were interested in limiting the companies' power and the extreme influence exercised by individual large property owners.

The municipal voting age was not changed. Although the 40-grade scale introduced by the reforms of 1907–1909 limited the number of votes a single voter could have, it did mean, according to speeches in the parliamentary debate, that power remained with the older and socially stable groups. Just as before, in connection with the reforms in the mid-nineteenth century, the economic criteria for suffrage were meant to supplement the age limits for voting, or at least there was a clear idea that the economic requirements could have the same consequences as the age threshold. Young people would be excluded from political influence.

At the same time, the political battle between two distinct principles—the liberal preference for the British-style lower-house parliamentarism and a conservative model that sought to preserve elite influence in the First Chamber and the equal status of the two chambers—was more important than the discussions about how the proposals should be designed in detail. However, a high de facto voting age was a central element in the political ambitions, as regards the right to vote in both Second Chamber and municipal elections.

Women's suffrage was not a crucial issue for the Riksdag before 1909, because both Liberals and Social Democrats prioritised the struggle for male suffrage. The implementation of women's suffrage was perceived by these to be dependent on first achieving universal male suffrage. The lack of interest in approaching the issue of women's suffrage should also be viewed in light of the fact that working, unmarried women in towns who were registered to pay tax already had the right to vote in municipal elections since the 1880s and could thereby also affect First Chamber elections, although the 40-grade voting scale in municipal elections made their influence extremely limited.[143] In addition, first Staaff and then Lindman took steps to broaden municipal suffrage for married women with income or property. The proposed amendment to the Appropriation Ordinance (the tax legislation) of 1908, put forward by the Lindman government, explicitly aimed to give more married women the right to vote in municipal elections and to enable them to serve as elected representatives in the municipalities.[144] This can be interpreted as a deliberate strategy by the Liberals and Lindman's government to conciliate the female suffragists. The inquiry into universal suffrage for women over 24 did not lead to any bill; that would have favoured the influence of the urban population in the political system and hence the working class. The government chose a more limited target group of married women with income or property when it gave priority to changing the tax legislation. It is characteristic of a paternalistic regime that the decision was based on women's husbands paying taxes (and being over 21 years old, from 1909 over 24). For women, the right to vote was linked to their marital status. When it came to men's suffrage, the ambition was also, as we have seen, that they should be the family breadwinners.

The 1911 election was a major breakthrough for the Liberals and Social Democrats, who increased their parliamentary representation dramatically. Control of the First Chamber, however, remained in the hands of the Right, and in the municipalities the 40-grade voting scale had the effect of limiting the impact of the Social Democrats and the Liberals. This set its stamp on the ensuing discussion of voting rights and voting ages during the 1910s. Large sections of the male working class were still excluded from voting by the various dividing lines.

Notes

1. Adult offspring living at home (*hemmasöner*, *hemmadöttrar*) were the sons and daughters who remained at home, usually as labour on the farm but without any income or wealth of their own, subject to the head of the household.
2. Nils Stjernquist, *Tvåkammartiden: Sveriges riksdag 1867–1970* (Stockholm: Sveriges riksdag, 1996), pp. 62–67; Göran B., Nilsson, "Folkval och fyrkval 1863–1909", Scandia 30:1, 1963;21.Göran B. Nilsson, "Den samhällsbevarande representationsreformen", *Scandia 35:2*, 1969; Göran B. Nilsson, *Självstyrelsens problematik: Undersökningar i svensk landstingshistoria 1839–1928* (Stockholm: Svenska bokförlaget, 1967); Ingemar Norrlid, "Kommunen som bolag? En studie i liberal rösträttspolitik före första världskriget", Scandia 36:1, 1970, pp. 80–83.
3. Stjernquist (1996, pp. 62–67), Göran B. Nilsson (1964, 1967, 1969), and Norrlid (1970, pp. 80–83).
4. Ibid.
5. Norrlid (1970, p. 82).
6. Ibid., pp. 50–53.
7. Riksdagstrycket, *Proposition 1896:41*; Ebba Berling Berling Åselius, *Rösträtt med förhinder: Rösträttsstrecken i svensk politik 1900–1920* (Stockholm: Acta Universitatis Stockholmiensis, 2005), pp. 41–45.
8. Riksdagstrycket, *Motion AK 1896:239*, p. 3.
9. According to the Constitutional Committee in 1906, the discussion of age limits at the turn of the century was based on the positions already taken in Conservative (1885, 1893) and Liberal (1899, 1900, 1902) political programmes and, according to the Committee, the requirements of paid taxes and military service were shared features in the Second House proposal in 1900. Riksdagstrycket, *Utlåtande KU 1906:7*, p. 190.
10. Riksdagstrycket, *Motion AK 1896:236, Motion AK 1896:149.*
11. Riksdagstrycket, *Motion AK 1896:238.*
12. Riksdagstrycket, *Motion AK 1896:234*, p. 2.
13. Ibid.
14. The requirement of tax payment was problematic because taxes were paid in arrears, which meant that people had to save some of their earnings for future payment of taxes. This was difficult for the poorer stratum of the population and, as we shall see, it was a recurrent issue in the debate.
15. Stjernquist (1996, pp. 60–62); Georg Andrén, *Sveriges riksdag: Historisk och statsvetenskaplig framställning*, Bd 9, *Två kammarsystemets tillkomst och utveckling* (Stockholm 1937) pp. 284–355. Hjalmar Branting, "Rösträtt och värnplikt: Kätterska strötankar", *SocialDemokraten* 1 July 1900; Berling Åselius (2005, pp. 77–78). For more on the significance

and implications of the conscription criterion see Anders Ahlbeck and Fia Sundevall, "Värnplikt, rösträtt och kön: Värnpliktsstrecket i debatt och praktik", in Annika Berg and Martin Ericsson (eds.), *Allmän rösträtt? Rösträttens begränsningar i Sverige efter 1921* (Göteborg & Stockholm: Makadam, 2021); Harald Hjärne, *Rösträtt och värneplikt: Föredrag vid ett den 9 oktober 1892 av Uppsala rösträttsförening anordnat möte mot urtima riksdagen* (Stockholm: Bibliografiska institutet, 1892); Berling Åselius (2005, pp. 42–45).

16. Riksdagstrycket, *Motion AK 1896:234*, p. 2.
17. Berling Åselius (2005, pp. 42–43).
18. Georg Andrén, *De ekonomiska valbarhetsvillkoren till första kammaren i 1866 RO: Deras tillkomst och motivering* (Göteborg: Wettergren och Kerbers förlag, 1933) pp. 30–35. See Chap. 2 above.
19. Christina, Carlsson Wetterberg, *Kvinnosyn och kvinnopolitik: En studie av svensk socialdemokrati 1880–1910* (diss. Lund: Arkiv förlag, 1986).
20. Berling Åselius (2005, pp. 18–20); Hans-Krister Rönblom, *Frisinnade landsföreningen 1902–1927: Skildringar ur den liberala organisationsrörelsens historia i vårt land* (Stockholm: Saxon & Lindström, 1929); Staffan Runestam, Förstakammarhögern och rösträttsfrågan 1900–1907 (Uppsala: Acta Universitatis Upsaliensis, 1966) Torbjörn Nilsson, *Elitens svängrum: Första kammaren, staten och moderniseringen 1867–1886* (Stockholm: Almqvist & Wiksell International, 1994).
21. Riksdagstrycket, *Motion AK 1899:221, 225, 226, 227, 163.*
22. Riksdagstrycket, *Utlåtande KU 1899:4*, p. 5.
23. Ibid.
24. Riksdagstrycket, *Motion AK 1900:173*, pp. 9–10.
25. Hjalmar Branting, *Tal och skrifter* 3: *Kampen för demokratin* 1 (Stockholm: Tiden, 1927), pp. 210–214 (*Socialdemokraten* 25 February 1902).
26. Riksdagstrycket, *Motion AK 1900:173*, p 1.
27. Ibid., p. 2.
28. Ibid.
29. Ibid., p. 3.
30. Ibid., p. 4.
31. Ibid., p. 8.
32. Riksdagstrycket, *Riksdagens skrifvelse 1900:86*; *Utlåtande KU 1900:8.*
33. Riksdagstrycket, *Riksdagens skrifvelse 1900:86.*
34. Arne Wåhlstrand, *Regeringsskiftena 1900 och 1902* (Uppsala: Almqvist & Wiksell, 1947), pp. 30–49, 56–57; Berling Åselius (2005).
35. H. L Hammarskjöld to F. W. von Otter, 28 November, PM no. 1, quoted in Wåhlstrand (1947, pp. 175–176).
36. Ibid., p. 176.
37. Riksdagstrycket, *Proposition AK 1902:65*, pp. 13–14.

38. Ibid., p. 15.
39. Ibid., p. 14. See Berling Åselius (2005) on the varying meanings of the concept of universal suffrage.
40. Riksdagstrycket, *Proposition AK 1902:65*, pp. 16–19.
41. Ibid., p. 22.
42. Ibid., pp. 22–26.
43. Ibid., p. 27.
44. Ibid., pp. 27–28.
45. Ibid.
46. Ibid., p. 29.
47. Ibid., p. 30.
48. Ibid., p. 3.
49. Fia Sundevall, "Ekonomi och rösträtt: Skatteskulder, konkurs och fattigvård som rösträttshinder", in Annika Berg and Martin Ericsson (eds.), *Allmän rösträtt? Rösträttens begränsningar i Sverige efter 1921* (Göteborg & Stockholm: Makadam, 2021).
50. Riksdagstrycket, *Proposition AK 1902:65*, pp. 27–28.
51. Ingemar Norrlid, *Demokrati, skatterättvisa och ideologisk förändring: Den kommunala självstyrelsen och demokratins genombrott i Sverige* (Lund: Liber/Gleerup, 1983); Norrlid (1970, pp. 50–51).
52. Berling Åselius (2005, pp. 20–21); Victor Lundberg, *Folket, yxan och orättvisans rot: Betydelsebildning kring demokrati i den svenska rösträttsrörelsens diskursgemenskap 1887–1902* (Umeå: h:- ström – Text & kultur, 2007); Hultin Rosenberg and Sundevall (2022).
53. Berling Åselius (2005, pp. 20–21), Norrlid (1983), Norrlid (1970, pp. 64–69), and Göran B. Nilsson (1969).
54. Riksdagstrycket, *Proposition AK 1902:65*, pp. 15–18.
55. Ibid.
56. Josefin Rönnbäck, *Politikens genusgränser: Den kvinnliga rösträttsrörelsen och kampen för kvinnors politiska medborgarskap 1902–1921* (Stockholm: Atlas, 2004); Christina Florin, *Kvinnor får röst: Kön, känslor och politisk kultur i kvinnornas rösträttsrörelse* (Stockholm: Atlas, 2006).
57. Rönnbäck (2004, p. 115).
58. Berling Åselius (2005, pp. 22–24).
59. Anna Wicksell, "De gifta kvinnorna och kommunallagarna", *Dagny: Tidning för svenska kvinnorörelsen* 1910:3, pp. 28–30.
60. Christina Carlsson Wetterberg, "Kvinnans rätt och nationens väl", in Lars M. Andersson (ed.), *Rätten: En festskrift till Bengt Ankarloo* (Lund: Nordic Academic Press, 2000); Kari Melby et al., *The Nordic Model of Marriage and the Welfare State* (Copenhagen: Nordic Council of Ministers, 2000).
61. Riksdagstrycket, *Protokoll AK 1902:21*, p. 3.

62. Ibid., p. 4.
63. Ibid., p. 4.
64. Riksdagstrycket, *Protokoll AK 1902:51*, pp. 40–41.
65. Ibid., p. 42.
66. Ibid., p. 43.
67. Ibid., pp. 43–44.
68. See, for example, Höjer, who expresses this especially pithily, Riksdagstrycket, *Protokoll AK 1902:51*, pp. 53–56.
69. Ibid., pp. 10–11, my italics.
70. Ibid., p. 11.
71. Ibid.
72. Ibid., p. 12.
73. Ibid.
74. Ibid., pp. 16, 22–23, 35; Riksdagstrycket, *Protokoll FK 1902:36*, p. 36. Bishop Gottfrid Billing argued for a further inquiry as a consequence of his opinion that the debates testified to a shared norm of a 25-year age limit together with some basic criteria of responsible behaviour: "The only thing about which there seems to be general agreement is that, in the event of a change in voting rules, the right to vote should not be granted until the age of 25, provided that the person concerned has not neglected his duties in respect of military service and taxes." Riksdagstrycket, *Protokoll FK 1902:36*, p. 53.
75. Riksdagstrycket, *Protokoll FK 1902:35*, pp. 26–29.
76. E.g., Riksdagstrycket, *Protokoll FK 1902:35*, pp. 16, 22–23, 35; Riksdagstrycket, *Protokoll FK 1902:36*, pp. 36, 53.
77. Kungl. Statistiska centralbyrån, *BiSOS R, Valstatistik XIV:3, Statistiska Centralbyråns underdåniga redogörelse angående valrätt till riksdagens andra kammare år 1900* (Stockholm: P. A. Norstedt & Söner, 1904).
78. "Fram för den allmänna rösträtten", Partistyrelsens cirkulär, 1903, Hjalmar Brantings arkiv 1889–1922, Arbetarrörelsens arkiv och bibliotek.
79. Branting (1927, pp. 186–189) ("Lika rösträtt – proportionella val").
80. Ibid., pp. 217–230 ("Allmänna rösträttsmotionen 1902").
81. Ibid., pp. 215–216 ("Det kungliga rösträttsförget", *Social-Demokraten*, 13 March 1902).
82. Berling Åselius (2005, pp. 46–48).
83. See note 173 above for the quotation from Riksdagstrycket, *Protokoll FK 1902:36*, p. 53.
84. Berling Åselius (2005, pp. 49–50) and Stjernquist (1996, p. 63).
85. From Wåhlstrand (1947, pp. 124–125, quotation p. 124).
86. Stjernquist (1996, p. 63).
87. Riksdagstrycket, *Proposition AK 1904:51*, pp. 16–17, 20. "In the laws of most countries there are provisions which deny suffrage to those who

enjoy or have enjoyed poor relief during a certain period of time before the election. It seems obvious to me that such a provision should not be absent here, and justice surely also requires that the consequence of loss of suffrage should affect not only a person who has received poor relief himself, but also a person whose wife or minor children have required poor relief as a result of his failure to take care of them [...] In my opinion, the requirements for this should not be excessive but should grant suffrage to a person who, for a certain limited time before the election, had supported himself and his family, even if he had not been able to repay the support previously provided."

88. Berling Åselius (2005, pp. 52–54).
89. Sam Clason, *Hvad gäller rösträttsfrågan: Statistik och anmärkningar* (Stockholm: Nordiska bokhandeln, 1902), pp. 21–28.
90. Ibid., pp. 34–35.
91. Berling Åselius (2005); Riksdagstrycket, *Proposition AK 1906:55*, p. 11; *Motion AK 1904:168*; Carlsson Wetterberg (1986, pp. 94–106, 140–146), Rönnbäck (2004), and Florin (2006).
92. See note 173 above for the quotation from Riksdagstrycket, *Protokoll FK 1902:36*, p. 53.
93. The differences in consequences for industrial workers and farm workers are examined in Chap. 8. What is most likely meant here is that many industrial workers and workers in the towns earned more than the limit of 800 kronor and lost out on the higher age limit, while farm workers did not earn as much and now benefitted from gaining the right to vote in elections to the Second Chamber without any minimum economic income and property requirement.
94. "Protokoll fört vid sammanträde med riksdagsgruppen, partistyrelsens verkställande utskott samt redaktörerna för partitidningarna söndagen den 5 februari för behandling av rösträttsfrågan", Gunnar Gerdners papper, nr 2:7–9, pp. 1–3. Handskriftssamlingen, Uppsala universitetsbibliotek.
95. Ibid., pp. 3–4.
96. Branting (1927, pp. 281–284) ("En konjunkturreform", *Social-Demokraten* 26 February 1906).
97. Manuscript, "Partistyrelsens förslag om författningsrevision, 1889–1922 91/4/7/1", Hjalmar Brantings arkiv, Arbetarrörelsens arkiv och bibliotek, Hjalmar Brantings arkiv. "Possibly from 1906" noted on the cover of the archive folder.
98. Berling Åselius (2005, pp. 54–56). Riksdagstrycket, *Motion AK 1907:20*; *Utlåtande KU 1906:7*, p. 154; Lars Gogman, "Material om rösträttsfrågan i ARABs samlingar", *Arbetarhistoria* 2019, pp. 73–90; Runestam (1966); Carlsson Wetterberg (1986, pp. 200–217). In the minutes of the

Social Democratic parliamentary group, however, it is clear that a number of members argued in favour of demanding both male and female suffrage, e.g. "Protokoll fört vid sammanträde med riksdagsgruppen, partistyrelsens verkställande utskott samt redaktörerna för partitidningarna söndagen den 5 februari 1906 för behandling av rösträttsfrågan", Gunnar Gerdners papper, nr 2:7–9, pp 1–3. Handskriftssamlingen, Uppsala universitetsbibliotek.

99. The right to impede the implementation of decisions for a fixed period, which can usually be annulled by a new decision.
100. Leif Lewin, *Ideologi och strategi: Svensk politik under 100 år* (Stockholm: Carlsson, 2017), pp. 90–103; Brita Skottsberg, "Den svenska diskussionen om parlamentarismen i samband med rösträttsfrågan 1904–1907", *Statsvetenskaplig tidskrift* 1934:2, pp. 130–152. See footnote 113 below.
101. Kungl. Statistiska centralbyrån, *BiSOS R, Valstatistik XIV:3* (see note 176 above).
102. Stjernquist (1996, pp. 67–81).
103. Riksdagstrycket, *Motion AK 1907:20.*
104. August Nilsson, *Rapport över den Socialdemokratiska riksdagsgruppens verksamhet under treårsperioden 1906–1908* (Stockholm, 1908), p. 10.
105. "Protokoll fört vid sammanträde med riksdagsgruppen, partistyrelsens verkställande utskott samt redaktörerna för partitidningarna söndagen den 5 februari för behandling av rösträttsfrågan", Uppsala universitetsbibliotek, Gunnar Gerdners papper 2:7–9. Handskriftssamlingen, Uppsala universitetsbibliotek. See also P. A. Hanson in *Fram* 1909, Valnummer I & II, which also cites Värner Rydén's critique of rule by old upper-class (gubbvälde) men and their anti-labour policies.
106. Branting (1927, pp. 326–341) ("Den Lindmanska författningsreformen 1907").
107. Gustav Möller, "Studier i valstatistiken", *Tiden* 1918:5, p. 203.
108. Riksdagstrycket, *Proposition 1907:28*; cf. Riksdagstrycket, *Proposition AK 1906:55*; Berling Åselius (2005, p. 20); Åke Holmbäck, "Karl Staaff: Anteckningar kring en biografi", *Svensk Juristtidning* 1966:42, pp. 42–44; Runestam (1966).
109. See Chap. 6 and Lindman's statement in the concluding debate.
110. Ibid.
111. Norrlid (1970, pp. 50–53, 82).
112. See, e.g., Riksdagstrycket, *Proposition 1907:28*, *Utlåtande SärU 1907:3.* This also cites the motion by Adelswärd mentioned below, *Motion AK 1907:216.*
113. Riksdagstrycket, *Motion AK 1907:216*, Theodor Adelswärd, "Tal i rösträttsfrågan 1907", "Tal i rösträttsfrågan vid möte med Åkerbo, Bankekinds och Henekinds valkrets valmän i Åtvidaberg den 13 januari

1907", "Inledningstal vid möte för diskussion af rösträttsfrågan anordnadt af Föreningen för studenter och arbetare i Stockholm söndagen den 28 April", all in Folder Egendomen 2, Plåtskåp, Theodors Adelswärds tal, Baroniet Adelswärds gårdsarkiv.

114. Adelswärd, "Inledningstal vid möte för diskussion af rösträttsfrågan anordnadt af Föreningen för studenter och arbetare i Stockholm söndagen den 28 April 1907", p. 5, Theodors Adelswärds tal, Baroniet Adelswärds gårdsarkiv.
115. "Tal i rösträttsfrågan vid möte med Åkerbo, Bankekinds och Henekinds valkrets valmän i Åtvidaberg den 13 januari 1907", p. 30, Theodors Adelswärds tal, Baroniet Adelswärds gårdsarkiv.
116. Ibid., pp. 30–31, also pp. 20–21. My italics.
117. Ibid., pp. 28–29. word crossed over in Adelswärds text
118. Ibid., p. 29.
119. Adelswärd, "Inledningstal vid möte för diskussion af rösträttsfrågan anordnadt af Föreningen för studenter och arbetare i Stockholm söndagen den 28 april 1907", pp. 7–8, Theodors Adelswärds tal, Baroniet Adelswärds gårdsarkiv.
120. Ibid., pp. 10–11.
121. Riksdagstrycket, *Motion AK 1907:216*, pp. 2–3.
122. Ibid., p. 4.
123. Ibid., p. 5.
124. Ibid., p. 9. Unmarried women over 21 with an income and paid taxes could vote in municipal elections.
125. Ibid., p. 10.
126. Rönnbäck (2004).
127. Per Albin Hansson, "Ungdomens medborgrätt", *Fram: Socialdemokratiska Ungdomsförbundets Organ* 1908:1, p. 2.
128. Ibid., pp. 2–3.
129. Rönnbäck (2004, p. 115) and Berling Åselius (2005, pp. 179–185); Ulla Manns, "Den gifta kvinnans frigörelse: Reflexioner kring rösträtt och myndighet i svensk kvinnorörelse", in Kari Melby (ed.), *The Nordic Model of Marriage and the Welfare State* (Copenhagen: Nordiska Ministerrådet, 2000).
130. Rönnbäck (2004, p. viii).
131. Riksdagstrycket, *Proposition 1907:28*, pp. 24–25; see also, e.g., *Protokoll AK 1907:8*, pp. 7–8; *Motioner AK 1907:208*, pp. 6–9.
132. Riksdagstrycket, *Motion AK 1904:168*, pp. 8–11; *Protokoll FK 1904:36*, pp. 58–61, *AK 1904:39*, pp. 63–69; *Beviljningsutskottets betänkande 1908:22*, pp. 6–10; *Protokoll AK 1908:53*, Branting's statement pp. 67–69.
133. Riksdagstrycket, *Proposition 1908:34*, pp. 41–53.
134. Ibid., pp. 44–45.

135. Wicksell (1910, pp. 28–30) and Rönnbäck (2004, p. 115).
136. Kungl. Statistiska centralbyrån, *BiSOS R, Valstatistik XIV:44: Valrätt till riksdagens andra kammare år 1900. Kvinnor över 24 år* (Stockholm: P. A. Norstedt & Söner, 1908), pp. i–x.
137. See Berling Åselius (2005, pp. 129–130) for an account of the grounds for disqualification, broken down by social group; *BiSOS R, Valstatistik XIV:4*, pp. i–x.
138. Mellquist (1974, pp. 112–113).
139. Berling Åselius (2005, pp. 183–186).
140. Kungl. Statistiska centralbyrån, *BiSOS R, Valstatistik XIV:4*, p. viii.
141. Minna, Harjula, "The Poor and Deservingness for Political and Social Citizenship: 'Universal suffrage' in Finland Since 1906", *Suffrage, Capital and Welfare: Conditional Citizenship in Historical Perspective*, Eds. Fia Cottrell-Sundevall, and Ragnheiður Kristjánsdóttir (Palgrave Macmillan, 2024), pp. 225–248; Cottrell-Sundevall, Fia, and Kristjánsdóttir, Ragnheiður, *Suffrage, Capital and Welfare: Conditional Citizenship in Historical Perspective*, Eds. (Palgrave Macmillan, 2024).
142. Berling Åselius (2005, pp. 183–186).
143. This probably also reduced the propensity to exercise the right to vote. The willingness to vote generally decreased with the number of votes, i.e. the fewer votes a person had, the less likely he was to vote; this was mostly noticeable in the towns. See, e.g., Kungl. Statistiska centralbyrån, *SOS Allmänna val, Landstingsmannavalen 1914* (Stockholm, 1915), pp. 22–23.
144. Rönnbäck (2004, p. 115); Christina Carlsson Wetterberg, *Jag saknar fruntimmer här: En biografi över Anna Bugge Wicksell* (Stockholm: Natur & Kultur, 2020), pp. 148–149; Wicksell (1910, pp. 28–30).

CHAPTER 4

Age Limits in the Political Game 1910–1917

The election to the Second Chamber in 1911 took place according to the new voting rules, and although it was a Conservative reform, the outcome was a breakthrough for what was called the Left. The First Chamber nevertheless remained Conservative, as the reform had preserved its position of power. Three distinct political blocs can be distinguished in the continued discussion of voting rights: the Social Democrats, the Liberals, and the General Electoral League (the Conservatives, also called the Right). A characteristic of this period in Swedish history was the considerable mobility between the political blocs, as regards both party and group formations in Parliament and the political affiliation of individual members of parliament.[1] For example, the Second Chamber member Erik Palmstierna left the Liberals for the Social Democrats in 1910 after being elected as a Liberal two years earlier, while Alfred Petersson "of Påboda" left the conservative government in 1909 to become a member of the Liberals. Carl Lindhagen was initially a Liberal but became a Social Democrat in the 1910s and later a member of the radical left party and subsequently changed parties again and became a Social Democrat.[2]

The election in 1911 brought about the fall of the Lindman government, leaving Karl Staaff to form a minority government. Under his leadership from 7 October 1911 to 17 February 1914, the suffrage issue was raised once again in the Riksdag. The Liberal government then fell on the defence issue in 1914. Staff's government was succeeded by a caretaker government of civil servants as office holders led by the Conservative

B. Sandin, *Voting and Eligibility Age in Sweden, 1866–1921*,
https://doi.org/10.1007/978-3-031-95276-0_4

Hjalmar Hammarskjöld (17 February 1914 to 30 March 1917). In the 1914 Second Chamber election, the Social Democrats increased while the Liberals declined, and the Right became the largest party in the Second Chamber. The economic crisis of 1917 and the social unrest, with hunger riots in 1917, led to a new Conservative minority government under Carl Swartz (30 March 1917 to 19 October 1917), after which Liberals and Social Democrats formed a majority coalition with Edén as prime minister between October 1917 and 10 March 1920.

In this chapter I shall examine the various approaches to the issue of voting restrictions based on age, from 1910 to the end of 1917. The premises were stated in the previous chapter. The Liberals and the Right had the same attitude to age limits for suffrage, but the Liberals and Social Democrats also shared the growing criticism of the voting restrictions. The political climate in this period was coloured by the First World War and the events leading up to it. The defence issue in its various aspects—mobilisation, non-alignment, and feeding the people—dominated the political conversation. But the suffrage issue was a recurring topic in the Liberals' and Social Democrats' political appeals. The women's suffrage movement was growing, with more members and local associations. The realisation that married women had the right to vote if they had an income and were registered to pay tax—what was called "the Wicksell discovery" (after Anna Bugge Wicksell)—stimulated women in their struggle for suffrage.[3] Universal male suffrage was perceived as having already been implemented in some sense. The fact that it was not really universal suffrage, as a result of the many restrictions, remained a bone of contention between Liberal and Social Democratic politicians, although from 1909 they agreed that women's suffrage must be on the political agenda.

Voting at Age 24 or from 21, for Men and Women

The various groupings among the Right were initially not very active in the debates after 1910. Those who did speak expressed support for the 1907–1909 reform, arguing, for example, that it was better if those who had the right to vote actually used it, rather than further extending suffrage.[4] The Social Democratic and Liberal proposals were designed on the foundation established in the period before 1911. The Social Democrats were decidedly in favour of women's suffrage and uncompromising with respect to the voting age and the abolition or relaxation of the restrictions. At the same time, the Social Democrats' motions revealed the scope of their demands. Although Branting and others played down the calls for a republic and the abolition of the First Chamber, far-reaching demands of this type were repeatedly heard from the left wing of the Social Democratic Party and later the left-wing socialists.

In 1912, Hjalmar Branting and others submitted a motion to the Second Chamber which clearly put the issue of the voting age on the agenda. The proposers began by questioning whether the 1909 decision would end the political conflicts and remove the suffrage issue from the political agenda.[5] They praised the Liberal government for including women in their latest proposal for an expansion of suffrage. That was a step in the right direction, but the struggle for democracy must continue and, according to Branting, comprise both the municipality and the state. The various restrictions were criticised and dismissed—the criteria of gender, tax payment, poor relief, recent migrants to municipalities, bankruptcy, military training, and finally,

> *the higher age threshold*, up to an actual average of *over 25*, introduced in connection with the 1907 extension of suffrage. No inconvenience whatsoever had previously been reported as a result of the voting age being the same as the age of civic majority, nor can any viable reason be cited, at least not in a country like Sweden, for excluding these four cohorts of men and women from the right to vote. On the contrary, we need our young people at the ballot box so that – with their optimistic faith in the possibility and necessity of rapid and effective reform – they can counterbalance the excessively anxious hesitation which has its full say right up to the late autumn of life.[6]

The proposal also called into question the thresholds still set for eligibility to the First Chamber. The barriers to women's eligibility and the income and property requirements had to be removed.[7] The Social Democrats demanded the right to vote from the age of 21 in elections to the Second Chamber and to municipal and county councils (and thus indirectly the First Chamber), the age of 25 for eligibility to the Second Chamber (unless legally incapacitated or under the guardianship of the poor relief board), and age 30 for eligibility to the First Chamber, which corresponded to current legislation. In this motion Branting called for women's suffrage, while Ola Waldén's motion on municipal suffrage in the Second Chamber emphasised that it also included married women. Waldén also made a point of the unreasonable consequence of the voting rules introduced in 1909 for municipal elections both in the country as a whole and in the big cities. The high voting age introduced by the decisions of 1907–1909 was not acceptable in the eyes of Social Democrats. A crucial argument was that the municipalities were not private entities or corporations but state institutions that required equal terms and responsibilities for all citizens.[8]

Suffrage at the age of 21 was perceived as fundamental in the Social Democrats' political platform, as a non-negotiable right. The demand emphasised that young people as individuals deserved the right to vote. The Social Democratic motions paint a picture of young people's contribution to the development of society which reflected a belief in the future and the potential for effective reform inherent in the younger generation. That contrasted with the hesitation that characterised politicians during the "late autumn of life", as Branting characterised them.

In a statement in the spring, the Constitutional Committee, which the Liberal minority government had appointed, took up a position on the Social Democrats' and the Liberals' motions for an extension of the right to vote. It concerned the demands for extended male and female suffrage from the age of 21 and eligibility from the age of 25 for the Second Chamber and 30 for the First Chamber, as well as the abolition of the voting restrictions and the 40-grade municipal suffrage.[9]

In the Committee's reasoning, the question of age played a fundamental role, based on the arguments that were heard at the turn of the century. The Committee referred to the bill proposing an extension of suffrage from 1902. A more mature age, it was noted, was an important "prerequisite for independence and judgement, and that it could therefore be considered justified to set as a condition of political suffrage a slightly higher age than the usual age of majority".[10] According to the Committee, there was "great agreement on this issue" of the appropriateness of a higher voting age.[11] The Committee also rejected the other calls for reforms, albeit acknowledging that the rules needed to be reviewed. Branting noted the willingness to revise the rules in his reservation, but once again he opposed the retention of the age threshold. He did not think that the extension of male suffrage had gone far enough. He regarded the age limits as a concession to the Conservatives' demands for guarantees.

> However, if these concessions can be regarded as being in some measure symptomatic of a nascent understanding of the legitimacy of these demands

> of ours, which are of such vital importance to the working class, the Committee still remains opposed to any radical extension of suffrage for men. The Committee therefore believes that the high age threshold should be maintained, essentially only because this concession has been made to the Conservative demand for "guarantees". Against this, no weight at all is attached to the fact that four annual cohorts of adult men are completely excluded from the right to vote.[12]

We thus see how the Social Democrats' demands were rejected, although the possibility was left open for some adjustment of eligibility requirements and an inquiry into certain issues. The age threshold that Branting had criticised as a concession to the Right was maintained by the majority of the Committee with reference to the political consensus on the matter, that obviously did not include the Social Democrats.

In 1912 and 1914 the Social Democrats motioned, among other things, for equal municipal suffrage and the abolition of all restrictions and the 40-grade scale. In these motions, comments were also made about the status of municipalities in relation to the state, testifying to a new view of the state and the meanings of citizenship. The motions substantiated the demands to abolish the 40-grade voting scale and give more powers to municipal government. The municipality was not a voluntary commitment but a part of the state and thus a civic commitment, underlined by the tendency towards increasing municipal self-government and responsibility. Given this, equal suffrage ought to apply to all political bodies. It was also in the municipalities that the influence of the Social Democrats was seriously tested; it actually grew under the stresses of war and shortages, despite the restrictions on suffrage.[13]

The Right and the Liberals, on the other hand, were in agreement about the voting age. They both argued that suffrage should be granted from 24/25, but the Liberals took a clear stand for women's suffrage, partly under the influence of the suffrage movement.[14] The suffrage issue was not resolved during Karl Staaff's prime ministership, and his government fell on the defence issue in February 1914. It was succeeded by a Conservative-dominated caretaker government under Hjalmar Hammarskjöld.

During the period 1914–1917, other political issues dominated, but the Social Democrats and the Staaff Liberals still negotiated on matters such as suffrage. This is shown, among other things, by the discussions between Liberals and Social Democrats in May 1915. The deliberations of

1915 were mainly about forming a future government. Staaff argued that the Social Democrats should consider forming a government themselves, and according to Oredsson, Staaff likewise "did not want a detailed joint programme for the two parties: a few points were enough. Municipal suffrage was particularly important, but there the Liberals were not committed to any policy. The issue would be raised at the national congress in the autumn".[15] Karl Staaff maintained that there was no question of universal suffrage, but that equal municipal suffrage could be contemplated. The tax line, that is to say, the requirement that voters had paid their taxes, had to remain although it could be relaxed somewhat.[16] It was on this basis that the rapprochement with the Social Democrats could be built, but the Liberals' new position regarding the 40-grade scale was not crystal clear. The agreement that was reached, according to a draft joint statement dated 22 May preserved among the papers of leading figures of the Liberal and Social Democratic Party, yielded meagre results: as regards the right to vote in elections to the Second Chamber, women should be put on an equal footing with men, the poor relief threshold would be revised so that temporary dependency did not affect the right to vote, and there was also a sentence that began: "Municipal suffrage …", but it remained unfinished.[17] On that point, the parties had not reached agreement.

Arvid Lindman observed in parliamentary debates in 1918 that the Edén the Liberal, as late as the summer session in 1914, believed that the voting scale needed to be revised, but "without the need to go all the way towards equal suffrage".[18] Oredsson argues in his book about Edén that the tricky question to resolve between the parties was not women's suffrage, nor was it equal municipal suffrage. The crucial issue was the tax threshold. But it was not until 1915 that the Liberals clearly approached the Social Democrats on the matter of the 40-grade voting scale.[19] In the negotiations between the Liberals and the Social Democrats after the parliamentary session in 1915, the issue of the tax threshold was the obvious stumbling block. Equal suffrage, i.e. the abolition of the 40-grade scale, was a possibility but did not constitute universal suffrage. Staaff could at most accept "some minor modification" as to whether political suffrage was also possible.[20] Oredsson's analysis is based on notes from the meeting between Edén and the Social Democrats, but he does not stress the differences in opinion between the Social Democrats and the Liberals.[21] They were not in agreement about everything. The high voting age and the tax threshold were still key issues for the Liberals, as was the question of the degree to which "universal suffrage" should actually be universal. In this respect the Liberals had a different view from the Social Democrats.

Having an income and being registered to pay tax were prerequisites for suffrage in the Liberal view of universal suffrage. The right to vote was linked to the ability to pay taxes. This meant that married women without an income would not be allowed to vote under the Liberal proposal. There will be reason to return to this in connection with the discussion in 1917–1918. "The Wicksell discovery", mentioned above, meant that married women with little income could be allowed to vote in municipal elections but were dependent on their husbands' right to vote.[22]

A discussion of this dependence of married women's suffrage surfaced, as we shall see, in connection with the suffrage proportions in the spring of 1918. The Social Democrats embraced the principle that the right to vote was tied to individuals and citizens regardless of income, and this included women. The Social Democratic women explicitly questioned this very dependence on men's suffrage. The emphasis on tax liability and the ability to pay the taxes levied constituted another difference of opinion, along with the issue of age limits. The closer cooperation with the Liberals meant that conflicts with left-wing groups within the party were now sharpened as Social Democrats at the same time began to demand stronger party discipline.[23]

Forming the Forces in 1917

During the First World War, Sweden was neutral in the great international conflict. The policy of neutrality observed by the government under Hammarskjöld was largely appreciated by the Liberals, although they were more positively inclined towards the Entente. A government of the Right under Lindman and Ernst Trygger did not appear to be an option. The food crisis, the defence budget, and the fact that the government has not managed to reach a trade agreement with the United Kingdom provoked criticism to varying degrees from Liberals and Social Democrats, but also from some Conservative politicians and representatives of industry. On this point, the labour movement and industry had a common interest in a better relationship with the Entente. The crisis became acute in connection with the budget decisions of 1917. The government fell on 30 March. A new government was formed with the moderate Right politician from Norrköping, Carl Swartz.[24]

Fig. 4.1 Soldiers on their way to a meeting in Söder in Stockholm in 1917. Could these young people be trusted in a politically charged situation? Source: Foto Axel Malmström. Arbetarrörelsens arkiv och bibliotek

The situation for the government was particularly troublesome. The food crisis had led to hunger demonstrations and riots. It was uncertain whether the rank and file of the military would be loyal in the long run (Fig. 4.1). The youth league excluded by the Social Democrats formed a Social Democratic Left Party. This new party represented critical voices that did not submit to party discipline, but they were scarcely a united group. Developments in Russia, along with the split of the Social Democratic Party, the food crisis, the constitutional issue (i.e. suffrage and the existence of the First Chamber) meant that the threat of revolution could be perceived as imminent. At the same time, bourgeois forces were mobilised, among other things, through the organisation of an armed defence corps in Stockholm.[25] The Social Democrat Erik Palmstierna was concerned about this but also about

> these "young socialists" to our left; they are fishing in murky water and playing with fire. Apparently, there is uncertainty about the military. Heard von

> Sydow [the Minister of Civil Affairs] the other day saying to Petersson, the former Minister of Justice, "We cannot trust the troops, that is the difficult thing in this situation" (Fig. 4.1).[26]

With 1 May 1917 drawing near, people were palpably nervous. Prime Minister Carl Swartz also considered a temporary ban on alcohol on 1 May. On 28 April an appeal was published in *Dagens Nyheter* in which the party leaders, including Trygger, Edén, and Branting, called for unity. May Day passed without any problems.[27] In the following months, both Liberals and Social Democrats acted through approaches to the government and calls in Parliament demanding equal and universal suffrage for men and women, along with the abolition of the 40-grade scale. A difference in nuance can be noted, however.

The Liberals called for universal and equal suffrage for all taxpayers, while the Social Democrats demanded this for "all irreproachable men and women".[28] Swartz responded in a speech on 5 June 1917. He explained that the government's primary task was to ensure that the people had food, whereas constitutional issues could wait until after the autumn elections.[29]

The Social Democrats' motions in the spring of 1917 demanded universal and equal suffrage from the age of 21 and called for the abolition of the 40-grade voting scale and the various economic thresholds. As before, they proposed eligibility for the Second Chamber from the age of 25 and for the First Chamber from the age of 30.[30] The rhetoric of these motions is particularly strident, as before, in terms of the criticism of the consequences of the restrictions at various political levels and the position of the First Chamber in Parliament, and also in the vivid descriptions of the threatening world situation. The fact that one in three voters was disqualified on account of some restrictions was questioned. The criticism was directed at the Right but also at the Liberals. The Social Democrats condemned the thresholds of poor relief, tax, and military training and emphasised, as before, that the age limit was not acceptable, with the same wording as before. They called for the abolition of all the thresholds.[31]

The Social Democrats also made it clear that the question of the abolition of the First Chamber was no longer on the immediate agenda. On that point there was a certain willingness to compromise. The most pressing reform was the abolition of the 40-grade voting scale and the property requirements for eligibility, and they approved the idea of proportional representation. In the latter respect too, there was a possibility of compromise. Branting had previously argued that proportional representation could be accepted if the First Chamber were simultaneously abolished (see Chap. 3). But the background now was different. The world situation was a palpable menace to those who opposed the people's demands for democracy.[32] The motion referred to the:

> gigantic military struggle that we are now witnessing between power groups fighting for world domination. In every country we now see with increasing clarity the struggle behind the trenches, which has been fought since long before these were dug, and which will grow with intensified strength into a mighty assault, when they have been filled in again and the defenders return to a starving and impoverished homeland. We have seen the strongest bulwarks of reaction in Europe collapse under the unanimous cries of the people for emancipation and self-government. The immediate future will certainly be characterized by a similar growing, triumphant rising of the supporters of democracy in all countries. It testifies to short-sightedness and poor statesmanship if the Swedish Right still insists on opposing the full and unrestricted right of representation for our people. By doing so, they only summon up against themselves the revolutionary forces of the people, of which historical testimony and current events can confirm that they ultimately defeat even the most self-assured reactionary power.[33]

At the same time, the Social Democrats were under criticism from the left wing of their own party—Ernst Hage, Carl Lindhagen, Ivar Vennerström—who voiced demands for more fundamental and comprehensive constitutional changes, the introduction of a republic, and the abolition of the First Chamber. [34] Lindhagen's paper on the revision of the constitution in early 1917 is an impressive review of all the various challenges that the transformation of society entailed.[35] Taken together, these motions expressed the mood within the left-wing opposition that did not submit to Social Democratic Party discipline and was consequently excluded in 1917.

In 1917, the Liberals moved in both the First and Second Chambers for women's suffrage from the age of 25 on the same terms as men, that is, with the thresholds retained. Perhaps for tactical reasons, the Liberals' proposals explicitly confined themselves to the issue of women's suffrage and refrained from commenting further on the suffrage restrictions. The right to vote for married women would also be dependent on their husbands not failing to meet the requirements for proper economic behaviour.[36] The family was thus the norm on which the proposals were based, with the same effect as the high age requirement. In this respect, the liberal proposal was solidly traditional when viewed in relation to the greater individualism reflected in the amendments to marriage law already implemented in 1915 and those that would come in 1921.[37] But the rhetoric was progressive. The motion was submitted in April and somewhat later, on 7 May, the Liberals went to Prime Minister Swartz with demands "to eliminate outdated preferences based on class and gender, on which we are now internally divided", according to the report in *Dagens Nyheter*.[38]

The Constitutional Committee examined the motions and rejected them with respect both to the age of eligibility and to the extension of women's suffrage. In its arguments about women's suffrage, however, the Committee was open for the possibility that it should perhaps be graded according to maturity and thus also according to age:

> The Committee has not found convincing reasons in the present motions either for the lowering of the age limit to 21 or for the removal of the restrictions on suffrage resulting from a state of bankruptcy, unpaid taxes, and failure to undergo military training. In the Committee's view, the age limit currently in force is well suited to the obvious requirement of a certain degree of maturity on the part of those who are to participate in political life.[39]

In its statement the Constitutional Committee argued that the difference in the age of eligibility between the two chambers should be greater and that the income requirements for eligibility to the First Chamber were fully justified.[40] In contrast, the Committee felt that different age limits for men and women could be considered if women should be granted the right to vote, because it was doubtful whether women "acquire as quickly as men the political understanding and the interest in related issues that is required for the exercise of suffrage". Such a decision should also take into account that the significant demographic surplus of women, especially in Stockholm but also in other towns, could have a negative impact on elections.[41]

The question of the size of the urban population was also important. The fact that women in the towns and cities would also be able to make greater use of their right to vote was also worrying, as it affected the issue of proxy voting between spouses, that is, that spouses could vote for each other in the event that one of them was prevented from voting for practical reasons. The idea of proxy voting was an issue where the great distances in rural areas appeared to be a good enough reason for women to prefer not to leave home to vote, a task that they could entrust to their spouse, and thus balance urban working women's easier access to the polling stations in urban environments.[42]

On 5 June 1917 the Constitutional Committee rejected all proposals for change, with the exception that it wished to look more closely at the proposals regarding poor relief put forward by Gerhard Halfred von Kock. He was critical of the fact that the dependence on poor relief, for one's own sake or for family members, should lead to the loss of suffrage. Both the Social Democrats and the Liberals expressed reservations with reference to their own motions. The Constitutional Committee now had a new chairman, the Liberal Nils Edén, who was thus overruled by the majority in the Committee, including the Social Democrats. At the same time, the Liberals emphasised in their reservation that, although their motion only concerned women's suffrage, they agreed with the motions proposed by the Social Democrats and von Kock about the need for an inquiry into how receipt of poor relief should affect the right to vote and the tax threshold.[43]

The opinion of the Constitutional Committee was published on the same day that Swartz declared that the question of a constitutional revision would have to be postponed until the autumn after the election. It is clear from his private notes from 1917, however, that this remained a burning issue even within the Right and the government. Internally, Swartz had explored whether it was appropriate and possible to set up a parliamentary commission on the constitutional question. Swartz's notes testify to his ambition to do this, but also reveal that he did not have undivided support from the Right party group in the Riksdag. The notes also testify to divisions within the parliamentary Right. Individual members declared themselves in favour of the introduction of women's suffrage and the abolition of the 40-grade voting scale. Others demanded guarantees in the form of increased state control of the municipalities' economy or threatened to resign if the 40-grade scale was abolished. It is clear from an undated draft of a speech that if any such parliamentary commission were to be set up, it did not need to consider the question of women's suffrage. A commission ought to be able to put forward proposals about to that effect immediately and concentrate on the problematic issue about the 40-grade scale and whatever other matters might arise.[44]

Carl Swartz's notes testify to a fear that Liberals and Social Democrats would push foreign policy to the left and support the Entente. The election results in October forced the formation of a new government, and a long negotiation process began that ended with Edén forming a government with the support of individual Social Democratic members. The government included Hjalmar Branting as minister of finance, Erik Palmstierna as minister of economic affairs, and Värner Rydén as minister of ecclesiastical affairs.[45] The basis for the government in October 1917 was an agreement on a common policy platform. On the suffrage issue, the parties now agreed to abolish the 40-grade scale but require payment of taxes. Municipal self-government would be defended against the Right's "demands for guarantees", modifying the poor relief threshold and the migration criterion, and introducing women's suffrage on the same terms as men. An inquiry was needed into the tax thresholds so that they did not affect the wrong "blameless" people.[46] There is no mention whatever of age limits, which ought to mean that there were no plans to change them. The starting point was thus voting from the age of 21, in other words, the demands on which the Social Democrats had built their policy.

The government declaration made it clear that the constitutional issue had priority along with the food supply and neutrality. Equal suffrage for men and women, the abolition of the 40-grade scale, and a review of certain suffrage thresholds were proposed, but with no suggested timetable. Equal suffrage, however, here meant "equal suffrage for all who pay taxes to the municipality",[47] which was the same as the Liberals' stance on suffrage and did not automatically comprise all women and men. This was not in line with the Social Democratic programme.

On 13 November 1917 the Government decided to set up a special expert inquiry into municipal suffrage, which then formed the basis for the government's bill in April 1918. Two of the investigators on the Suffrage Committee were Social Democrats, who also made it clear that their principle was that suffrage should be universal. Members from the Righ abandoned their seats on this committee in protest against its fixed mandate, but the Social Democratic members took part while making it clear that they still believed that universal suffrage should not be based on the principle of taxation. The proposal that was drafted was based on the Liberal programme and received some support, with reservations, from the Social Democratic members.[48] Suffrage was still related to a person's contribution to the municipality as a tax-paying citizen.[49] The idea of the municipality as a company seemed to live on. And so the ground was ready

Fig. 4.2 The 1917 riots: a young man is led away by police who had instructions from the government to keep a special eye on the youth. Source: Foto Axel Malmström. Arbetarrörelsens arkiv och bibliotek

for a continued discussion about the age limits for voting. Could the 40-grade voting scale be abolished without also changing the age limits? As we shall see, this remained a controversial issue (Fig. 4.2).

Concluding Reflections

The discussions of universal and equal suffrage after 1910 reflected differing views on the meaning and importance of voting restrictions. The age limit played a minor role in the debate and in the political negotiations. The discussions of the matter did not result in any large volumes of text. At the same time, the lines of conflict were clear. The Liberals argued for women's suffrage, while maintaining the restrictions concerning economic status and behaviour, and they proposed an age limit for voting in parliamentary elections from the year after turning 24. They shared the position of the Right on these matters. The Social Democrats, on the other hand, had a general demand to abolish the voting thresholds (except for people under the guardianship of another person or the poor relief board) in addition to the demand for women's suffrage. They thus maintained the demand for voting from the age of 21 in both municipal and parliamentary elections. This also meant that they did not accept that married women's suffrage should be dependent on having a tax certificate and an income.

Social Democrats and Liberals differed in their demands for women's suffrage. In the Liberal vision, women's suffrage would be designed with the same restrictions as for men. Married women's suffrage was further restricted, for example if the husband had been declared bankrupt, had failed to pay his taxes, or had received poor relief. On this point, the Liberals' position on suffrage had also been shaped by notions of the family and dependency within the family. Women's suffrage depended on how the criteria of responsible behaviour affected their husbands' right to vote. Other differences concerned the Liberals' hesitation to abolish the 40-grade voting scale in municipal elections, and their differing views on the voting age. The Social Democrats objected to the Liberals' view that tax payment should be the central basis for the right to vote. Their stance was thus much more radical than that of the Liberals, emphasising the right of the individual per se. The insistence by the Liberals (and the Right) on payment of taxes as an essential criterion would have excluded many married women without an income of their own. In addition, the Liberals' proposal for voting from the age of 24 meant that *unmarried* women would not be allowed to vote until they had reached the age of 25, even though they were actually of legal age and could vote in municipal elections. There was yet another difference between the Social Democrats and the Liberals.

The Constitutional Committee rejected all proposals for change as late as 1917, and both the Social Democrats and the Liberals registered dissenting opinions, citing their motions. The Liberals were open to the possibility of an inquiry into the voting thresholds, in which respect they came closer to the Social Democrats. One could interpret the Liberals' position to mean that they initially wanted to focus on women's suffrage and avoid a discussion of the thresholds but were at least prepared to indulge the Social Democrats by suggesting that a couple of the thresholds could be reviewed. When it came to age limits and the tax threshold, however, Liberals and Social Democrats were far apart. At the same time, the Right was rather divided but in some parts they favoured extending suffrage to married women.[50]

The situation was thus rather unclear in the broad area represented by the left—the Social Democrats and Liberals. Part of the left demanded far-reaching constitutional reforms, a republic, and the abolition of the First Chamber, in addition to the calls for universal and equal suffrage for tax-paying citizens or universal and equal suffrage for all citizens from the age of 21. The Social Democrats lacked government competence and experience, and the Liberals did not have a clearly formulated political position on municipal suffrage, although after 1915 they were prepared to question the 40-grade voting scale. In addition, there were diametrically different views on an appropriate voting age. It was all these issues that awaited a solution. And they were connected together, as we shall see.

Notes

1. Sverker Oredsson, *Nils Edén: Demokratins statsminister* (Stockholm: Ekerlid, 2017), p. 65.
2. Josefin Hägglund, *Demokratins stridslinjer: Carl Lindhagen och politikens omvandling, 1896–1923*, diss. (Huddinge: Södertörns högskola, 2023).
3. Christina Carlsson Wetterberg, *Jag saknar fruntimmer här: En biografi över Anna Bugge Wicksell* ([Stockholm]: Natur & Kultur, 2020), s. 148–149, pp. 148–149; Konrad Hagman, *Sveriges kommunallagar: Förordningarna den 21 mars 1862 jämte en mängd andra till kommunallagstiftningen hörande författningar* (Stockholm: Froléen, 1911), p. 44.
4. Riksdagstrycket, *Motioner FK 1912:94*, pp. 1–3; *Motion AK 1912:271*, with the same demands. Reference was also made in support of this to the Riksdag paper no. 137 of 1908.
5. Riksdagstrycket, *Motion AK 1912:307*, "Af herr Branting m.fl., angående utvidgad politisk valrätt och valbarhet", p. 1.
6. Ibid., p. 6, italics in the original. See also Riksdagstrycket, *Motioner AK 1912:316* (Lindhagen et al.).
7. Riksdagstrycket, *Motion AK 1912:307*, p. 8.
8. Riksdagstrycket, *Motion AK 1912:182*, pp. 5–14; see pp. 10–11 on the cities; Riksdagstrycket, *Motion AK 1912:307.*
9. Riksdagstrycket, *Utlåtande KU 1912:32.* The statement relates to bills 281, 307, 316 tabled in the Second Chamber.
10. Ibid., p. 3.
11. Ibid., p. 4.

12. Ibid., pp. 13–14.
13. Riksdagstrycket, *Motion AK 1912:182*, *Motion AK 1912:307*; Kjell Östberg, *Kommunerna och den svenska modellen: Socialdemokratin och kommunalpolitiken fram till andra världskriget* (Eslöv: Brutus Östlings bokförlag Symposion, 1996), pp. 97–104.
14. Josefin Rönnbäck, *Politikens genusgränser: Den kvinnliga rösträttsrörelsen och kampen för kvinnors politiska medborgarskap 1902–1921* (Stockholm: Atlas, 2004), pp. 113–141, 169–188. The Liberals' suffrage bill of 1912 is an impressive demolition of the arguments against women's suffrage and its normative foundations.
15. Oredsson (2017, p. 123).
16. Ibid., pp. 122–123. Nils Edén, "Regeringsproblemet och vänstersamverkan 1913–1923", F 9956 c:7, Edéns arkiv, Handskriftssamlingen, Uppsala universitetsbibliotek; Ingemar Norrlid, "Kommunen som bolag? En studie i liberal rösträttspolitik före för- sta världskriget", *Scandia* 36:1, 1970, pp. 100–112.
17. Untitled "Dokument om underhandling och uttalande om samverkan mellan båda vänsterpartierna 22/5 1915"; "Partipolitik, Diskussionerna om vänstersamverkan", Värner Rydéns arkiv, vol. 20 F II 2–5 (e 9189) F II m, Riksarkivet. See the same document in "Förslag till förhandlingsgrundval, Förhandlingar med Liberalerna", Hjalmar Brantings arkiv 1889–1922 91/4/7/1, Arbetarrörelsens arkiv och bibliotek. The same documents can be found in "Liberalernas handlingar", Edéns arkiv, Handskriftssamlingen, Uppsala universitetsbibliotek.
18. Riksdagstrycket, *Protokoll AK 1918:71*, p. 26.
19. Oredsson (2017, p. 123) and Norrlid (1970, pp. 100–112).
20. "Kommentar till sammanträde i regeringsfrågan vid 1915 års riksdags slut", Edéns arkiv, Handskriftssamlingen, Uppsala Universitetsbibliotek.
21. Oredsson (2017, pp. 123–124).
22. Carlsson Wetterberg (2020, pp. 148–149).
23. Carl Göran Andræ, *Revolt eller reform: Sverige inför revolutionerna i Europa 1917–1918* (Stockholm: Carlsson, 1998), pp. 218–242.
24. Oredsson (2017, pp. 136–141); Per T. Ohlsson, *1918: Året då Sverige blev Sverige* (Stockholm: Bonnier, 2017); Sven Anders Söderpalm, *Storföretagarna och det demokratiska genombrottet: Ett perspektiv på första världskrigets svenska historia* (Lund: Gleerup, 1969); Steven Koblik, "Between Reform and Revolution", *Scandia* 42:1, 1976, pp. 115–132.
25. Oredsson (2017, pp. 140–142); Erik Palmstierna, *Orostid: Politiska dagboksanteckningar 2, 1917–1919* (Stockholm: Tiden, 1953), pp. 49–56; Lars Berggren och Kjell Östberg, "Reformism eller revolution: Arbetarrörelsen inför rösträttsbeslutet 1918–19", i Ulrika Holgersson och Lena Wängnerud (red.), *Rösträttens århundrade: Kampen, utvecklingen och framtiden för demokratin i Sverige* (Göteborg & Stockholm: Makadam, 2018).

26. Erik Palmstierna, Orostid: Politiska dagboks anteckningar 2. 1917–1919 (Stockholm: Tiden, 1953), p. 53.
27. "Carl Swartz anteckningar 1917–1920", Släkten Swartz i Norrkoping BVb:21, Stadsarkivet i Norrkoping.
28. Oredsson (2017, pp. 142–145); Branting's question of 27 April 1917 quoted from Oredsson, p. 141; "Förslag till förhandlingsgrundval 1917", Hjalmar Brantings arkiv 1889–1922, Arbetarrörelsens arkiv och bibliotek; Edén, "Författningsfrågan", Gunnar Gerdners samling vol. 4, Edéns papper, Handskriftssamlingen, Uppsala universitetsbibliotek; Edén, "Förhandlingar mellan liberaler och soc. demokrater", Gunnar Gerdners samling vol. 4, Edéns papper, Handskriftssamlingen, Uppsala universitetsbibliotek.
29. Oredsson (2017, p. 144) and Andræ (1998, pp. 137–144).
30. Riksdagstrycket, *Motion AK 1917:378*, *Motion 1917 AK 1917:87*, *Motion AK 1917: 37*.
31. Riksdagstrycket, *Motion AK 1917:378*, p. 8.
32. Ibid., passim, quotation p. 10.
33. Ibid., p. 10.
34. Riksdagstrycket, *Motion AK 1917:390*.
35. Riksdagstrycket, *Motion AK 1917:289*, *Motion AK 1917: 400*.
36. Riksdagstrycket, *Motion AK 1917:408*, *Motion FK 1917:130*. The thresholds that the Liberals wanted to retain are stated in *Motion AK 1917:408*:

    a. any person who is under guardianship or in a state of bankruptcy;
    b. a married woman who has not gained a judicial separation of the joint estate after divorce and whose husband is in a state of bankruptcy;
    c. any person in receipt of assistance from poor relief during the current or the previous calendar year for himself or for his wife or minor children;
    d. a married woman whose husband is in receipt of assistance from poor relief during the current or the previous calendar year for herself or for the spouses' minor children;
    e. any person who has not paid the taxes imposed on him to the state and the municipality which have fallen due for payment during the last three calendar years;
    f. a married woman who has not gained a judicial separation of the joint estate after divorce and whose husband has not paid the taxes imposed on him to the state and the municipality which have fallen due for payment during the last three calendar years;
    g. any man liable for military service who has not completed the training incumbent on him up to the end of the last calendar year.

    For guidance at elections there shall be an electoral roll; and, as specifically stated in the Electoral Act, the right to vote shall be based on the conditions prevailing at the time when the electoral roll was established, even if a change occurs before the election.

37. Christina Carlsson Wetterberg, "Kvinnans rätt och nationens väl: Debatten kring 1920 års giftermålsbalk", i Lars M. Andersson (red.), *Rätten* (Lund: Nordic Academic Press, 2000); Zara Bersbo, *"Rätt för kvinnan att blifva människa – fullt och helt": Svenska kvinnors ekonomiska medborgarskap 1921–1971* (Växjö: Linnaeus University Press, 2011); Bente Rosenbeck and Hanne Sanders, *Det politiska äktenskapet: 400 års historia om familj och reproduktion* (Göteborg & Stockholm: Makadam i samarbete med Centrum för Danmarksstudier vid Lunds universitet, 2010).
38. Oredsson (2017, p. 143), *Dagens Nyheter* 8 May 1917.
39. Riksdagstrycket, *Utlåtande KU 1917:36*, p. 5.
40. Ibid., p. 8.
41. Ibid., p. 9. "According to figures obtained by the Committee, while the number of men listed in the electoral roll for the election to the Second Chamber in 1911 was 1,349,201, no fewer than 1,526,340 women were listed who had reached the age of 24 at the time of the census of 31 December 1910. For every 1000 men there was thus a national average of 1131 women. According to these figures, women constitued an even larger majority in the cities: in Stockholm 1421, in other places 1273 women for every 1000 men."
42. Ibid., p. 10.
43. Riksdagstrycket, *Utlåtande KU 1917:36*, p. 19.
44. "Carl Swartz anteckningar 1917–1920", Släkten Swartz i Norrköping BVb:21, Stadsarkivet i Norrköping.
45. Oredsson (2017, pp. 148–158, 208).
46. "Anteckningar från de gemensamma överläggningarna [...] delegerade för liberala och socialdemokratiska partiledningarna", October 1917, Värner Rydéns arkiv, vol. 20 F II, pp. 2–5 (e 9189), Partipolitik, Diskussionerna om vänstersamverkan, Riksarkivet; "Anteckningar av Edén i regeringsfrågan 1917 och författningsfrågan hösten 1918", Gunnar Gerdners papper 1:1, Handskriftssamlingen, Uppsala universitetsbibliotek.
47. "Anteckningar av Edén i regeringsfrågan 1917 och författningsfrågan hösten 1918", Gunnar Gerdners papper 1:1, Handskriftssamlingen, Uppsala universitetsbibliotek.
48. Riksdagstrycket, *Proposition 1918:290*; Andræ (1998, pp. 143–254).
49. Oredsson (2017) and Andræ (1998, pp. 243–244).
50. Riksdagstrycket, *Motion FK 1912:94*, pp. 1–3 (see also *Motion AK 1912:271* with the same demands, referring to the parliamentary paper 1908:137); *Motion AK 1912:311*, *Motion AK 1912:317*, *Motion AK 1914:251* and *250*; see also *Motion AK 1917:390*; *Utlåtande KU 1914:28*, pp. 4–25; *Motion AK1914:243*, *Motion FK 1914:87*, *Motion AK 1914:227*, *Motion AK 1914:243*.

CHAPTER 5

Voting Rights with Guarantees: Political Negotiations in 1918

In the spring of 1918 the question of the voting age became topical again. It was now taken for granted that the government's proposals for a suffrage reform would apply to both women and men. Instead, other issues were at the centre of political debate and cross-party compromises. The proposals for reshaping the right to vote constituted a whole in which the different parts were played off against each other. The issue of the voting age also reflected the requirements for completed military training, being willing and able to pay taxes, and having the capacity for social responsibility. This is evident from the debate that took place in Parliament about how the various initiatives on the suffrage issue should be interpreted and how the consequences should be evaluated. The 40-grade economic voting scale, the criteria of responsible behaviour, gender, and class were intimately linked in the debates, even though they referred to such different aspects of citizens' lives. Nor can they be fully understood unless they are interpreted in the light of the age boundaries that applied in different spheres of society.

The government proposed a reform of both parliamentary and municipal suffrage. In this chapter we follow the age issue in the political debate during 1918 until the negotiations in the special committee in which the question of age limits was brought to a resolution that could be presented to Parliament. I shall first describe the bills and then the debate in the spring and autumn of 1918. Then I draw attention to the dynamics of the special parliamentary committee.

B. Sandin, *Voting and Eligibility Age in Sweden, 1866–1921*,
https://doi.org/10.1007/978-3-031-95276-0_5

Voting Rights and Suffrage Thresholds Reconsidered

The Edén government's bill regarding the right to vote in elections to the Second Chamber, presented at the end of February 1918, rested on the same intellectual foundation as the previous Liberal proposals. The Liberal prime minister Staaff's 1914 proposal was also appended to the bill. The same voting restrictions would apply to men and women and the voting age would be 24. This, then, was still the meaning of universal and equal suffrage in the Liberal interpretation in the spring of 1918. However, they suggested that the tax and poor relief thresholds should be reviewed, which hints at an opening towards the Social Democrats' demands.[1] They explicitly opposed the suggestion for an initially higher voting age (33) for women that the Moderate Women's Suffrage Association had submitted.[2] The notion that women should be less politically mature than men was rejected on the grounds that the proposed age limit (24) was set relatively high.[3] Implicitly accepting that both men and women below 24 were less politically mature but there was no other gender difference. Hence the surplus of women in the population was not a problem from a democratic point of view, with reference to the Liberal motions of 1914:

> That women on average should develop later in relation to men in those respects which are important for the assessment of their political maturity is a claim that is surely difficult to verify; and it does not seem justified to set the age limit for women higher than 24 on this basis. As regards the surplus of women as a reason for lowering the age limit for them, and the fears about the disadvantageous effects of this surplus, I may refer to the response to these fears in the motion from 1914 appended to these minutes.[4]

With this statement, the argument put forward by the Constitutional Committee in June 1917 was dismissed. We thus see a significant continuity in the Liberals' stance, which was based on a high voting age and thus also a restrictive attitude to women's suffrage, framed as it was by the limitations that applied to men's suffrage. There was a strong link between the criteria of responsible behaviour and what Berling Åselius calls the marriage criterion for women.[5]

In the spring of 1918, a proposal was also put forward about municipal suffrage and the abolition of the 40-grade voting scale. In a bill of 16 April, Edén returned to the issue of municipal suffrage after the Committee had delivered its opinion in support of a thorough reform of the 40-grade scale, and the voting rights of companies and the estates of deceased persons. The government accepted the Committee's proposal and suggested voting from the year after a person reached the age of 21. The 40-grade scale would be abolished. The proposal also limited the municipal tax threshold to concern only the taxes due for the last three years. As previously pointed out, tax was paid in arrears, which created serious problems. The proposal also included concessions, probably to satisfy wealthy rural interests. In deliberations in municipal government that touched on issues of "land valued in *mantal*" (taxable farming units, even very small ones), only members who owned such land were allowed to speak and vote.[6] The latter proposal testifies to a need that was felt to limit the political influence of people who owned no property. The issue of guarantees for property ownership was thus still alive.

How were these proposals received? The question of the age of voting and eligibility was considered to be of some importance because it influenced the "interests" that could have an impact on the work of the chambers. The Liberal member Theodor Adelswärd, whom we met above, proposed a motion on municipal suffrage on 7 May 1918, explicitly stating how this could affect the First Chamber. He supported a change in municipal suffrage towards greater democracy, with the abolition of the 40-grade scale.[7] However, it was important to him that the special character of the First Chamber as an upper house should be preserved. He suggested a higher voting age and county electoral assemblies as corporations appointing members to the First Chamber. Adelswärd's proposal is one that can be recognised from the suffrage discussions of the 1910s. The motion had the same feel, and much the same wording, as the one he tabled in 1907. He thought that a voting age of 30 would be quite appropriate given that it was the same for all social strata, but the high age limit had the advantage that it could

> sift out from the electorate those elements which, in terms of behaviour and outlook, are still least stable and authoritative and thus least suited to appoint members of the First Chamber. I base this on the premise that the task of this chamber is to be the restraining element in the representation of the nation, and to ensure against sudden changes and the excessive influence of temporary opinion […] about 85 per cent of the voters would be married or, in other words, the kind of persons who have started a family and, as a rule, are settled and often with a home of their own, and for these reasons

> must be presumed to be properly qualified to elect members of the First Chamber.[8]

The high voting age thus reflected a willingness to favour stable elements and settled families. He did not comment further on the eligibility criteria because, as he said, they obviously needed to be reformed. But he did emphasise the differences between the chambers. The First Chamber should be designed as a regulating and restraining force for conservation, through specific eligibility criteria in which a "favoured position" should be granted to insight and education, experience and expertise.[9] Here too, then, we see a hint of ideas about more corporative representation, despite the fact that Adelswärd had doubts about other proposals for the representation of special interests.

Among the proposals from the Right that Adelswärd cited and criticised is the one dated 2 May and signed by Conservative member Sam Clason, who urged for the bill to be rejected. The administration and organisation of the municipalities and the role of the First Chamber were so important that they deserved a comprehensive inquiry before any decision could be made. The comments provide a fascinating insight into the thinking, among other things, about how age limits could counterbalance the abolition of other suffrage restrictions. Here too, the argumentation can be recognised from the discussions around the turn of the century. Clason suggested that certain corporations and groups should be given greater influence. This was reflected in the suggestion that a stronger vote should be granted to groups with greater competence, maturity, understanding, and responsibility in municipal matters, and people with closer ties to the municipality where they lived. The basic reasoning was therefore about the principles of "vote enhancement", that is to say, guarantees of increased influence *not* based on income and the value of property. On that point, some right-wing interests had realised that reform was imminent. As we saw in Chap. 3, Sam Clason was committed to these issues as early as 1902.

Clason first mentions "owners and users of land" because they were permanently attached to the municipalities and could be assumed both to take responsibility for and to suffer the consequences of decisions taken, in a way that made them different from the mobile population. Then came the group that could be identified as having a fixed and responsible position in the municipalities: tradesmen, civil servants, practitioners of arts and sciences, and certain qualified groups of workers. However, it was also suggested that those who paid large sums in tax ought to have more votes, as should those with insurance responsibilities for others as employers.[10] Axel Schotte, who was a Liberal and a minister in the government, waxed ironic in a letter about the disparate proposals concocted by the Right, which hit out in every direction. Yet he noted with satisfaction that the Right appeared to have accepted that the 40-grade scale was no longer a possible basis for suffrage.[11]

Alongside these criteria based on ties to and status in the municipality, responsibility, and competence for which the Right argued, they also emphasised higher age and the role of breadwinner. Higher age evidently went hand in hand with these other qualifying criteria.

> The emphasis should be on greater maturity and experience. This foundation is a higher age. In many cases, moreover, this is probably also associated with a more lasting attachment to the municipality than in younger years, when professional training, studies, the propensity to try out different things, the difficulty of gaining permanent and secure employment in certain fields, make for a more mobile life. At a certain age in life, however, this mobility ceases to a large extent, marriages are entered into with the consequent obligations which bind a person to a particular activity and locality, by which time some maturity and experience have been gained, which constitute special conditions for participating wisely and thoughtfully in municipal decisions. As an appropriate age limit for obtaining vote enhancement on this basis, the age of 35 seems to stand out. The inquiry can also take into account the position of breadwinner as a basis for an enhanced vote, especially in cases involving more extensive responsibility. The importance of the home as a foundation of society is not contested by anyone, and maintaining one's own home is usually a proof of a capacity to work and a sense of responsibility, beside which it brings new duties. If the home raises a growing generation, duties are increased and responsibility is heightened. Good homes make it much easier for the municipality to fulfil its tasks. It is therefore in the interests of the municipalities, from various perspectives, to provide the family with appropriate recognition of this through influence.[12]

On this point—the importance of a higher age limit for voters—there is also a noticeable continuity in the argumentation both from the Right and the Liberals, as well as the idea of an enhanced vote for citizens of more mature age, and the idea that the right to vote strengthens family interests. The conflicting views espoused by the champions of suffrage—the Social Democrats and Liberals—is also demonstrated in this way. There were basically two different ways of assessing the meaning of universal suffrage: whether it should protect the status quo and the family through a higher voting age, or represent voters as individuals, with the right to vote at the age of 21. The voice of the left-wing Social Democrat Vennerström was also heard in the debate. He responded with a motion on the introduction of a unicameral system and the abolition of the First Chamber. Without further comment, he assumed that the voting age should be 21, as in the Social Democrats' proposal. In his speech, however, he criticised the Social Democrats' willingness to compromise with regard to sweeping constitutional reforms.[13]

The Constitutional Committee's statement from 20 April supported the government's proposal,[14] with the reference to the importance of women in society outside the home, in business, and in general welfare work. Women's efforts in the home and the general crisis also justified women's suffrage on an equal footing with men.[15] It was the same ideas that were the foundation for the new marriage legislation.[16] Judging by the minutes of the Social Democratic parliamentary group, they accepted the idea of proxy voting with reference to the forthcoming decision about the ability of sailors to vote in elections. However, they objected to women losing their right to vote if their spouses had not paid their taxes.[17]

It was therefore somewhat inconsistent that the Committee did not propose any changes to the voting restrictions and explicitly maintained in its proposal that a married woman also lost her right to vote if, for example, her husband had been declared bankrupt. The proposed reform thus testifies to the divisions within the parties on the left, as was also pointed out in a reservation from the right and in the discussions in the chamber. The proposal also demonstrates some continuity regarding the various elements of the suffrage reforms. Gender, age, the 40-grade voting scale, and the criterion of responsible behaviour were all, as we shall see, closely linked to each other, even though they concerned such different aspects of the citizens' lives.[18] The bill passed the Second Chamber but was defeated in the First Chamber. The Social Democrats and the Liberals had fundamentally different views of the appropriate long-term solution. The opposition of the Right in the debate was solid, but they declared themselves willing to accept an unconditional inquiry into municipal suffrage. This was the same stance as in 1917.[19]

The discussion in Parliament also illustrated the connection between the 40-grade scale and the age limits. The compromise reached in 1907–1909 when the decision had created various thresholds to restrict the right to vote in elections to the Second Chamber and to the First Chamber (the 40-grade scale), was now challenged by the government's bill. It included no new guarantees to compensate for the proposal to abolish the 40-grade scale. Some of the speeches in parliamentary debates illustrate this. We also see that the demand for women's suffrage could be interpreted differently. Gender, age, and class all interacted in a way that made women's suffrage problematic.

Karl Johan Ekman, member for Jönköping, argued in the First Chamber that suffrage for middle-class women was different from suffrage for women in the working class and in rural areas. Educated women in the white-collar class made an independent contribution to society, whereas young women working in factories and in the countryside arguably did not have the same interests. The sphere of these women was limited to the family which, according to him, did not justify giving them the vote. According to Ekman, men were perfectly capable of looking after women's interests, as had been demonstrated in a matter such as the protective legislation on night work. In contrast, educated women in the white-collar class had sufficient economic independence and political judgement to exercise political suffrage.[20]

> On the other hand, I do think that we must have serious doubts in this respect about the thousands of young women who are employed in factories and who largely have their interests exclusively in the home or in their own circle of acquaintances, and even less so, I believe, that any real political interest can be expected in the majority of rural women. Even more than urban women, they are more attached to the home, to domestic chores, and to the personal interests there. At all events, I do not believe that there is any real need for political suffrage for these women until a slightly older age than that established for the political competence of men, because there are surely no real personal or economic interests to safeguard for these women at an earlier stage in life.[21]

He did not think that such a "significant" group of voters could be granted suffrage before it was certain that they had "firm convictions and real interests".[22] In addition, he questioned whether the competence of women in female spheres was an argument for letting them participate in political life.

> I do not believe much in what is said about this, that it should be so extremely valuable to get women to participate in political life solely because

> they have a better knowledge of the home and certain matters that are close to female activities. I believe that such interests are just as well safeguarded by men.[23]

His argument was also directed against the bourgeois women's movement, which emphasised that it was as representatives of the home that women should be given the right to vote, but also against the Social Democratic women who had previously struggled against the ban on night work. They did not think that men had any right to determine the conditions under which women worked, and they had expressed serious doubts about the ban on night work for women.[24]

In the Second Chamber the government bill received a mixed reception from both the Right and the Social Democrats. Age and family formation tended to be presented as the key selection criteria. Erik Räf, member of the Lower House on the Conservative side, summed up his position briefly and pithily, but with a clear nod to the working class:

> the greater maturity that comes with greater age, marriage, and so on – all without regard to other class differences – should be accorded greater political and municipal influence than those of immature age and so on – to whatever class they may belong – greater influence for the good worker than the good-for-nothing, etc.[25]

He was critical of the government bill because it would mean that the composition of the First Chamber would be based on municipal suffrage from the age of 21, which was contrary to the role of the First Chamber in preventing hasty and immature decisions. Räf also stressed how important it was that the government should design a better "guarantee structure", pointing out that this must be based on the importance for the municipality and the state "of the family, the more settled population, the house owner – whether he is an ordinary manual labourer, an employer, or a tradesman, a tenant of an independent farm".[26] But for the same reason he believed that it was dangerous to abolish the voting scale without raising the voting age. In his argumentation, then, property and other qualifications were replaced by age as a selection criterion.

Former prime minister Arvid Lindman also objected to the bill. He expressed his suspicions that it was part of a plan to abolish the First Chamber, first by introducing equal municipal suffrage, then universal municipal suffrage, and then abolishing the First Chamber.

> A person must be absolutely blind who does not see that this is the path of development. The very fact that the supporters of a unicameral system thus see the radicalization of municipal suffrage as the surest way to achieve their goal ought surely to open the eyes of those who support a real bicameral system as to where the current path is leading.[27]

With the abolition of the 40-grade voting scale, the low voting age in municipal elections would have such dramatically negative consequences for the bicameral system and the First Chamber's role as an upper house, according to Lindman. The First Chamber risked having a lower voting age than the Second Chamber (the bill tabled by the government for the reform of suffrage to the Second Chamber was based on a voting age of 24), which yielded unreasonable consequences. Here Lindman's argument clearly showed that the voting scale for municipal elections replaced age requirements and was crucial for the possibility of maintaining the special position of the First Chamber. The same logic about the relationship between age limits and the income-graded voting scale was behind the reforms of 1907–1909. This was the reason for the low voting age in municipal elections and the high voting age in elections to the Second Chamber. If Parliament was to abolish the 40-grade scale, which had been introduced in 1907–1909 by the government led by Arvid Lindman, the voting age of 21 in municipal elections would pose a threat to the special status of the First Chamber and its role in the parliamentary system. He thus opposed the government bill.

> Moreover, how can one conceive of a voting system which allows the right to vote in elections to the First Chamber to begin at an earlier age than to the Second, and which also in other respects gives the less circumspect and less experienced elements of the population a greater influence on the composition of the First Chamber than on that of the Second, which furthermore bases the whole difference in character between the chambers on some now rather meaningless rules on eligibility, on indirect elections, and a slightly longer term of office for the First Chamber? How can one imagine that such a system is capable of giving us a real upper house and a real bicameral system? [...] The realization that the government here is on a dangerous path in this case has also recently begun to gain ground even in some liberal circles. It has thus been openly acknowledged, from quarters which are said to be quite close to the present government, that it is inappropriate to maintain the 21-year limit for voting in elections to the First Chamber, while simultaneously looking in the same direction for qualifications for a real

> upper house and also specifying certain such qualifications. It can thus surely be considered to be admitted that the government's bill does not measure up in this regard. Quite simply, it is unreasonable.[28]

In his reasoning Lindman also emphasised that the development in the municipalities was worrying as the municipalities had increasingly broadened their social responsibilities. It was an economically risky policy that caused him to fear for the future, because those who depended on municipal support did not contribute to the same extent and might want to pass the costs on to others.[29] He also hinted at a rift among the Liberals in their view of the voting age of 21, and he deplored the situation of the farming population in industrialised municipalities where responsible and settled groups were at risk of becoming a minority. One should consider, he argued, additional votes for certain groups, "chiefly among them the farmers, those who own and farm the land".[30] On the latter point, he apparently shared the belief that agricultural interests should be given greater influence of the kind already expressed in the bill, that gave holders of agrarian property a privileged position in matters when decisions effected such land.

The left-wing members Hage and Vennerström argued that the government bill was a serious departure from the personality principle. The bill made women's suffrage dependent on their paying tax, and moreover dependent on the economic position of their husbands.[31] Vennerström supported Hage's reservation against the Committee's opinion:

> Because the vote here is for or against the personality principle. It is the case that the Liberal gentlemen, with the assistance of some of the government socialists, have violated an old democratic principle on this point within the government, namely, the personality principle. They want to make a married woman's right to vote dependent on her husband's payment of taxes. They thus would equate the married woman with the ox and the ass, in the same way as in ancient times the woman used to be considered part of the man's economic property. I believe that the Second Chamber should be prepared to abandon that principle and give women the vote as persons and as citizens without linking a woman's economy in any way to that of her husband.[32]

One of the Liberal members, Axel von Sneidern, defended himself by saying that Branting shared their view. It could also have unreasonable consequences if a woman were given the right to vote while her husband was disqualified. Moreover, women were jointly responsible for any economic problems the spouse may have. He felt that the Liberals on the Committee were not being portrayed fairly:[33]

> For it can be said that if women were to be given the vote without being affected by the tax criterion, they would actually be rewarded in a way. They would then to a large extent obtain a right to vote that men do not enjoy, since it is unfortunately the case that the tax criterion affects an enormous number of cases. It is true that if a woman has a careless husband, she may be wrongly deprived of her right to vote, but we also unfortunately have cases where men lose their right to vote because the wife does not run the home in such a way that the man is able to pay his taxes.[34]

In this speech too, the normative basis was the family as a social and political unit; von Sneidern thought it unreasonable that different grounds for disqualification should apply to women and men—within the same family. The latter was considered particularly problematic if a carelessly managed family economy affected both spouses equally hard, not just one of them. This argument is in line with the view of the family as a political unit, even if the spouses are entitled to vote as individuals.[35]

The discussion in the Second Chamber was conducted against the background of an understanding that the First Chamber had already decided to reject the bill. The criticism was sharp, and it had some impact on the Second Chamber because a clear majority accepted Hage's proposal for a rewording. Even among those in favour of the government bill, then, there were critical voices.[36] There was a divide between the Liberals and the Social Democrats that concerned both the conditions for women's suffrage, and the class limitations and social thresholds restricting the right to vote—and in all this age played a significant role.

But this was not the only line of conflict. The Social Democrat Arthur Engberg ironically summed up the Right's proposal to compensate for the abolition of the 40-grade scale through extra votes and new thresholds:

> It is essentially the following five circumstances that will constitute the criterion of greater competence: (1) belonging to a particular social class or skill in a particular profession, (2) a certain age, (3) married status, (4) higher education, with the introduction of the threshold of high school graduation, and (5) fulfilment of positions of civic trust. If one now combines all these points, it must be said that if the 40-grade scale was designed to consolidate political power within the propertied class in this country, then the

system to which the Right is now fumbling its way is doubly designed to consolidate political power where it already lies.[37]

The lines in the debate were slightly shifted, but basically they remained in place. The requirement of a certain age carried a multitude of social meanings that summed up the cultural and economic dimensions of the conflicts (Fig. 5.1). Engberg also declared that Lindman was right in his

Fig. 5.1 This cartoon from 1914 was still relevant in 1918, the conflict was the same. Denied to vote, allowed to serve. We will not take away the voting restrictions for unworthy elements dependent on poor relief, underaged, with tax debts, or recent migrants to municipalities. In 1918, however, the exclusion of women was central in the political agenda (Source: Drawing. Östergötlands Folkblad 31 augusti 1914, Kungl. biblioteket)

concerns. The call to abolish the 40-grade voting scale was an attack on the First Chamber in its present form, "a First Chamber that always looks after the interests of the propertied class in the first place, although it disguises its concern for the interests of this class in the misused name of the fatherland".[38]

It can thus be observed that those who were critical of the government's proposal for municipal suffrage were at the same time inclined to accept that some fundamental changes were also on the way regarding women's suffrage, the voting thresholds, and the 40-grade scale. The government bill had now come significantly closer to the Social Democratic position. The proposal to revise the voting thresholds, on the other hand, had moved further away from the common ground on which Liberals and Conservatives had stood in 1914–1916. However, members of municipal councils who owned rateable *mantal* land (i.e. farmers) were also offered greater influence in matters concerning such land.

At the same time, we see that the issue of the voting age was also raised as a consequence of the proposals for new electoral laws at the municipal level. The forthcoming abolition of the 40-grade scale gave new energy to the question of raising the voting age. In the arguments for this raise it is easy to recognise the previous positions of the Right and the Liberals. Now the idea was also put forward that the voting age in elections to the First Chamber should be even higher in order to ensure that settled families had the greatest voting power. The voting age suggested by the government for elections to the Second Chamber was, as before, 24. The changes at municipal level concerned the segment of the population over the age of 21 who could prove that they had paid their taxes. It was the latter aspect that was questioned by a Conservative like Clason. Apparently, not all Conservatives found it reasonable that the right to vote should be based on tax payment according to the Liberal model. But the prerequisite, in his view and that of the others who proposed motions in Parliament, was that the voting age be raised instead, as compensation for the extension of suffrage. We see here how the relationship between the ability to pay taxes and the criterion of responsible behaviour was made into a concrete link to the voting age, in what was perceived as a reasonable exchange. That question now became central when opposition to women's suffrage seemed somewhat less compact among the Conservatives. The irony of the Liberals' and Conservatives' emphasis on the family as a foundation, of course, is that if married women were given the vote, each family would get two votes. That point would be made in discussions during the autumn of 1918.

Compromise or Victory?

The constitutional issue came up again in autumn 1918, while the different positions on the left and right were being debated. In *Dagens Nyheter* there was discussion about the possibilities of a rapprochement between the Right and the Liberals, and within the Social Democrats Gustav Möller and Per Albin Hanson debated the implications of the social revolution. This also involved taking a stance in relation to the Social Democratic Left Party. The government parties assessed and in this way marked their boundaries to the right and the left. In October the need arose to convene an extraordinary session of Parliament to discuss the possibility of a salary supplement for civil servants to cover the higher prices and other issues resulting from the crisis. The postponement of military exercises as a result of the ravages of the Spanish flu was another important matter that required a decision by Parliament. There were dramatic political developments in Russia and Germany, and the food shortage in Sweden rendered the political situation explosive.[39] When the suffrage issue was raised again, the voting age was also debated, and of course it was included in the bill on municipal suffrage. According to the historian Carl Göran Andræ, it was one of the topics in the discussions between the parties from the beginning.[40]

There is good reason to look more closely at the part played by the voting age. The Social Democrats demanded that the extraordinary session of Parliament deal with the suffrage issue. Prime Minister Edén discussed the matter with the leaders of the Right in September and October. The primary position of the Right was that another inquiry into the matter should be set up and that the question could be dealt with in the spring 1919 session. That was Swartz's suggestion in conversation with Edén. He was doubtful whether the Right was prepared to accept equal and universal municipal suffrage, that is, to abolish the 40-grade voting scale and limit the tax payment criteria. How the First Chamber could be preserved was also up for discussion. Yet it was not obvious that the issue could and should be dealt with in the autumn. An extraordinary session of Parliament did not have a mandate to propose amendments to the constitution.[41]

Judging by Lindman's notes from 6 November, Edén's contacts with the leaders of the Right prompted First and Second Chamber members of the Right to discuss the suffrage issue together. The comments suggest a positive attitude towards negotiations about the possible abolition of the voting scale, on condition that the Right could also obtain guarantees of "sound municipal administration and a real bicameral system". The need for a voting age of 35 was mentioned, and demands for extra votes, possibly special electoral corporations. In his notes from 11 November, Lindman reported discussions with Edén about a proposal before the 1919 session involving equal municipal suffrage but requiring paid municipal taxes. For the First Chamber "one could envisage a voting age of 30", women's suffrage from 30 with a gradual adaptation to the same terms as for men. For elections to the Second Chamber, the tax criterion would be replaced by tax deduction from wages. According to Edén, Lindman promised to raise the issue with his party colleagues. This discussion seems to have taken place on 13 November, judging by some sporadic notes in which members of the Right spoke about the possibility of scrapping the 40-grade scale and about their hesitation with regard to women's suffrage.[42]

The Social Democratic parliamentary group's representative council also met on 13 November, the same day that Lindman talked to the members of the Right. Branting presented an action programme for a reform of municipal suffrage and a revision of the constitution at the next session of Parliament. On these points the plan was clear. But the wording in the minutes about how far the reform should go was not as clear. According to Branting, the government planned to table a bill "on universal and equal suffrage, possibly equal municipal suffrage without tax thresholds".[43] The discussion between the parties on the left was obviously still going on. On 14 November, according to Lindman, Edén returned with information that they intended to take up municipal suffrage at the current session. The idea was that the question of suffrage to the Second Chamber, which was a constitutional issue, would be "recorded in the minutes as a stated opinion". According to Lindman, Edén wanted to keep the tax requirement but acknowledged that many Liberals and Social Democrats wanted to abolish it. Edén did not feel that the time was ripe or that there were sufficient guarantees for such a reform. Lindman expressed his annoyance that the government had not waited for proper negotiations with the Right. He also noted that the Social Democrats did not want revolution and that the government intended to stick together but therefore had to offer something substantial. On 15 November, Lindman observed in conversation with the parliamentary group that it was now too late for negotiations with the Liberals. The government had made up its mind. It was just a matter of waiting for the bill to come.[44]

These issues from the discussions within the Farmer's Party's parliamentary group, as initiated by Edén's proposals, show that the age requirements that were suggested ranged from 24 for municipal suffrage to 35 for elections to the First Chamber and guarantees that could mean, among other things, a limitation of municipal self-government and increased control of the municipalities' finances, tax thresholds, and so on. Notes from the discussion within the Right group on 6 and 13 November show a wide spread in opinions, from total refusal to accept women's suffrage or any talk of suffrage in general, but also positive attitudes to women's suffrage and the abolition of the 40-grade scale, but with demands for guarantees for the control of municipal expenses, a voting age of 35, and extra votes. There were also calls for guarantees to safeguard the position of the First Chamber. A second sheet appears to summarise the demands. This certainly seems like a statement of the maximum demands:

> Municipalities (1 vote for property) + 1 for age 35, Guarantees: 1) Stronger control and restriction of expenditure and tax reduction and taxation rights. 2) municipal council 3)? establishing the scope of self-government 4) age 24. Towns (1 vote for higher income) + 1 for age 35. 1st Chamb 1) appointed by county councils 2) partly corporation voting 3) reduction of towns' representation in relation to rural areas.[45]

The Social Democrats had intensive discussions about what demands should be made, which in some cases also included the call for a republic, for example, from the Stockholm branch of the Social Democratic Party. Demands like these were made in the central circles of the party, but in the final negotiation within the government the focus was on the demand to abolish the municipal tax thresholds.[46] The Social Democrats in the government pushed the issue that the political situation made it impossible to set up an enquiry to further explore the possibility of constitutional reform, as has been suggested by the conservatives. The decisions could not be postponed until the regular Parliament. In the internal discussions, the question arose of abolishing the tax thresholds and introducing equal suffrage. But the negotiations with Edén had not resulted in a definite solution.[47]

In Germany, the empire fell and the political situation in Sweden became critical, partly as a result of the left-wing socialists' demands for political action. The executive committee of the Social Democratic Party decided to demand a statement from the cabinet. Between 12 and 14

November 1918, the cabinet formulated a joint communiqué, while Edén also held talks with the leaders of the Right. In practical terms, this meant that Edén did not wait for the discussions with the Right to finish, which was described later in the parliamentary debate as a betrayal.[48] The communiqué agreed to women's suffrage, the abolition of the municipal voting scale, and the abolition of the tax threshold in elections to the Second Chamber. Edén had also accepted that the municipal tax threshold should be limited. At the same time, there were Liberal writers who explicitly believed that it was time to abolish all the thresholds, which surely strengthened the Social Democrats' negotiating position and increased the antagonisms.[49]

The discussions among the leaders of the Social Democratic Party led them to accept the general framework of the reform. Branting felt he could allow a certain tax threshold. That was the price to be paid to preserve the alliance with the Liberals. Rydén, for his part, argued that the threshold should be abolished but could accept a compromise on the demands for universal municipal suffrage, and consent to its being based on liability to pay municipal taxes.[50] The decision of the Social Democratic parliamentary group's representative council was along Rydén's lines. According to Rydén's diary, it was he who negotiated with Edén about the wording of the final communiqué, and for Edén the tax threshold was a fundamental criterion. In the communiqué the issue was resolved by emphasising equal municipal suffrage for all taxpayers. Loss of suffrage due to non-payment of taxes would soon become a minor problem once the forms for tax collection were improved. With regard to political suffrage, the tax threshold would be abolished and the poor relief threshold would only affect those who received permanent support.[51]

The government's ambitions to reach a decision on municipal suffrage during the extraordinary session of Parliament and to arrive at an agreement on the foundation for a full review of the constitution were presented 14 November. The text did not mention the ages for voting or eligibility, only the call for universal and equal suffrage for municipal taxpayers.

In the discussions between Edén and Lindman, as we saw above, it was clear that the voting age was a central part of the preliminary negotiations. Did the voting age also play any part in the discussions between the Social Democrats and the Liberals? This was the issue on which they had embraced such different views since the days of the "People's Parliament" and on which the Liberals were actually closer to the Right. Rydén's diary does not contain any direct comments on age, nor do other sources for these negotiations. But the communiqué exists in two versions, the published one and a preliminary draft that is archived among Rydén's documents. In the draft there was initially a sentence about the age limits for voting in elections to the Second Chamber, which reflected the Social Democrats' basic political programme. It was crossed out in the draft and was not included in the final version. The sentence "The bankruptcy and poor relief thresholds will be abolished, and the age threshold will be lowered from 24 to 21" was deleted. In one of the versions the wording about the tax threshold is also softened somewhat with reference to a future inquiry.[52] This deletion suggests that the Social Democrats were already prepared to compromise on the age demand, but that tax payment remained a troublesome issue (Fig. 5.2).

The Social Democrats under Branting's direct leadership avoided the demand for a republic at a dramatic meeting with the local branch in Stockholm, citing, among other things, that the king was in favour of reforms. The Social Democrats and the Trade Union Confederation also marked their distance in other ways from the left-wing socialists and backed the government's various measures to maintain order.[53] The government returned with a bill on 22 November 1918.[54] The discussions had now been narrowed to concern only age limits and tax thresholds. The proposed voting age was 21 and the 40-grade voting scale was to be abolished. It was this combination of voting conditions against which Lindman and other Conservatives had reacted so strongly a few months earlier because it could have dramatic effects on the composition of the First Chamber.

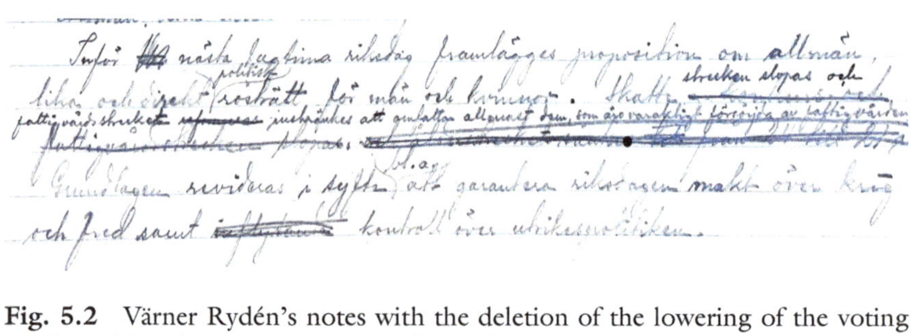
Inför nästa lagtima riksdag framlägges proposition om allmän, lika och direkt politisk rösträtt för män och kvinnor. Skattestrecken slopas och fattigvårdsstrecket inskränkes att omfatta allenast dem, som äro varaktigt försörjda av fattigvården.
Grundlagen revideras i syfte bl.a. att garantera riksdagens makt över krig och fred samt kontroll över utrikespolitiken.

Fig. 5.2 Värner Rydén's notes with the deletion of the lowering of the voting age from 24 to 21 years. (Source: Utkast till regeringskommuniké, Rydéns ministertid, Värner Rydéns arkiv vol. 24, F IV:b, Riksarkivet)

But the differences between the Social Democrats and the Liberals were not insurmountable. On the same day the Social Democrat Erik Palmstierna noted in his diary some positive phrases about Prime Minister Edén's impressive ability to keep all the different interests together,

> from Påboda to the extremes in our party. [...] Påboda was extremely doubtful about the abolition of the municipal tax threshold. He found it illogical and would rather have accepted universal suffrage with some increase in the age limit. There is undeniably something to be said for this.[55]

His words suggest that the Social Democrats were prepared for a compromise, which could certainly include the question of age limits. This is also evidenced by Värner Rydén's notes from the negotiations within the government, where the old Social Democratic demand for a voting age of 21 in elections to the Second Chamber was deleted before the publication of the joint communiqué. They did not want to make any direct challenge to the positions of the Right and the Liberals.

The premise of the bill was that the voting age in municipal and state elections would be 21 and the number of grounds for disqualification would be reduced to declaration of legal incompetence and failure to pay municipal tax (thus excluding those who did not have an income, and this could differ from one municipality to another depending on different tax adjustments according to the "basic deduction"). The proposed age of eligibility for county councils was 25. The bill also entailed that married women (without an income of their own) would be given municipal suffrage if their husbands were liable to pay tax. That meant proposing the abolition of the 40-grade voting scale.[56]

Women's suffrage was designed with the municipalities in mind. The linkage between a married woman and her husband's economic status was incorporated, along with a justification for this which was reminiscent of arguments expressed earlier in the year by Adelswärd and Clason about the meaning of the higher age. Settled status was associated with family responsibilities and stability, values put forward in an argument that, as we have seen, was connected to age. A settled family did not move away from problems as the mobile young working-class population did. And their vote strengthened the position of family as a political entity.

> This application of the principle of equal municipal suffrage may be considered to be capable of significantly strengthening the position of the settled

> population within the municipalities. The fact that the wives of municipal taxpayers also gain the right to vote obviously places the emphasis in municipal decision-making on those within the municipality who have formed a family and are thus most strongly tied to the common interests of the municipality.[57]

Here, then, the right to vote enjoyed by men paying municipal taxes led to the proposal that their wives be allowed to vote. Thus suffrage for married women is not a consequence of their being perceived as individuals in their own right, but is dependent on their being settled and married to men with a taxable income. In this bill too, there was in reality an inbuilt age norm because the marriage age was generally high.[58] I will return to that in Chap. 7.

The most interesting thing about this argument is that women's suffrage was used here to reinforce the argument about the settled population and the family as the basis for municipal suffrage. Married women would strengthen the votes for the family that Conservatives wanted to link to older male breadwinners some 20 years earlier. In this way, the suffrage bill was built on the basic principles argued by both Conservatives and Liberals about the importance of the influence of settled families. This could also be achieved through female suffrage.

Men and unmarried women who did not have a tax certificate or were exempt from paying tax after income adjustment, or who had unpaid taxes, would not be able to vote in municipal elections with this bill. It also emphasised that voting by proxy would make it possible for women who were prevented by their housework from attending municipal meetings and elections to transfer their votes to their husbands. Tax payment systems would also be reformed, it was suggested, so that fewer people would have problems paying their taxes on time.[59]

The bill emphasised that the issue had to be resolved immediately during the extraordinary session and could not wait until the 1919 session. The democratic transformation and the events of the past month could have serious consequences if action were not taken.

> And no one who is following with serious attention what is now going on within broad strata of Sweden's population could fail to understand that a delay, even as brief as until the ordinary 1919 session of Parliament, could be disastrous for the state of Sweden. As the war is now unmistakably drawing to a close, there is an irresistible demand to implement the constitutional

> changes whose necessity has been brought to full maturity by the experiences of the war years. When in country after country in Europe the old forms of government are overturned within a few days or hours, the people of Sweden feel that the moment has come to take a decisive step for the revision of the constitution which it has found for years to be increasingly ineluctable. It is of the utmost importance that the powers of government should take action right now if they wish to ensure that the democratic movement will not be affected by distrust of their ability to meet the demands of the time, a distrust that could have very serious consequences. In view of the call at this time for swift and resolute action, it is necessary immediately to draw up the guidelines by which a Swedish constitutional reform should be implemented.[60]

Although the initial idea had been that in 1918 it would only be possible to propose a change to the rules for municipal elections, this also affected the First Chamber. The system of suffrage for the Second Chamber also had to be considered in preparation for a decision in the next session of Parliament. The government stated in the bill that core of the political work "consists of a series of suffrage reforms: the abolition of the economically graded scale for municipal suffrage, which is now in force in Sweden alone among all civilized countries; political suffrage for women; and the revision of the so-called poor relief and tax thresholds". The head of the ministry also rejected all the proposals received for a reform of the graduated voting scale, for example, with extra votes.[61]

In formal terms, the positions were deadlocked. At the same time, the political situation was dramatic in this agitated atmosphere. Would the matter once again fall foul of the conflict between the First and Second Chambers? At the same time, the discussion had been simplified in some respects—it now mostly concerned the voting age and various aspects of economic guarantees, rather than women's suffrage. The bill recommended giving women the vote, with the argument that the family should be regarded as a fundamental unit in the electorate, as had long been asserted in the political discourse of both Liberals and Conservatives. But the question of the voting age persisted in the debate that followed the bill.

Right-Wing Criticism and Left-Wing Mobilisation

In Parliament it was members of the Right who presented alternative proposals. The 1918 bill naturally aroused great interest in the daily press, where the issue was also set in a broader political context. As before, in my analysis of how the arguments about the voting age were shaped, I consider the possible openings that they implied.

Suffrage was a politically loaded issue, as is evident from the reactions that came from the Right when its representatives were quoted in the papers. Arvid Lindman, delivering a public lecture cited in *Svenska Dagbladet*, criticised the government's handling of the matter. He said the Liberal government was taking advantage of the crisis to carry out a major transformation of society using threats and coercion. He urged them to seek consensual solutions. The government had given way to insurrectionists and lacked "the courage and power to keep these gentlemen at bay". According to Lindman, "a government formed to pursue liberal policies had ended up pursuing socialist policies". A consensual solution, he realised, would admittedly entail "a far-reaching democratization of our constitution, but it would prevent as far as possible a fatal democratic degeneration".[62]

Lindman's speech focused on the proposal for municipal suffrage. He objected to the idea of equal municipal suffrage for all taxpayers regardless of whether "they had fulfilled their tax obligation or not". On this point, the demands from the Right were unshakable. In formal respects the government's proposal "maintained in name the connection between the right to vote and the obligation to pay tax, but in reality removed it". Lindman also declared that it could not be "objectionable to democracy to raise the voting age in municipal elections to 24, as this hits everyone equally". In this context he also proposed settled status as a criterion which would deny suffrage to anyone who had not been a resident of the municipality for at least two years. Here we also see an emphasis on measures to ensure that it was primarily the "stable elements" that were given the vote, thus rewarding settled status, maturity in age, and payment of taxes. Despite the critical views, the article was given a conciliatory headline in *Svenska Dagbladet*—it was not clenched-fist politics.[63]

It was in the same spirit that the Conservative member Trygger gave a speech in the First Chamber. The morning after, 27 November, *Svenska Dagbladet* reported it in full. The article underscored Trygger's main thesis, that it was necessary to raise the age of municipal suffrage because the guarantee of influence for the more stable elements of society that came with the 40-grade voting scale was about to be abolished.

> The nature of municipal undertakings is such that not only the majority should prevail but that there should be due regard for maturity and experience. It is not just a matter of fairness between individuals, but also towards the municipality, and a reasonable distribution of municipal influence is necessary. If one wishes to be impartial, one should say that the graduated scale has in large measure enabled very good municipal administration. Under it, it has been possible to implement a municipal voting age of 21, while elections to the Second Chamber require an age of 24. The leadership of the municipalities will now be stripped of its more moderate and experienced elements.[64]

A higher voting age could allow for equal municipal suffrage for taxpayers. The speech thus signalled both a firm demand and a willingness to accept a reform of the 40-grade scale, provided the voting age was raised. A corresponding willingness to negotiate was signalled by the newspaper *Skånska Socialdemokraten*, which accepted the idea of a higher voting age for parliamentary elections, given that a decision there could be adjusted later once democracy was "largely" implemented.[65] However, comments on the voting age were far from being a dominant feature of the reactions in the press, which mainly concerned broader questions about the need for suffrage reform.

The opinion pieces of the Right in the press were accompanied by a series of motions in Parliament which to some extent accepted certain basic premises in the proposal but simultaneously argued for different models to guarantee social stability and order. In several of the motions, the voting age was at the centre of the argumentation.[66]

This was the case, for example, with Bernard Nilsson of Landeryd, who proposed that the voting age for municipal elections should be 24 and that people should have an additional vote from the age of 35. This was the best solution, in his opinion, as it would affect everyone "in society in every way and thus cannot be opposed by anyone from a social point of view. Such a provision, however, is undoubtedly likely to provide some opportunity for the more mature elements of society to assert their rights in local and county councils and likewise in the First Chamber".[67] The same demands were made in motions by a number of members of the First and Second Chambers: Karl Johan Ekman, Erik Räf, Ernst Trygger, Arvid

Lindman, Sam Clason, to name just a few.[68] In all these motions, the voting age played a significant part.

Karl Johan Ekman, a member for the Right from Jönköping, began his motion with a look at the development of society. He lamented the growth of individualism, which had created a class society, a class-based mass society. He also noted that the working class had come furthest in its organisation into a political unit, which risked becoming the class with the potential to oppress those classes that had not yet reached the corresponding degree of organisation and development. In the transformation to the new society, national unity must be maintained. The new society would be based not on property or money but on personality. The right to vote therefore had to be universal, but arranged so that it did not lead to class oppression. The right to vote being universal did not mean that it should be equal.[69] The difference can be summed up in terms of the development of personality that accompanies a higher age. Individuals in the mass change with age and increasing experience, and this is what democracy should be based on. Ekman described it as "a blatant assault" on democracy if it did not take advantage of "the difference that high age brings":

> Personality is not a dead thing; it evolves. The individuals in the mass are not manufactured pawns, one immutably similar to the other, in the municipal and political power game; they develop, under otherwise normal conditions these individuals over the course of their lives gain an ever-increasing accumulated fund of insight, experience, and maturity of judgement in the area where they live. Democracy cannot fail to recognize this difference in determining the age when the right to vote should begin, whether it is fixed at 21 or 24. It cannot then be contrary to the essence of democracy if a further increase in influence is granted, for example, at the age of 35.[70]

The individual's experience and maturity with increasing age was what prompted Ekman to suggest an extra vote for those who had reached the age of 35. He observed that this could not be perceived as unfair since it affected everyone equally but protected the younger working class from exerting too much influence. Volatile and irresponsible youths risked escaping the consequences of their actions. The municipalities could be bankrupted, leaving the burden on the older generation.

> If such increased influence is not guaranteed to the older, more experienced, and more settled elements of society, whatever class or group they belong to, it will be felt as an insulting injustice that the younger, more inexperienced,

> and more volatile elements, where they are more numerous, should be able to seize all the power and make the older ones subordinate to them. In addition, in the municipalities there is the danger that, after these young people have plunged the municipality into debt or other difficulties, through a misguided municipal policy, they themselves, by virtue of their greater mobility and greater ease in finding a livelihood elsewhere, can avoid the consequences of their actions by moving away and thus throw the entire burden on the older ones who have established themselves in a more permanent manner and cannot so easily escape. Moreover, this additional vote is of such a kind that it does not belong to any particular class or party as its exclusive privilege. It is open to all, as soon as they reach the age that qualifies them to exercise it. It will be granted to every voter as he attains the set higher age in the same way as the first vote is granted to everyone who reaches the set lower voting age.[71]

This conflict between different age groups had the greatest consequences in urban environments and industrial communities, Ekman argued. The younger ones tended to move away from the countryside so that the additional votes were not so significant, but the problems were palpable in "the towns and in the more numerous industrial municipalities in the countryside".[72] That the threat from the young was palpable in the towns could be substantiated by statistical data:

> According to the latest available data, the total number of persons in the towns entitled to vote in the municipality of residence was 459,000. Of these, 244,000 or 53% are over 35 years old and 215,000 or 47% under 35. When one considers that in the former group there are a large number of elderly people or weak and infirm persons, who cannot exercise their right to vote or can do so only with difficulty, while the second group includes young, energetic people aged 21 to 35, it is clear which of these groups would gain the upper hand after the introduction of universal suffrage.[73]

Here, the generational conflict appears dramatic—the volume and vitality of the younger generation is presented as a threat to the stability of society. Ekman thus proposed universal suffrage with greater influence "for older experienced and more permanent elements within society".[74]

Admiral Lindman and Mr Trygger proposed identical motions in the Second and the First Chamber respectively. These drew attention to the various complications entailed by the government's proposal, but both were open to the possibility of re-evaluating the voting restrictions. The central remaining requirements were that voters had to be liable to pay tax in the municipality and could prove that they had paid their state tax; also, they could be disqualified for having been declared legally incapacitated or bankrupt or for having a criminal record. Married women would also be entitled to vote under certain conditions. However, the motions still insisted that the undistributed estate of a deceased person should have a vote. They proposed a voting age of 24 in municipal elections but also a higher eligibility age of 34.[75] At the same time, the wording of the motions hints at a certain resignation about the possibility of reaching agreement on the age limits.

> As regards the right to vote in elections to these electoral colleges, it has appeared desirable to us to strengthen the voting rights of citizens whose age, experience, and insight ought to render increased influence. But because we have ascertained that no sympathy can be expected from the left-wing parties in Parliament for such a demand, however well-founded it may be, we confine ourselves to the demand that the right of eligibility to the electoral colleges in question should not come until the year after a municipal voter has reached the age of thirty-four. Such a provision cannot be said to benefit any one social class at the expense of another, besides which it has been adopted in truly democratic constitutions.[76]

Clason's motion in the First Chamber was more explicit about the question of age as a decisive factor. He referred to his earlier motion and rejected the bill as a reasonable basis for sound municipal administration. He also rejected the linkage of the voting age to the age of majority.

> The principle in the government bill, of equal municipal suffrage for all those liable to pay municipal tax, having reached the age of 21, is based on the fiction that all municipal taxpayers from the age of 21 have equal understanding and competence to assess municipal issues in a clear-sighted manner. That fiction is false. On reaching the age of majority, a man or a woman usually has little experience of municipal matters and nothing like the same experience as the more mature. For that reason alone it is wrong to give the former the same power over municipal decisions as the latter.[77]

Like Räf before him, Clason went on to argue that a number of comparable countries in Europe had a high voting age. He also observed that the reason the voting age in Sweden was tied to the age of majority was that the graded voting scale gave a greater influence to more mature voters.

Without any grading of suffrage, it was unreasonable to give the vote to anyone who had just become an adult man or woman.[78]

Age is also important in his continued argumentation. However, he questions tax liability as a criterion for suffrage. The personality principle on which a potential extension of suffrage would be based could (and should) not be dependent on tax payment and thus a certain level of income:

> If, on the other hand, it is maintained a certain age should be required for municipal suffrage, higher than the age of majority, a certain minimum period of residence in the municipality and full payment of taxes by those liable for municipal tax, it seems questionable to me whether tax liability itself can be maintained in all circumstances as a condition for the right to vote. For if the principle of personality is accepted as the basis for municipal suffrage, it will be inconsistent, as I pointed out in my motion to this year's ordinary session of Parliament, to allow personality to begin with the income that entails tax liability; and the impropriety of this becomes all the more obvious when even now this tax threshold varies in different municipalities according to the amount of the tax-free deduction granted in each municipality. Thus, in one municipality the right to vote will begin at an income limit of, say, 550 kronor, and in another at a limit of 700 kronor, and the same person will be granted or denied the right to vote as he moves from one municipality to another.[79]

Since municipalities—and here he is probably thinking mainly of urban municipalities—had different deductions, suffrage based on tax liability would have different meanings in different municipalities. In this respect Clason disagreed with both the Liberal and the Conservative positions, instead coming closer to the Social Democratic stance. He also pointed out that this was even more unreasonable given that unmarried and married people could be taxed differently, and taxation could also differ depending on the size of the family. In addition, there were deductions of various kinds. This could mean, for example, that an unmarried person gained the right to vote earlier than a married person, or a childless person could vote before the father of a family could. He thus concluded that tax liability could not be the basis for municipal or parliamentary suffrage, and he foresaw the need for an increasing influence for people with greater maturity and experience, which he also considered to entail, with reference to his earlier motion, enhanced votes for "certain municipal voters".[80]

He noted, however, that there was currently no hope of implementing the principle of greater influence for greater maturity and experience. This was what led him to stress the need to grant more voting power to people of higher age.

> On the other hand, I renew my call for increased voting rights at higher age and specify it as follows: that two votes should be granted to those entitled to vote in the municipality who have reached the age of thirty-five. Such a system, which would give increased influence within any shade of opinion or social class to anyone who has acquired a greater measure of experience in the school of life, can only be of benefit to the development of society.[81]

The idea of a higher voting age had united Liberals and the Right, summing up essential elements in the idea of how a democracy with guarantees could be built. The government's proposal for a voting age of 21 in municipal elections, with no thresholds, and the abolition of all thresholds preventing for men and women from voting in elections to the Second Chamber, was clearly problematic for these critics of the bill. Moreover, the speeches in the debate give the impression that municipal suffrage and the defence of the status of the First Chamber were perhaps just as important for the advocates of guarantees as was the right to vote in elections to the Second Chamber.

Prime Minister Edén clearly distanced himself from the proposals to raise the voting age. On 2 December *Svenska Dagbladet* reported on a speech delivered by Edén at the end of November to the Stockholm Liberal Association at the Cirkus theatre in Stockholm. In the speech he responded to parts of the Right's motions, declaring that the government's proposal was a "minimum programme, of which individual parts may not be pruned". The tone was brash and aggressive. There was no room for compromise Regarding the proposal for special electoral colleges for the First Chamber, with voting only from the age of 34, he declared: "I may as well start by saying outright that any thought of a settlement along such lines is completely out of the question." The government proposal was, in all respects, the only solution to the constitutional issue and the profoundly serious situation. It cannot be called a threat to tell the truth that the world is at boiling point, he argued. The Right had to give up its positions on matters such as the tax payment thresholds, and he rejected the list of demands.

> They want to raise the voting age to 24, they put forward new demands for a substantial transformation of the municipal council as an institution, they question in a strange manner the right of county administrative boards to review certain decisions in the municipalities, and the entire municipal reform is dependent on future decisions about the issue by the First Chamber. [...] Finally, for the reformation of the First Chamber, they have brought up the idea of special electoral assemblies to which no one would be able to vote until the age of 34, but along with this they retain the demand for municipal suffrage.[82]

Edén's bill (supported by the Liberals and Social Democrats) was based on the same premises as the proposal from the Right, that suffrage should be enjoyed by citizens who were liable to pay taxes if they had actually fulfilled their tax payments for three years. In these respects, the Liberals and the Right had been in agreement for a long time. Here, however, Edén opposed the idea of electoral colleges, the reform of municipal councils, the review of municipal decisions by the country administrative boards, and the high ages for voting and eligibility. The Conservative proposals thus included the idea of curtailing local self-government as an additional guarantee if suffrage were to be extended.

Arvid Lindman's notes from the discussions in the parliamentary group of the Farmers' Party provide some justification for Edén's fears, as we saw above. The Right was prepared to demand far-reaching requirements when it came to raising the voting age.[83]

In the following weeks the Social Democrats also campaigned intensively in their local organisations to gain support for their line on the suffrage issue. Per Albin Hansson, like Nils Edén, described the bill as a minimum programme. The large-scale mobilisation led to more radical proposals including the disestablishment of the church and the partition of large estates. Värner Rydén gave a speech in Jönköping, and Per Albin Hanson spoke in Linköping about the social revolution and threatened strikes to coincide with the vote on the bill in Parliament. He hinted at the possibility of more subversive measures, such as transforming the Riksdag into a national assembly. Möller organised "spontaneous" demonstrations in Malmö, Västerås, Halmstad, Karlstad, and Landskrona in support of the government bill, to coincide with the start of negotiations in what was called the third special committee.[84] At the same time, it was clear within the Social Democratic Party that the various unions of the Trade Union Confederation were not in the mood for a major strike or a revolution.[85]

The reactions to the bill show, on the one hand, that the relative positions of the left and the right were deadlocked. Yet it was evident from the debate that the parties on the Right were prepared to accept women's suffrage and to abolish the 40-grade scale. The voting thresholds were important to the Right, as was the idea of additional votes and a high age for voting and eligibility. A high voting age had previously been a distinct possibility also for the Liberals in previous proposals from the Liberals. But they had become highly dubious about the voting thresholds and the 40-grade scale. They shared this position with the social democratic parties. The bill thus challenged a central aspect of the right-wing parties' struggle for democracy with guarantees and the preservation of the First Chamber.

The political crisis, the unrest in Sweden and the problems with food supply, along with the mobilisation taking place in the outside world, led the Riksdag to appoint a special joint committee of the two chambers to reconcile the various proposals. On 27 November the matter was referred to the third special committee. This had 12 full members and 12 alternate members. Among the Social Democrats there was a left-wing socialist, Ivar Vennerström, who declared his loyalty to the left.[86] He later registered a dissenting opinion in the minutes of the committee.

Harsh Words and Building Consensus

This section considers the work of the third special committee. The aim is to gain a greater understanding of the premises for the agreement that led to a voting age that differed from the age of majority.

Negotiations in the committee began on 3 December. Branting was elected chairman, with the Liberal Kvarnzelius as vice-chairman; in both votes the Right saw its candidate Trygger defeated. In the initial negotiations, the minutes of the committee testify that the issue of women's suffrage was not broached, nor was the 40-grade suffrage scale. These were no longer important matters of conflict.[87] Now, the differences concerned were, among other things, the tax threshold and universal suffrage, as well as the timetables for the reforms. Following the chairman's proposal, a small delegation of ten people was appointed on 4 December to continue the negotiations. The first meeting was scheduled for 5 December.[88]

According to Palmstierna, the ten-man delegation excluded "the stubborn farmers", which was a good thing, but

> we offered universal municipal suffrage against raising the age to 24. The Right insisted on postponing the reform of the First Chamber and an election to the Second Chamber for the constitutional changes, before the 40-grade scale is definitively abandoned, thus making the raising the age for first-time voters to the First Chamber an ultimatum.[89]

This account from a Social Democratic perspective suggests a certain willingness to appease the Right in order to achieve universal suffrage. There is already a hint of this in Rydén's notes about the negotiations with Edén. That the Right formulated their demands as an ultimatum is wholly consistent with other statements. The threshold of fulfilled tax payment remained a stumbling block that recurred in the negotiations on 6 December, when the committee also decided that a smaller group of four people should continue the discussion. The chairman Branting and the Liberal vice-chairman Kvarnzelius were appointed from the left, which meant that Edén did not take part in these talks. The Right was represented by the former prime minister Carl Swartz and the councillor Adolf Dahl from Kristianstad.[90] Carl Swartz was the person on the Right who was perceived as most willing to negotiate and who had shown himself in Parliament to be most open to finding a solution to the constitutional problems, according to Hugo Hamilton, the speaker of the First Chamber.[91] What role did age play in the negotiations and how did the committee justify its proposals to Parliament? How was it possible to reach a joint statement and a proposal to Parliament?

What Happened in the Special Committee?

Our sources for the negotiations in the special committee are relatively limited but still give a picture of the direction taken by the discussion. We can find information about the negotiations in the diaries of Hamilton and Palmstierna. These provide subjective data about negotiations in which they themselves participated, noted in chronological order, as well as secondary input about the discussions in the special committee. The texts were probably edited before they were published. Two other actors have also left documentation that may be more useful: the former prime minister Carl Swartz, who was one of the delegates, both in the smaller ten-man group and in the final four-man group, in which he led the conservatives; and Arvid Lindman, who was in the special committee's original and ten-man groups, but did not take part in the final four-man group. We may assume that he also had frequent contact with Carl Swartz. In addition, the Speaker of the First Chamber, Hugo Hamilton, ensured that he was closely informed of the progress of the discussions. Among Swartz's papers there are five sheets of notes relating to these talks. The notes appear to have been kept as the negotiations proceeded. Lindman's notes, evidently written during the negotiations and dated day by day, record and comment on what was said.

The first three pages of Swartz's notes summarise the central bones of contention. His observations concern the obligation to pay municipal taxes and the voting age to the First Chamber.[92] The notes do not provide any information on whether this meant that the other voting restrictions were unproblematic and taken for granted, or simply less controversial. Swartz's demands concern age and tax payment, which reflects the demands put forward in the parliamentary motions of the Right as crucial guarantees of the social order. Swartz likewise presents the demands as fair and therefore fully ensuring a democratic balance between rights and obligations. The high voting age would allow the First Chamber to represent the older, more mature part of the population. Swartz also stressed here that a difference in voting age and eligibility age was not sufficient to guarantee the influence of the "circumspect" people. At the same time, the proposal was based on the personality principle, which was the basis of the proposal from the left. Below is my transcript of Swartz's notes:

> *Agreement*
> Municipal tax liability
> Voting age 24
> Voting age to the First Chamber 34
> Municipal tax liability
> Basis: the rights requirement
> Civil rights should be based on the fulfilment of civil obligations
> All possible consideration for when failure to pay tax is not of one's own making. Given this, no objection can be made to the establishment of this condition.
> (NB. Private: it is of the utmost importance to be accommodating here – it is always open (after democratization [comment inserted in the text afterwards]) to later change, if this isreally desiable.
> Voting age 24, wholly democratic demand.
> The personality principle is fully satisfied.
> Gentler transition. Even at the age of 24, in the case of equal municipal suffrage, the right to decide is given to the broad strata.

> These thus have in their power if they find desirable to lower the voting age to 21. But the upheaval will not be so hasty.
> Conditions not as pressing here as elsewhere. A more cautious approach ought to be desirable for everyone. Norway and Denmark.
> Electoral age to the First Chamber 34
> This demand is likewise wholly democratic.
> Apt to allow the FC to appear as representing older people – i.e. representation of the more circumspect in the population.
> This is not sufficiently expressed with equal suffrage – but different age of eligibility for 1st chamber compared to 2nd c.
> The raising of the voting age necessary for special electoral colleges – these should, however, be appointed at the same time and for the same period of office as the county councils.[93]

Here Swartz has reasoned about his arguments for the voting age and the citizenship that payment of taxes entailed. While realising that once universal suffrage was introduced, the majority could change the age limits, he thought that the transition to democracy could be secured through a compromise. He also assessed the relationship between the chambers in terms of age. At the same time, he was concerned about the options if no agreement was reached.

Swartz had considered the possibility of a breakdown in negotiations. He made notes about two separate scenarios under the heading "No agreement. How to act then?" The notes indicate that these options were not so attractive. The bill was not acceptable, but neither could it be rejected without negative consequences. Swartz foresaw the possibility of civil war and rebellion, or at least a deep division in the country should the bill be rejected. Nor was there any government alternative, and the threat of a general strike could lead to even worse consequences in the long run, with the introduction of a unicameral parliament and a republic. Also, a win, with the demands of the Right being accepted, was not something that could prevent further democratisation. It is thus intriguing to note his resignation about maintaining the positions of the Right, and also his palpable fear of the threat of a major strike and civil war.

> Accept the bill?
> = total capitulation with accountability w ref. to the effects ~~in the consequences~~ of rules in a spirit of which one cannot approve.
> ~~Abdication of the right for the future~~ Making it more difficult for the Right to argue its views on constitutional issues in the future.

> Unity not real, only apparent.
>
> Deep malaise within broad layers of the population.
>
> Reject the bill? ~~What is gained. Government~~
>
> What is at risk?
>
> Government resignation certain.
>
> Can another government be formed?
>
> Pure Right government – Trygger?
>
> = rebellion – otherwise impossible to achieve – neither L-n nor I willing
>
> T. can no more form a government now than before, now less than ever!
>
> K. does not address him.
>
> Caretaker government?
>
> Impossible other than under extraordinary pressure of events – note 1914, c.14 days of effort.
>
> But in the event of a change of government, the new government must be ready immediately, otherwise impossible to maintain order.
>
> General strike begins at once – its effects impossible to foresee in current conditions.
>
> Probably: powerful reaction from the bourgeois elements in the country, then probably with civil war.
>
> In any case: deep divisions within the people – two bitterly hostile camps in the country. Unhappy for our future development.
>
> If the battle is lost – much more far-reaching democratization – republic and unicameral system?
>
> If the battle is won – democratization is not prevented – within a couple of years the left will be in the majority in the First Chamber too.[94]

The negotiations in the committee show that the raising of the voting age had become the crucial parameter. The committee only discussed age, tax liability, and paid taxes as the basis for voting and eligibility.

Arvid Lindman's notes enable us to follow the dynamics of the meetings from 3 December until 8 December. His notes relate both to the meetings of the Conservative group in the committee (which he designates as the Right), the initial discussion, and the negotiations in the committee, and they take the form of a dialogue between different speeches and viewpoints. The notes appear to have been made sequentially. The presentation here follows the arrangement in the notes. The reports begin with a picture of disagreement and harsh words from individual members on both sides. Branting and Swartz were restrained. The people on the left emphasised that the bill was not negotiable. Those on the other side declared that the motion that Lindman and Trygger had tabled in Parliament constituted the Right's proposal. Members on the left pointed out that the working class had so far shown great self-restraint but hinted that the mood could become more revolutionary, and there was even the threat of strikes. Lindman, citing his own statement, criticised the leaders of the left for fuelling the antagonisms, while Trygger added that "if there are people who want to force their demands through with revolution, there may be those who will prevent revolution."[95]

The Right specifically underlined that their proposal was not conservative but was intended to ensure the maturity of the electorate and that payment of tax was not up for negotiation. The tax criterion was the same for everyone and had to be retained. Swartz asserted that "we understand full well that the time has come for a democratic reform of the constitution. [...] Cannot accept the removal of the tax payment obligation for those who are able to pay. One should now give to the more mature – later one can go further." Maturity refers here to the fact that the Right's motion proposed a higher voting age, which prompted Harald Hallén to ask ironically whether maturity was to be synonymous with being on the Right.

The demand for tax payment was not only questioned by the Social Democrats but also by a Liberal member who pointed out that this caused problems for crofters and pensioners. At the same time, tax obligations involved a certain degree of reasonable control of newcomers that was positive, according to Clason. Tax liability was defended by the Right.[96] At the same time, some positions were qualified in an internal meeting of the Right, with a declaration that it concerned those who could afford to pay but, "out of carelessness, indifference, contumacy, failed to pay".[97] Branting noted that there was some willingness to compromise on the part of the Right: "We can see that the difference is not so great but for the working class impossible to relinquish the tax threshold. The tax threshold has a terrible effect. It will make no impression on the country if the injustice of this is not removed."[98]

Branting did not comment on the opinions concerning maturity and age, but Vennerström did, questioning the high voting age of 27–30 for county council elections and 24 in municipal elections as hinted by a person on the Right. The position of the First Chamber was the recurring issue. On the second day, the tone seemed less confrontational. This was when Branting suggested that the matter should be further treated in a smaller delegation of ten members.[99]

In the internal meeting of the Right after the committee meeting, the different lines in the discussion were made more concrete. Several of the members were clearly in favour of universal municipal suffrage. The doubts concerned whether it was possible to drop the demands for paid taxes, and the idea was broached of requiring a certificate from those liable to pay tax. The practical implementation of such a system was questioned, which led to the following statement: "Extremely difficult to determine whether a person can or cannot pay tax. Universal suffrage at age 24."[100] Age was consistently related to the issue of tax payment. Age was likewise a central factor in the discussion of the position of the First Chamber, and it was also presupposed that electoral colleges would be established in such a way that the voting age in county council elections could be different from that in municipal elections. According to Lindman's notes, the voting ages suggested were in the 30–35 range, with possible additional votes after the age of 35, and this was balanced against the economic restrictions:

> Clason: Can contemplate universal municipal suffrage.
> Widell: Certification of 35-year-old voters on oath. Negative certificate can be issued, that a person may not vote on account of failure to pay through carelessness, indifference, contumacy.
> Thus a person owing one or two years' tax can tender such a certificate.
> Ekman: 1st chamb the problem. Voting age county council 35 or an additional vote for 35-year-olds.
> Roth [misspelled, likely Rooth]: Extremely difficult to test whether a person can or cannot pay taxes. Universal suffrage age 24.
> Trygger: Hildebrand's proposal for payment 1 year out of 3 better.
> Bjälbo [Pettersson]: impossible to give up tax payment
> Hammarström: [...] The cardinal issue: 1st chamb. – Real guarantees needed.
> [...]
> Skottlandshus [Nilsson of]: wisest to reach an agreement
> Ollas Erickson: Think we can get voting age 24. Inquiry into tax payment.
> [...]
> Dahl: Easy to get 24, the Social Democrats want the tax threshold more than the Liberals
> [...]
> Widell: The tax payment threshold is the most important politically. Suffrage can be made the same for 1st & 2nd chamb.
> [...]
> Ollas: It would be throwing in the towel if one abandoned the tax obligation.
> Hildebrand: Age 30 all right for 1st chamb. Could one contemplate electing ½ the number of county councillors next year the other ½ the following year
> [...]

Swartz: What can we get: age 24 without a special electoral college, or an electoral college 30 years + 21 otherwise.[101]

In the following committee meeting there was a review of the voting rules in other countries. Lindman also noted statements about which taxes were commonly neglected and how complicated the tax system was, which made it difficult to evaluate the defaults. Here we see that universal suffrage was also perceived to be capable of benefitting sections of the rural population.

Wants universal suffrage so as to include sons living at home, crofters, beneficiaries. Then [female] servants will also be included.

Would like to have a real criterion of responsible behaviour, but have to abandon it if and when it proves impossible.[102]

This is the only occasion the women's suffrage is mentioned in the notes. In the next meeting of the Right group, three different alternative models were considered as a basis for the discussion. The document is not entirely clear. However, the priority model appears to be based on a voting age of 24 in municipal elections and 34 in election to the First Chamber, as well as guarantees for the First Chamber.

When the ten-man delegation met on 5 December, the discussion concentrated on the reform of the First Chamber and the timing of elections to it. Dahl, as a member for the Right, played the county councils against the First Chamber.

(Con) Dahl: we want to detach 1st C from the county councils, to get a higher voting age.
(Soc Dem) Branting: have not envisaged more than 24
(Soc Dem) Olof Olsson: can't agree to 34
(Lib) Kvarnzelius: County councils conservative. Would be more practical to have a higher age of eligibility
(Lib) Alexanderson: Higher age will soon disappear. What could be contemplated would be to raise eligibility qualifications for county councils.
(Soc Dem) Branting: 1st C should be the great council of the Swedish municipalities.
Parliament to supplement part of 1st C not 1st C itself.
(Soc Dem) Victor Larson: can agree to 23/24 in return for univ. munic. suffrage.
Lindman: ...

> (Lib) Kvarnzelius: univ. munic. suffrage, age 24, County councils 30, 1st chamb eligibility 35.[103]

However, after this exchange of views which took the discussion of age several steps forward, it was found that the perceptions of the tax threshold were incompatible. The parties on the left agreed that the right to vote should be universal.

At the internal meeting of the Right, several proposals were formulated about the idea of universal municipal suffrage from the age of 24, a tax threshold of at least three years, a residence requirement, the right to vote in county council elections from the age of 30, or from the age of 24 but with an additional vote from the age of 30, and electoral colleges for the big cities.[104] One of the members noted that it was tactical "to hold on to the county councils as electoral corporations" and urged caution about universal municipal suffrage, while John Erlandsson was noted to have said, "Universal suffrage not so dangerous. We gain a lot by it."[105]

When the delegation met again on 6 December, the questions came to a head and Lindman was now very curt in his presentation of the discussion.

> Dahl: proposals made about tax payment. Rejected by Branting and Alexandersson.
> Branting; have you thought of univ. munic. suffrage?
> Dahl: can we agree to 1 year's tax payment with checks?[106]

Hjalmar Branting, Herman Kvarnzelius, Carl Swartz, and Adolf Dahl then met to deliberate privately, with the result that the committee arrived at an agreement when it met on 8 December. That discussion cannot be followed in any notes.

The solution suggested by the reduced committee was an adjustment of municipal suffrage so that voting would no longer be based on payment of taxes. For those who were liable to pay tax, however, a certain remnant of the requirement of responsible behaviour was preserved. The voting age would be decided in the following sessions of Parliament for the Second Chamber 1919 and 1921 along the lines proposed by the Right and (before them) the Liberals, that is, the year after reaching the age of 23 (i.e. 24), with the same age of eligibility. The voting age for county councils would be raised to 27. The First Chamber would be chosen by electors appointed by the municipalities, "but the right to vote here will be subject to the same conditions as in the election of county councillors".

Stockholm and Gothenburg were separate constituencies in the election of electors, as these were not part of any county council. The voting age would be the same as the age of eligibility.[107]

The voting ages were raised for municipal and county council elections and thus for the First Chamber. In contrast, the voting age for the Second Chamber was lowered by one year. This higher age was what made universal suffrage acceptable to everyone, that is, without the requirement of tax payment but with documented payment of tax in one year out of the last three. This had clear advantages for the Liberals and the Right as well since more groups in rural areas acquired the right to vote. The Right also gained a hearing for its demand for proxy voting and for the appointment of county councillors by electors, and the high voting age of 27 for county council elections.

Figures 5.3, 5.4, 5.5, and 5.6. The different political perspectives on the Liberals' and Social Democrats' proposals for constitutional reform in November 1918 are reflected in the headlines of the daily press.

There would thus be universal and equal suffrage for men and women, but the requirement of one year's tax payment was retained for voting in municipal elections. For voting in elections to the Second Chamber, the restrictions on account of bankruptcy, legal incapacity, and receipt of poor relief were also retained. The Right successfully achieved some of its demands, with the retention of certain thresholds and the preservation of the First Chamber, along with guarantees of a high voting and eligibility

Vänstersocialisterna ge sig ej.

Inbjuda socialdemokraterna till fortsatt diskussion.

Proletariatets diktatur icke f. n. aktuell.

Fig. 5.3 The left-wing socialist will not give in and invite the Social Democrats to further talks. The dictatorship of the proletariat is currently not on the agenda. (Source: "Vänstersocialisterna ge sig ej", Dagens Nyheter 17/11 1918)

Amiral Lindman talar på Auditorium: Ingen den knutna nävens politik.

Högern har ställt sig på den ståndpunkt, där det liberala partiet stod för endast ett par veckor sedan.

Ett föredrag om författningsfrågan hölls på måndagen i Auditorium, som var till sista plats fullsatt, av amiral Lindman. Mötet öppnades av dr Karl Hildebrand, vilken med några ord hälsade de närvarande välkomna och överlämnade ordet åt amiral Lindman, som framträdde, hälsad med applåder.

Aldrig så liten eftertanke säger, att en verklig första kammare ej kan skapas på regeringsförslagets grund.

med förslag om effektiva reformer för utskyldernas indrivning. Huru pass effektiva dessa nya former äro, får framtiden utvisa. Det går naturligtvis mycket bra att vidtaga införsel i lön för lagstadda tjänare och stadigvarande arbetare, men hur vill man på den vägen nå lösarbetarna, den som är här i dag och där i morgon?

Fig. 5.4 No clenched fist politics, say Admiral Lindman. Now on the position the Liberals were a couple of weeks ago. A real First Chamber cannot be based on the government proposal. (Source: "Amiral Lindman talar", Svenska Dagbladet 26/11 1918)

age, along with electors for county councils, the expansion of the council institution at the municipal level, and an initial period of proxy voting for spouses.[108]

Before the large delegation of the committee made its decision, support for the proposal was established in the various party groupings, first in the so-called group of ten and then in the various party groups. Edén, who had not been involved in the final negotiations and who was the person who would be presenting the decision, had misgivings of some kind, according to Palmstierna.[109] Palmstierna also hinted at doubts on the part of the Social Democrats. Fredrik Thorsson and Östen Undén had some objections. Thorsson, according to Palmstierna, was concerned that:

> in a time when, during the development of revolutionary forces, others are going down to a voting age of 20 for men and women, in Sweden the voting age is being raised with our assent. In addition, it worried him that a remnant of the tax payment threshold in municipalities had been retained. The

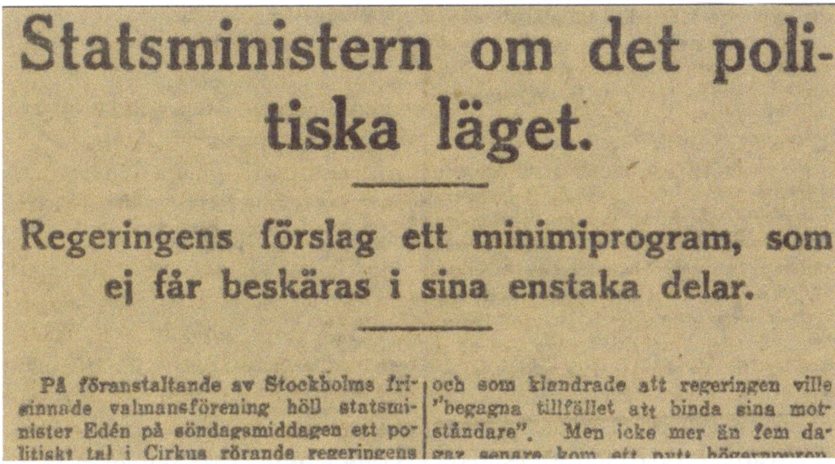

Statsministern om det politiska läget.

Regeringens förslag ett minimiprogram, som ej får beskäras i sina enstaka delar.

På föranstaltande av Stockholms frisinnade valmansförening höll statsminister Edén på söndagsmiddagen ett politiskt tal i Cirkus rörande regeringens ... och som klandrade att regeringen ville "begagna tillfället att binda sina motståndare". Men icke mer än fem da-

Fig. 5.5 The prime minister on the state of affairs. The government proposal is a minimum programme that cannot be deprived of its part. (Source: "Statsministern om det politiska läget", Svenska Dagbladet 2/12 1918)

Ett manifest från socialisterna.

"Det vi gått i strid för är i verkligheten vunnet."

Författningsreformen innebär Sverges demokratisering.

T Socialdemokratiska partistyrelsen, Landsorganisationens representantskap och Socialdemokratiska riksdagsgruppen ha på måndagsaftonen utsänt följande manifest:

Fig. 5.6 What we fought for is won. The constitutional reform makes Sweden a democracy. (Source: "Ett manifest från socialisterna", Dagens Nyheter 9/12 1918)

> higher age for the county councils, on the other hand, was swallowed unexpectedly easily.[110]

Palmstierna also stressed that the agreement had its defects and blemishes. However, there was nothing that could not be corrected. According to him, Swartz had also hinted as much to Branting. In Palmstierna's diary the decision appears as a step on the way to a new Right party welded together under new leadership. Trygger's and Lindman's time was over.[111] In the joint meeting of the Social Democratic party executive and some trade union organisations, the agreement was also accepted. Branting presented the compromise and said that it was impossible to achieve any more, and the alternative of riding roughshod over the Right in Parliament was not feasible. Rikard Sandler, however, felt that the compromise, "particularly with regard to the age threshold, was exceedingly unattractive. As regards the tax payment threshold, it is on the right track but as far as the age threshold is concerned, it is a step backwards. It is an unattractive and irrational solution".[112] Other speakers had objections of various kinds, but the compromise was nevertheless deemed reasonable and extremely beneficial for the Social Democrats. "A real capitulation on the part of the Right."[113] The Social Democratic parliamentary group accepted the proposal after Branting announced that the parties on the Right had approved it; so too did the party executive and the Trade Union Confederation, as well as the Railwaymen's and Typographers' Unions.[114]

In Lindman's notes, however, it appears that it was difficult to win support for the agreement among the Social Democrats. According to Lindman, Branting had some trouble getting them to accept the threshold of one year's tax payment, and he was therefore forced to return to the Right's party group for further negotiations.

> Branting informed Swartz that the tax payment for one year is encountering tough (?) opposition from the party executive and others and asks if it could be abolished and replaced with a one year higher age for voting in county council elections. Swartz said *he* cannot agree to this. They could possibly force the proposal through anyhow, but then it would be an act of violence and would be labelled as such.
>
> Dahl informs us that Zweigbergk told him that this proposal was a dreadful anomaly, to have a higher age for county councils than municipalities. They might prefer to raise the municipal ages instead. Stockholm & Gothenburg different is downright unreasonable.[115]

For the Social Democrats, there was no option but to accept the compromise, according to Palmstierna, otherwise they would have lost the chance of social legislation to benefit the working class, besides which it weakened the revolutionary movement, partly thanks to the "highly accommodating" behaviour of the Right.[116]

The speaker of the First Chamber, Hugo Hamilton, described in his diary the changing moods through reports from Swartz. Initially, Swartz was quite concerned —there was the threat of conflicts and a general strike that might render negotiations impossible—but gradually became more positive once the discussions were under way. At the same time,. Hamilton expressed his surprise that the small delegation was able to reach an agreement, "oddly enough, one might well say".[117]

Just before the final meeting of the small delegation, there was apparently great nervousness. Edén, according to Hamilton, was not prepared to promote a "consensual peace". Swartz and Dahl, as representatives of the Right, anticipated being steamrollered without agreement. However, both Branting and Kvarnzelius returned with the message that they accepted the committee's suggested compromise. Among the Right, there were some misgivings about the decision, but at the same time a "more conciliatory atmosphere" made itself felt. Hamilton nevertheless took the opportunity to criticise Branting's "comical" proposal for a joint statement by the committee, "the craziest thing imaginable", and his lack of organisational skills. According to Hamilton, "neither the Right nor the Liberals would hear of it, and even Branting's own people thought it was rather too much". He was irritated by Branting's broad brushstrokes about the Entente and the progress of democracy, the socialisation of society, and the causes of the World War.[118] It is revealing to look at how it was presented, since Branting's text established the shared foundation for the decision. It interwove the arguments for reform put forward by the right and the left, albeit in Branting's wording, and it also built on the tone set in the government bill, aiming at a consensual approach.[119]

The introduction takes a clear stand against the "distorted picture" of social revolutions and the reversal of class domination that could be witnessed in the contemporary world. Democracy was advocated with reference to US President Woodrow Wilson. Branting observed that the global situation and the calls for social revolution in different parts of the world made the issue acute.

> The great masses among the nations, who desire peace, have turned against the whole system of government which they blame for this disaster. These peoples, brought to despair by their sufferings during the war and by their complete defeat in the struggle, have now begun a radical political and social transformation by means of revolution. In some countries and from certain elements of society, attempts are even being made, instead of the initially proclaimed civil equality, to reintroduce class domination, but upside down; The new privileged groups would be the lower layers of the old society, while those who formerly had privileged status are condemned to lose their rights
>
> [...]
>
> Such a distorted picture of social revolution, however, in no way alters the fact that a common feature recurs everywhere in what is happening in this tremendous historical crisis, when an old era is coming to an end and a new one is being born. These peoples who have blindly followed their leaders through the misery of war all the way to complete destruction, are now setting up as their highest standard the profound and healthy watchword spoken by the President of the United States in his speech when the United States joined the war: The world must be made safe for democracy. The people are demanding to take their destinies into their own hands in order to secure peace and to establish a better society for life in the future. The great social demands are thus linked to the political ones.[120]

Branting noted that the committee's left-wing majority could support the government proposal as a unifying minimum programme, and that it was implemented within the framework of the extraordinary session of Parliament. The right-wing parties had also accepted the basic elements of the proposal,

> that participation in municipal life should be based on the principle of equal suffrage, and that the right of companies and other such corporations to vote must be abandoned, and agreement has been reached about the extension of political suffrage to women, and also about a significant restriction of the so-called poor relief threshold.[121]

The reasons for setting a higher voting age now also became a shared and reasonable starting point. A shift in power to the younger age groups could be limited by raising the voting age.

The criticisms, on the other hand, have concerned the fact that, since the graduated voting scale indirectly granted a stronger influence to greater maturity and experience, its replacement with equal suffrage would mean an excessive increase in power for younger age groups. An adjustment on this would be warranted, and it ought to be made by raising the voting age.

> But even if such an adjustment were approved, the fact would remain, with respect to the right of municipal corporations to vote in elections to the First Chamber, that such a shift in influence in favour of the younger electorate could not be regarded as leaving room for the necessary assurance that prudence and maturity of understanding that ought to have an influence in elections to the First Chamber in order to further its special duty according to the constitution. To rectify this anomaly, no other way appeared open but to transfer the right to vote for the First Chamber from county councils and borough councils to joint electoral colleges, appointed by municipal voters with a substantially increased age limit, thirty-four years.[122]

The arguments for higher voting age and eligibility age limits are thus accepted here. According to the committee, the municipal restriction on recipients of poor relief had been a stumbling block, but it was accepted in a modified form because it was a principle cherished by the rural population.[123]

This meant that the voting age was modified for both chambers and that in the bill presented to Parliament the right to vote was no longer based on tax payment, which meant that new groups of rural inhabitants were included. In order to respond to the criticism that the voting age was too low, a higher age was also established for county councils: This forced a special arrangement for elections in the larger municipalities:

> Since it has nevertheless been argued that this age [23] would be far too low, if the principle of universal suffrage is applied, for the election of the corporations which are to appoint members of the First Chamber, the committee has considered it necessary to accommodate this view to some extent by proposing that the right to vote and to be elected to these corporations should not come until the age of 27. As a consequence, however, in the larger cities which do not participate in county councils, the right to elect members of the First Chamber has had to be removed from the urban council and transferred to specially appointed electors.[124]

The committee's proposal, as we know, followed the group's suggestion to raise the age limit for municipal suffrage (described as a "certain increase", p. 33) and elections to the Second Chamber. Some changes would also be made to the residence requirement, the poor relief disqualification, and the tax payment threshold, as well as proxy votes for spouses. It was also suggested that the 40-grade voting scale should be abolished, along with voting by corporations and the estates of deceased persons.[125]

In this narrative, which came to form the basis of the parliamentary decision, the actual solution to the democratic problem, with reduced influence for people with "maturity and experience", was to deny the vote to younger citizens until the year after they reached 23, in municipal council and Second Chamber elections and, 27 in county council elections and First Chamber elections. According to what the Liberal minister Eliel Löfgren said in the parliamentary debate in the spring of 1918, the opposition to women's suffrage concerned the numerical superiority of women in different age groups. Still, in his view there was no objective reason for this, as it did not affect the development of society. He did point out, however, that with a voting age of 27, the numerical difference was less noticeable and hence, implicitly, less problematic.[126] Perhaps the numerical superiority of women in the population played a certain part in the compromise on age limits when a voting age of 27 was established as the compromise between the position of the Social Democrats and that of the Liberals and the Right. However, there is no direct evidence of this in the discussion.

Branting hereby also gained legitimacy for this description and turned it into a shared narrative about the birth of democracy and the conditions for its application. The text accepts and indeed advances the positions of the left but demarcates itself from left-wing radicalism, while simultaneously inscribing and legitimising the positions of the Right. Not everyone was happy, however. The committee's decision led to reservations from Vennerström of the Social Democratic Left Party, who attended the initial meetings of the committee and there expressed his dissatisfaction with the portrayal of working-class youth as immature.

The criticism reflected some of Thorsson's fears about the reactions of those to the left of the Social Democratic Party. The voting age was at the centre of the criticism. The young generation that the Right and, perhaps to some extent, the Liberals were concerned about was, in this description, the very foundation on which a new and positive society would be constructed. "These socially awake, knowledge-seeking, vigorous young age groups have been the driving forces in the work of organising and educating the people", but were now ranked as inferior citizens. The democratic breakthrough was restricted and marred by a compromise which meant that no fewer than 400,000 citizens lost their right to vote. Moreover, the remaining thresholds meant that civil rights were still a matter of money, as Vennerström wrote in his reservation. He also stressed that the conservative guarantees of changes in municipal budgets were a blow to the interests of the small people and would consolidate the interests of private capitalism.[127] Vennerström was not satisfied and would return with criticism and suggestions for changes in the following years.

Concluding Reflections

The negotiations in the third special committee of the Riksdag in the autumn of 1918 show that the higher age limit was the key to the solution of the parliamentary deadlock. Behind the closed doors, the discussion boiled down to the two fundamentals: age and economy. It may also help us to understand the political process in broader terms. Before the decision of 17 December, the government had tried in the spring of 1918 to pass proposals for a reform of voting rights for both municipal and Second Chamber elections that included equal and universal suffrage for men and women. This had failed against the First Chamber's opposition to women's suffrage. That observation has been a key element in previous research.

By all accounts, however, other matters were more important. The age of the electorate was absolutely crucial, as my study shows. The opposition still concerned the guarantees that could be assured through voting restrictions. Basically the same issue was on the agenda from 1900 to 1909: the relationship between the Second and First Chambers. The government bills were based on the foundation shared by the Liberals and the Right, namely, a high voting age, although the Liberals and the Social Democrats were in agreement on women's suffrage. At the same time, the proposals in 1918 were based for a long time on voters and their spouses paying tax and displaying good civic behaviour. In reality, this meant that married women's right to vote was conditional on earning their own income and having a husband who was entitled to vote. It was not a question of universal suffrage for either men or women. The targets were not very ambitious. The high voting age of 23 or over was the absolute normative basis for the suggested age limit for elections to the Second Chamber, and even higher ages were proposed. The discussion still reflected a fear of the working-class youth in the towns and cities and now, by all accounts, also those working in the mills in industrial communities all over the country. A top priority was to ensure the participation of the married population. On this point, Liberals and the Right were in complete agreement. Restricting the right to vote to families stands out in the debate as the crucial guarantee that the bourgeois parties needed.

It is in this light that the proposal in the autumn of 1918 to abolish the 40-grade voting scale became problematic, because it was based on the established voting age of 21. This had major implications because the composition of the First Chamber would be influenced by 21-year-old voters without the guarantee provided by the income scale, which shifted influence to the wage-earning (and older, married, and responsible) segment of the population. The income scale was thus perceived, as I noted earlier, to have the same effect as the higher voting age for the Second Chamber. In other words, this meant that the composition of the First Chamber would be determined by the young unmarried working-class population from the age of 21. In one fell swoop the First Chamber would become more democratic than the Second Chamber, which had a voting age of 24, and its distinctive character in relation to the Second Chamber would be undermined. Probably more than the question of women's suffrage, this was the key issue in the conflict in the spring of 1918 and the reason why no agreement on suffrage reform could be reached that time.

In the spring and autumn of 1918, the Right repeatedly suggested the compromise of holding further inquiries, but this met with limited enthusiasm. Political developments in the outside world and in Sweden during 1918 meant that the question of the legitimacy of the political system was questioned and the matter could no longer be postponed. The negotiations in Parliament and later in the special committee tackled precisely these problems. The agreement was based on equal suffrage, which was combined with a high voting age (and eligibility age) and a slow turnover of members in the First Chamber. The terms of office also meant that many eligible voters would have to wait years to cast their vote. The right to vote in municipal and Second Chamber elections became general, in other words, not limited by the citizens having to pay taxes, but in the case of municipalities it was combined with the obligation to have paid taxes in one of the last three years. Because the voting age for municipalities and county councils differed (23 and 27 respectively) and because the First Chamber was elected by the county councils (directly or through electors), the position of the First Chamber in Parliament was guaranteed. The adjustment of the age limits made the compromise possible in 1918. The age of the electorate was the link in politics that made it possible to resolve the deadlock between the different political levels—local, regional, and national elections. At the same time, things had moved quickly towards the end of the process. Was this decision—described in retrospect as a democratic breakthrough—a good one? After all, it excluded significant groups of citizens. In the next chapter we shall follow how the decision was evaluated in connection with the final debate in Parliament.

Notes

1. Riksdagstrycket, *Proposition 1918:104.*
2. Moderata kvinnornas rösträttsförening was a women's organisation affiliated to the Farmers' Party. See Ebba Berling Berling Åselius, *Rösträtt med förhinder: Rösträttsstrecken i svensk politik 1900–1920* (Stockholm: Acta Universitatis Stockholmiensis, 2005), pp. 188–191.
3. Riksdagstrycket, *Proposition 1918:104*, p. 29: "The association considered that certain categories of women in Sweden, before all women achieved the right to vote, needed a transitional period during which, by acquiring information about the vital issues of the state and society, they could prepare to exercise the influence that political suffrage entailed. The envisaged age limit was 33, which would be lowered year by year until it reached the age limit set for men."
4. Ibid., p. 30.
5. Berling Åselius (2005, pp. 181–188).
6. Riksdagstrycket, *Proposition 1918:290*, pp. 3, 49–50.
7. Riksdagstrycket, *Motion AK 1918:416*, pp. 1–7.
8. Ibid., pp. 7–8.
9. Ibid., p. 8.
10. Riksdagstrycket, *Motion FK 1918:171*, pp. 1–9.
11. Gunnar Gerdner, *Krigsslut, vänsterseger och reformer: Axel Schottes "regeringsrapporter" till David Bergström 1918–1920* (Uppsala, 1960).
12. Riksdagstrycket, *Motion FK 1918:171*, p. 19, italics in the original; see also Riksdagstrycket, *Motion AK 1918:401*, pp. 1–3, with the warning that the suggestion in the bill is only the first step in the expansion of popular influence.
13. Riksdagstrycket, *Motion AK 1918:399*, pp. 1–9.
14. Riksdagstrycket, *Motion AK 1918:401*; *Utlåtande KU 1918:122.*
15. *Utlåtande KU 1918:122*, pp. 6–9.
16. Christina Carlsson Wetterberg, "Kvinnans rätt och nationens väl", i Lars M. Andersson (red.), *Rätten: En festskrift till Bengt Ankarloo* (Lund: Nordic Academic Press, 2000); Kari Melby m.fl., *The Nordic model of marriage and the welfare state* (Köpenhamn: Nordiska ministerrådet, 2000).

17. “Protokoll 10 April 1918”, Socialdemokratiska riksdagsgruppen, Protokoll 1918–1923, vol. A 2:2, 1918–1920, Arbetarrörelsens arkiv och bibliotek.
18. Riksdagstrycket, *Motion AK 1918:401*, pp. 10–12. See also Clason et al. FK 1917:171; *Protokoll AK 1918:71*, p. 27. The Social Democrats voted in favour of the Constitutional Committee’s proposal on female suffrage but expressed a dissenting opinion against the voting restrictions; see “Protokoll 25 April 1918”, Socialdemokratiska riksdagsgruppen, Protokoll 1918–1923, vol. A 2:2, 1918–1920, Arbetarrörelsens arkiv och bibliotek; Rönnbäck (2004).
19. Carl Göran Andræ, *Revolt eller reform: Sverige inför revolutionerna i Europa 1917–1918* (Stockholm: Carlsson, 1998), p. 244.
20. Riksdagstrycket, *Protokoll FK 1918:27*, p. 65.
21. Ibid., p. 65.
22. Ibid.
23. Ibid.
24. Josefin Rönnbäck, *Politikens genusgränser: Den kvinnliga rösträttsrörelsen och kampen för kvinnors politiska medborgarskap 1902–1921* (Stockholm: Atlas, 2004); Christina Carlsson Wetterberg, *Kvinnosyn och kvinnopolitik: En studie av svensk socialdemokrati 1880–1910* (diss. Lund: Arkiv förlag, 1986).
25. Riksdagstrycket, *Protokoll AK 1918:71*, p. 10.
26. Ibid., p. 12. See also the following speech in the debate.
27. Ibid., p. 28.
28. Ibid., pp. 28–29.
29. Ibid., pp. 24–25.
30. Ibid., p. 27.
31. Riksdagstrycket, *Protokoll AK 1918:45*, pp. 1–6.
32. Ibid., p. 6.
33. Ibid., pp. 4–6.
34. Ibid., p. 4.
35. Elin Hinnemo, *Inför högsta instans: Samspelet mellan kvinnors handlingsutrymme och rättslig reglering i Justitierevisionen 1760–1860 (Uppsala: Acta Universitatis Upsaliensis, 2016)*. Compare here the negotiations on women’s responsibility for the household and their separate legal competence in an earlier period.
36. Riksdagstrycket, *Protokoll AK 1918:45*, pp. 6–11.
37. Riksdagstrycket, *Protokoll AK 1918:71*, p. 72.
38. Ibid., p. 79. See also Riksdagstrycket, *Protokoll AK 1918:78*, pp. 1–6.
39. Andræ (1998, pp. 244–248).

40. Ibid., pp. 247–251, quotation pp. 250–251; Sverker Oredsson, Nils Edén: Demokratins statsminister (Stockholm: Ekerlid, 2017), pp. 238–248.
41. Edén's diary, 10 October, Gunnar Gerdners papper, nr 1:1, Handskriftssamlingen, Uppsala universitetsbibliotek; Lindman's notes, loose sheets, "Samtal med Edén", 11 October 1918, "Redogörelse för samtal med Edén", 17 September 1918, untitled 1 October, untitled comprising 11, 13, and 14 November, including a note that "women's suffrage must be taken" without further comment. Further notes from 11 and 14 November, in addition "Samtal med Edén" 14, 15 November 1918, 4 sheets. These include a discussion of the poor relief threshold and universal suffrage and the note "Women's suffrage done". See Lindmanska samlingen, Riksarkivet. On women's suffrage see also the draft of a speech in the chamber by Prime Minister Carl Swartz, probably in the spring of 1917, in which the issue of women's suffrage appears to be the least controversial, "Maskinskrivet tal, folder, Anteckningar 1917–1920", Släktens Swartz i Norrköping BVb:21, Norrköpings stadsarkiv.
42. Lindman's notes, loose sheets, untitled, 1 October, comprising 11, 13, and 14 November; further notes from 11 and 14 November, Lindmanska samlingen, Riksarkivet. Lindman's notes including a note that can also be followed in fair copy in Gerdner's excerpts; see "Arvid Lindman: Strödda anteckningar och promemorior", Gunnar Gerdners papper 2:10–11, Handskriftssamlingen, Uppsala universitetsbibliotek.
43. "Protokoll 13 November", Förtroenderådet, Socialdemokratiska riksdagsgruppen 1918–1920, Arbetarrörelsens arkiv och bibliotek.
44. Lindman's notes, "Samtal med Edén", 14, 15 October 1918, four sheets, Lindmanska samlingen, Riksarkivet.
45. Lindman's notes, 1? November 1918, two loose leaves, Lindmanska samlingen, Riksarkivet. Also "Arvid Lindman: Strödda anteckningar och promemorior", Gunnar Gerdners papper 2:10–11, Handskriftssamlingen, Uppsala universitetsbibliotek.
46. Gunnar Gerdner, "Ministären Edén och författningsrevisionen 1918", in Axel Brusewitz (ed.), *Statsvetenskapliga studier till Statsvetenskapliga föreningens i Uppsala tjugofemårsdag 7/11 1944* (Uppsala: Almqvist & Wiksell, 1944), pp. 272–277.
47. Ibid., pp. 269–272.
48. "Edéns dagbok rörande regeringsfrågan 1918", Gunnar Gerdners papper, nr 1:1, Handskriftsavdelningen, Uppsala universitetsbibliotek.
49. Gerdner (1944, pp. 279–280).
50. Ibid., p. 281, 13 November, Socialdemokraternas förtroenderåd, Gerdner samling 2:9, Handskriftssamlingen, Uppsala universitetsbibliotek.

51. Regeringskommunikén den 14 november 1918, Bilagor Värner Rydéns dagboksanteckningar 11–15 November 1918, reproduced as an appendix in Gerdner (1944, pp. 295–296); "Dagboksanteckningar, Rydéns ministertid", Värner Rydens arkiv vol. 24, F IV:b. Riksarkivet; "Utkast till regeringskommuniké, Rydéns ministertid", Värner Rydéns arkiv vol. 24, F IV:b, Riksarkivet.
52. Gerdner (1944, pp. 295–296); "Utkast, Rydéns ministertid", Värner Rydens arkiv, vol. 24, F IV:b, Riksarkivet.
53. Andræ (1998, pp. 253–260).
54. Riksdagstrycket, *Proposition Urtima 1918:34.*
55. Erik Palmstierna, Orostid: Politiska dagboks-anteckningar 2. 1917–1919 (Stockholm: Tiden, 1953), p. 245.
56. Riksdagstrycket, *Proposition Urtima 1918:34*, pp. 42–47. See also the problems this raised regarding rural crofters and tenant farmers who did not have a taxed income, e.g. *Motion AK 1918:53.*
57. Ibid., p. 47.
58. Klas Åmark, "Familj, försörjning och livslopp under 1900-talet", in Helena Bergman and Peter Johansson (eds.), *Familjeangelägenheter: Modern historisk forskning om välfärdsstat, genus och politik* (Eslöv: Brutus Östlings bokförlag Symposion, 2002).
59. Riksdagstrycket, *Proposition Urtima 1918:34*, p. 47.
60. Ibid., p. 43.
61. Ibid.
62. "Amiral Lindman talar på Auditorium. Ingen den knutna nävens politik", *Svenska Dagbladet* 26 November 1918, p. 6.
63. Ibid.
64. "En behärskad remissdebatt i författningsfrågan. Starka uttryck från högerpartierna för samförstånd", *Svenska Dagbladet* 27 November 1918, p. 9; see also the report on Clason's speech the same day, p. 10. Comparisons of the democratisation process between Sweden and other countries and how suffrage was restricted by criteria such as tax liability and age also recur frequently in newspapers at this time. For example, there are reports of ongoing reforms in Italy, Germany, Britain, the Netherlands, Denmark, and Finland (see also articles from earlier, e.g. 1910–1917), and sometimes these countries are held up as explicit comparative examples in the argumentation (*Svenska Dagbladet* 27 November 1917, pp. 9–11, and "Reflexioner över läget", *Dagens Nyheter* 25 November 1918, p. 4, where it is noted that Denmark at this time had a voting age of 35.
65. Cited in *Dagens Nyheter* 17 November 1918, p. 12.
66. Riksdagstrycket, *Motion Urtima AK 1918:58*, p. 2, *Motion Urtima FK 1918:20, Motion Urtima AK 1918:55, Motion Urtima AK 1918:56,*

Motion Urtima FK 1918:16, Motion Urtima FK 1918:18, Motion Urtima FK 1918:19.

67. Riksdagstrycket, *Motion Urtima AK 1918:58*, p. 2.
68. Ibid., p. 2, *Motion Urtima FK 1918:20, Motion Urtima AK 1918:55, Motion Urtima AK 1918:56, Motion Urtima FK 1918:16, Motion Urtima FK 1918:18.*
69. Riksdagstrycket, *Motioner Urtima FK 1918:16*, pp. 2–3.
70. Ibid., pp. 3–4.
71. Ibid., pp. 3–4, italics in the original.
72. Ibid., p. 4.
73. Ibid.
74. Ibid.
75. Riksdagstrycket, *Motion Urtima FK 1918:20, Motion Urtima AK 1918: 55.*
76. Riksdagstrycket, *Motion Urtima AK 1918:20*, pp. 9–10.
77. Ibid., p. 1.
78. Ibid., pp. 1–2.
79. Ibid., pp. 3–4.
80. Ibid., pp. 4–5.
81. Ibid., p. 6.
82. "Statsministern om det politiska läget. Regeringens förslag ett mini-miprogram som ej får beskäras i sina enstaka delar", *Svenska Dagbladet* 2 December 1918, p. 7. According to Hamilton, speaker of the First Chamber, Edén had promised to be willing to compromise about the government bill at the Cirkus meeting. "Hugo Hamiltons dagböcker juni–dec. 1918", p. 156. Gunnar Gerdners papper 3:1, Handskriftssamlingen, Uppsala universitetsbibliotek.
83. See note 333.
84. Andrae (1998, pp. 258–260).
85. Ibid., pp. 262–263.
86. In the discussion in the Social Democratic parliamentary group's representative council about which candidates to appoint to the special committee, Värner Rydén and Erik Palmstierna were critical of the nomination of Vennerstrom: "He could cause a lot of difficulty for the left in the committee." The chairman (Branting) explained that "we did not want to be accused of excluding a party". Vennerstrom had said that he would be loyal to the left. See "Protokoll, 25 November 1918", Socialdemokratiska riksdagsgruppen, Protokoll 1918–1923, vol. A 2:2, 1918–1920. Arbetarrörelsens arkiv och bibliotek.
87. Tredje särskilda utskottets protokoll, Andra kammar riksdagens arkiv, Riksarkivet. On women's suffrage, see also draft speeches to the chamber by Prime Minister Carl Swartz, probably from the spring of 1917, in

which the issue of women's suffrage appears to be the least controversial, Maskinskrivet tal, folder, Anteckningar 1917–1920, Släktens Swartz i Norrköping BVb:21, Norrköpings stadsarkiv.

88. Andrae (1998, pp. 260–261). According to Palmstierna, the proposal to form a smaller delegation of ten people came from Swartz. See Palmstierna (1953, p. 253).
89. Palmstierna (1953, p. 253); Andrae (1998, p. 261).
90. Andrae (1998, pp. 261–262).
91. Hugo E. G. Hamilton, *Dagböcker 1917–1919* (Stockholm: Norstedt, 1956), p. 241.
92. Loose sheets, torn out, unnumbered, pp. 1–3, "Anteckningar 1917–1920", Släkten Swartz i Norrköping arkiv, BVb:21, Norrköpings stadsarkiv.
93. Ibid.
94. Ibid., crossing out and emphasis by Swartz.
95. "Särskilda utskottet 3", 3 December 1918, 4 December 1918, Lindmans anteckningsbok, Lindmanska samlingen, Riksarkivet.
96. Ibid.
97. "Högern i utskottet", 1 December. Lindmans anteckningsbok, Lindmanska samlingen, Riksarkivet.
98. "Särskilda utskottet 3", 3 December 1918, 4 December 1918. Lindmans anteckningsbok, Lindmanska samlingen, Riksarkivet.
99. Ibid.
100. "Högern i utskottet", 1 December, Lindmans anteckningsbok, Lindmanska samlingen, Riksarkivet.
101. Ibid.
102. "Utskottet", 4 December, 1 p.m., Lindmans anteckningsbok, Lindmanska samlingen, Riksarkivet.
103. "Hela delegationen", 5 December, 11 a.m., Lindmans anteckningsbok, Lindmanska samlingen, Riksarkivet. Party affiliations added.
104. "Utskottshögern", 6 December 1918, Lindmans anteckningsbok, Lindmanska samlingen, Riksarkivet.
105. Ibid.
106. "Delegationen", 6 December, Lindmans anteckningsbok, Lindmanska samlingen, Riksarkivet.
107. "Tredje särskilda utskottets Protokoll" 8 December 1918, Andrakammarriksdagens arkiv, Riksarkivet.
108. "Utskott", 8 December, 1 p.m., Lindmans anteckningsbok, Lindmanska samlingen, Riksarkivet.
109. Palmstierna (1953, p. 254).
110. Ibid., p. 256.
111. Ibid., pp. 256–257.

112. "Protokoll fört vid gemensamt sammanträde med socialdemokratiska partistyrelsen, Landsorganisationens representantskap och representanter för järnvägsmanna-, lokmanna- och typografförbunden den 7–9 dec. 1918", p. 2, Gunnar Gerdners papper 1:13, Handskriftssamlingen, Uppsala universitetsbibliotek.
113. Ibid., pp. 2–3.
114. "8 dec 1918", Socialdemokratiska riksdagsgruppen 1906–1918, Gunnar Gerdners papper 2:9, Handskriftssamlingen. Uppsala universitetsbibliotek; "Protokoll 8 dec. 1918", Socialdemokratiska riksdagsgruppen, Protokoll 1918–1923, vol. A 2:2 1918–1920, Arbetarrörelsens arkiv och bibliotek.
115. "Högerledamöter i KS", 7 December, 11 a.m., Lindmans anteckningsbok, Lindmanska samlingen, Riksarkivet. Otto von Zweigbergk was a liberal politician and a member of the Constitutional Committee 1918–19 and editor-in-chief of *Dagens Nyheter*.
116. Palmstierna (1953, pp. 256–257).
117. Hamilton (1956, quotation p. 351).
118. Ibid., pp. 342–356. Nils Herlitz, who later became Professor of Political Science and a member of the First Chamber, was the committee secretary; according to him, the statement was written by Hjalmar Branting but significantly changed after objections from the bourgeois side. See Stjernquist (1996, p. 86), citing Nils Herlitz, "Författningsrevisionen 1918", *Svenska Dagbladet* 12 December 1958, and Herlitz, "Från författningsutskottets arbete 1918", *Svenska Dagbladet* 18 December 1958.
119. For a broader context, see Pasi, Ihalainen, *Springs of Democracy*, (Finnish Literature Society / SKS 2017), pp. 381–392.
120. Riksdagstrycket, *Utskottsutlåtande Urtima 1918:1*, p. 25.
121. Ibid., p. 27.
122. Ibid.
123. Ibid.
124. Ibid., p. 30.
125. Ibid., pp. 33–36. See also Riksdagstrycket, *Riksdagens skrivelse Urtima 1918:40*.
126. "Finally, if it is in fact the case that it is not any lack of political maturity among women but their numerical superiority that is frightening, the dissenters have also had material to propose a certain age limit to even out this disproportion. It has been ascertained that, with an age limit of 27, the eligible voters of both sexes would be approximately even in number." See Riksdagstrycket, *Protokoll FK 1918:27*, p. 26.
127. Vennerström, Riksdagstrycket, *Utskottsutlåtande Urtima 1918:1*, p. 117.

CHAPTER 6

Did We Do the Right Thing?

The bill was passed in December 1918. It passed the First Chamber without a vote. In the Second Chamber, Ivar Vennerström called for the raising of the voting age to be rejected. Another left-wing socialist, Ernst Hage, opposed the voting age for county council elections, while one member from the Right wanted to change the proposal to decrease the tax payment threshold. He said he was speaking on behalf of the "settled population", those who would be affected by the people who had not paid their taxes. All these motions were rejected by a large majority.[1] But how great was the consensus on the bill? How did members of parliament actually perceive the compromise and the concessions that had had to be accepted by both sides in the conflict? Opinions differed on the wisdom of the decision. With hindsight, had the committee done the right thing? Was the price of democracy too high? What was the significance of the higher voting ages?

The Social Democrats were quick to celebrate the compromise as a victory. Even before the bill was passed, they published "A manifesto from the Socialists" in *Dagens Nyheter* on 10 December. Some of the triumphant subheadings: "What we have fought for has actually been won" and "The constitutional reform means the democaratisation of Sweden". The rhetoric was high-flown and celebratory. The labour movement's steady and unwavering struggle had made it a great victory, finally succeeding in carrying out a reform which definitively made Sweden democratic:

B. Sandin, *Voting and Eligibility Age in Sweden, 1866–1921*,
https://doi.org/10.1007/978-3-031-95276-0_6

> The executive committee of the Social Democratic Party, the representatives of the Trade Union Confederation, and the Social Democratic parliamentary group issued the following manifesto on Monday evening: Our minds have been filled with great anxiety because of a widespread and well-grounded fear that the Right, relying on its old power privileges, would even now refuse to accede to the demands of a unanimous popular opinion for full democracy, largely in agreement with the unifying minimum programme put forward at the right time by the government. It is all the more satisfactory, then, to be able to announce today that we have succeeded in reaching such an agreement in the Constitutional Committee that in some respects it represents an even more radical democratisation than that proposed by the government, while at the same time fully maintaining the rapid pace in implementing what was one of the best points of the government bill. The reform of municipal suffrage proposed by the Constitutional Committee does not confine itself to equal suffrage linked to tax liability, but also takes the full step towards universal suffrage. The oligarchy entailed by the 40-grade scale will therefore soon be a thing of the past. A new First Chamber will see the light of day as soon as possible, with elections based on universal and equal suffrage."[2]

It was also noted that the age of oligarchy was over in the municipalities and that the thresholds for voting in elections to the Second Chamber were abolished, which meant that the number of working-class voters in cities such as Stockholm, Gothenburg, Malmö, Norrköping, and Linköping more than doubled. The enthusiasm, on the other hand, was not as great and undivided throughout Parliament, although no member was willing to revoke the decision. Most of the criticism came from the Right and from the left-wing socialists.[3] In this chapter I shall describe how the compromise reached in the third special committee in the autumn of 1918 was presented and evaluated by the parliamentary parties before the two chambers voted. Various aspects of the compromise were scrutinised, whether they were good or bad, and who was responsible for the decision to which the parties in Parliament were now bound after the negotiations. A firm decision was essential, but the various actors needed to explain—to the rest of Parliament, to their own party groups, and to their voters—why they had accepted the compromise. This also gave an opportunity to criticise their opponents.

It was therefore a solemn moment, but also an urgent one—for purely practical reasons: the Christmas recess was about to begin. Hamilton, speaker of the First Chamber, wrote irritably in his memoirs that it was high time to make a decision. Members had ordered tickets home for the Christmas holidays.[4] It was thus a special final meeting of Parliament to deal with this sensitive issue before the members boarded the trains to go home. The emphasis in my analysis here is, as before, on how people viewed the significance of age limits in the larger political context.

The Debate on 17 December

In the First Chamber and the Second Chamber, the meetings began with a presentation of the motions submitted to amend the bill. As regards the age limits, Vennerström's and Trygger's motions represented two opposing poles, but of course they also disagreed on other points. The Conservative member Trygger suggested that the voting age for tax-paying residents of the municipality should be the year after reaching 24, provided a person had paid municipal taxes for three years. He did not accept the basis of the compromise that had been reached. Nor did Vennerström, who proposed the right to vote from the age of 21. There was thus in reality, as usual, a five-year difference between left and right in the voting age they demanded, besides which the member on the Right also wanted to retain the criteria of tax liability and paid taxes.[5]

Prime Minister Edén opened the debate in the First Chamber. He noted that the compromise had gone further than the government had suggested. He stressed that the government was prepared for compromises as long as the basic democratic ideas were not distorted. The bill had been a minimum programme and the extension was fully in line with the government's ambitions. Payment of taxes had been the basic premise for the government bill, but it had also included the wives of tax-paying men, yet now the compromise had ended in a proposal for universal suffrage for Swedish citizens. However, Edén did not regret that the voting age had become more restrictive than in the government bill, which is perhaps explicable given that the final result was quite close to the Liberals' and Conservatives' previous stance on the voting age. In this regard, he emphasised that the compromise on municipal suffrage actually lowered the age limit for elections to the Second Chamber.[6]

> We find it fully justified that, in connection with the extension of municipal suffrage to make it universal, the age limit for gaining the right to vote has now been raised by two years, and we accept it all the more gladly in that it presupposed introducing the same age limit for voting in elections to the

> Second Chamber, thus adding a new annual cohort to the electorate of this Second Chamber.[7]

He also accepted the introduction of a poor relief threshold when it came to municipal suffrage, similar to that for parliamentary suffrage since the right to vote now became universal. This meant that those who were permanently dependent on poor relief did not have the municipal right to vote that they otherwise had as citizens. At the same time, it seems somewhat inconsistent that he lamented the remnants of the tax payment threshold.[8] He was also in favour of the expansion of the municipal council as an institution, but his strongest objection was to the higher voting age in county council elections, which he viewed as completely unjustified in relation to the functions of the county councils, given that the electoral procedure was unwieldly and difficult to organise. The government, he argued, would not oppose the proposal for two reasons: firstly because it made the county councils the basis for the First Chamber, and secondly because the higher age limit satisfied those who had demanded guarantees for the special status of the First Chamber:

> with this arrangement the county councils have nevertheless been retained as electoral corporations for the First Chamber, which we must regard as the happiest of the various suggested possibilities with respect to Swedish tradition and Swedish social conditions, and the second reason [for accepting the committee's proposal] is that it has clearly been impossible to find any option other than this special age limit for voting in elections to the First Chamber that would satisfy those who unconditionally demanded special so-called guarantees for the formation of that Chamber.[9]

Subsequently, Edén stressed that such a decision was fully in accordance with the basic principles of democracy, "since the higher age limit for the electors of the First Chamber has a uniform effect for all classes of society and thus differs completely from the monetary scale which has applied hitherto, and which is now finally being abolished".[10]

The exclusion of adult citizens over 21 from voting was described here as compatible with democratic principles because it was the same for all classes of society. We may assume that Edén thought the same about the restriction of voting to the Second Chamber. The crucial factor in the argumentation was that the higher age limit guaranteed the special status of the First Chamber in the Riksdag. However, he deplored the provision in the transitional rules on proxy voting for spouses.[11] Obviously, Edén felt that he wanted to express both praise and criticism of the compromise proposal, which was not entirely in accordance with his ambitions as expressed in previous proposals and in the government bill. At the same time, he was not in a position to question the compromise. It is therefore significant that he marked his dissatisfaction while simultaneously urging unity, and he praised the Riksdag for its ability to carry the issue to a solution.

In the Second Chamber, the debate was opened by Schotte, the minister of civil affairs. He too stressed immediately that the expansion of the reform was in fact entirely in line with the ambitions of the Liberals (the government). He believed, however, that the raising of the age limit did not really have any direct benefits, but it was offset by the lowering of the age limit for the Second Chamber. However, he did have misgivings about the age limit being set at 27 for county council elections. But since this age limit affected everyone equally, Schotte said, there could be no objections on principle. He also thought that the technical solution for the tax payment threshold in municipal elections was less fortunate, but he was satisfied with the solution for the Second Chamber because it affected the rules when people moved to a different municipality. He also expressed some doubt about proxy voting. He observed with satisfaction that the Liberals could now embark on important social reforms, such as the legislation on working hours.[12] The Speaker of the First Chamber, Hamilton, made a speech in which he underlined that this was the end of the Liberals' long struggle for democracy and a victory for the tradition of liberal ideas. He touched upon age limits, but only parenthetically.[13]

The situation was quite different for Trygger, the Conservative member in the First Chamber. He began with a long account of how the situation had degenerated under the pressure of world events, combined with the threatening actions of the government and the left. This was not a reasonable starting point for an objective, sober, and thoughtful discussion.[14] The draft legislation had therefore not undergone sufficient scrutiny. He also criticised the representatives of industry whose statements, "made by eminent men in our economic life, have given the appearance of supporting the government proposal, the meaning and consequences of which they were undoubtedly not in a position to assess objectively and thoroughly".[15]

He pointed out how the proposal seemed ill-considered and carelessly constructed, for example, regarding the consequences for the First

Chamber. It was a rushed job badly executed. He pointed in particular to the form of the age limits for municipal suffrage. The best thing would have been to postpone the matter. There was nothing to rejoice about in this compromise, which involved such great sacrifices on important points. He expressed some satisfaction that the First Chamber would be based on the county councils and a high voting age, albeit not high enough, and he was of course also critical of other aspects of the reform. It was with a heavy heart that he would vote in favour.[16] Other Conservative members echoed his tone. It is also noteworthy that conservatives criticised industry leaders for backing suffrage reform. In the "Gothenburg telegram", the Wallenberg Group had expressed its support for reform as a way to preserve peace in the labour market.

> There has already been talk about the appeal that has come to the leaders of the Right from Gothenburg. I personally believe that it testifies to political immaturity and a certain degree of irresponsibility. Elsewhere, pressure has been exercised more sagely. It has operated without being seen. I would by no means say that this pressure has had an impact on our negotiators, but it has strengthened our opponents and thereby made it more difficult to reach an agreement.[17]

The rift between the different elites and within the Right was obvious. It was also clear from Swartz's speech in the Second Chamber in which, although he expressed some understanding for the concerns and the viewpoints, he defended, without going into detail, the compromise and its ultimately positive significance for the development of society.[18] Other speakers were heard underlining the fear of what the Social Democrats, together with the left-wing socialists, would do when universal and equal suffrage gave them power. It was not the right to vote that was the problem, but the long-term consequences.[19] The tone suggests that the decision was perceived as a capitulation to the demands of the left, with alarming consequences for the future.

The next speaker in the Second Chamber after Schotte was Axel Lindman, the Conservative former prime minister and architect of the legislation of 1907–1909. He questioned the way the suffrage issue was raised in an extraordinary session of Parliament without prior information that it would be on the agenda, but also with reference to the provisions of the constitution. He also pointed out that the political pressure resulting from the international situation, visits from workers' groups, proclamations, the talk of threats and "circumventing the constitution", was significant. He said the government's concession was "unauthorised" and he compared the government's actions to a coup. The result was a poorly prepared, hastily achieved compromise with unforeseeable consequences. The heavy burden of responsibility lay on the Social Democrats, who had tried to undermine the First Chamber. He emphasised that this naturally reflected the actually incompatible positions of the Social Democrats and the Liberals. The outcome was a bad bicameral system. He called the proposal a mockery, a monstrosity, especially in its original form.[20] Age criteria play a key role in his argumentation:

> Already last spring, when the bill was tabled, the government did not want to do anything about the formation of the First Chamber. They refused to take any account of the First Chamber, despite the fact that equal municipal suffrage was introduced and the voting age in municipal elections was kept at 21. Thus, the right to vote for the foundational electoral college of the First Chamber was based on the age of 21, and in this government bill it was the same. It ought to be even more essential here to think of the First Chamber, since the requirement of tax liability has been abolished. But the government paid no heed to this, and so the outcome is a bicameral system which I have described on another occasion as a monstrosity, a mockery of a bicameral system. [...] The very fact that the First Chamber should be based on an age of 21, while the voting age for the Second Chamber is 24, should be sufficient reason to show the truth of what I said here on a previous occasion. However, any idea of raising the age was rejected by the government, and they did not want to hear about it or do anything along those lines.[21]

The crux of his criticism was that the ill-conceived proposal had been aimed at creating equality between the chambers, not a difference in character. Lindman shared the criticism of the compromise. The left had tried by every means to pressure the right to change its position. In the end, the only thing left to fight for was the age limit. He stressed that the age of voting was 28 which was the practical consequence of the voting limit from the age of 27.[22]

> When everything else was given away, this higher age was all that was left. For one must suppose that higher age brings more maturity, more experience, more circumspection on the part of voters when they elect county councillors. [...] I would say that I do not believe that it would have been

> of any benefit if we had made any further progress, and I am pleased that, in the end, it has nevertheless been possible in this case, as a result of the work of the Right in the committee, to achieve the age of 28 for the county councils.[23]

Perhaps a demagogical twist to emphasise the successes of the Right. In other contexts it tended to be the left-wing socialists that underlined that aspect in their critique. That Age was also affected by the parliamentary terms for the First Chamber, which, as he observed with some satisfaction, had now been extended to eight years. This also meant that some voters had to wait up to eight years to vote after reaching the age of 27. He was also pleased that the municipal voting age was raised to 23, although it would have been better if it had been 24, because in the 21–24 age group there were many people without sufficient experience and stability. He deplored the fact that the age level in the compromise had been pressed down to 23. A higher age could not be considered undemocratic, he emphasised, just as the Liberals had done.[24]

He then expressed his discontent with the removal of tax thresholds and his satisfaction that the Right had succeeded in its struggle to retain at least some of these voting restrictions. After this critical and partly aggressive and disappointed analysis, he asked himself why he had now accepted the compromise. He noted that a majority of the population, as reflected in the distribution of seats in Parliament, wanted something other than the right-wing parties. The narrow right-wing majority in the First Chamber would not be able to obstruct the trend in the long run as a consequence of economic development "and its impact on the present source of comfort". He ended by pointing out that this had been a great sacrifice on the part of the Right and that the compromise had gone further than he had wished, but the Right had in this way taken responsibility for the development of society and not abused its position. He finally appealed for consensus and unity, so that the compromise would not be further undermined.[25]

Hjalmar Branting objected to Lindman's description in his speech and emphasised the government's sense of responsibility and the shortcomings of previous governments in the work for reform. Of course, he also drew attention to the global situation and the impossibility of postponing the issue further. The time had come and the government had an obligation to act. He stressed that the government had accommodated the Right instead of being confrontational, as previous right-wing governments had been. They were taking responsibility for the shared future of the nation. Democracy had to be implemented, but it was possible to compromise about the forms.[26] He was also highly critical of the left-wing socialists who denied the value of the changes that had been decided on.

He was pleased that the requirement of paid taxes for voting in elections to the Second Chamber had been abolished and that only a vestige remained of the poor relief threshold. Admittedly, the requirement of paid taxes for municipal suffrage remained, but this was essentially symbolic, not much of a guarantee "beyond this one little stick", the one remaining restriction.[27] The most serious criticism had concerned the age limits, he noted, but on that point he thought a compromise was reasonable when a solution began to emerge. He stressed that the voting age for men to the Second Chamber had been lowered at the same time. That was the significant change.

Branting reasoned in much the same way about the raising of the voting age for county council elections. This was balanced by the removal of the 40-grade scale. Moreover, he said, the right to vote was acquired as young people passed through the different age groups, although with a slight delay. He also pointed out that very few young people under 27 would die before they had an opportunity to vote, so there was little risk that they would be denied the right to vote. The group affected by such excess mortality was so marginal that it was irrelevant.[28] Here, he belittles the criticism of the compromise and renders the Social Democrats' previous position invisible. Later in the debate, the Social Democratic member Engberg returned to the issue of the high age for voting in elections to the county councils and hence the First Chamber. In his view, a large share of those who were unable to vote until they reached the age of 27 would have been disqualified because they would otherwise have been prevented by one or more of the economic thresholds.[29] Branting thus did not take the arguments of the left-wing socialists seriously, but he also opposed the arguments from the Right for a further rise in age limits.[30] Branting went on to argue that this democratic breakthrough would now make it possible to begin to implement social reforms of various kinds.[31]

This was not how the left-wing socialist Fredrik Ström in the First Chamber interpreted the compromise, or Vennerström in the Second Chamber. On the contrary. It was a victory of the bourgeoisie, with the support of the Social Democrats. Ström did acknowledge that universal suffrage was a step in the right direction, but it was the only victory the people had won. He then mentioned the raising of the voting age to 23 and the retained tax threshold. He was also critical of the high voting age limit for elections to the First Chamber and the county councils. The age limits were a class law, he argued, aimed at the working class, which made universal suffrage an illusion, a pretence. It excluded large groups that already had the right to vote and would now lose it. This was all the more serious because the average life expectancy of the working class was so much lower, and thus their potential to influence society was severely limited, just when they were in their prime.[32] It was a long speech, but it is worth quoting because Hjalmar Branting in the Second Chamber took the time to comment on the significance of the age of eligibility in somewhat condescending terms.

> [The compromise] excludes six or seven age classes, comprising first all those under the age of 27 who have hitherto had the right to vote, about 300,000 capable, decent citizens in their prime, and as many more as would now have gained the right to vote; in other words, a total of 600,000 citizens. This, it must be said, is an immense number, a number so large that these age classes and groups of citizens now excluded could in fact tip the balance in many of the elections that will take place. But it is not just that a large number of people are excluded here that makes the principle of universal suffrage, which they claim to have accepted, a mere pretence: it is also the case that, by excluding these age classes, these rules will particularly affect the working class, whose members have an average lower life expectancy and, moreover, in these younger years, take a keener interest in public affairs and especially in political matters than in older years. This may seem like an exaggeration, but it is not, if you consider the situation that in the trade unions and in the workers' educational associations, in their political organisations, in the temperance societies, etc., a very, very large percentage of the members are in fact people under the age of 30.[33]

A higher voting age was thus scarcely something that affected all social classes equally and thus scarcely a democratic reform. These arguments were also heard in the Second Chamber, where Vennerström argued emphatically that the higher age limit for workers meant that they had fewer opportunities to influence society through elections.

> Go to the big factories, go to a town like Eskilstuna, and look at the life expectancy in the groups of industrial people who earn their living in this treadmill! If you know this, you will naturally understand that the rise in the age limit means that for these categories of citizens the number of elections

> in which they have the right to vote will be substantially lower than the number of elections in which the classes who are in a better position are allowed to vote, with their longer life expectancy and therefore greater opportunities to participate in major political decisions later in life.[34]

Vennerström also turned to the Social Democrats and pointed out that the young were the very core of the Social Democratic movement. He warned that this could benefit the undemocratic elements of the movement, leading to a greater hostility to society. He claimed that the young people in Branting's party "even use such strong words as to say that democracy is now assassinating Sweden's mature and awake youth".[35]

Ström moreover perceived the bill as being particularly aimed at the left-wing socialists.

> In particular, it will be an emergency law against the left-wing socialists, who precisely in these age groups between the ages of 20 and 30 have their large, predominant majority of voters, but the whole compromise will bear the mark of an emergency law vis-à-vis one political party, and the very fact that this emergency law has been passed, by all the other parties in mutual agreement, gives this compromise and especially this age provision an even more odious character.[36]

I shall return later to the demographic situation in the growing industrial environments to which this comment alludes. This critical tone in Ström's argumentation also recurs in his overall analysis of the compromise, which in his view was a capitulation of the more right-leaning socialists to the parties on the Right, giving up the demand for a voting age of 21. He also questioned whether it was necessary, given the division of the right and the possibility of a revolt by the working class, which was now left in the lurch by its leaders.[37] However, he predicted that the battle now would be not only about constitutional democracy, but also about economic and social democracy. That struggle would be fought outside Parliament in "the battle in the labour market. That was where the workers would wage their struggle which, although it could enable a bourgeois muster, it would above all be a proletarian and socialist gathering".[38] Slightly later, Dahl, one of the members from the Right who had taken part in the negotiations, admitted that Ström was correct about the nature of the compromise, saying that the Right had made significant gains through the compromise, and defended himself against criticism from other members on the Right. At the same time, he criticised the Liberal Otto von Zweigbergk, who in turn argued that the age limit of 27 was not so important and that it would hardly be possible to retain it for any length of time. Dahl positioned himself against the extreme faction of the Right, which clearly illustrates the division within the Right.[39]

Other speakers emphasised what they saw as some odd consequences of the decision, for example, that a person who was too poor to be taxed was given the right to vote while a person who was lagging behind in his tax payment lost the right to vote. It was better not to be liable for tax. One speaker challenged the logic by which voting from the age of 27 was believed to preserve the distinctive character of the First Chamber. It was rather the age of eligibility of 35 that effectively preserved the elitist character of that chamber.[40]

Karl Johan Ekman, who had been particularly active in the debates during 1917–1918, made a passionate speech in favour of "the higher age" for exerting influence in municipal and county councils because it meant that the personalities became more distinctive: "They evolve; age brings greater insight, greater experience, greater thoughtfulness, and greater stability in all circumstances."[41] As he had done in previous years, he warned of the one-sided dominance of the working class that he judged to be the consequence of the new voting rules. He predicted that the farmers would begin to organise to a greater degree to counter this.[42]

Mr Möller of the Social Democrats contributed to the debate with a broad description of how it would have been possible to achieve a reform by force, if people had wanted. But they had chosen a different path that was more successful. Democracy was implemented in a way that saved everyone great suffering. Now that democracy was secured, the Social Democrats could begin the work of developing socialism. On the matter of age, he stated that there could be no objective justification for any of the suggested ages, 23, 24, 25, or 27. The big problem was the residue of the tax payment threshold, which was the sole concession to the Right that there was reason to regret.[43]

Concluding Reflections

How is this debate to be understood? It showed, first of all, that there was significant conflict within the Right but also, of course, a conflict between the Social Democratic Party and the left-wing socialists. Secondly, there was a hint of a future division between the Social Democrats and the

Liberals and within the Social Democratic Left Party. There were also insinuations of the threat of revolution among the Social Democratic members who spoke in the debate.

Thus, the polarisation was clear, and the members questioned the motives of their opponents. However, the vast majority of those involved finally declared themselves prepared to support the decisions, accompanied by some high-flown words about the nation and the fatherland and hopes for a spirit of cooperation. The members were speaking to more than one auditorium.

The parties differed in their views of age limits. For the Social Democrats and the Liberals this was not an important issue compared to the great successes they had now achieved, but both parties suggested that the higher age limit for the First Chamber and for the county councils was not logical. That view was shared by the left-wing socialists. The Liberals, meanwhile, thought that the voting age of 23 was reasonable for the municipalities and the Second Chamber. The Social Democrats likewise defended the voting age for the Second Chamber and the municipalities, although they indicated a willingness to return to the issue.

It should also be emphasised that the ages of eligibility and the thresholds concerning who could be elected were only exceptionally commented on in the parliamentary debates. This is important because the eligibility requirements, economic thresholds, and age limits were the factors that gave the First Chamber its elitist character in the late nineteenth century. The 1909 decision lowered the economic thresholds, and members of the First Chamber were now remunerated. Yet the age limit was the same as what it had been in 1866. However, the remuneration was significant because it replaced a system in which the members had to support themselves in Stockholm while the Riksdag was in session. This prevented a large majority of the population from seeking election. At the same time, for the Right, the higher voting age in municipal and county council/First Chamber elections was absolutely crucial for defending the special status of the First Chamber.

Not everyone in the Right perceived the defence of the high age limit as a successful strategy; many would have preferred to see a different solution with stricter tax thresholds. The Right also thought that the suffrage issue could have waited until the regular session of Parliament and felt unreasonably hard pressed to reach an agreement and support a decision. They believed that the calm of a spring session would have allowed a better compromise. At the same time, the Right Party leader Lindman's contribution to the debate suggests a clear realisation that the battle was lost in the long run. The left—the Liberals and Social Democrats—would ultimately win the battle over the forms of democracy.

Everyone seems to have been aware that the decision was not well-thought-out and that it was extremely rudimentary, simple but perhaps communicable for precisely that reason. The committee's proposal actually went further than the original bill in terms of universal suffrage (all citizens, not just taxpayers). Still, the Liberals tried to portray this as part of their original strategy. The Social Democrats omitted to mention that they had considered conceding an even higher voting age, perhaps if they had been forced to do so in the negotiations in return for the abolition of the remaining tax payment threshold.

The age criterion was thus absolutely decisive for the form of the compromise, defining the character of the First Chamber and also of the Second Chamber, as well as the relationship between the chambers. The threat to the First Chamber was averted by raising the voting age. Ideas about the younger generation and the different opinions about who was excluded played a significant part in the discussion. There is good reason to consider these views because they affected not only the discussion during the time when the suffrage issue was resolved, but also in the entire period from the late nineteenth century to the democratic breakthrough. The discussion appears to have been occasioned by the demographic trends in the big towns and cities, where young people—unmarried workers—of the very ages excluded by the reform were becoming increasingly numerous. It was hinted early on that the reform was not neutral in social and class terms. The debates during 1917–1918 emphasised population growth in the rural Swedish mill towns. It is therefore necessary to examine demographic trends too. Public statistics give us a good opportunity at least to approach this issue. It is also worth examining other aspects of social development, crime, and family formation.

The parliamentary debate gives us yet another reason to do this. Branting's argument for accepting the compromise was based on the fact that it was better to accept a higher voting age in municipal and county council elections than to retain the 40-grade voting scale, along with a lowering of the voting age by one year, from the year after turning 24 to the year after turning 23 for the Second Chamber. And municipal suffrage was no longer based on tax liability, having become much more universal. Perhaps it was not so serious for the Social Democrats that young people were now excluded until after the age of 27 in the elections to the county councils and the year after the age of 23 in Second Chamber elections, since many people with few votes in municipal elections had not actually used their votes, for various reasons, as we shall see in the following chapter.

Therefore, we may ask how many people were excluded under the new rules in relation to how many could theoretically have voted at the age of 21 with the 40-grade voting scale.

In the following chapter, we shall first look at the political and cultural significance of the suffrage policy, with its demographic and social conditions, and then make some calculations of the different possible outcomes of the voting ages. After that we shall return to examine whether the decision to raise the voting age was socially neutral—whether it affected everyone in the same way. While the parliamentary debates give clear indications that the problem was the working-class population of the big cities and the mill towns, the politicians claimed, as later research has done, that the age criteria were neutral. But was this really the case?

Notes

1. Nils Stjernquist, *Tvåkammartiden: Sveriges riksdag 1867–1970* (Stockholm: Sveriges riksdag, 1996), pp. 85–90, p. 90; for a detailed presentation of the debate see Pasi Ihalainen, *Springs of Democracy*, (Finnish Literature Society / SKS 2017), 280–401.
2. "Ett manifest från socialisterna. Det vi gått i strid för är i verkligheten vunnet. Författningsreformen innebär Sveriges demokratisering", *Dagens Nyheter* 10 December 1918, p. 10.
3. Riksdagstrycket, *Protokoll Urtima AK 1918:17.*
4. Hugo E. G. Hamilton, *Dagböcker 1917–1919* (Stockholm: Norstedt, 1956), p. 350; "Hugo Hamiltons dagböcker juni–dec. 1918", pp. 165–166, Gunnar Gerdners papper, 3:1, Handskriftssamlingen, Uppsala universitetsbibliotek.
5. Riksdagstrycket, *Protokoll FK Urtima 1918:10*, pp. 5–6.
6. Ibid., pp. 5–7.
7. Ibid., p. 7.
8. Ibid., pp. 7–8.
9. Ibid., p. 8. See also Schotte's letter from Easter 1919 in which he emphasises that the only defect in the decision was the voting age of 27 for county council elections, Gerdner, Gunnar, *Krigsslut, vänsterseger och reformer: Axel Schottes "regeringsrapporter" till David Bergström 1918–1920* (Uppsala 1960), pp. 125–134.

10. Riksdagstrycket, *Protokoll Urtima FK 1918:10*, p. 9.
11. Ibid.
12. Riksdagstrycket, *Protokoll Urtima AK 1918:17*, pp. 6–9.
13. Ibid., pp. 33–34.
14. Riksdagstrycket, *Protokoll Urtima AK 1918:10*, pp. 11–13.
15. Ibid., p. 13.
16. Ibid., pp. 13–18.
17. Ibid., p. 20.
18. Riksdagstrycket, *Protokoll Urtima FK 1918:11*, pp. 24–27.
19. Ibid., pp. 30–34.
20. Ibid., pp. 9–13.
21. Ibid., p. 13.
22. Ibid., pp. 12–13.
23. Ibid., p. 13.
24. Ibid., p. 16.
25. Ibid., p. 18
26. Ibid., pp. 20–24.
27. Ibid., pp. 25–27, quotation p. 27.
28. Ibid., p. 28.
29. Ibid., pp. 76–79.
30. Ibid., p. 29
31. Ibid., pp. 30–33.
32. Riksdagstrycket, *Protokoll FK Urtima 1918:10*, pp. 42–46, *Protokoll Urtima AK 1918:17*, pp. 60–71.
33. Riksdagstrycket, *Protokoll FK Urtima 1918:10*, p. 43.
34. Riksdagstrycket, *Protokoll AK Urtima 1918:17*, p. 64.
35. Ibid., p. 66.
36. Riksdagstrycket, *Protokoll FK Urtima 1918:10*, p. 44.
37. Ibid., p. 45.
38. Ibid., p. 46.
39. Ibid., pp. 45–47.
40. Ibid., pp. 64–65.
41. Riksdagstrycket, *Protokoll Urtima FK 1918:11*, p. 3.
42. Ibid., pp. 3–4.
43. Riksdagstrycket, *Protokoll Urtima AK 1918:17*, pp. 44–49.

CHAPTER 7

The Same for Everyone? Demographics in Politics

In the previous chapter I noted that the principle of a high voting age, around 25, in the first decade of the twentieth century became a central issue in the discussion of male suffrage in elections to the Second Chamber. Establishing a high voting age was one of the political measures that came to the fore when Conservative and Liberal interests responded to the demands of Social Democrats and some Liberals to extend suffrage from the age of majority. During the debates in Parliament the Right and the Liberals returned to the question of population development. The discussion from the turn of the century to the 1910s focused on the big cities, but during the period after 1915, when the issue became acute, the debate concerned just as much the young mobile population in smaller industrial towns and communities. It is therefore worth paying attention to demographic development in both short-term and longer-term perspectives. To understand why different political parties and individual members of parliament rallied behind the high voting age, one can delve deeper into the social and economic transformation and into the cultural meanings of the suffrage issue. That is the purpose of this last empirical chapter.

Let us begin with some questions. Did the debates in Parliament about potential voters reflect social changes that also affected how the meaning, opportunities, and problems of democracy were perceived? How did the population under and over the age of 25 differ in social and cultural terms? Did young people in the towns move around, and when did they get married? Did the working class not pay its taxes, and what was crime like in

B. Sandin, *Voting and Eligibility Age in Sweden, 1866–1921*,
https://doi.org/10.1007/978-3-031-95276-0_7

different population groups? Were young people more revolutionary and did they constitute a threat to the state apparatus? These are descriptive questions that need to be answered to enable us to approach the overall question: Was a higher voting age really the same for everyone?

The Well-Behaved Family

The steadily growing political impact of the left in elections, as we have seen in the previous chapters, made suffrage into a burning issue. The analysis of the parliamentary debates shows that the idea that the right to vote should be restricted to people of a more mature age was in fact fundamental to the discussion of how the right to vote should be limited and who should be allowed to participate in general elections. Age was associated with notions that certain groups of the population were married and supporting a family at about the age of 25, had a permanent residence and were experienced, responsible citizens. This also reflects a conviction that family responsibilities were the central foundation for citizenship.[1] Other criteria that were specified concerned this norm of good civic conduct and responsibility, and identified deviations from the social norm: unpaid taxes, failure to take part in military training, a criminal record, dependence on poor relief, and having gone bankrupt.

Bishop Billing's statement in the 1902 parliamentary debate contained a pithy expression of the relationship between the higher voting age and the supplementary requirements. He pointed out the few things on which the members agreed, as he saw it.

> The only thing on which there seems to be general agreement is that, in the event of a change in voting rules, the right to vote should not be granted until the age of 25, provided that the person concerned has not failed in his duties regarding military training and tax liability.[2]

Through an age limit, as envisaged in the discussions, the right to vote in elections to the Second Chamber would be denied to the population under the age of 25: young, unmarried men in towns and cities—and, of course, women. That was the outcome of the parliamentary decision of 1907–1909 as I have shown in the earlier chapters. At the same time, the agreement could be reached if the established voting age of (21) was coupled with income and wealth-graded voting rights and with the requirement of paid taxes, which had the same effect on who could vote at a higher voting age. Thus the right to vote in municipal elections continued to be dependent on income with the 40-grade voting scale, and this indirectly influenced the First Chamber. In rural municipalities, which were a crucial topic of debate, the problem was not the young generation, which was not considered to be so numerous, but the number of votes the companies enjoyed and the influence of particular wealthy individuals. In the urban municipalities this issue had been partially resolved in the 1860s by limiting the number of votes a person could have. The discussion was mainly about the right to vote for tax-paying male citizens, which of course makes it clear that the good and bad norms were also gender- and class-coded from the beginning. They were male and/or female, but also associated with age. Schematically, the norms can be illustrated as dual opposites:

- Responsible–Irresponsible or unable to take responsibility
- Experienced–Inexperienced
- Competent/educated–Incompetent/ignorant
- Mature–Immature
- Well-behaved–Badly behaved/
- Stable–Mobile/not taking responsibility for decisions and their consequences
- Independent–Dependent
- Rational – Emotional

At the same time, these dichotomies were challenged by the women's suffrage movement, which from the early twentieth century fought for equal suffrage for women with reference to their work for the family—the home—which was the foundation for women's contributions to society and the state.[3]

There was also, however, an age norm built into this, because the right to vote was primarily related to women's responsibility for the family and the central role of motherhood. It was thus all about married women. This meant that the personality principle was negotiable within the women's movement as well. However, the qualities of motherhood were perceived as essential for women regardless of marital status. Motherhood and building a family were the very basis of the demands for legitimate political influence expressed by the National Association for Women's Suffrage (LKPR). This was not only a matter for the family but also for the state.[4]

After 1907, municipal laws allowed married female voters to hold municipal office, and married women with an income or property could vote after the changes in tax legislation in 1908, but within the framework set by the 40-grade scale.[5] Here too, then, a class perspective can be discerned. People with small incomes found it difficult to make their voices heard in the municipalities, despite the voting age of 21, but they were able to increase their influence gradually.[6] The Social Democratic women, like the Social Democratic Party from 1909, argued for a voting age of 21 for all elected bodies for each individual, while the National Association for Women's Suffrage and the Liberals demanded the right to vote on the same terms as men, that is, 25, and with graded votes.[7]

The Social Democrat Kata Dalström spoke at a suffrage meeting in Stockholm in 1911, where the following critical comment was reported, "In addition she pointed out the damage caused by the raising of the age threshold from 21 to 24 years, depriving thousands of young people of their right to vote." She also protested against the "hassle thresholds" and the effect they had in towns and rural areas. The poor relief thresholds would affect women the most and the tax payment threshold would hit men hardest. She also emphasised that the struggle of working-class women was different from that of the upper-class women, which meant that they could not be in the same organisation. "They are primarily suffragists – we are first and foremost social democrats, and only secondly suffragists." The meeting ended with a call for full political equality with men and the removal of voting restrictions.[8] In addition, before the 1911 elections, the differences between the left and the moderate suffragists sharpened before the 1911 elections when it was decided that the movement would support the parties that worked for women's suffrage.[9]

The umbrella organisation for women's suffrage, the LKPR, was largely driven by women from the bourgeoisie. After what was called "Wicksell's discovery", the movement also propagated that married women had the right to vote even if they had only a small income, and that married women should exercise their right, and their policy was that women should be able to vote on the same terms as men.[10] From that perspective the emphasis on marriage and responsibility for the family ignored the unmarried women who also earned their own wages and paid taxes and thus had municipal suffrage, albeit limited, and women without income.

There were also critical perspectives in the debate around the turn of the century that formed an important background to the interest in the norm of the (well-behaved) family in the suffrage debate. In parallel to suffrage, several other political topics were hotly debated, issues in which the male breadwinner was critically scrutinised. This concerned men's responsibility for bringing up children, the fact that men visited prostitutes, that women helped to support the family through paid work, and that men did not always provided for their children, but evaded their responsibilities as the breadwinner. In these debates too, there was a criticism not only of married men, but also of unmarried fathers and self-supporting women. Negligent breadwinners became an established and critiqued notion.

During these years there was criticism—and finally repeal—of the infanticide ordinance (1918) according to which a search could be conducted for the fathers of illegitimate children. A series of child laws were created which allowed the state to support single mothers in various ways and to act *in loco parentis.* The state assumed the parental role when the biological parents or providers did not meet expectations. In this process there was also a review of the legislation on fostering and adoption. Prostitution, child welfare, and marriage as an institution were subjects of broad and critical debate, as was the way in which working-class families looked after their children. To a large extent the discussion involved a critical scrutiny of working-class men, as well as unmarried mothers.[11] LKPR, the middle-class-dominated women's suffrage movement, was also engaged in issues such as prostitution and legislation on working hours. For these women, the suffrage issue was embedded in a broader social commitment to create a society in line with the bourgeois view of the family, but it also set its stamp in different ways on other parts of the labour movement and the temperance movement.[12]

Yet neither does the image of the family as a purely male-dominated sphere match the ideals of the time. Change was coming. According to the law of 1734, a married woman was wholly subordinate to her husband, but with the reforms of marriage legislation in 1915 and 1920, marriage became a union between two fully equal parties. Civil marriage was introduced in 1908, and in 1921 married women were made legally competent. It also became easier to dissolve a marriage. Men and women had the same rights and obligations within a marriage. Ownership was individualised which was also reflected in the design of the tax legislation and which meant that more married women were able to vote as has been pointed out above. The discussion of the right of married women to vote in the period from 1904 to 1910 was largely based on premises of civil law which established that women had entire disposal of their own income and property within marriage.[13] At the same time as this breakthrough for a more individualistic attitude, gender differences and the view of the family as the foundation for the construction of society were accentuated. In the words of Christina Carlsson Wetterberg, "women became the bearers of modern society's conflict between the need for individual freedom and rights on the one hand, and the need for the care and stability that the family continued to represent on the other."[14] This discussion had begun in the late nineteenth century and was partly conducted within the framework of a joint Nordic commission which led to different legislation in the different Nordic countries. In Sweden the marriage legislation was amended in 1915 and 1921.[15]

At the same time, the women's movement vigorously and explicitly questioned the notion that women's responsibility in the family meant incompetence, ignorance, or lack of independence. They also stressed that this was a responsibility for society that went beyond the individual family, it was a central contribution to the nation[16] This was pointed out by the women's suffrage movement but also, for example, by Liberals in Parliament such as Theodor Adelswärd and Social Democrats such as Carl Lindhagen. In the debate in 1902, Sigfrid Wieselgren pointed out that women were generally both more responsible and less criminal than the men who the raising of the voting age would exclude. From that perspective, it was illogical to exclude women from the right to vote, he said.[17]

Through high age requirements for the right to vote, it was thought that problems linked to the younger and unmarried population could be avoided, along with other social problems typical of urban environments. In the very first debate, these links were cited by Hjalmar Hammarskjöld to justify his proposal of a higher voting age, and before him the Liberal leader of the National Coalition Party, Sixten von Friesen. There were several dimensions to the problems, as indicated by a reading of the parliamentary debates; these reflect the fact that the population of the towns and cities was growing with it an increasing political influence for urban environments. In addition, the discussion concerned the fact that the population cohorts in their twenties had not started a family and showed signs of greater criminality and other deviations from the norms. Let us therefore first look more closely at what the population statistics can say about the growth of cities and the proportion of unmarried and married people, and then return to the youth issue.

Urban, Unmarried, and Mobile

The urban share of Sweden's population increased dramatically between 1870 and 1913. In 1870 the population of the towns made up about 13 per cent of the total in Sweden. In 1890 the population of the towns was already about 25 per cent of the total, and by 1913 it had reached 40 per cent. After the big cities—Stockholm, Gothenburg, Malmö, Norrköping—there were a whole series of small towns with up to 30,000–35,000 inhabitants and a number of smaller mill towns with a population employed in industry. In agriculture there was no corresponding increase in the number of people employed. Farmers and agricultural labourers, according to the economic historian Arthur Montgomery, seem to have been about the same number in 1910 as 40 years earlier, and during this period there was a sharp decline in the proletarian underclasses in the countryside. This is explained by industrialisation and emigration. When emigration declined, this also had consequences for the towns that grew with the migration from the countryside.[18] This affected the size of the young population aged 25–30 especially. In this section I present the population development in towns, with the emphasis on the size and marital status of the different age groups. It is also worth pointing out that the development of the towns towards the end of the nineteenth century was also an expression of the demographic transformation that fundamentally reshaped society, social structures in Sweden. The suffrage issue was coloured by all this.[19]

The vigorous population growth in the first half of the nineteenth century and the declining child mortality had its main impact on the towns after the 1890s. After the turn of the century it became even more tangible. This was a recurring theme in the Central Bureau of Statistics' reflections on "congestion in the labour market".

> Throughout the nineteenth century the 1870s show by far the largest absolute increase in the number of people in midlife or, as can be seen from the table, 286,000 people. The troublesome congestion in the labour market resulting from this triggered the great emigration of the 1880s, and for that reason the increase in the working-age population in that decade was only 16,000. Since then, however, the growth has increased again; in the 1890s it was, one could say, about normal or 216,000 people, and during the decade 1901–10 it was slightly larger than normal, 265,000. In the last decade, 1911–20, however, the increase in the population of working age was of an unforeseen size. The age group in question grew during this

> decade by no less than 374,000 people, an increase of 113%. The reason can be found partly in the reduced emigration and partly in the improved mortality.[20]

The report on the 1920 census states that this had had major consequences for young people in particular. Between the ages of 20 and 30 the younger generation had great difficulty in starting a family and in asserting themselves in the labour market.

> What this large increase in the number of hands seeking work in the last decade means for the individual in the congestion of the labour market goes without saying. Especially for the young, who have to carve a path for themselves, start a family and a home, the difficulties are currently great. [...] The important ages from 20 to 30 have grown by close to 100,000 people in the last decade, corresponding to 26.1% of the whole population during the time in question, and from 35 to 45 by no less than 115,000, or 30.2% of the entire increase.[21]

The report notes that the age cohorts immediately under this, those aged 10–20, were smaller, suggesting that population growth was slowing down. It goes on to stress that the size of the youth group seemed different in different towns and was clearly different for women and men. The explanations were obvious: "different birth rates, slower or faster population growth, more industry with mainly male or mainly female workers, an educational institution or garrison located in the city, etc." (Fig. 7.1)[22]

What did this mean, then, for this group of young people who were in danger of being excluded from the democratic processes? From the census of 1920, it appears that in many towns the young generation had difficulty establishing themselves. It was thus these whose right to vote was now restricted. This concerned the three big cities but also the group of towns listed as largest in the public statistics.[23] Additionally, the surplus of women in the towns was significant, which affected the elections after the decisions of 1918–1921.

> According to the above-mentioned data, there were 319,217 men and 406,116 women among those entitled to vote. In relative terms, this represents 44% and 56% respectively of the total. The female electorate is thus much more numerous than the male one. For 1,000 men entitled to vote, there are no fewer than 1,272 women in the towns altogether. However, the variations in this respect between different towns are quite naturally large, as

Fig. 7.1 Workers at the Fritsla weaving mill after completing their day's work. In rural small towns, young newcomers could become a dominant element in the population. At the end of the nineteenth century, the mill had 1000 employees and was Västergötland's largest workplace. (Source, Unknown photographer. Arbetarrörelsens arkiv och bibliotek)

> can be seen from a glance at the table showing the distribution of persons entitled to vote in towns of different sizes, presented on the next page. In the big cities, thus, the female electorate is a very large majority. For every 1,000 men entitled to vote, there are 1,326 women, while in the larger towns (those with 5,000–10,000 inhabitants) the proportion of the sexes is only 1,219 women to 1,000 men. In the whole country there were only 8 towns at the time of the election in question where the number of male voters outweighed that of women, and of these towns all but Haparanda are recent formations.[24]

Towns and urban communities grew vigorously during the last decades of the nineteenth century. Big cities like Stockholm, Gothenburg, and Malmö increased their population by 30–40 per cent between 1860s and 1910, but smaller towns also experienced strong population growth, as Table 7.1 illustrates.

Table 7.1 Population of the biggest cities and towns 1800–1910

Year	*1865*	*1890*	*1900*	*1910*
City				
Stockholm	133,361	246,454	300,624	342,323
Gothenburg	43,346	104,657	130,619	167,832
Malmö	21,720	48,504	60,857	83,375
Norrköping	22,032	32,826	41,008	46,416
Gävle	12,138	23,484	29,522	35,203
Helsingborg	6602	20,410	24,670	33,348
Örebro	8713	14,547	22,013	30,098
Eskilstuna	5088	10,909	13,663	28,371
Karlskrona	15,977	20613	23,955	27,448
Jönköping	9262	19,682	23,143	26,971
Uppsala	9815	21,511	22,855	25,960
Borås	3218	8106	15,837	21,541
Lund	9437	15,023	16,621	20,139

Source: *Statistisk tidskrift* 1912

Before we examine the development in Stockholm, Gothenburg, and Malmö from 1880 to 1920 more closely, let me illustrate the difference between Stockholm and the country as a whole in a population pyramid. The population pyramid for Sweden in 1900 shows that the size of cohorts from the youngest to the oldest was falling, as expected. To some extent, the effects of emigration are also noticeable in the cohorts from 25–35, which stands out as slightly smaller than expected. The contrast with the population pyramid for Stockholm, is striking. It was precisely population groups from roughly 20–30 years of age, with a large proportion of unmarried person, that was largest, differing from the national age group relationships, as shown in Fig. 7.2 below.

As Table 7.2 demonstrates, the cohorts 20–30 are more significant in Stockholm than in the countryside. It is also important that the cohorts of infants in Stockholm were less prominent and significant, while in the towns, generally, those cohorts were larger than in Stockholm.[25]

With this background, it is essential to take a closer look at the population development not only in Stockholm but also in Gothenburg and Malmö as well as in some of the smaller cities with strong population growth as demonstrated in Table 7.1. Was it only a Stockholm phenomenon or did it also affect other urban areas in a way that can explain the

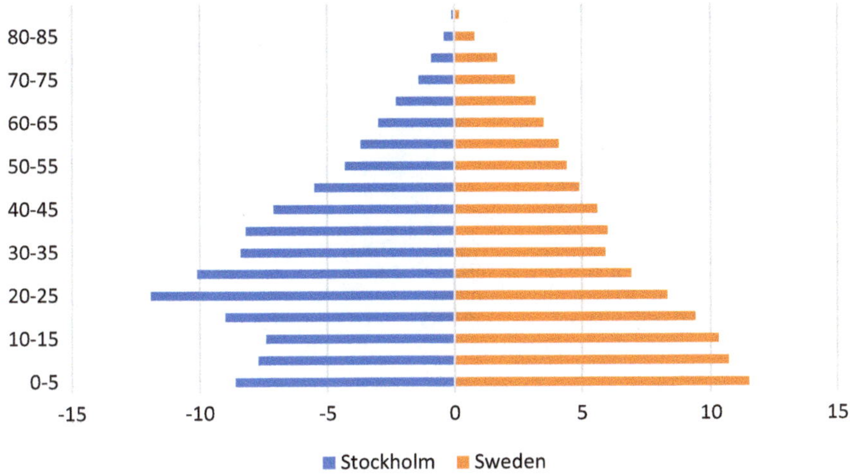

Fig. 7.2 The population of Sweden and Stockholm in 1900 by age groups (percentages). (Source: Kungl. Statistiska centralbyrån, Bidrag till Sveriges officiella statistik A, Befolkningen: Tredje avdelningen 1900 (Stockholm: P.A. Norstedt & Söner, 1910), s. 66–68. Tabell 4 och 5)

focus in the parliamentary debates on the young, unmarried, and urban population?

The age distribution that characterised Stockholm's population development from 1870 to 1920 can also be observed in Gothenburg and Malmö, which developed in a similar way but with a certain lag. In all three cities, significant groups of people were in their twenties throughout the period. But it was mainly from 1900 onwards that these age groups set their distinctive stamp on the demographic profile. The data come from censuses from 1870 to 1920 (Figs. 7.3, 7.4, and 7.5).

The share of unmarried men and women under 30 was also a large majority. Only in the age cohort 30–35 was the proportion of married and unmarried men and women together roughly equal, although fewer women married.[26] As Table 7.3 shows, this was a general phenomenon, but it was even more noticeable in urban environments such as Stockholm (Table 7.4).

The large unmarried population was perceived in the statistics analyses as showing that things were not quite right. Young adults had difficulty obtaining a reasonable income and they had not been able to emigrate

Table 7.2 Age distribution per 1000 inhabitants in rural areas and Stockholm

Age	*1806–1855*	*1880*	*1890*	*1900*	*1910*	*1920*
	Countryside					
0–5	129	124	115	118	115	10
5–10	110	110	112	111	110	102
10–15	102	99	105	107	105	105
15–20	93	100	92	94	94	96
20–25	85	83	69	77	76	82
25–30	75	67	62	64	66	70
30–35	70	60	55	55	61	63
35–40	62	58	51	57	55	58
40–45	56	52	50	54	48	54
45–50	50	52	45	48	51	49
50–55	45	48	45	44	47	42
55–60	38	47	44	42	41	43
	Stockholm					
0–5	84	97	111	85	86	62
5–10	69	68	83	77	68	71
10–15	70	66	68	74	63	78
15–20	81	84	72	89	81	102
20–25	110	117	104	119	119	106
25–30	113	110	113	101	114	101
30–35	104	90	101	84	94	87
35–40	87	80	78	82	72	74
40–45	72	70	61	71	62	58
45–50	57	60	53	55	60	57
50–55	47	46	45	43	52	48
55–60	35	39	37	37	39	46

Source: Kungl. Statistiska centralbyrån, Folkräkningen den 31 december 1920, III (Stockholm: P. A. Norstedt & Söner, 1926), pp. 20–21

either, according to the compilation of population statistics in 1910, which noted

> the still very high number of unmarried adults (over the age of 15) [...] For the year 1910 the adult unmarried population is now found to number as much as 294,310 per million, and, as far as is known, this group of the population has never before been so numerous in our country. This can naturally be attributed partly to the fact that emigration in several recent years has been comparatively small. The unmarried young people who used to emigrate now stayed at home for a few years – yet without finding in their home country much more opportunity than in the past to marry.[27]

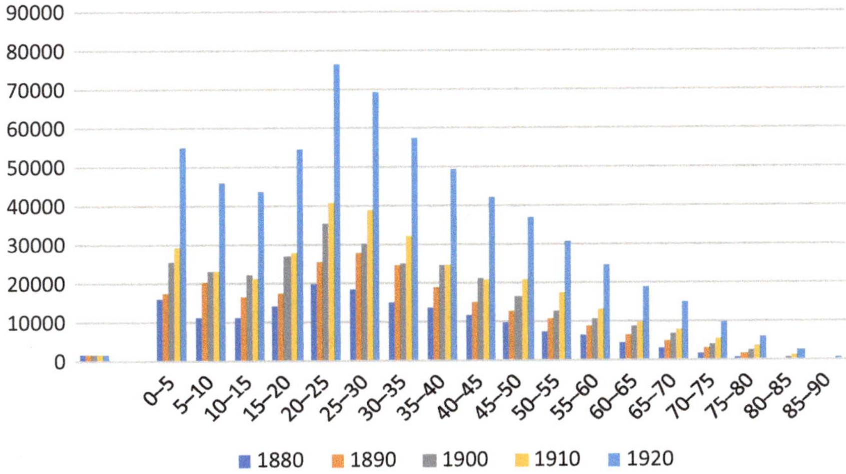

Fig. 7.3 Population development in Stockholm 1880–1920 by age group. (Sources for Figs. 7.3, 7.4 and 7.5. Kungl. Statistiska centralbyrån, BiSOS 1870 A, Befolkningen: Tredje avdelningen (Stockholm: P. A. Norstedt & Söner, 1871), s. 1, BiSOS 1880 A, Befolkningen: Tredje avdelningen (Stockholm 1881) s, 1, tabell 1, BiSOS 1890 A, Befolkningen: Tredje avdelningen (Stockholm 1892), s. 73–75, Tabell 5, BiSOS A, Befolkningen: Tredje avdelningen 1900 (Stockholm 1991), s. 68–70, tabell 3, SOS, Folkräkningen den 31 december 1910: II. Folkmängdens fördelning efter kön, ålder och civilstånd (Stockholm 1913), s. 10–17, SOS, Folkräkningen den 31 december 1920: III. Folkmängden efter ålder, kön, civilstånd och födelseort (Stockholm: P. A. Norstedt & Söner, 1926), s. 18–25, tabell 2)

As we have seen above, the young and unmarried generation moved to the towns, and the population increased in certain age groups.

The formation of families within the working class in the towns and cities was an issue that also left its mark on social settings in the nineteenth century and created the concept "Stockholm marriage". During the nineteenth century, it affected, among other things, legislation on poor relief and business as well as the development of schools and laws on child labour, as previous research has shown.[28] Stockholm led the development and exerted a powerful attraction on younger immigrants.

The population of the cities was consequently not self-reproducing. The large population increase in the early nineteenth century created waves of large population growth in certain periods. At the end of the nineteenth century it was the grandchildren of the generation of 1815–1835 who moved to the towns or emigrated. Their presence in the

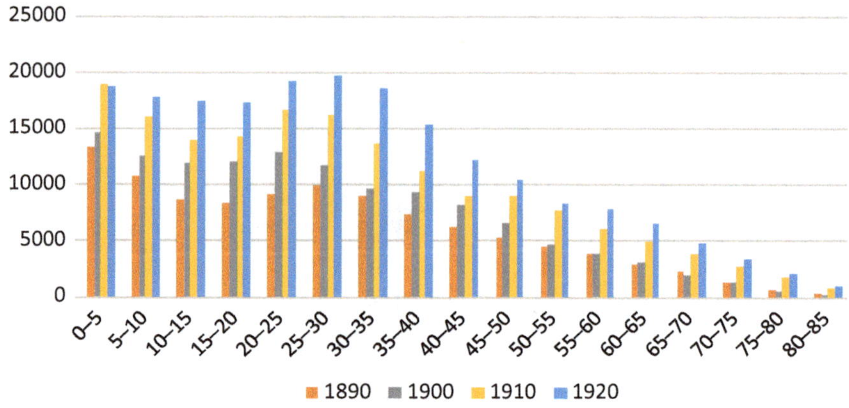

Fig. 7.4 Population development in Gothenburg 1890–1920 by age group. (Sources: see Fig. 7.3)

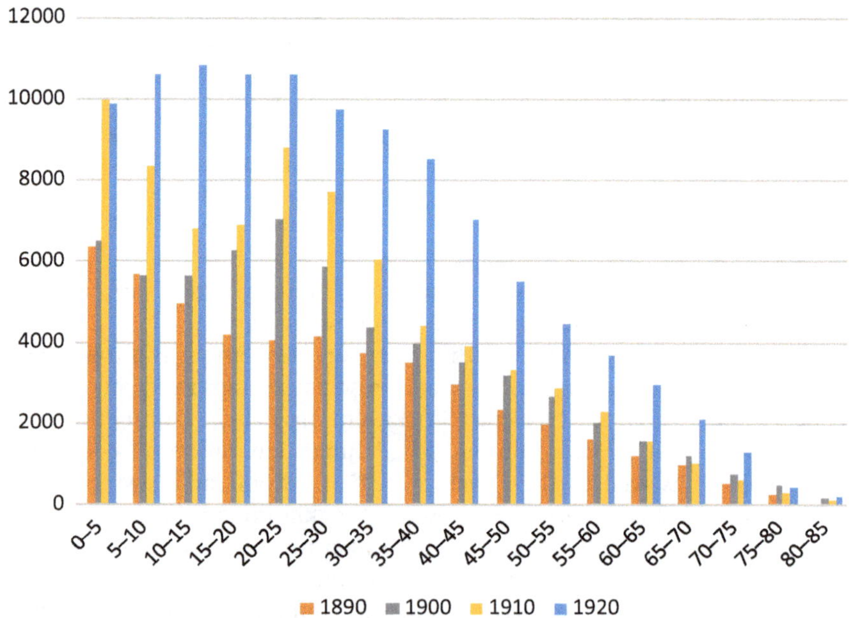

Fig. 7.5 Population development in Malmö 1890–1920 by age group. (Sources: See Fig. 7.3)

Table 7.3 Percentage of married in different age groups in Sweden 1900–1910

	Unmarried men		*Unmarried women*	
Age	*1900*	*1910*	*1900*	*1910*
15–20	99.98	99.98	98.87	98.89
20–25	91.89	93.19	80.41	80.24
25–30	60.60	61.97	51.52	51.37
30–35	35.26	36.34	34.83	34.69
35–40	23.03	24.24	26.50	27.24
40–45	17.06	18.23	22.40	21.53
45–50	13.46	15.26	19.39	19.83
50–55	10.19	13.31	18.09	18.11

Source: Kungl. Statistiska centralbyrån, *Folkräkningen den 31 december 1910*, II, p. 47

Table 7.4 Percentage of married people in the church-registered population of different ages in Stockholm 1870–1910

Year	*Of the total population*	*Population above 15*	*20–25*	*25–30*	*30–35*	*35–40*	*40–45*	*45–50*		*65 over*
Men										
1870	28	39	4	23	46	58	63	65	63	50
1880	28	38	4	29	50	62	67	67	66	55
1890	30	42	5	31	55	65	71	71	68	57
1900	30	41	5	29	54	66	72	72	70	57
1910	32	42	5	32	53	64	73	73	71	57
Women										
1870	23	28	11	26	40	48	44	44	28	9
1880	24	30	11	30	44	50	45	45	32	11
1890	26	34	12	33	47	54	51	51	37	15
1900	26	33	12	31	45	52	53	53	40	17
1910	27	33	13	34	46	52	51	51	42	19

Source: Kungl. Statistiska centralbyrån, SOS, Folkräkningen den 31 december 1910: II, s. 47. The population of married 10-20 was below 1 per cent.

towns was the background to the suffrage debates and was the force behind the controversy about young people's suffrage and democracy. The marriage age and the proportion of married people in the population in Stockholm, Gothenburg, and Malmö also show that they married late, and many of them not at all.

The discussion in Parliament about marriage as a reasonable measure of social stability and civic virtue could reflect a reaction to the share of the population that was not married. It may be worth recalling that in 1900 the discussion about the voting age was raised in earnest in Parliament, and that 1910 was the year after the voting age for men in elections to the Second Chamber was raised to 24, and 1920 was the year before the voting age for the Second Chamber was set at 23 for men and women and was raised to 27 for county councils and the First Chamber. The population figures for Stockholm, Gothenburg, and Malmö are shown in Figures 7.6, 7.7, and 7.8. The data are divided into unmarried men (including formerly married men) and married men, and unmarried women (including formerly married women) and married women.

An analysis of census data on the population of smaller towns shows that the pattern was similar as the bigger cities, but not everywhere. The 1910 census gives an overview of the age distribution of the population in towns (Fig. 7.9).

The censuses illustrate how all cities and towns, even small ones, were affected by the range of age groups mentioned in the parliamentary debates, but with different impacts depending on the industrial structure and the presence of military or civil educational institutions. The different urban centres were also in slightly different phases of development. Stockholm had been affected first, ever before the 1870s, after which Gothenburg and Malmö were affected in a similar way from the 1890s. From 1900, the group of people in their twenties was an important feature of these cities. The statistics from 1910 regarding the smaller towns show similar patterns in many places, and from 1920 additional towns were noticeably marked by the younger and unmarried age groups. It is also clear that the difference between men's and women's employment in industry had an impact. Examples of population pyramids provide a good illustration of these processes in a small sample of towns. The point is not that these places were completely dominated by young unmarried adults, but that they were frequent enough and developing along such directions all over the industrialising country to be cited as a problem in parliamentary debates (Fig. 7.10).

Judging by the parliamentary debate, politicians were aware of the size and effects of these population groups and took them into consideration in their proposals for changes in suffrage. Other contemporaries, such as Gustav Sundbärg, the demographer and author of the great inquiry into emigration, were convinced of the importance of demography for political

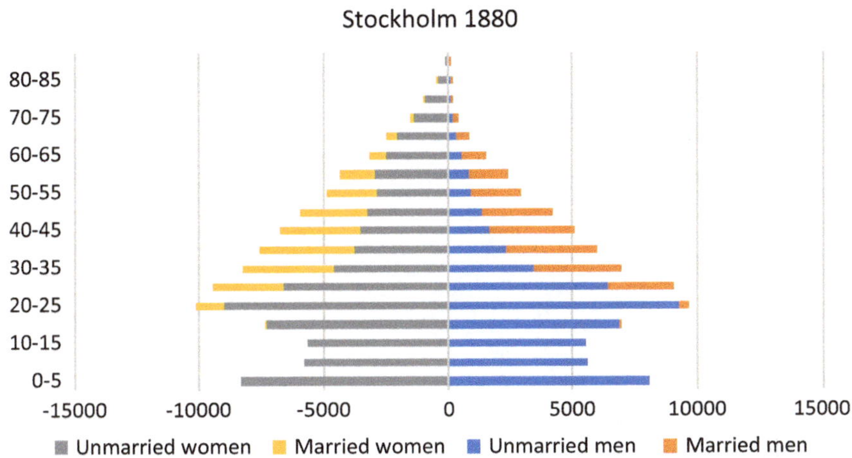

Fig. 7.6 a. Stockholm 1880, age groups, gender, marital status. b. Stockholm 1890, age groups, gender, marital status. c. Stockholm 1900, age groups, gender, marital status. d. Stockholm 1910, age groups, gender, marital status. e. Stockholm 1920, age groups, gender, marital status. (Sources for Figs. 7.6, 7.7, and 7.8: Kungl. Statistiska centralbyrån, BiSOS 1870 A, Befolkningen: Tredje avdelningen (Stockholm: P. A. Norstedt & Söner, 1871), s. 1,BiSOS 1880 A, Befolkningen: Tredje avdelningen (Stockholm 1881) s, 1, tabell 1, BiSOS, 1890 A, Befolkningen: Tredje avdelningen (Stockholm 1892), s. 73–75, Tabell 5, BiSOS A, Befolkningen: Tredje avdelningen 1900 (Stockholm 1991), s. 68–70, tabell 3,SOS, Folkräkningen den 31december 1910: II. Folkmängdens fördelning efter kön, ålder och civilstånd (Stockholm: P. A. Norstedt & Söner, 1913), s. 10–17, SOS, Folkräkningen den 31 december 1920: III. Folkmängden efter ålder, kön, civilstånd och födelseort. (Stockholm: P. A. Norstedt & Söner, 1926), s. 18–25, tabell 2)

development. The higher birth rate in the nineteenth century had caused older institutional forms and rules to burst. In 1902 Sundbärg wrote:

> The cohorts of the years 1816–1835 are more remarkable in our population statistics than all the others. [...] The effect of this can be detected in a great many areas, far beyond what is usually conceived. When they reached school age, these cohorts filled all the schoolrooms and made education a burning

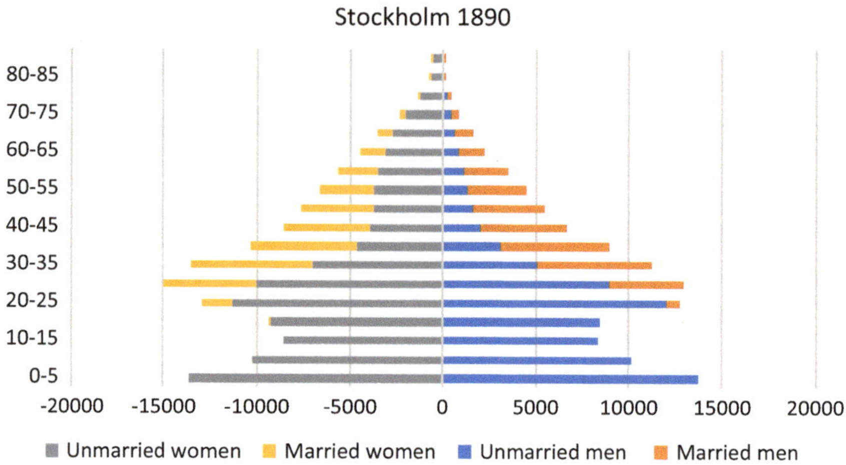

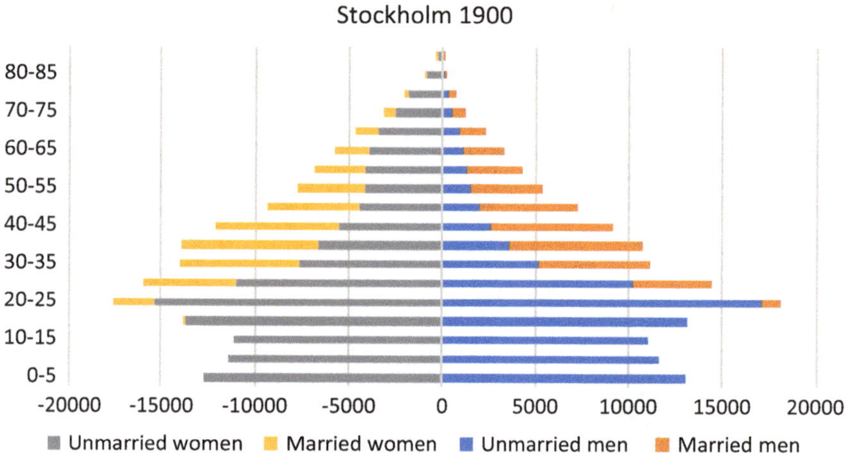

Fig. 7.6 (continued)

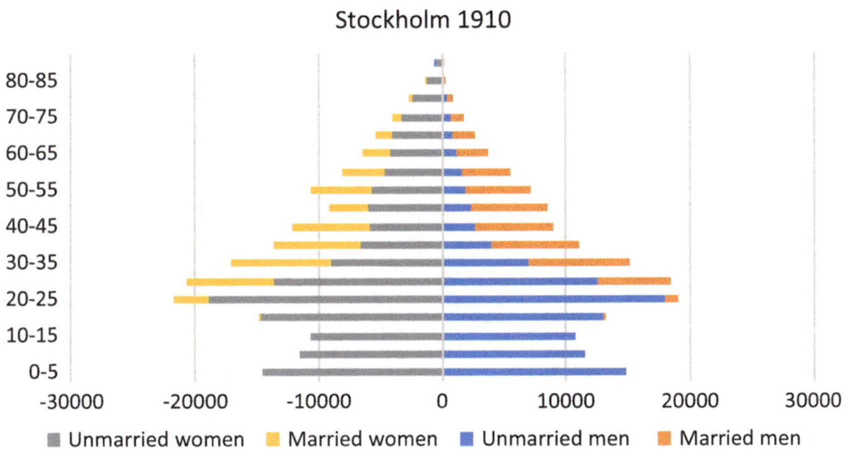

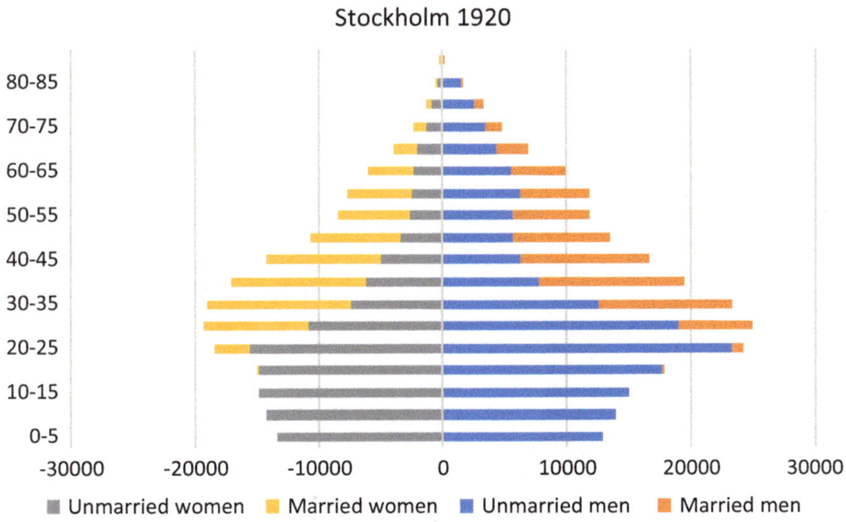

Fig. 7.6 (continued)

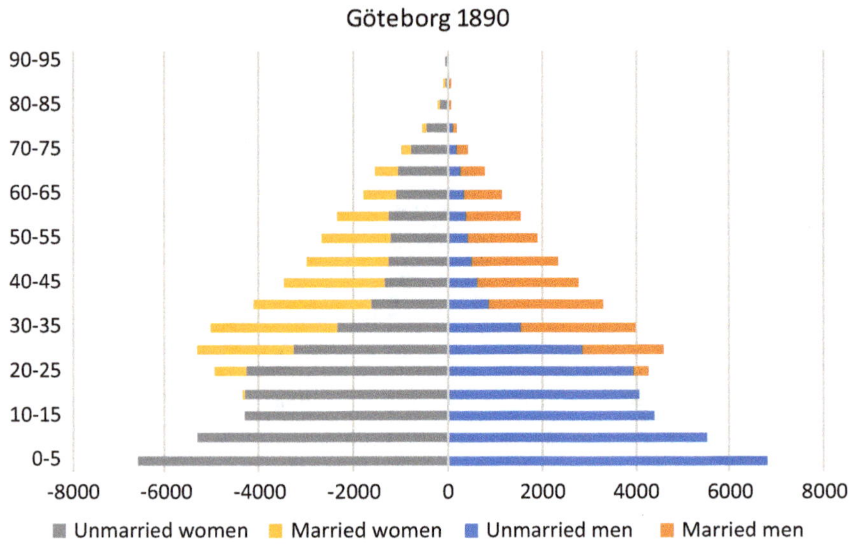

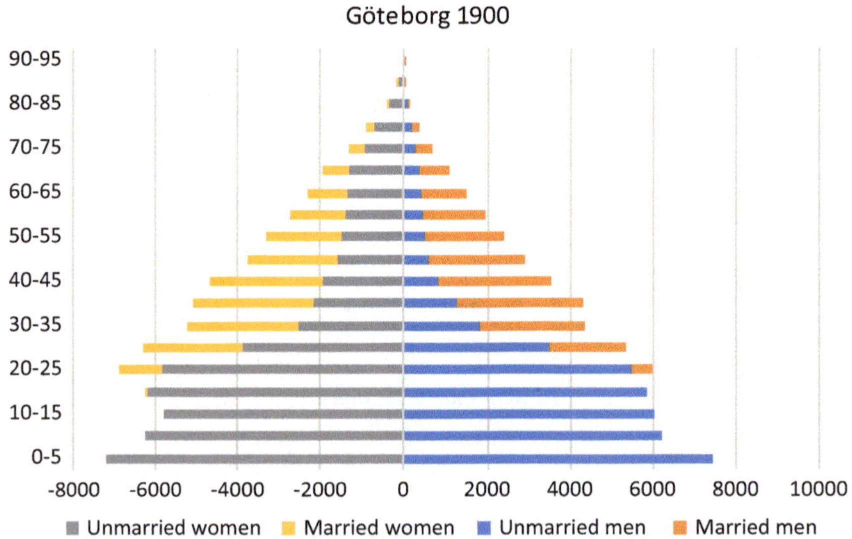

Fig. 7.7 a. Gothenburg, 1890, age groups, gender, marital status. b. Gothenburg, 1900, age groups, gender, marital status. c. Gothenburg, 1910, age groups, gender, marital status. d. Gothenburg, 1920, age groups, gender, marital status

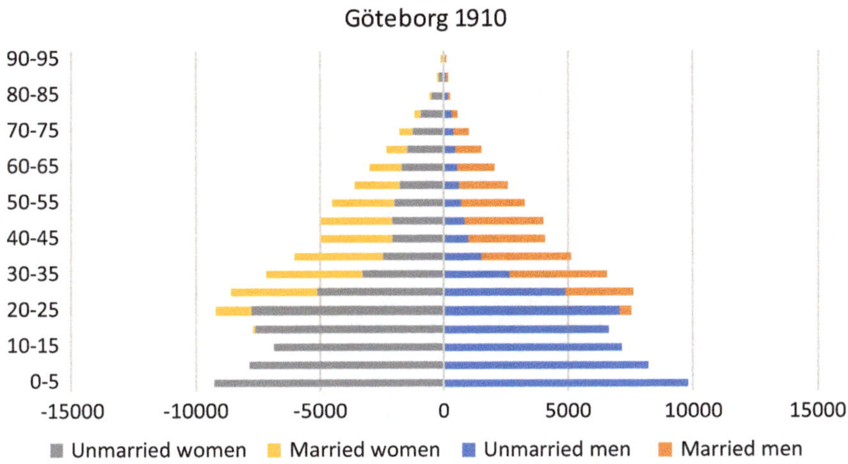

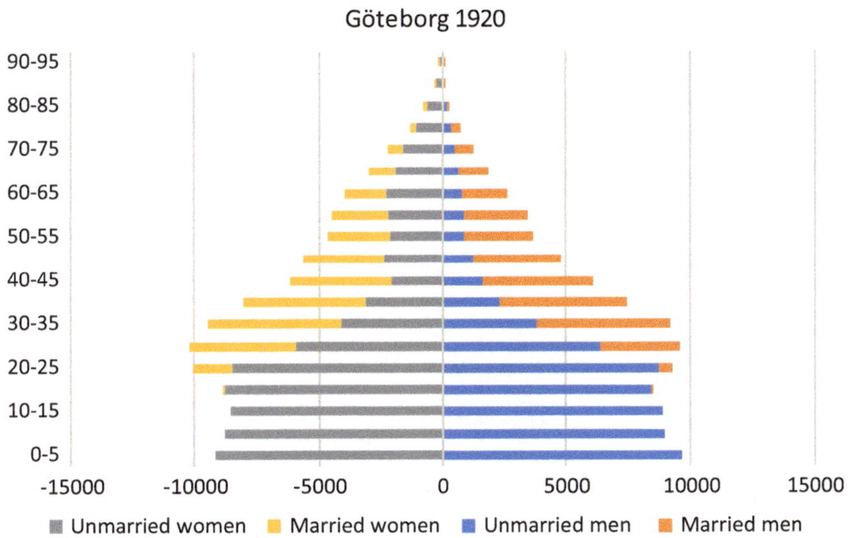

Fig. 7.7 (continued)

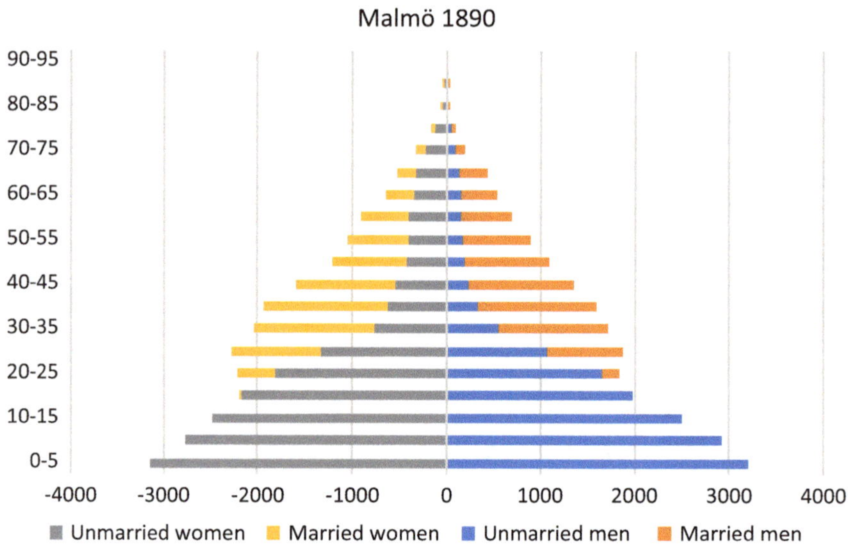

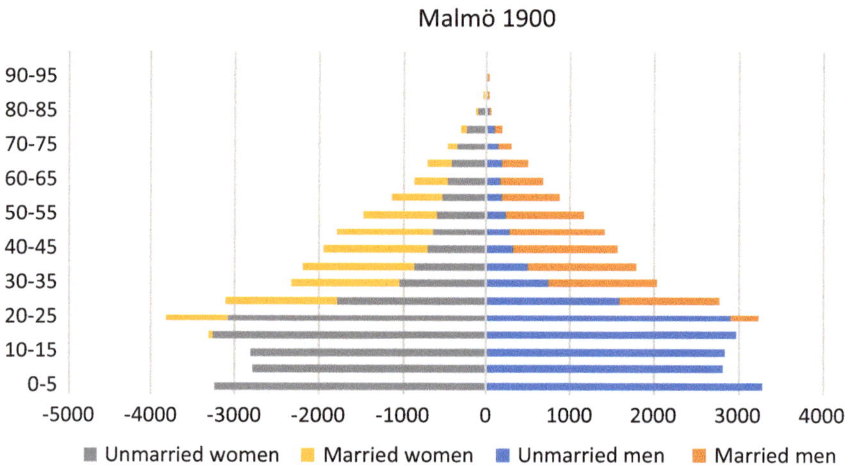

Fig. 7.8 a. Malmö 1890, age groups, gender, marital status. b. Malmö 1900, age groups, gender, marital status. c. Malmö 1910, age groups, gender, marital status.d. Malmö 1920, age groups, gender, marital status

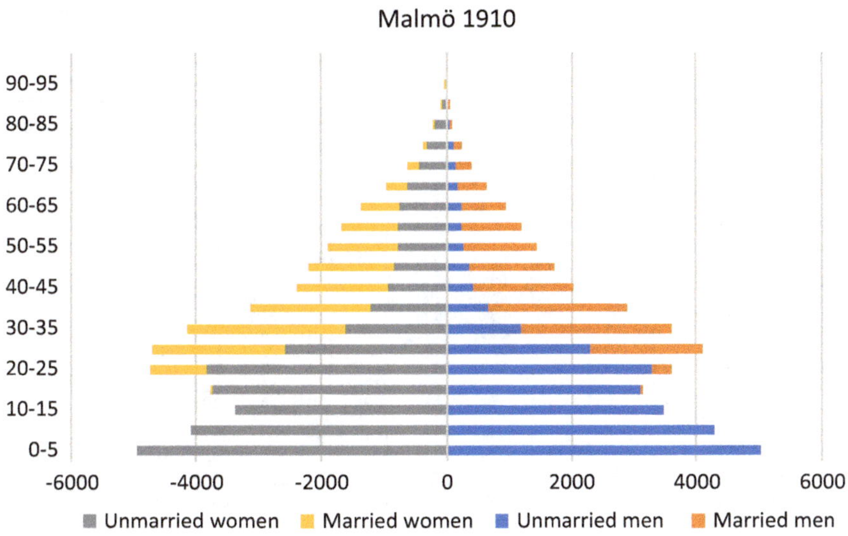

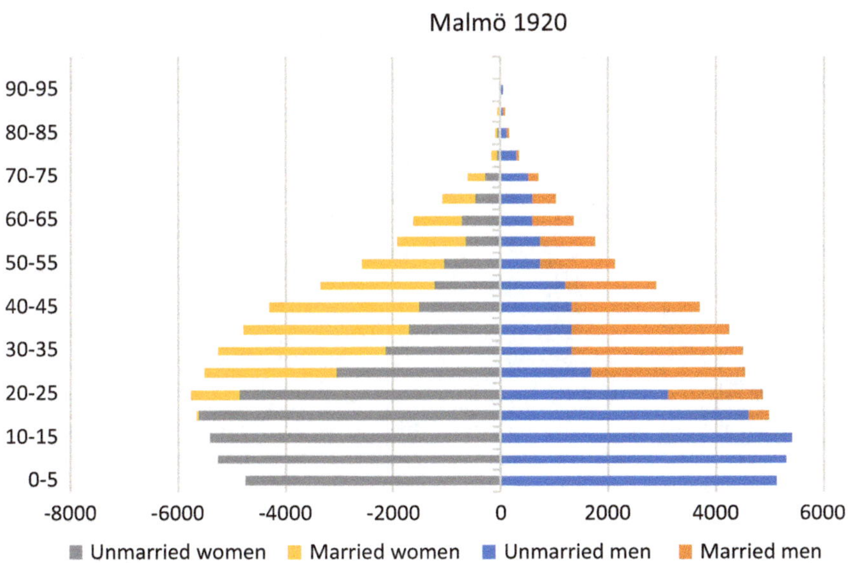

Fig. 7.8 (continued)

Ålder, år	1 Stockholm	2 Göteborg	3 Malmö	4 Norrköping	5 Gävle	6 Hälsingborg	7 Örebro	8 Eskilstuna	9 Karlskrona	10 Jönköping	11 Uppsala	12 Borås	13 Lund
0—5 .	86·1	113·4	119·4	97·4	111·2	102·7	109·3	111·2	106·6	114·6	84·1	125·5	105·2
5—10 .	67·7	95·7	100·2	91·5	108·4	97·2	94·2	113·0	82·5	100·9	70·5	107·6	91·0
10—15 .	62·9	83·7	81·9	85·6	100·4	85·9	89·6	105·6	74 7	91·4	72·4	95·1	82·1
15—20 .	81·5	85·2	82·6	87·8	98·0	87·7	91·1	95·2	115·6	91·4	98·6	84·8	85·9
20—25 .	119·1	99·7	100·0	93·8	89·4	99·3	106·1	87·4	136·8	94·0	118·7	96·4	86·3
25—30 .	114·1	96·6	105·4	82·1	79·4	94·3	94·2	77·6	98·1	81·6	91·5	91·0	90·8
30—35 .	93·9	81·7	92·7	79·9	75·8	88·8	79·7	77·9	76·5	73·5	69·2	80·2	80·5
35—40 .	72·6	66·8	72·2	66·9	61·1	70·4	68·8	71·3	56·5	61·2	55·8	69·4	62·9
40—45 .	61·8	53·8	52·8	60·4	56·6	57·2	56·1	58·9	47·6	52·8	52·7	52·8	55·4
45—50 .	60·6	53·2	47·0	57·6	52·4	52·6	54·5	57·2	45·1	53·2	57·8	49·3	51·4
50—55 .	52·0	46·4	39·7	50·4	45·0	47·5	44·0	40·9	44·6	49·1	51·8	43·5	45·5
55—60 .	39·5	36·7	34·7	39·0	35·5	36·5	33·3	32·4	31·1	35·1	47·5	31·4	48·4
60—65 .	29·7	30·1	27·6	33·8	28·7	27·8	26·0	24·7	26·1	30·7	39·3	25·3	35·5
65—70 .	23·8	22·8	19·0	28·6	24·8	21·8	21·3	19·7	21·4	26·1	35·7	19·5	31·1
70—75 .	17·0	16·6	12·4	21·4	15·6	15·7	13·8	13·9	17·7	19·5	25·5	14·1	22·9
75—80 .	10·7	10·6	7·4	14·3	10·2	8·7	10·2	8·0	11·1	14·0	16·6	8·5	13·6
80 o. över	7·0	7·0	5·0	10·0	7·5	5·9	7·8	5·1	8·5	10·9	12·3	5·6	11·5
0—15 .	216·7	292·8	301·5	274·5	320·0	285·8	293·1	329·8	263·8	306·9	227·0	328·2	278·3
15—50 .	603·6	537·0	552·7	528·0	512·7	550·3	550·5	525·5	575·7	507·7	544·3	523·9	513·2
50 o. över	179·7	170·2	145·8	197·5	167·3	163·9	156·4	144·7	160·5	185·4	228·7	147·9	208·5
Summa	1 000	1 000	1 000	1 000	1 000	1 000	1 000	1 000	1 000	1 000	1 000	1 000	1 000

14 Västerås	15 Halmstad	16 Linköping	17 Karlstad	18 Sundsvall	19 Landskrona	20 Kalmar	21 Uddevalla	22 Falun	23 Kristianstad	24 Söderhamn	25 Ystad	26 Södertälje	Ålder, år
114·8	112·3	100·5	121·5	93·2	109·9	113·2	123·0	110·9	97·2	107·5	110·0	119·9	0—5
101·2	105·0	88·8	107·7	91·6	106·0	99·0	112·1	98·8	77·6	105·5	93·8	106·6	5—10
86·1	94·5	82·5	91·2	87·9	95·1	88·7	96·9	89·2	80·3	101·8	81·7	89·0	10—15
87·9	91·9	83·7	87·5	111·4	92·5	80·7	84·0	94·1	106·4	99·0	102·7	79·7	15—20
102·4	93·1	90·1	93·8	104·7	97·2	82·5	80·6	96·0	129·1	92·9	129·6	75·2	20—25
90·8	84·3	85·2	91·2	84·1	81·7	81·2	77·1	88·6	93·7	82·4	86·6	86·7	25—30
82·8	73·3	77·4	85·4	68·4	76·2	83·8	73·2	77·3	79·5	68·8	71·8	86·5	30—35
66·5	63·7	62·6	63·2	57·0	61·6	61·0	64·0	61·4	63·1	49·0	56·2	71·6	35—40
57·7	52·5	57·0	51·3	54·7	52·0	54·6	49·9	54·8	53·0	50·5	47·8	58·9	40—45
52·2	52·1	52·9	48·5	58·7	54·0	53·8	52·7	56·6	48·4	52·2	50·0	52·1	45—50
41·3	47·9	54·2	40·8	54·8	47·4	47·8	43·7	44·1	44·9	44·9	42·4	42·1	50—55
34·0	36·8	45·6	34·6	43·4	37·1	41·4	35·4	35·7	32·1	39·2	36·8	36·3	55—60
28·4	29·5	41·9	27·1	34·3	28·9	31·6	31·6	32·4	29·7	38·5	32·7	30·1	60—65
21·8	24·1	34·0	23·8	23·9	22·5	27·8	27·6	25·5	26·0	28·5	24·8	27·4	65—70
15·9	19·0	23·6	16·2	16·1	18·7	23·8	21·1	16·7	18·0	17·8	17·5	18·4	70—75
9·4	10·6	12·8	10·6	9·6	10·0	17·1	16·1	9·7	12·3	12·6	10·4	10·9	75—80
7·3	9·4	7·7	6·6	6·2	9·2	12·5	11·0	8·2	8·7	8·9	6·2	8·6	80 o. över
302·1	311·8	271·3	320·4	272·7	311·0	300·9	332·0	298·9	255·1	314·8	285·0	315·5	0—15
539·8	510·9	508·9	520·4	539·0	515·2	497·6	481·5	528·8	573·2	494·8	544·7	510·7	15—50
158·1	177·3	219·8	159·2	188·3	173·8	201·5	186·5	172·3	171·7	190·4	170·3	173·8	50 o. över
1 000	1 000	1 000	1 000	1 000	1 000	1 000	1 000	1 000	1 000	1 000	1 000	1 000	

Fig. 7.9 Age distribution in Sweden's towns and cities in 1910. (Source: Kungl. Statistiska centralbyrån, SOS, Folkräkningen den 31 december1910: II. Folkmängdens fördelning efter kön, ålder och civilstånd (Stockholm: P. A. Norstedt & Söner, 1913), s. 30–31)

issue. When they reached working age, they burst the guilds (1840s) and forced legislation on freedom of trade, without which these masses of people could not have been kept alive. When they reached the age of marriage, their abundance forced people to marry later and ultimately [...] caused the great exodus. The superabundant class of "all others", which was outside the popular representation of the time, burst the constitution of the four estates of the realm (1850s and 1860s). And as they have now reached old age in our days, they fill our poorhouses and charitable institutions and raise the issue of disability and old age insurance.[29]

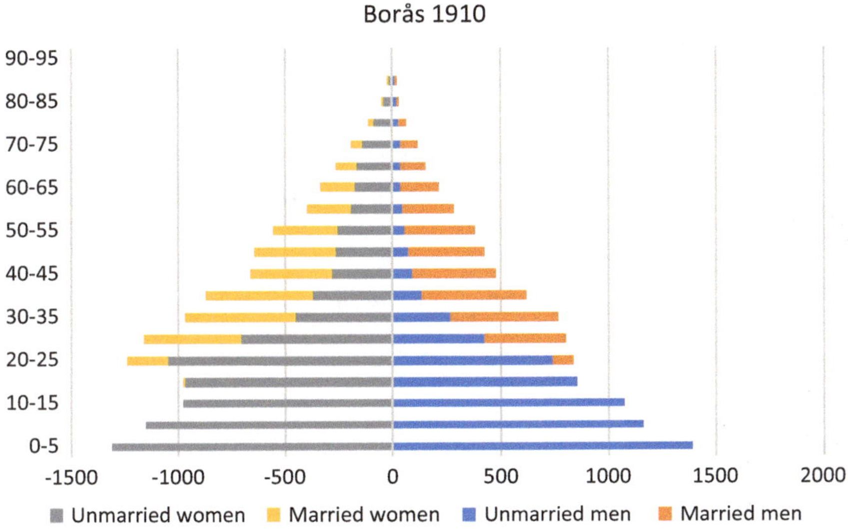

Fig. 7.10 Age distribution in five-year groups, gender and marital status in the smaller towns of Sweden, 1910 and 1920. a. Borås, 1910. b. Borås, 1920. c. Eskilstuna 1910. d. Eskilstuna, 1920. e. Gävle, 1910. f. Gävle, 1920. g. Helsingborg, 1910. h. Helsingborg, 1920. i. Jönköping, 1910. j. Jönköping, 1920. k. Kristianstad, 1910. l. Kristianstad, 1920. m. Linköping, 1910. n. Linköping, 1920. o. Lund, 1910. p. Lund, 1920. q. Norrköping, 1910. r. Norrköping, 1920. s. Sundsvall, 1910. t. Sundsvall, 1920. u. Uppsala, 1910. v. Uppsala 1920. w. Örebro, 1910. x. Örebro, 1920. (Source. Kungl. Statistiska centralbyrån, SOS, Folkräkningen den 31 december 1910: II. Folkmängdens fördelning efter kön, ålder och civilstånd (Stockholm: P. A. Norstedt & Söner, 1913), s. 54–64, tabell 4, SOS, Folkräkningen den 31 december 1920: III. Folkmängden efter ålder, kön, civilstånd och födelseort (Stockholm: P. A. Norstedt & Söner, 1926), s. 50–64, tabell 4)

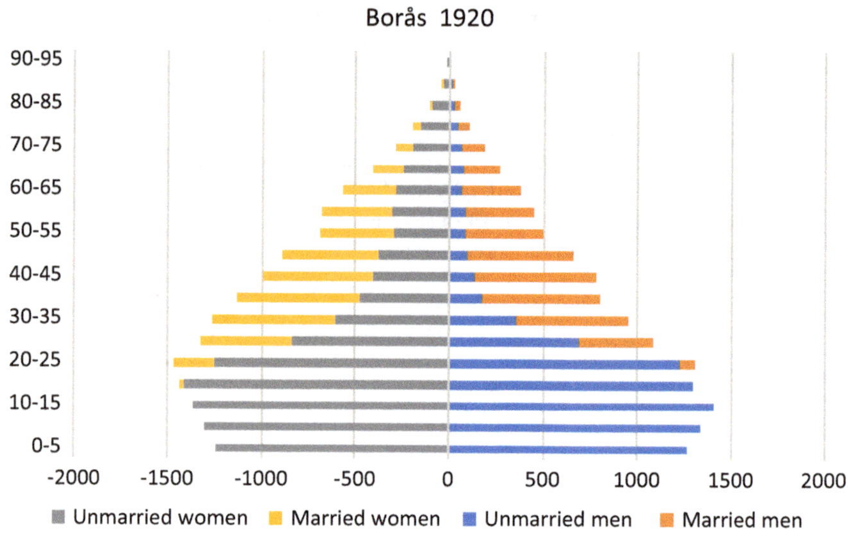

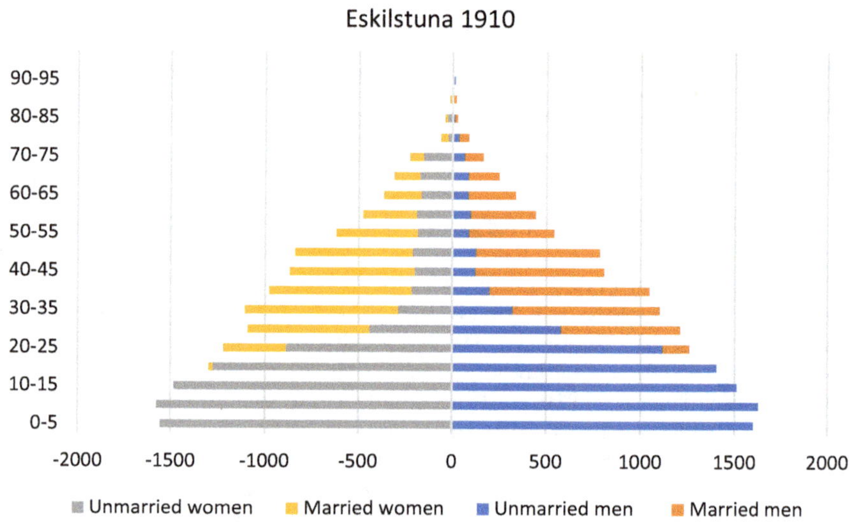

Fig. 7.10 (continued)

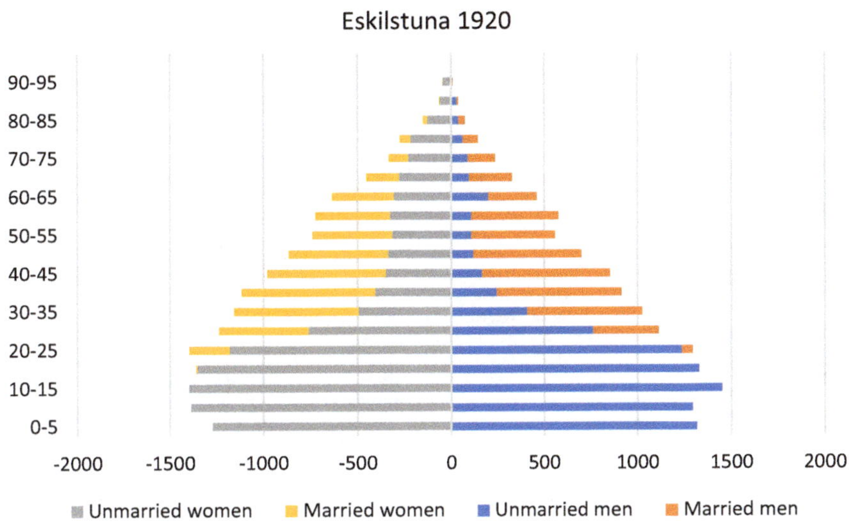

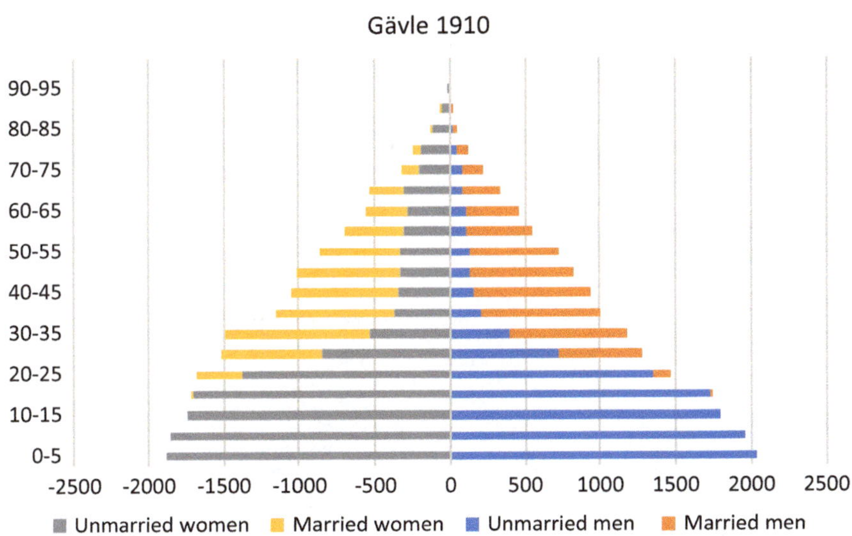

Fig. 7.10 (continued)

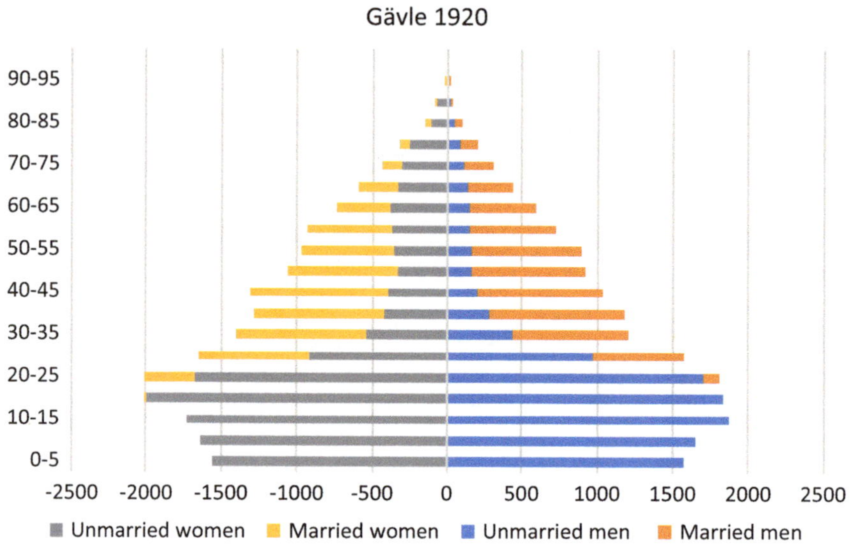

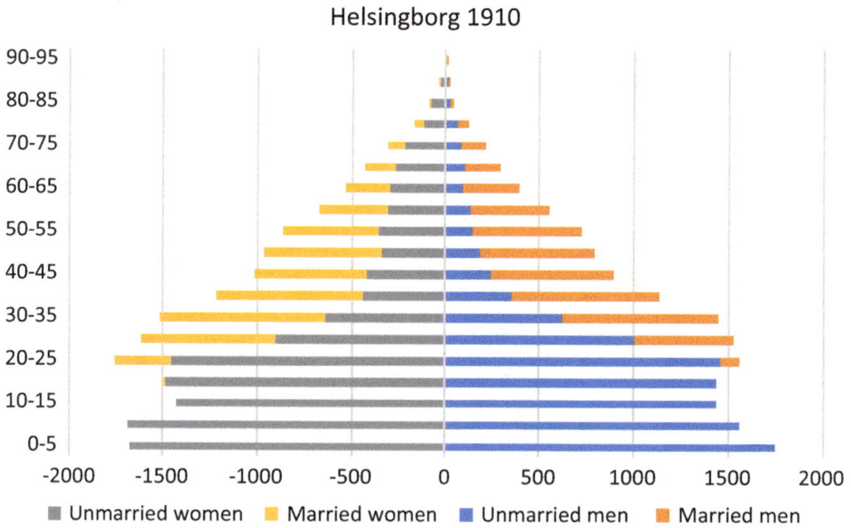

Fig. 7.10 (continued)

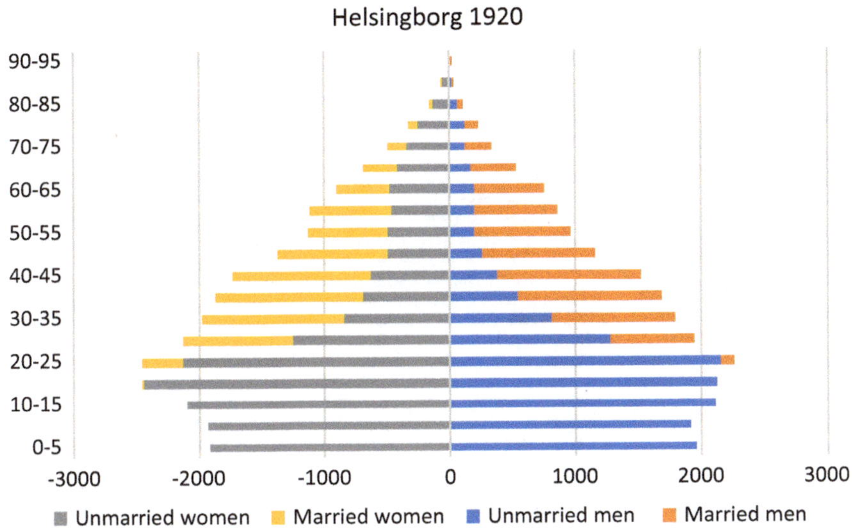

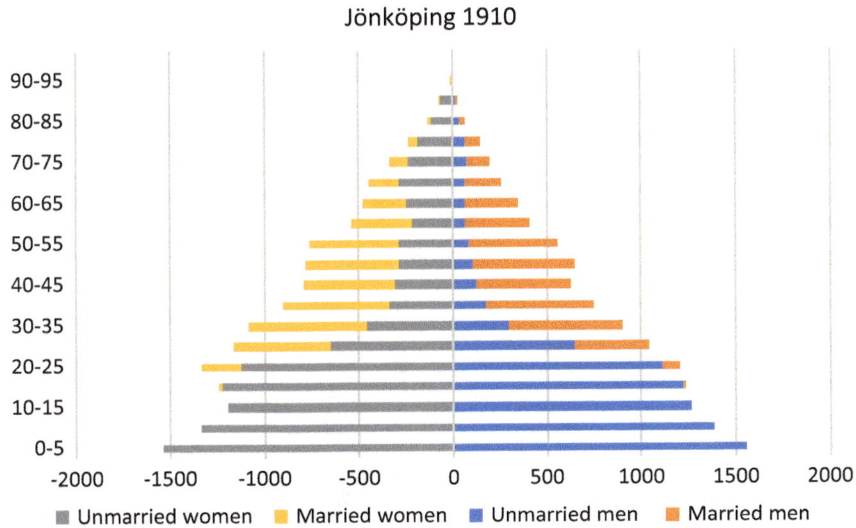

Fig. 7.10 (continued)

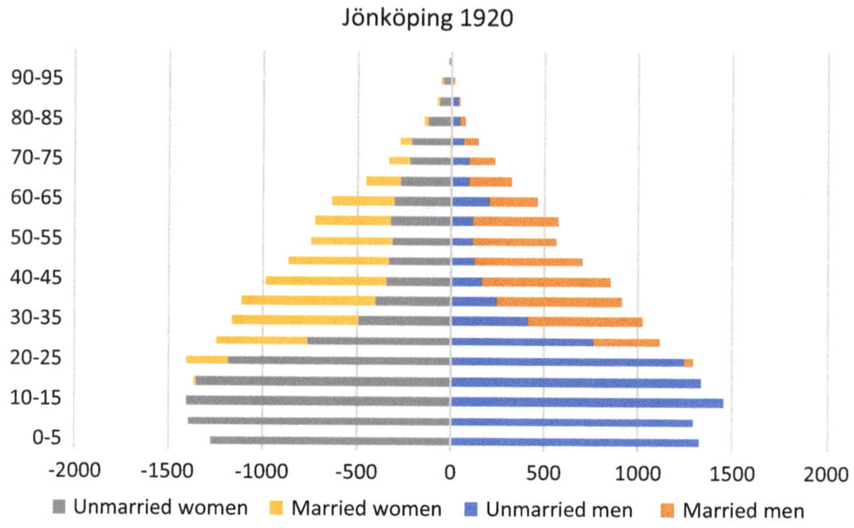

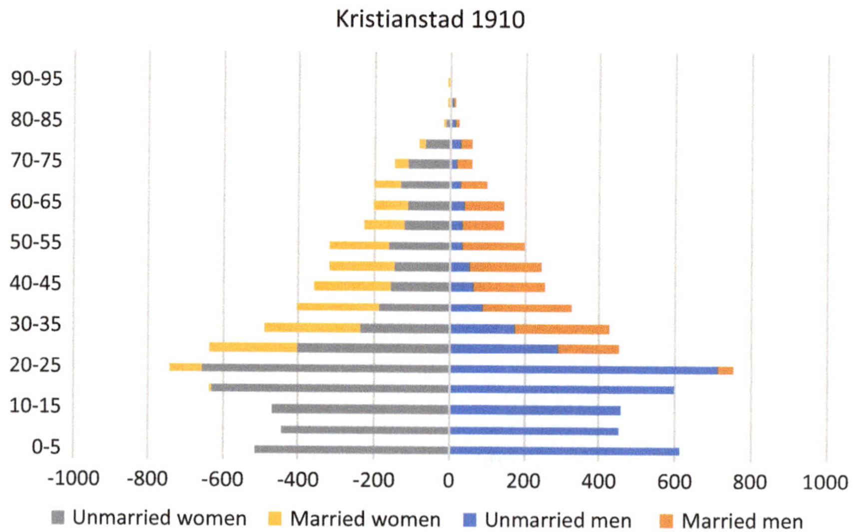

Fig. 7.10 (continued)

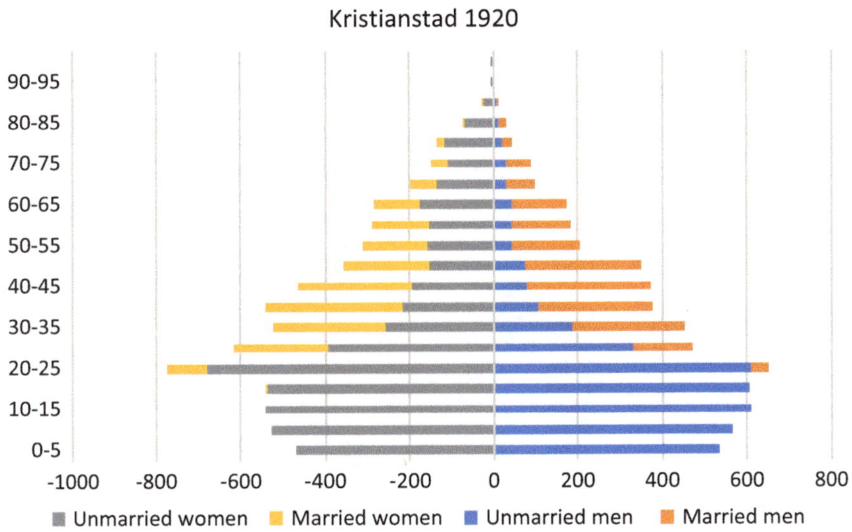

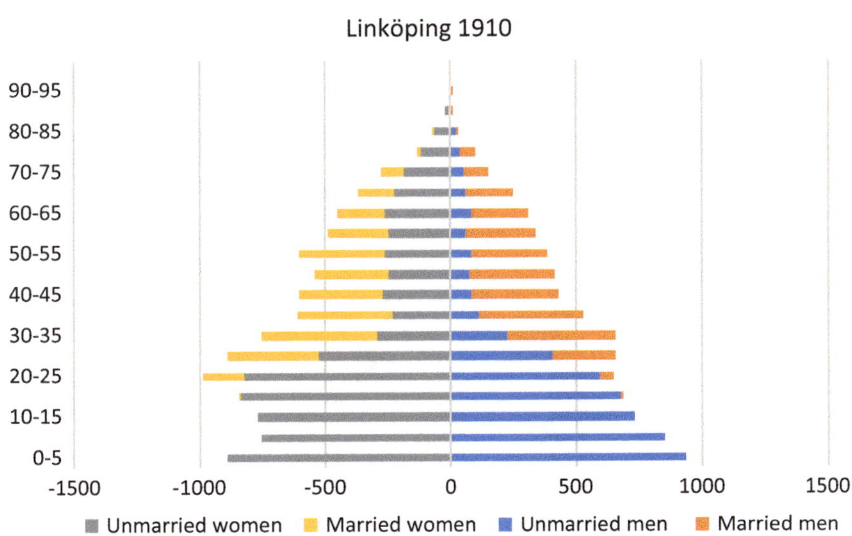

Fig. 7.10 (continued)

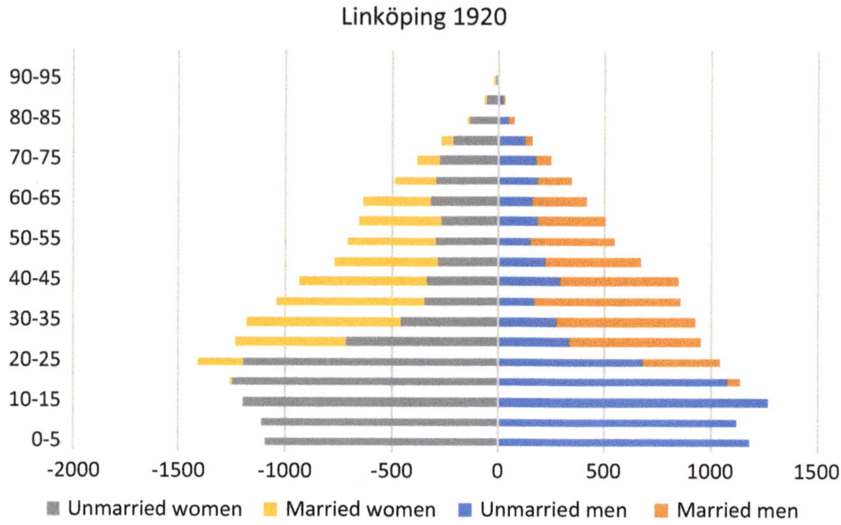

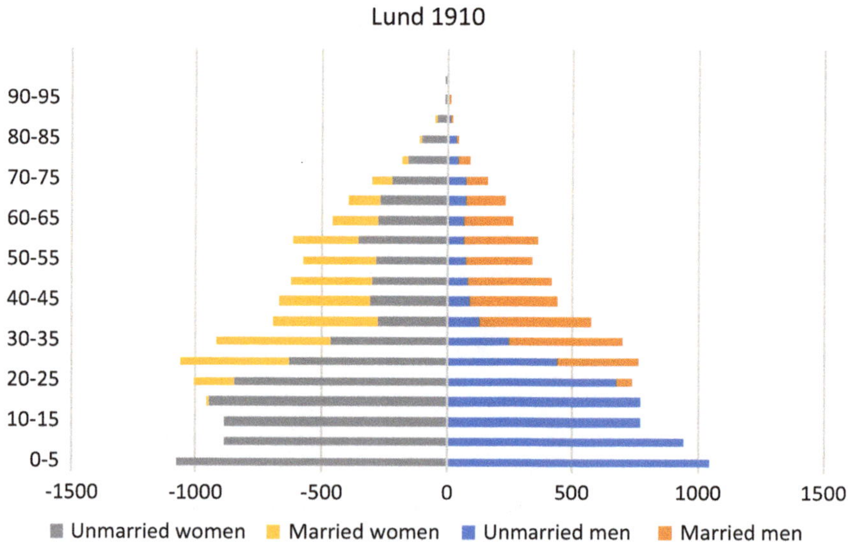

Fig. 7.10 (continued)

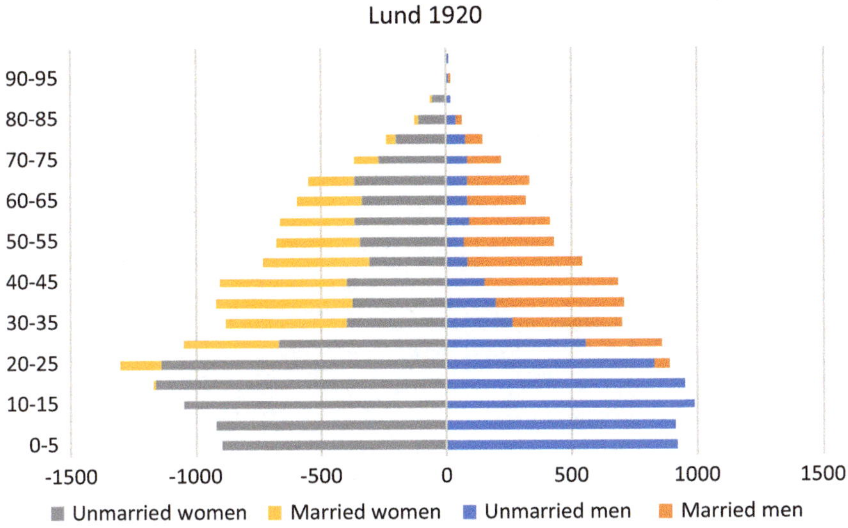

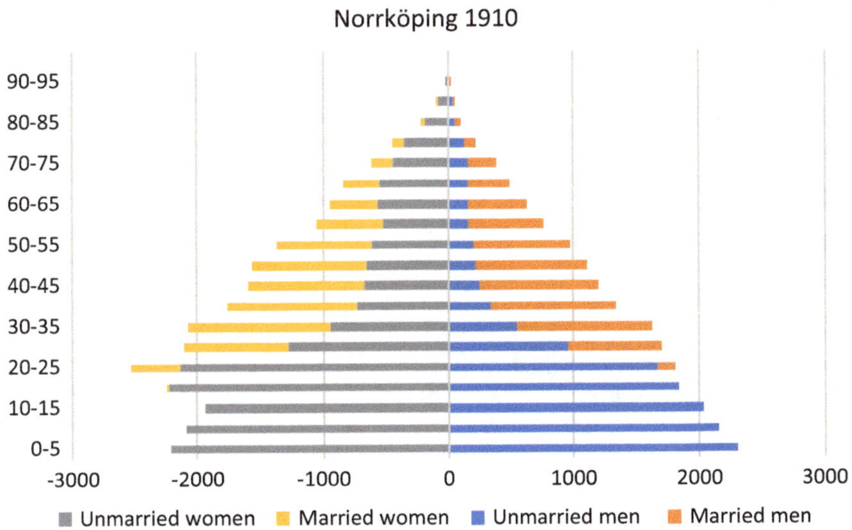

Fig. 7.10 (continued)

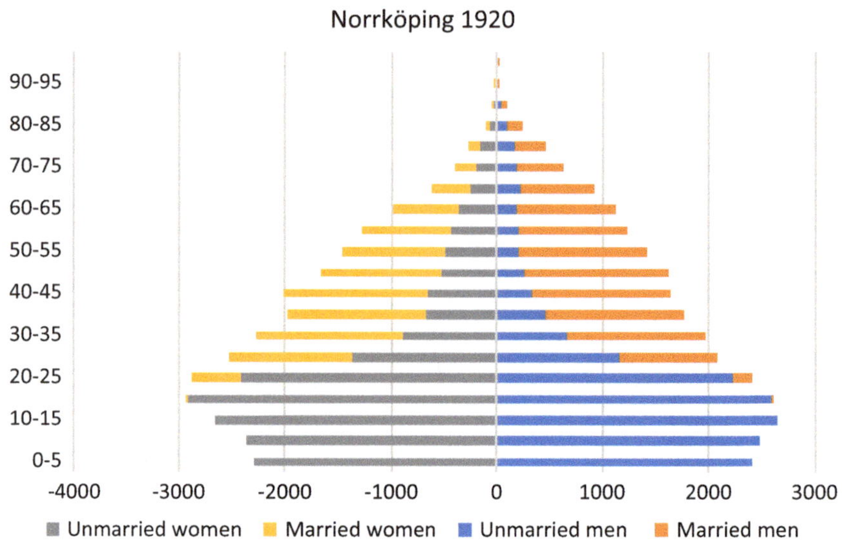

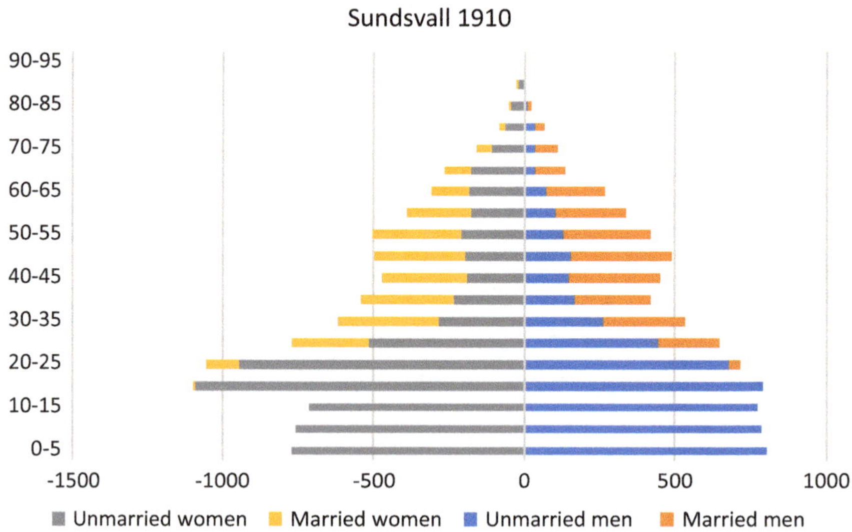

Fig. 7.10 (continued)

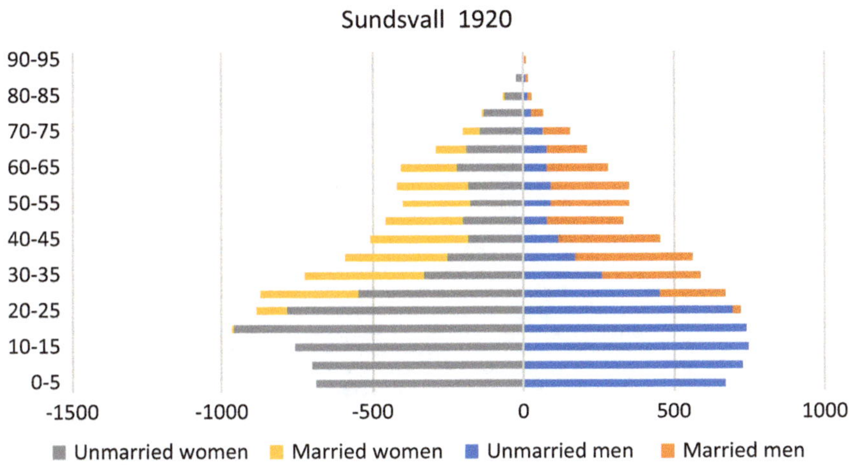

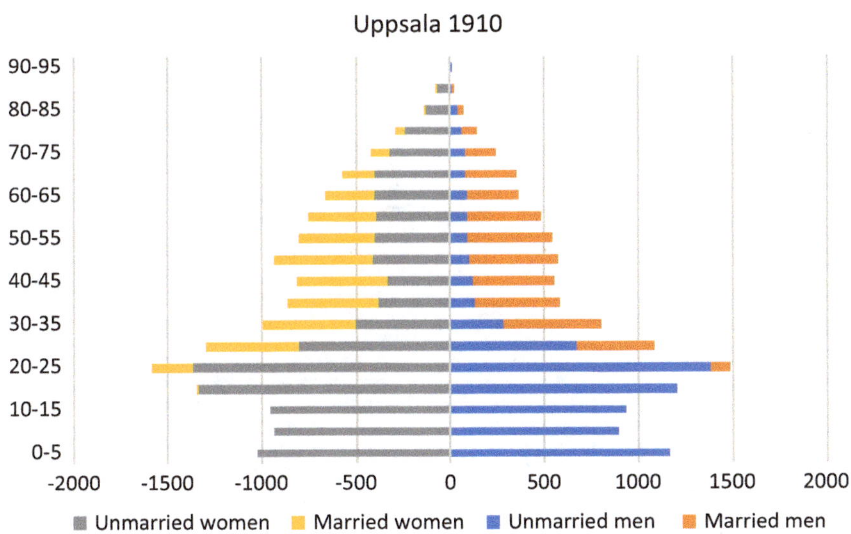

Fig. 7.10 (continued)

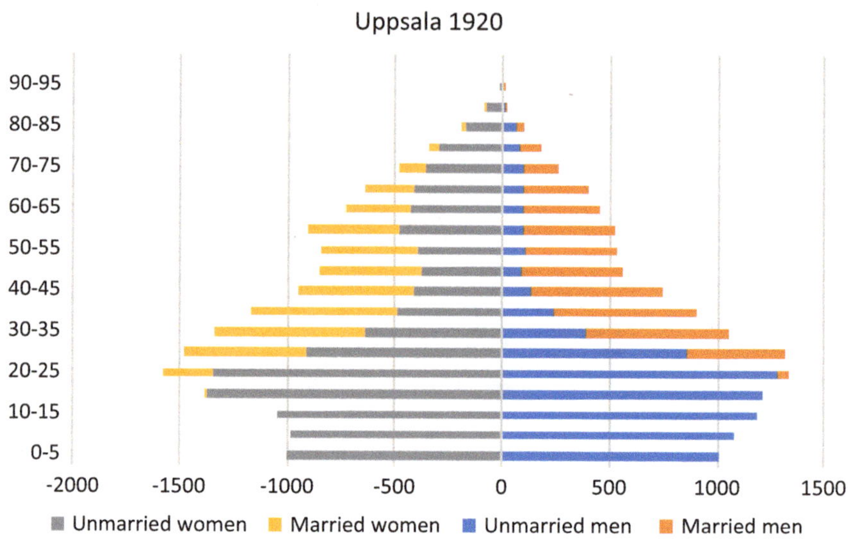

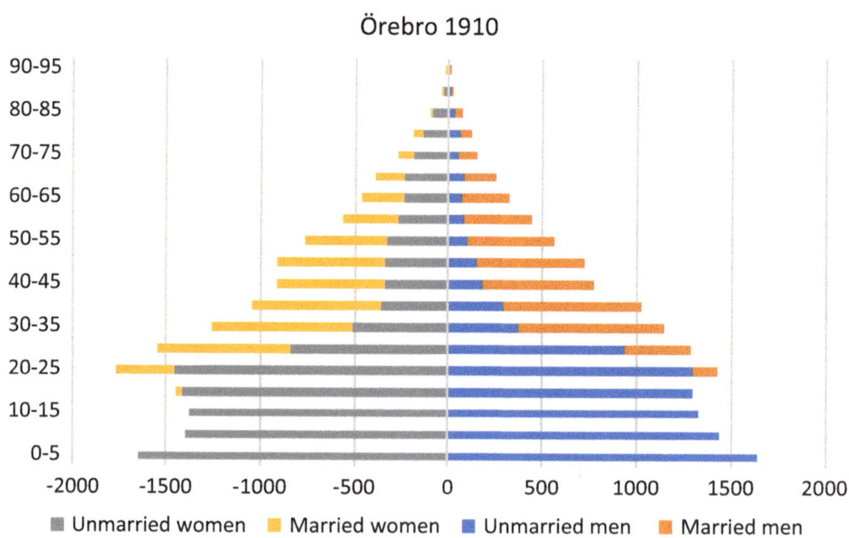

Fig. 7.10 (continued)

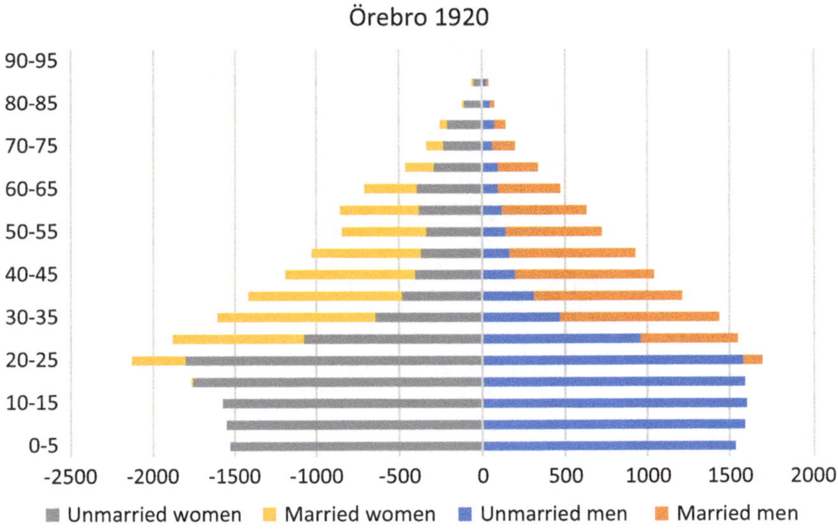

Fig. 7.10 (continued)

In this book, I have thus followed how the grandchildren of the large population cohorts of the nineteenth century influenced the suffrage issue at the end of the nineteenth century and in the first decades of the twentieth century. The situation could be summed up in terms like those of Gustav Sundbärg: *at this time, the large number of grandchildren meant that the issue of the right of the working class to participate in the representation of the people could no longer be ignored, but it could be delayed*. The emigration inquiry discussed population development, rural stagnation and the growth of industry, late marriages, extramarital births, workers' wages, and the rise of socialism. Sundbärg was critical of many aspects of development in Sweden, including political measures and social conditions in the country and in towns. He also mentions suffrage parenthetically. He seems to think that broader suffrage would be a good thing. He notes that Sweden was lagging behind when it came to improving economic conditions that could limit emigration, which was "a result of the unpleasant fact that universal suffrage was introduced too late here".[30] By universal suffrage, he was referring to male suffrage.

As we have seen in this and the previous section, the age distribution of the population was interpreted in the light of a debate about marriage and family formation, and the importance of family responsibilities in society.

This was contrasted with the behaviour of young unmarried people. At the start of the twentieth century, discussions about the young generation took on partly different dimensions. In the next section I discuss the living conditions of the young generation, how it was perceived and became the subject of other official interventions. These too were dimensions of the suffrage issue. They concerned how far the authorities and the political leaders could trust the young generation.

Young and Norm-Breaking

It was thus no coincidence that around the turn of the century there was also a vigorous debate about the conditions in which children grew up, and legislation was passed on adoption and child protection of various kinds. The young generation was large and highly noticeable in urban settings. The government also set up inquiries into "depraved" (*vanartade*) children and criminal youth. These inquiries, which were discussed above in connection with the so-called child laws, also led to the creation of child welfare boards in the big towns and cities and to the establishment of institutions for young people who were considered criminal.

> However, in view of the increasingly heard demand from the general public to curb, as far as may be possible, the crude and refractory violence of which youths, especially in the towns but also in the countryside, have often been guilty in recent times, the committee, not daring to trust that the replacement of corporal punishment with fines, which can be the sentence imposed for such acts of violence, would be sufficient to curb these crimes, will not omit to express its conviction as to the need for greater severity in short-term prison sentences through the addition of corporal punishment in the cases concerned.[31]

This statement probably referred to underage youths, but the essence of the debate concerned the increasing crime rate among young people in the cities. There are several aspects to this discussion. It was about delinquency and criminality among younger children up to the age of 14, which was considered to be a result of neglect on the part of young parents in the working class. A statistical analysis of the conditions of illegitimate children (the cohort born in 1898) showed that the majority of these had slightly more mothers aged 20–25 than mothers aged 25–30. A significant percentage of the children were later made legitimate through marriage. Unwed mothers were subject to particularly harsh criticism.[32]

Youth delinquency was also believed to be increasing. The 1902 Child Welfare Act was intended to remedy the problem of criminal and delinquent young children in the big towns. It was not until the passing of the new Child Welfare Act of 1924 that the legislation became national. This development, which is well described in previous research, shows that the towns and cities were perceived as the problem.[33] The image presented in Parliament, portraying the younger urban population as particularly unreliable and irresponsible, could be substantiated by the public statistics while at the same time reflecting a general concern about the consequences of broad changes in society—the consequences of industrialisation and urbanisation. But the debate was also explicitly about those prosecuted for crimes.

Firstly, it may be noted in general that Stockholm dominated in the total volume of people arrested for crimes and misdemeanours around the turn of the century. Of the men detained in Sweden in 1901, for example, 2381 of the total 4745 were from Stockholm; the corresponding figures for women were 718 for Sweden as a whole and 521 for Stockholm.[34]

As regards marital status, 2603 persons are reported as having been sentenced in 1905, to take an example that was fresh when the matter was debated in Parliament. Among these, 2130 (81.8%) were unmarried, 386 (14.8%) were married, and 87 (3.4%) were widowers, widows, or divorced.[35]

Around the end of the nineteenth century, the number of people sentenced for crimes such as assault, drunkenness, and theft increased. Generally speaking, the age groups from 18 to 30 were overrepresented, especially those aged 21–25. The statistics also showed that a large overrepresentation of unmarried men committed these crimes and misdemeanours and that the cities (chiefly Stockholm and Gothenburg) dominated in the statistics. This is also true in relation to the size of the age groups.[36] The statistics naturally reflected a complex reality in which both the organisation of the judiciary and the forms of surveillance had implications for how this population group was portrayed and perceived.

Young people and unmarried people attracted attention as a social problem, and as we have seen, they were not welcomed as participants in the political process. At the same time, the period between when young people left home to enter working life and when they established a family of their own could be long. Most young people had started working between the age of 14 and 16, and young people were counted as adults from the age of 16, for example, in public statistics on occupation and causes of death.[37] The high marriage age thus meant that both men and women had a long period of time in which they supported themselves before they married or started cohabiting. It is thus a long transitional period of adolescence, no less than ten years, between leaving the family of origin and starting a family of one's own. This was probably the picture of the experienced working-class youth to which Branting referred in his speech on the motion to the People's Parliament in 1893. In addition, it should be stressed that up to 20 per cent of women did not have children at all and a large share of both the male and the female population remained unmarried. Against this background, the proposal for an extra vote for married men over the age of 25 or 35 would also have major consequences for men's political citizenship. Of the female population aged over 15, some 45 per cent were unmarried, thus accounting for a large proportion of women in working life.[38] The proposals of suffrage for married women with an income or property of their own should also be understood in relation to these conditions.

It should also be emphasised that the last vestiges of authority exercised by heads of household and employers were disappearing even before the end of the nineteenth century. Domestic servants, shop assistants, farmhands, transport workers, office staff, and others were not subject to the traditional domination of a head of household.[39] It is also worth noting that a person under a head of household was not deprived of the right to vote after 1862. There was a provision to this effect in previous municipal constitutions, and it was actually valid in Stockholm until 1898.[40] Young people in the cities lived as lodgers or shared flats with each other, as is evident from contemporary social reports by Gustav af Geijerstam and, for example, in the stories of the popular author Elin Wägner. In addition, certain young workers or office employees were expected to wear a particular style of dress, which required a degree of frugality that was made possible by life as a lodger or sharing a home with other young people in a similar situation.[41] Young employed unmarried workers could have a high level of consumption. But we must assume that this group was relatively strong financially precisely by virtue of being single. Historian Edvard Bull, in his studies of the Norwegian working class in Kristiania (Oslo), describes their situation:

> The accounts show a fairly generous economy, with carriage rides and photography, drinks and cakes for his sweetheart. But when [the man in question] got married and had a large number of children around him, his income did not rise significantly and the generous economy disappeared.[42]

Real wages for the Swedish working class grew more vigorously than in other European countries, which meant that the thresholds set for voting (in elections to the Second Chamber and municipal councils) were formally within reach for many workers. However, as we saw earlier, the share of persons entitled to vote was lower than in other comparable European countries as a result of voting restrictions.[43] At the same time, 800 kronor a year was not a high wage to support a family with children on one income. Once a couple started having children, it was not possible for the wife to work to the same extent, and the dependency ratio increased as the family grew larger. Married people over the age of 25 were portrayed in the parliamentary debate as being more socially stable, meeting the standards that applied to a family. But these were families living under great social and economic pressure, which meant that the various economic restrictions on suffrage and eligibility could leave many of these families unable to satisfy these requirements. According to Gustav Sundbärg, the author of the emigration inquiry, the trade union movement was also affected by this conflict; the young workers pushed up union fees to levels that the older married men found difficult to manage.[44]

Conservative and Liberal politicians marked their distance from the mobile young unmarried wage-earners when they emphasised the importance of a higher voting age. However, these young workers were the section of the potential electorate that was best-off financially in the expansive economy that prevailed in the late nineteenth century and the early twentieth century. Families with just one income probably had to struggle more and risked falling behind with their tax payments and were thus disqualified from voting. The conflict with the discourse is palpable. Young adults, those under the age of 25, were associated in the political discourse with lack of social stability and responsibility, while the group of married men over 25 were associated with responsibility and competence. For those who did not live up to the requirements of responsible behaviour, criteria were formulated to exclude them from participation in democracy. Those who were best off in the working class were also excluded from voting by the age limits, while those with the most problematic situation economically and socially were among the beneficiaries of the extended suffrage, although in reality they were excluded by the economic thresholds.[45] This gives a slightly different meaning to the restrictions on the right to vote.

At the same time, it is difficult to evaluate exactly who was unable to exercise the right to vote. The official statistics confirm the increasing

Table 7.5 Persons entitled to vote in parliamentary elections as a percentage of the total for the whole country 1887–1902

	Countryside	*Towns*
1887	80.6	18.4
1893	79.7	20.3
1902	74.8	25.2

Source: Kungl. Statistiska centralbyrån, BiSoS 1900–1902 R,Valstatistik XV: Riksdagsmannavalen 1900–1902 (Stockholm, 1903), pp. 11–12

Table 7.6 Eligible voters as a proportion of the male population of legal age, 1893–1902

	Countryside	*Towns*	*National average*
1893	23.3	25.6	23.7
1902	26.4	32.6	27.7

Source: Kungl. Statistiska centralbyrån, BiSoS 1900–1902 R,Valstatistik XV: Riksdagsmannavalen 1900–1902 (Stockholm, 1903), p. 11–12

influence of the towns and cities during the late nineteenth century, as shown in Table 7.5. In 1902, just over a quarter of all eligible voters were living in towns or cities after an increase of some 26 per cent in just the last three years before 1902 (Table 7.6).[46]

The development had also resulted in a large difference in the number of eligible voters in each constituency, but the most significant factor was the large number of eligible voters who were unable to vote in elections to the Second Chamber because they had yet to pay their municipal taxes. In 1902, 8.3 per cent of rural voters had lost their right to vote. For urban voters the corresponding figure was 19.1 per cent. Compared with the 1899 elections, the number of rural voters who had not paid their taxes had increased by 31 per cent, whereas the figure for the corresponding urban voters had increased by 55.8 per cent. This meant a great disparity between different counties in the number of people who were really eligible to vote. The share of people who were disqualified for this reason ranged from 0 to 43 per cent in different towns, but mostly around 25 per cent were excluded on account of unpaid taxes.[47] In the bigger cities as many as 54 per cent of voters were disqualified, while the situation was better in smaller towns, but among these were also places with a high percentage of voters disqualified for failure to pay taxes. Here is an extract from the survey by the Central Bureau of Statistics:

> The first group includes Stockholm, with its significant number of 41,235 (62.9%) with outstanding municipal tax debts who would otherwise be entitled to vote, which is 16,898 more than the number of persons entitled to vote. If the former are not counted, the corresponding number for other towns in the group is 12,997 (37.4%), consisting of Gothenburg with 7,633 (45.3%), Malmö with 2,967 (32.0%), Norrköping with 1,314 (30.9%), and Gävle with 1,083 (24.7%). Of the towns in the other group, Sundsvall with 662 (32.7%) has the highest relative number, and Karlskrona with 745 (27.5%) comes next. The last place is occupied by Växjö with only 17 (2.7%) and the second last by Kristianstad, 38 (3.8%).[48]

A significant and increasing percentage of the urban population were and remained disqualified from voting during the period when population growth was at its strongest and the debate about voting restrictions was at its most intense. The above data refer to the period before 1909, when those who were not allowed to vote in municipal elections also lost the right to vote in parliamentary elections. Ebba Berlin Åselius has analysed the data in the official statistics for the later period 1914–1920 and has shown that, for that period too, the people excluded from voting in parliamentary elections were to be found in the constituencies of the big cities and towns: Norrköping/Linköping, Stockholm, Gothenburg, Malmö, Helsingborg, Landskrona, and Lund, but also in parts of Norrland, Medelpad, and Blekinge. The most common reason for exclusion was still the same: unpaid taxes. More people were excluded in industrial constituencies than in rural constituencies and, in general, the working class was hit hardest by the tax thresholds. Rural workers were also affected by the residence thresholds, having recently moved into a constituency. The middle class, freehold farmers, tenants, and elementary school teachers were hit the least.[49]

But how old could those who did not pay their taxes have been? Was it the young, who ought to have been well enough off, relatively speaking, or was it stable, well-behaved, and slightly older working-class men who were married and had to provide for a family and thus must surely have been less well off? Taxes were paid retrospectively by the taxpayer, which meant that he or she was responsible for putting money away for the purpose. This, of course, was a problem. In 1903 the Central Bureau of Statistics, on behalf of the government, carried out an inquiry into the consequences of a possible change in men's suffrage, on the premise that parliamentary elections would be based on those who were entitled to vote in municipal elections. They asked about the differences in outcomes if the voting age was 21 or 25, and how large a percentage would be disqualified on account of unpaid taxes. The study showed that, of the male population over the age of 18 who had not paid their taxes at the end of August 1900, the proportion was 26.9 per cent of urban taxpayers and 5.3 per cent of rural taxpayers.[50] Here it was clear that the requirements for tax payment that were discussed in Parliament had greater consequences in the towns, but as we shall see below, those under the age of 25 paid their taxes to a greater extent than those over 25.

The problem of unpaid taxes was greatest in the big cities. In Stockholm, 40.6 per cent of taxpayers were behind with their payments, and in Gothenburg 46.8 per cent. The average for other towns was 16.8 per cent. This meant that the absolute number of people with unpaid taxes in Stockholm was "larger than in all the other towns together and almost as large as in the whole of the rest of Sweden".[51]

However, since some of these were underage (people were liable to pay tax from the age of 18 but did not have municipal suffrage until the age of 21), the failure to pay taxes was examined for the group aged over 21 (those with municipal suffrage) and for the group of men over 25 (the voting age proposed in the 1902 bill for elections to the Second Chamber). Raising the voting age would curb the increase in the number of voters, it was noted. If the payment of *mantal* duties (a tax on property) was additionally taken into account, the difference between town and country in the increase of eligible voters became considerable. "The growth in the number of eligible voters, which in the former case is, relatively speaking, 2.5 times as great for rural areas as for urban, is in the latter case, likewise in relation to the previous number of eligible voters, four times as large."[52] The rural population would thus be less affected by a combination of a higher voting age and the requirement of paid taxes.

It was found, however, that the actual payment of state tax was generally better than the payment of municipal tax, especially among men over the age of 25.[53] However, in the towns the number of taxable men over 25 who were behind in their payments of state tax and who were also obliged to pay *mantal* duties was larger than in rural areas:

> the share of people in arrears in rural areas was 9.6% and in the towns 67.9%, and of those also in arrears with other crown taxes, 1.8% in rural areas and 19.7% in the towns. The number of people in arrears is thus highest in the former category, or the poorer population. As for the latter category, it should be mentioned for the sake of comparison that, among men entitled to vote over the age of 25, 7.4% in rural areas and 40.6% in the towns are in arrears with municipal taxes.[54]

The statistics do not give a detailed picture of the economic conditions of the age group under 25. Yet it appears to be the urban population over the age of 25 who failed to pay state and municipal taxes, whether out of inability or negligence, though to different extents. The politicians who urged these demands for voting restrictions must have been fully aware that raising the voting age combined with requirements of tax payment would exclude many potential urban voters. That was the purpose of the inquiry. It was also clear that such demands were more favourable to the rural political influence than that of the expanding urban population.

The pattern persisted after the reforms of 1918–1921. Moreover, the remaining economic thresholds affected men and women in different ways. Dependence on poor relief, with the consequent loss of suffrage, was to a greater extent a rural phenomenon that affected women more than men, whereas in the towns it was men who lost the right to vote as a result of the tax threshold, as Fia Sundevall has shown.[55] Of course, this also affected the elections. In the municipal elections in 1919, the first to be based on the new regulations, it was in urban environments that voters aged over 23 lost their right to vote for the municipal council and the county council as a result of the tax criterion. Women in rural areas were affected more by the poor relief threshold. In the big cities, the effect of the tax threshold was palpable.[56] Industrial settings appear to have had a special status.

> The relative number of men entitled to vote was almost always significantly higher in the towns and in many cases, especially in the counties of Östergötland, Gävleborg, and Västernorrland, the difference was considerable. Only in three counties, Stockholm, Blekinge, and Södermanland, did men in the countryside have a less favourable position than in the towns. The reason for this, as far as the first of these counties is concerned, is the large number of people ineligible to vote in the populous, highly industrialised municipalities in the neighbourhood of Stockholm, especially in Solna and Sundbyberg, where the men have largely failed to pay their taxes.[57]

For those over 27, the effect of the tax payment threshold was reduced, while the proportion affected by the poor relief threshold increased, which is explained by the fact that more of the elderly were dependent on poor relief. But age was also significant when it came to tax payment. The tax threshold affected people aged 23–27 to a greater extent than those over 27.[58] Perhaps this is another circumstance suggesting that newly formed family units had trouble making ends meet.

But the groups of young people could certainly also be perceived as more of a threat than the older married and settled population. The social movements that emerged during the nineteenth century largely grew by recruiting young people seeking an identity and a place in society during a time of dramatic transformation. The popular movements were based on a critique of established norms and values, but responsible behaviour and social stability were also central values. The free churches, the cooperative movement, the trade unions, and the temperance movement certainly demanded discipline and responsibility from their members, but they also questioned the prevailing political and economic conditions.[59] Social democracy and other socialist or anarchist movements also emerged as concrete threats to the state. Foreign events testified to this, but there were also Swedish examples. The *Amalthea* incident, when young socialists blew up a boat housing strike-breakers in 1909, could fuel the idea of a link between young people and radicalism as a threat to society. The young socialist movement that emerged in the late nineteenth century also drew inspiration from anarchism and recruited youngsters with a radical rhetoric and revolutionary romanticism. A leading representative such as Hinke Bergegren came into conflict with the establishment in many arenas, from politics to sexual morals.[60] The security police therefore also found it important to keep an eye on radical movements in Stockholm. The labour movement was under close surveillance for a long time, even after the Social Democrats ended up in government, and the meetings of anarchists and later of young socialists attracted considerable interest.[61]

The young socialists also found themselves in conflict with the Social Democrats, who did not accept them as the youthful working-class avant-garde of the revolution. The conflict concerned everything from rhetoric to strategy. The rift was profound because the Social Democrats could not accept an independent youth movement, according to the historian Henrik Berggren. This also influenced the relationship between the Social Democrats and the other socialist youth movement formed in 1903. They too refused to follow the party's lead. The youth association did not receive much support from the party leadership, which ignored them, for example in connection with the meeting of the Socialist International in Copenhagen. The relationship between the youth association and the party was fraught. The youth association's rhetoric was youthful and individualistic, glorifying itself in a manner that challenged the labour movement's identity as a collective.[62]

The high age limits did not have the same consequences for the population as a whole. The questioning of young people's maturity and competence as voters was part of a broader critique and debate about the family, marriage, and class society. All this was a reflection of social changes and increasing conflict between social classes and between urban and rural areas, not only due to general cultural differences but also as a result of the growing and increasingly young urban population. Laws affecting children and young people, marriage, and protective measures were visible political expressions of this, leading, in due time, to the construction of welfare institutions. The debate thus revolved around a demographic regime based on a high marriage age, a low frequency of marriage, and a high, albeit declining, birth rate—features that continued from the late nineteenth century into the early twentieth century. Yet that would change. The marriage age began to fall, and the number of children decreased, although it was still influenced by the large generations of the nineteenth century. Those excluded from voting by the decisions of 1918–1921 would also be viewed differently.[63]

The high age limits were not the same for everyone. The discussions and decisions around the first decade of the twentieth century excluded women in various ways, but initially it was just as much a matter of limiting the influence of the urban male working class and then the entire group of young workers, both male and female. The aim was, in part, to deprive a generation of young unmarried people in the towns and cities of any political influence, and to favour the older married population, in so far as they behaved responsibly. It was thus also a blow aimed at the working class that had been mobilised politically, in an attempt to preserve a bourgeois cultural order and its view of society. The population described as exemplary by virtue of their married status did not always pass the other criteria of good behaviour. The rules were obviously designed to exclude them. For these reasons, it was also natural that the Liberals and the Right should try to limit the influence of the urban working class after the reforms of 1918–21 by making the voting age higher than the age of majority.

Who Was Excluded by the Age Limits?

We can thus observe that the reforms of 1918 to 1921 took place against the background of a significant demographic shift towards the cities and the industrial communities, which underlines and explains why the voting age could be assigned such an important role in the debate. The population pyramids presented above illustrate the shift. This is also reflected in the differing views on how the voting age affected the ability of the various parties to pursue their politics. It is precisely for this reason that it is worth examining what the age limits meant in concrete terms.

The reforms of 1918–1921 were fundamentally based on the compromises and decisions made in 1907–1909 in which, although the Right and the Liberals did not have the same opinion about the design of the reform, there was a consensus on the appropriateness of a high age limit, with the requirement to have reached the age of 24 in the year before the election. The previous voting age for men was 21. In her study, Berling Åselius examined the consequences of the thresholds during the period 1909–1921. She emphasises that the proportion of men entitled to vote in elections to the Second Chamber increased only marginally, mainly on account of the criteria of unpaid taxes, having recently moved to a new constituency, and being in receipt of poor relief. The urban share of the total number of people entitled to vote did not grow after the reform. It favoured rural areas. In the parliamentary elections of the 1910s, about 20 per cent of the population was excluded. To a large extent it was the working class that was affected. In the big cities and industrial towns, the proportion of disqualified voters was therefore very high—up to 50 per cent in some districts. On average 85 per cent of the rural electorate was qualified to vote, as against only 63 per cent of urban voters.[64] However, Berling Åselius does not consider the age limits, that is, the number of people excluded by the higher voting age. It should be emphasised here that when the reforms were passed, politicians were fully aware of the consequences of the thresholds discussed. The government inquiries had made that very clear.[65]

What difference did the age limits make? The first election after the reform was held in 1911, which allows us to calculate the difference between the number and proportion of men (and women) who could have voted if the voting age had remained at 21 instead of 24, and if women from the age of 21 had also been included, instead of the envisaged age of 24. The figures are based on the population according to the

1910 census and should thus give a reasonable picture of the consequences in the 1911 elections to the Second Chamber. Of course, this was also influenced by the gender distribution of the population. It concerned about 181,430 people aged 21–24, or about 12 per cent of the adult male population in the whole country of 1,521,370. The youthful character of the urban population meant that this had greater consequences in the towns than in the countryside. Therefore, in the towns where the young population was larger, a larger percentage of the potential voters was excluded, about 14 per cent of the male population.[66] The population structure meant that decisions were not neutral as regards class or geography. I have compiled my calculations in Table 7.7. Women are also included to illustrate how they would have been affected if they had been allowed to vote on the same terms as men in the 1911 election.

Young male industrial workers between the ages of 21 and 24 in both urban and rural areas generally had a higher income than the 800 kronor required to vote before 1909—provided they had paid their taxes. The 1909 reform meant that they lost the right to vote in the next election. At this time it was exceptional for rural workers to earn more than the income threshold for voting; having been excluded from voting before 1909, they now benefitted in part from the reform.[67] This also affected Social Democratic policy.[68] Gustav Möller's study from 1918 also demonstrated that the tax threshold excluded significant groups of urban workers from voting in the period after 1909, as the tax payment threshold disqualified them. He also drew the long-term political conclusion: that it was of the utmost importance that the Social Democrats could recruit among agricultural labourers, who otherwise tended to vote for bourgeois parties.[69]

What, then, was the effect of the decisions of 1918–1921? Table 7.8 shows the corresponding figures based on the population in the 1920 census. Here we can see the effect of a lowering of the voting age in Second Chamber elections, to 23, in relation to the outcome if the decision had followed the Social Democrats' original demand for a voting age of 21. The voting age in municipal elections was also raised, from 21 to 23, and they no longer had a direct impact on the First Chamber, where the voting age was now 27 through elections to the county councils. The 1920 census allows us to estimate who was allowed to vote in the 1920 election under the old rules and those who were no longer eligible to vote in the 1921 election. There is a certain discrepancy, but it ought not to distort the general results.

Table 7.7 Proportion of the population in urban and rural areas and in Stockholm, Malmö, and Gothenburg excluded by the raised voting age in the 1911 elections, in absolute terms (in thousands) and as a percentage of the population

1911	*Countryside*			*Towns*			*Stockholm*			*Göteborg*			*Malmö*		
	Men	*Women*	*Sum*	*Men*	*Women*	*Sum*	*Men*	*Women*	*Sum*	*Men*	*Women*	*Sum*	*Men*	*Women*	*Sum*
Total population	2067	2088	4155	631	736	1368	154	188	342	78	90	168	39	45	84
Population over 21	1150	1192	2322	371	472	843	100	133	233	45	57	101	22	28	50
Population between 21–24	129	122	251	53	60	113	16	19	33	6	7	14	3	4	7
% Population without franchise over 21	11.2%	10.3%	10.8%	14.2%	12.8%	13.4%	15.6%	14.1%	14.4%	13.8%	13.0%	13.4%	13.2%	14.0%	14.1%

Source: Kungl. Statistiska centralbyrån, *Folkräkningen den 31 dec 1910*: II. *Folkmängdens fördelning efter kön, ålder och civilstånd* (Stockholm, P. A. Norstedt & Söner, 1913), pp. 1–6, reworked from table 2

The figures for women are hypothetical but demonstrate how many women would have been excluded if granted voting rights on the same terms as men

Table 7.8 Proportion of the population in urban and rural areas and in Stockholm, Malmö, and Gothenburg that were excluded from voting in the 1921–1922 elections to municipal councils, the Second Chamber, and the county councils (First Chamber) in absolute numbers (in thousands) and as a percentage of the adult population

	1920								
	Countryside			Towns			Stockholm		
	Men	Women	Sum	Men	Women	Sum	Men	Women	Sum
Total population	2087	2074	4161	811	932	1743	187	190	377
Population 0–20 år	906	857	1763	314	318	632	61	64	125
Population 21 år and older	1181	1217	2399	497	614	1111	126	126	252
Municipal and AK 21–23[a]	104	95	198	46	54	100	11	15	26
County/FK i 21–27[a]	225	210	436	106	123	227	27	34	61
Municipal and AK 21–23[a, b]	8.8%	7.8%	8.3%	9.3%	8.7%	9.0%	9.0%	11.8%	10.4%
County/FK 21–27[a, b]	19%	17%	18%	21%	20%	20%	21%	27%	24%

	Göteborg			Malmö		
	Men	Women	Sum	Men	Women	Sum
Total population	96	106	202	53	60	114
Population 0–20	38	37	75	22	22	44
Population 21 and older	59	69	127	31	38	70
Municipal and AK 21–23[a]	6	6	12	3	3	6
County/FK i åldern 21–27[a]	13	14	28	7	8	14
Municipal and AK 21–23[a, b]	9.8%	8.8%	9.3%	9.4%	9.0%	9.2%
County FK 21–27[a, b]	23%	21%	22%	21%	21%	21%

FK = first kammaren AK = second kammaren

[a]Adults without voting rights to different assemblies

[b]Percentage of adult population

Source: Kungl. Statistiska centralbyrån, *Folkräkningen den 31 december 1920*: III. *Folkmängdens fördelning efter ålder, kön, civilstånd och födelseort. Äktenskapen efter varaktighet och efter makarnas ålder* (Stockholm: P. A. Norstedt & Söner, 1926), reworked from tables 1–2

As the table shows, in Sweden as a whole about 600,000 people aged 21–27 were unable to vote in elections to the county councils and hence the First Chamber, while about 150,000 men actually lost the right to vote in municipal elections. A larger proportion of the population in the towns than in the countryside was affected by the decisions. The high voting age in elections to county councils and the First Chamber excluded almost 20 per cent of the urban population, the group aged 21–27, while those aged 21–23 excluded from voting in municipal and Second Chamber elections amounted to roughly 10 per cent. Since the new voting rules for municipalities applied from the municipal elections of 1919, the result was that in the 1921 elections, people aged 21–27 had no influence in county council elections. This was the same for men and women. Women aged 21–23 who had enjoyed municipal suffrage before 1921, provided that they had paid taxes, now lost their right to vote. A large majority of these women were probably unmarried, at least those in the towns, given the high marriage age, but it is of course uncertain whether these women in rural and urban areas were registered as taxpayers and had paid their taxes. On the other hand, lowering the voting age from 24 to 23 meant that an additional annual cohort of men was included among the voters (Fig. 7.11).

Concluding Reflections

When suffrage was extended, a large proportion of men and women were excluded from voting as a result of the age limits that were put in place. This issue was very much shaped by the political debate about social development in cities. My analysis makes it likely that the ambition was also to establish rules that in various ways disadvantaged urban workers, even though—in formal terms—the rules were neutrally designed. The same also applied, of course, to the requirement to have paid taxes in one of the last three years and not to have been dependent on poor relief, as pointed out by Ebba Berling Åselius.[70] In the years following 1921, it was these requirements that applied to people aged 23–27, thus excluding mainly urban men on account of unpaid taxes and urban women dependent on poor relief.[71]

The high voting age was a reaction to the fact that the urban population was increasing, which meant a greater political influence in general for towns and cities. It also reflected a fear of the population cohorts in their twenties who had not yet started a family and showed signs of greater criminality and other deviations from social and political norms. The

Fig. 7.11 By the time of the 1920 election, youthful enthusiasm was a common motif in labour movement flyers, although the voting age would exclude many young people. (Source, Drawing by E. Widholm. Arbetarrörelsens arkiv och bibliotek)

demand for responsible behaviour—payment of taxes and being able to support oneself—instead risked excluding those who were politically prioritised—adults in families with responsibility for children but unable to pay their taxes. There was a clear link between the social development and the political measures.

Cities such as Stockholm, Gothenburg, and Malmö saw a dramatic increase in population between 1880 and 1920, but smaller towns also experienced rapid population growth. Moreover, the marriage age in general was relatively high. A large majority of the population did not marry until after the age of 25, and many, especially women, did not marry at all. Both men and women had a long period before getting married. For young people as a rule, there was a transition period of around ten years between leaving home and starting a family of one's own. A large part of the population, both male and female, remained unmarried.

The decisions and debates in the first decades of the twentieth century excluded women in various ways, but they were just as much concerned with limiting the influence of the urban working class. The measures reflect a growing establishment of a bourgeois cultural order and a bourgeois view of society. It was the responsible married population that had to be included with the introduction of the new democratic order. The regulations were designed to exclude those who did not fit into the culture of responsible behaviour. At the same time, it is ironic that the workers' culture at this time also emphasised responsible behaviour. This was a culture firmly rooted in the established and well-educated strata of the working class, but also among the youth movement with its drive for self-improvement.[72] It would be interesting to examine the extent to which these groups also began to embrace the core values that characterised the suffrage debates.

Notes

1. In her thesis, Monika Edgren has pointed to changes in the concept of the family and the new meanings it acquired during the nineteenth century. See Monika Edgren, *Tradition och förändring: Könsrelationer, omsorgsarbete och försörjning inom Norrköpings underklass under 1800-talet*, diss. (Lund: Lund University Press, 1994).
2. Riksdagstrycket, *Protokoll FK 1902:36*, p. 53.
3. Christina Florin, *Kvinnor får röst: Kön, känslor och politisk kultur i kvinnornas rösträttsrörelse* (Stockholm: Atlas, 2006), pp. 28–30.

4. Josefin Rönnbäck, *Politikens genusgränser: Den kvinnliga rösträttsrörelsen och kampen för kvinnors politiska medborgarskap 1902–1921* (Stockholm: Atlas, 2004), pp. 186–210, 211–242.
5. Riksdagstrycket, *Proposition 1908:34*, pp. 44–45; Anna Bugge Wicksell, "De gifta kvinnorna och kommunallagarna", *Dagny:Tidning för svenska kvinnorörelsen* 1910:3, pp. 28–30; Rönnbäck 2004, p. 115; Konrad Hagman, *Sveriges kommunallagar: Förordningarna den 21 mars 1862 jämte en mängd andra till kommunallagstiftningen hörande författningar* (Stockholm: Fröléen, 1911) n 1911, p. 42.
6. Kjell Östberg, *Kommunerna och den svenska modellen: Socialdemokratin och kom Munalpolitiken fram till andra världskriget* (Eslöv: Brutus Östlings bokförlag Symposion, 1996), pp. 131–164.
7. Rönnbäck (2004, pp. 113–144).
8. *Morgonbris* 1911:11, p. 7.
9. Christina Carlsson Wetterberg, *Jag saknar fruntimmer här: En biografi över Anna Bugge Wicksell* ([Stockholm]: Natur & Kultur, 2020), pp. 154–155.
10. Ibid., pp. 148–149; Wicksell (1910).
11. Helena Bergman and Peter Johansson, *Familjeangelägenheter: Modern historisk forskning om välfärdsstat, genus och politik* (Eslöv: Brutus Östlings bokförlag Symposion, 2002); Tommie Lundquist, *Den disciplinerade dubbelmoralen: Studier i den reglementerade prostitutionens historia i Sverige 1859–1918*, diss. (Göteborg: Göteborgs universitet, 1982); Frida Stéenhoff, *Den reglementerade prostitutionen ur feministisk synpunkt* (Stockholm: Björck & Börjesson, 1904); Christina Carlsson Wetterberg, *– bara ett öfverskott af lif –: En biografi om Frida Stéenhoff (1865–1945)* (Stockholm: Atlantis, 2010); Maria Sundkvist, *De vanartade barnen: Mötet mellan barn, föräldrar och Norrköpings barnavårdsnämnd 1903–1925* (Uppsala: Hjelm, 1994); Gena Weiner, *De räddade barnen: Om fattiga barn, mödrar och fäder och deras möte med filantropin i Hagalund 1900–1940* (Uppsala: Hjelm, 1995); Cecilia Lindgren, *En riktig familj: Adoption, föräldraskap och barnets bästa 1917–1975* (Stockholm: Carlsson, 2006); Sundkvist 1994; Riksdagstrycket, *Protokoll FK 1902:35*, pp. 26–29; Bengt Sandin, "History of Children's Well-Being", in Ben-Arieh Asher et al. (eds.), *Handbook of Child Well-Being: Theories, Methods and Policies in Global Perspective* (New York & London: Springer, 2014); Svanström, Yvonne, *Offentliga kvinnor: prostitution i Sverige 1812–1918* (Stockholm: Ordfront 2006); Rebecka, Lennartsson, *Malaria urbana: om byråflickan Anna Johannesdotter och prostitutionen i Stockholm kring 1900* (Diss. Uppsala: Univ., 2002); Rebecka, Lennartsson, Den sköna synderskan: sekelskiftets Stockholm: betraktelser från undersidan. (Stockholm: Norstedt 2007).

12. Rönnbäck 2004, pp. 189–210; Ronny Ambjörnsson, *Den skötsamme arbetaren: Idéer och ideal i ett norrländskt sågverkssamhälle 1880–1930* (Stockholm: Carlsson, 1988).
13. See, e.g., Riksdagstrycket, *Proposition 1908:34*, pp. 41–53.
14. Carlsson Wetterberg (2000, pp. 59–81), quotation p. 63.
15. Ibid., pp. 43–62.
16. Rönnbäck (2004, pp. 169–242).
17. Riksdagstrycket, *Protokoll FK 1902:35*, pp. 26–29, Lindhagen, Adelswärd, Wieselgren.
18. Maths Isacson and Mats Morell, *Industrialismens tid: Ekonomisk-historiska perspektiv på svensk industriell omvandling under 200 år* (Stockholm: SNS förlag, 2002); Arthur Montgomery, *Industrialismens genombrott i Sverige* (Stockholm: Skoglunds bokförlag, 1947); Johannes Daun, *Vägen till den moderna familjen: Fruktsamhet i den växande industristaden Borås cirka 1830–1930*, diss. (Göteborg: Göteborgs universitet, 2016), pp. 49–58, 64–67, 74–76; Hans Nilsson and Lars-Göran Tedebrand, *Familjer i växande städer: Strukturer och strategier vid familjebildning i Sverige 1840–1940* (Umeå; Demografiska databasen, 2005), pp. 94–105; Bo Kronborg and Thomas Nilsson, *Stadsflyttare: Industrialisering, migration och social mobilitet med utgångspunkt från Halmstad 1870–1910*, diss. (Uppsala: Uppsala universitet, 1975).
19. Gustav Sundbärg, *Emigrationsutredningen: Betänkande i utvandringsfrågan och därmed sammanhängande spörsmål* (Stockholm: Nordiska bokhandeln, 1913); Daun 2016, pp. 49–58, 64–67, 74–76; Nilsson and Tedebrand 2005, pp. 94–105; Kronborg and Nilsson 1975.
20. *Folkräkningen den 31 december 1920: III. Folkmängden efter ålder, kön, civilstånd och födelseort. Äktenskapen efter varaktighet och efter makarnas ålder*, Kungl. Statistiska centralbyrån, Sveriges officiella statistik (Stockholm: Statistiska centralbyrån, 1926), pp. 10–11.
21. Ibid.
22. Ibid. See also Daun (2016, pp. 49–58, 64–67, 74–76); Nilsson and Tedebrand (2005, pp. 94–105).
23. Ibid., p. 10.
24. Kungl. Statistiska centralbyrån, Sveriges officiella statistik, *Allmänna val 1921, Kommunala valen 1920*, p. 5.
25. Kungl. Statistiska centralbyrån, *Folkräkningen den 31 december 1920, III* (Stockholm: P. A. Norstedt & Söner, 1926), pp. 20–21.
26. Stockholms stads statistik, *Statistisk årsbok för Stockholms stad 1920*, Table 31, "Åldersfördelningen inom befolkningen vid slutet av åren i % av befolkningen i Stockholm samt andelen ogift/gifta av medelfolkmängden 1901–1910" (Stockholm: Stockholms stads statistiska kontor, 1920).
27. Kungl. Statistiska centralbyrån, *Folkräkningen den 31 december 1910*, II, tables H–K, quotation p. 42.

28. Edgren 1994; Margareta Matović, *Stockholmsäktenskap: Familjebildning och partnerval i Stockholm 1850–1890* (Stockholm: LiberFörlag, 1984); Bengt Sandin, *Hemmet, gatan, fabriken eller skolan: Folkundervisning och barnuppfostran i svenska städer 1600–1850* (Lund: Arkiv, 1986); Gunnar Qvist, *Kvinnofrågan i Sverige 1809–1846: Studier rörande kvinnans näringsfrihet inom de borgerliga yrkena*, diss. (Göteborg: Göteborgs universitet, 1960).
29. Gustav Sundbärg, "Rikets folkmängd åren 1750–1900", *Statistisk tidskrift* 1903:2, pp. 169–70.
30. Sundbärg (1913, p. 830).
31. *Betänkande och Förslag afgifna af den af Kongl. Maj:t den 16 Oktober 1896 tillsatta komitén för utredning af frågan om åtgärder för beredande af lämplig uppfostran dels åt minderåriga förbrytare dels ock åt vanartade och i sedligt afseende försummade barn.* I. *Betänkande och förslag angående minderåriga förbrytares behandling* (Stockholm: K. L. Beckmans Boktryckeri, 1908), p. 95; Sundkvist 1994. For a disussion of "Stockholm marriages" see e.g. Matović (1984), Edgren (1994).
32. Kungl. Statistiska centralbyrån, *Statistiska meddelanden*, serie A, Bd 1:5, Utom äktenskapet födda barn (Stockholm: P. A. Norstedt & Söner, 1916), pp. 33–48, 88–89.
33. Ulrika Norburg, *Fängelse, skola, uppfostringsanstalt eller skyddshem? Åkerbrukskolonien Hall för pojkar år 1876–1940*, diss. (Linköping: Linköpings universitet, 2015), pp. 76–68.
34. Fångvårdsstyrelsens underdåniga berättelse, *BiSOS G, Fångvården: Ny följd XLIII* (Stockholm: P. A. Norstedt & Söner, 1903), pp. 4–5, table 2, "Personer, häktade för brott och förseelser år 1901".
35. Justitiestatsministern underdåniga ämbetsberättelse 1905, *BiSOS B, Rättsväsendet: Ny följd XLVIII:2 1905* (Stockholm: P. A. Norstedt & Söner, 1906), p. v.
36. Ibid., tables 4, 5, 6; Justitiestatsministerns underdåniga ämbetsberättelse 1899, *BiSOS B, Rättsväsendet: Ny följd XLII:2 1899* (Stockholm: P. A. Norstedt & Söner, 1900); Hanns von Hofer, *Brott och straff i Sverige: Historisk kriminalstatistik 1750–2010, diagram, tabeller och kommentarer* (Stockholm: Kriminologiska institutionen, Stockholms universitet, 2011), chapters 2–3.
37. Kungl. Statistiska centralbyrån, *SOS, Folkmängden och dess förändringar: Dödsorsaker år 1918* (Stockholm: P. A. Norstedt & Söner, 1923), p. 13.
38. Klas Åmark, "Familj, försörjning och livslopp under 1900-talet", i Helena Bergman och Peter Johansson (red.), *Familjeangelägenheter: Modern historisk forskning om välfärdsstat, genus och politik* (Eslöv: Brutus Östlings bokförlag Symposion, 2002), pp. 243–253. See also Riksdagstrycket, *Protokoll FK 1918:27*, p. 49. "Between the ages of 20 and 30, two thirds

are still unmarried, between the ages of 30 and 60, on the other hand, two-thirds are married – in certain ages as much as 70 per cent. During the same time, the number of unmarried people decreases, while the number of widows increases, and from age 60 up to death widows outnumber married women. We thus see that, although 70 per cent of Sweden's women get married, before age 30 and after age 60 the vast majority are unmarried."

39. Edgren (1994, pp. 132–160).
40. Hagman (1911, p. 42).
41. Gustaf af Geijerstam, *Anteckningar om arbetarförhållanden i Stockholm* (Stockholm: Samson & Wallin, 1894); Ulrika Knutson, *Den besvärliga Elin Wägner* (Lund: Historiska Media, 2020); Elin Wägner, *Norrtullsligan: Elisabeths krönika* (Stockholm: Ljus, 1908); Elin Wägner and Helena Forsås-Scott, *Pennskaftet* (Stockholm: Svenska Akademien i samverkan med Atlantis, 2003).
42. Edward Bull quoted from Lars Olsson, "Barns arbete och arbetets barn", in Karin Aronsson (ed.), *Barn i tid och rum* (Malmö: Liber, 1984), p. 158. Gustaf af Geijerstam, *Anteckningar om arbetarförhållanden i Stockholm* (Stockholm: Samson & Wallin, 1894).
43. Erik Bengtsson, *Världens jämlikaste land?* (Lund: Arkiv förlag, 2020), pp. 76–77.
44. Sundbärg (1913, p. 833).
45. Fia Sundevall, "Ekonomi och rösträtt: Skatteskulder, konkurs och fattigvård som rösträttshinder", in Annika Berg and Martin Ericsson (eds.), *Allmän rösträtt? Rösträttens begränsningar i Sverige efter 1921* (Göteborg & Stockholm: Makadam, 2021).
46. Kungl. Statistiska centralbyrån, *BiSoS 1900–1902 R, Valstatistik XV: Riksdagsmannavalen 1900–1902* (Stockholm, 1903), p. 11.
47. Ibid., pp. 14–15.
48. Ibid., p. 15.
49. Ebba Berling Åselius, *Rösträtt med förhinder: Rösträttsstrecken i svensk politik 1900–1920* (Stockholm: Acta Universitatis Stockholmiensis, 2005), pp. 124–133. See also Georg Andrén, *Sveriges riksdag: Historisk och statsvetenskaplig framställning, Bd 9, Tvåkammarsystemetstillkomst och utveckling* (Stockholm 1937), and Otto Grönlund, "Den allmänna politiska rösträtten och valen till riksdagens andra kammare åren 1911–1921 i statistisk belysning", *Statsvetenskaplig tidskrift* 27:3, 1924, pp. 214–267.
50. Kungl. Statistiska centralbyrån, *BiSOS R Valstatistik XIV:3: Valrätt till riksdagens andra kammare 1900* (Stockholm, 1904), pp. viii–x.
51. Ibid., quotation p. viii.
52. Ibid., p. x.
53. Ibid., p. xi.

54. Ibid., p. xii. "Data on unpaid taxes (crown taxes and municipal taxes) refer to the end of August 1900, the time of the year from which, under the current constitutional provision, elections to the Second Chamber begin." See ibid., p. xii.
55. Sundevall (2021, pp. 87–120).
56. Kungl. Statistiska centralbyrån, *SOS 1919, Kommunala valen 1919* (Stockholm: P. A. Norstedt & Söner, 1920), pp. 4–13.
57. Ibid., p. 6.
58. Ibid., pp. 12–13.
59. Sven Lundkvist, *Folkrörelserna i det svenska samhället 1850–1920* (Stockholm: Sober, 1977), pp. 91–94; Ambjörnsson 1988; Henrik Berggren, *Seklets ungdom: Retorik, politik och modernitet 1900–1939*, diss. (Stockholm: Tiden, 1995), pp. 93–98. Torkel Jansson, *Adertonhundratalets associationer: Forskning och problem kring ett sprängfullt tomrum eller sammanslutningsprinciper och föreningsformer mellan två samhällsformationer c:a 1800–1870* (Uppsala: Uppsala universitet, 1985).
60. Yngve Tidman, *Spräng Amalthea! Arbete, facklig kamp och strejkbryteri i nordvästeuropeiska hamnar 1870–1914* (Lund: Lund University Press, 1998), pp. 9–39; Berggren 1995, pp. 93–98.
61. Jenny Langkjaer, *Övervakning för rikets säkerhet: Svensk säkerhetspolisiär övervakning av utländska personer och inhemsk politisk aktivitet, 1885–1922* (Stockholm: Acta Universitetis Stockholmiensis, 2011), pp. 131–157.
62. Berggren (1995, pp. 76–92).
63. Bengt Sandin och Jonathan Josefsson, "Age as a yardstick for political citizenship: Voting age and eligibility age in Sweden during the twentieth century", Continuity and Change 2022:2, s. 257–280.
64. Berling Berling Berling Åselius 2005, pp. 124–133.
65. Kungl. Statistiska centralbyrån, *BiSOS R, Valstatistik XIV:4: Valrätt till riksdagens andra kammare år 1900. Kvinnor över 24 år* (Stockholm, 1908), p. i; *BiSOS R, Valstatistik. XIV:3: Valrätt till riksdagens andra kammare 1900* (Stockholm, 1904).
66. Kungl. Statistiska centralbyrån, *Folkräkningen den 31 december 1910: II. Folkmängdens fördelning efter kön, ålder och civilstånd* (Stockholm, 1913), pp. 1–6, table 2.
67. Gösta Bagge, *Wages, Cost of Living and National Income in Sweden 1860–1930*, vol. 2, *Wages in Sweden 1860–1930* (London: P. S. King, 1933); Kungl. Kommerskollegii Afdelning för Arbetsstatistik, *Arbetsstatistik L:1: Till belysning af Landtarbetarnas arbets- och löneförhållanden i Sverige år 1910* (Stockholm: P. A. Norstedt & Söner, 1911).
68. Berling Åselius 2005, pp. 103–123; Lotta Gröning, *Vägen till makten: SAP:s organisation och dess betydelse för den politiska verksamheten 1900–1933*, diss. (Uppsala: Uppsala universitet, 1988).

69. Möller (1918).
70. Berling Åselius (2005, pp. 124–133).
71. Kungl. Statistiska centralbyrån, *SOS, Allmänna val: Kommunala valen år 1919* (Stockholm: P. A. Norstedt & Söner, 1920), pp. 5–18; Sundevall 2021.
72. Björn Horgby, *Egensinne och skötsamhet: Arbetarkulturen i Norrköping 1850–1940* (Stockholm: Carlsson, 1993); Ambjörnsson (1988), Berggren (1995).

CHAPTER 8

Political Age Limits

Previous historians have not paid much attention to the raising of the voting age in connection with the suffrage reforms of 1918–1921 and before this in 1907–1909, with the exception of recent research on voting restrictions after 1921, which has led to the present study of the period before 1921. It has merely been observed that the higher voting age was an element in the compromise that enabled the decisions or that the voting age was socially and politically neutral. It did not leave any particular social class or gender or any part of Sweden at a disadvantage. Arguments like this were also heard in the contemporary conservative and liberal rhetoric. This is what my study has questioned. In this chapter I will point to the short-term relationship between the political processes and its fixation with the voting age but also the underlying understanding of age as a signifier of a married state and social stability in the short term as well as an expression of the long-term demographic transformation.

Previous scholars, except Ludvig Beckman, have not problematised the fact that Sweden deviated from the main lines of European development during the nineteenth century in its interest to raise the voting age. The low voting age during the nineteenth century had made Sweden exceptional, and when demands for democratic reforms increased at the end of the century, it led to a discussion of whether the voting age should be raised. This distinctive development gives us a unique opportunity and insight into how the political participation of young citizens and their role in society was looked upon.

B. Sandin, *Voting and Eligibility Age in Sweden, 1866–1921*,
https://doi.org/10.1007/978-3-031-95276-0_8

The constitutional transformation of Europe during the nineteenth century mainly benefitted the bourgeois strata while limiting or excluding lower social classes in various ways. This was also the case in Sweden, but the country retained the low voting age that had applied to the old Diet of the four estates, supplemented by economic voting restrictions and strict eligibility requirements. The new system was heavily dependent on the previous system of representation. In other countries the voting age was higher, but often in combination with other restrictions. In those countries the voting age was lowered when the democratisation process gained momentum, but in Sweden it was raised.

The voting age has been at the centre of this study. The cultural and social significance of the age limits has been examined and related to other restrictions on suffrage. I have also analysed the political processes that raised the issue of age and the economic and demographic changes that propelled them.

Age limits were relevant in various ways to the discussion of municipal suffrage and the right to vote in elections to county councils and the two chambers of Parliament. Age limits also affected relations between these different political levels. In this study, therefore, I have examined both national political suffrage (the Second Chamber) and municipal suffrage (which affected the county councils and the First Chamber) in a slightly longer temporal perspective. I started with the abolition of the Diet of the four estates. The provisions established by the constitutional decisions of 1863 and 1866 were based on the rules of the old Diet. They were challenged by social development in both rural and urban areas. The conflicts over the age limits for voting are an example of how social development undercut the legitimacy of institutions that were based on previous decisions and regulatory systems.

In connection with the 1907–1909 reform, the justification cited for the decision to raise the voting age was that it guaranteed social stability and order, together with a number of other voting restrictions (the "thresholds" or "lines") and with the introduction of a proportional representation system, it was thought that power would largely remain in the hands of the same people, but with an opening for new groups. This created the conditions for a compromise that first granted universal suffrage to men in 1909 and then gave women universal suffrage in 1921 while retaining the First Chamber and the monarchy. This meant that authority in society was shifted. The age limits were a crucial aspect of the endeavour to counteract what some perceived as the negative consequences of democracy

My analysis has shown how the issue of the voting age was interwoven with other aspects of the desire to achieve democracy with guarantees. The 40-grade economic voting scale, the criteria of responsible behaviour, the gender difference, the different economic thresholds and the age thresholds were intimately linked. The restrictions also reflected the age structure of society. The suffrage issue concerned age limits in society as they were reflected in relations between the classes and the genders, and also in the outlook on different generations, young people, the family, and marriage. At the same time, social development was affected by urbanisation and industrialisation. Gender and class were coded in terms of age as was economy and location. This was particularly noticeable in the towns and cities, where the youth cohorts under the age of around 25 were especially noticeable, at least from the 1890s until the beginning of the 1920s. The rise of this population group was a long-term consequence of the demographic transition from 1819 to 1830. Around 1900 these young people began to be perceived and described in new terms, as a generation associated with a range of social problems. Their presence in the towns, and the social conditions in which they lived, changed the political dynamics and the relationship between those who ruled and those who demanded the chance to participate in the political processes. My analysis shows that the shifting age limits enabled the political compromises that led to the decisions in 1918–1921 to introduce a more democratic constitution. The expansion of democracy was thus closely linked to measures intended to limit the electorate by excluding the young, that is, all those under the age of 24.

International research has emphasised the different roots of the suffrage issue and of democracy in different social processes, within the working class and in changing elites, as well as the dependence on both long-term social changes and more dynamic and conflict-driven events. Scholars have also studied the interaction between different aspects of the institutional transformations of society. These were not synchronised processes and could have incompatible effects. Some historians and political scientists have argued for a historicising perspective and for a consideration of class, ethnicity, and gender. The matter of the age has not been ascribed the same explanatory value in such earlier analyses.

That the development could be contradictory and the outcome, the consequences of the decisions, not always in line with the intentions of the actors, is another important insight in earlier research. In this study I have taken note of this approach, but with a focus on the aspect of the politics surrounding the democratic processes that research, both inside and outside Sweden, has neglected, namely, that of age and generation. As a consequence of my analyses, it is also obvious that space mattered; it was a conflict between urban expansion and rural social and economic interests. In this concluding chapter I shall first consider the significance of age limits and the part they played in the political processes. I then examine the age limits in relation to the family, young people, and finally the impact of the demographic trends.

The Meanings of Age Limits

When the demands for a higher voting age began to be formulated, it was as a reaction to the calls by the Social Democrats and the suffrage movement for an extension of the right to vote. The "People's Parliaments" in which Liberals and Social Democrats were active also challenged the hegemonic power of the Riksdag to formulate the conditions for a suffrage reform. They could not agree, however. Using radical political actions, the Social Democrats were campaigning to extend suffrage from the age of 21. The Liberals argued for an expansion of the electorate, but at the same time defended the idea of democracy with guarantees that power would remain in the hands of those currently exercising it. They argued for a higher voting age. This could limit the electorate to include only the socially stable and older strata of the population. Cooperation with the Social Democrats was not successful at this point.

The Liberals' demands for a larger electorate—by removing or lowering the economic requirements while simultaneously balancing this by raising the voting age—is a perfect example of how calls for the expansion of democracy went hand in hand with ideas about how the influence of certain age groups could be limited. The discussion of the voting age, along with the introduction of other restrictions on suffrage, was part of an offensive political strategy on the part of the political establishment, both Liberals and the Right.[1] The strategy included demands for proportional representation instead of majority elections and a defence of the status of the First Chamber. Maintaining the position of the First Chamber was intimately linked to an issue crucial for the Right, namely, power over municipal and county councils. Parts of what we regard as right-wing parties were also interested in implementing certain changes to the electoral system because the votes of companies in the municipalities were an obstacle for their electorate in rural industrial communities. Right-wing parties and Liberals also saw the need for suffrage reform because some of their potential core voters were excluded from the political system as well.

Around 1900 the proposals for a higher voting age were based on the idea that suffrage should be linked to social maturity, independence, and sound judgement, summed up in the notions of the married man's responsibility for a family. This was one of the basic arguments for having a voting age higher than the age of majority established in the eighteenth century. When most young men came of age they were not married. The voting age was associated with a family headed by a male breadwinner. This left out an entire large group of young working-class people who normally supported themselves from the age of 15 or 16. Marriage as the norm, of course, also meant excluding other "non-legalised" types of family, such as those held together by independent and self-supporting women. Here the debate also reflects an increased cultural emphasis on the bourgeois family with its morals and gender roles.

The idealisation of the bourgeois family was also linked to calls for social reforms aimed at compensating for what was perceived as the lack of responsibility and good parenthood in the young working class. The meanings of parenthood in different social classes were part of this discussion of the family as the foundation of society. The women's suffrage movement also stressed the importance of motherhood as a foundation for women's civic status and suffrage. Marriage as the norm was central to the discussion of women's suffrage, as Ebba Åselius has shown in her doctoral dissertation about the suffrage thresholds in Swedish politics.[2] A high voting age was intended to favour the political influence of the family.

Up until 1909, the right to vote in elections to the Second Chamber was based on municipal suffrage and the restrictions that applied to local elections. The new thresholds for voting in elections to the Second Chamber, introduced in 1909, were thus also a consequence of the fact that this was no longer based on municipal suffrage.[3] The voting age for men in municipal elections was 21, and although there was no poor relief threshold, in reality the economic voting scale excluded young age groups and poor people from real political influence. With a higher voting age and the exclusion of those who did not pay tax or received poor relief, the economic criteria for voting in Second Chamber elections could be abolished. The requirement to have completed military training and the bankruptcy criterion were new thresholds. Voting restrictions to the Second

Chamber were thus also constitutionally protected from 1909 onwards and required two consecutive decisions by the Riksdag and an election between the decisions. Municipal suffrage did not have this protection against change, which means that, as long as this was a prerequisite for voting in elections to the Second Chamber, there was a risk that sudden upheavals in political opinion could also affect the composition of the Second Chamber. This was the rational for no longer linking voting rights in Second Chamber elections to municipal suffrage.

With regard to municipal suffrage, the discussion of a higher voting age came to be related to the restrictions on voting resulting from gradation according to income. The 40-grade voting scale meant that the voting age in municipal elections could remain at 21 as it had been since 1866. When introduced in 1909, the scale effectively excluded large groups of workers, men and unmarried women, from exercising influence corresponding to their number, in municipalities and in elections to the First Chamber. The personality principle for voting gave way here to an idea that was corporatist and contributivist. The right to vote and exert influence was granted to those who had income, wealth, and real estate, who paid tax and were not a burden on the social welfare institutions (poor relief) of the local community.[4]

The argument about the qualities associated with age played a major role in shaping the new voting regulations. The 40-grade voting scale was likewise an implicit age threshold, deliberately favouring the influence of stable (responsible, tax-paying) patriarchal families—implicitly, men over 25. It was considered politically risky to grant too much influence to the younger generation and the less responsible sections of the working class.

The decisions of 1907–1909 were a victory for Lindman and the Right. They had achieved proportional representation and the reform of the income thresholds for municipal elections. The thresholds of age and tax payment became crucial criteria for excluding working-class voters. The decisions also show how central the First Chamber was in the politics of Swedish voting rights. The influence over the First Chamber and municipal elections is a key to understanding why Sweden was so late in giving votes to women and introducing universal and equal suffrage. Another essential idea was that the municipality should be a kind of voluntary association in which a person's influence corresponded to his contribution. Municipal suffrage was thus perceived as more important than and different from the right to vote in elections to the Second Chamber.[5] On these premises, the First Chamber could also remain a reflection of stable, mature, and long-term responsibility. Although this reduced the influence of the companies, it meant that established agricultural interests could dominate the First Chamber.

The voting age in elections to the Second Chamber was raised in 1909 to 24 (reaching the age of 25 in the year the election was held), combined with other restrictions. The decision to raise the voting age was a confirmation of the idea of the patriarchal family as the foundation for influence in society. The suggestions for additional votes at a higher age underlined this, as did other proposals for votes for various corporations, such as those with a higher degree of education or social responsibility.

The Intersection Between Age, Gender, and Class

The raising of the voting age for elections to the Second Chamber was occasioned by developments in the big cities with growing populations of young adults. This meant that the increasing weight of the cities in the electorate after 1866 was perceived as especially problematic, since a large share of the urban population consisted of young, unmarried workers. This led to a discussion about the need to curb the influence of the cities.

In rural municipalities, the electoral system had a different problem. The great influence of companies prompted supporters of the Right and the Liberals to find a way to limit the number of votes cast by big capital owners.

The demographic development in the cities could also be grounded in a broad discussion of the different meanings of the social issue. The discourse was shaped by the way society was described by the public statistics of the time, and perhaps by how it was experienced in everyday life. More and more young people were moving to the cities and the expanding mill towns, and these large cohorts were no longer emigrating as much as before. After 1900, we also see that population development in the smaller towns played a more significant part in the debate.

Payment of state and municipal tax, that is to say, being registered for tax, was the actual foundation for the right to vote in municipal elections and thus for the Second Chamber, but this was affected by municipal decisions about adjustment of taxation level for low incomes. The adjustments that municipalities could make at the local level thus meant that low income individuals risked losing their right to vote. Furthermore, it could be different in different communities.

The suffrage thresholds, the qualifications to vote, became the criteria for what was regarded as socially and politically normal. The idea was the normal family: responsible, settled, mature, and well-behaved. The suffrage thresholds were concrete expressions of what was regarded as deviant, abnormal, that which could not be rewarded with civic trust in the form of the right to vote for the Second Chamber. The debate was simplified into a matter of age limits, but it concerned the family as the basic social unit. The debate juxtaposed voting rights as an individual right and the institutions to which they were attached, the family and marriage. The crucial importance of the marriage norm is also evident in previous research, but this study has shown that this concerned not only relations between women and men but also the family in a broader sense, as an expression of the relationship and difference between the generations. By drawing attention to the central role of age limits for the suffrage issue, the study had identified new dimensions.

When the voting age became so culturally charged, the political conflicts between the political groupings that formed around the suffrage issue became multifaceted. From 1910 it was not only a conflict between the Right and the Left (Liberals and Social Democrats), but also between Social Democracy and the Liberals/Right. The contrasts between the Liberals and the Social Democrats were deep and significant in their view of age limits and tax payment as selection criteria for citizenship (voting rights). The Liberals were closer to the Right, with whom they also competed for rural voters. This meant that the conflicts also bore the imprint of the cultural conflict between town and country. There was also the problem of the uneven industrialisation; a characteristic of Sweden was that there were many mill towns, industrial communities in rural areas, and there was vigorous growth of conurbations with a young urban working class.

It was thus not only a struggle for women's suffrage but also an effort to defend the bicameral system and the status quo through voting restrictions and age limits. At its core, the suffrage struggle was also a story about the family as the basis for political influence. The subordination of women was of course questioned in the suffrage struggle, along with the ideas about women's immaturity, their lack of competence and knowledge, on which their subordination was based. But that struggle likewise reflected a conflict between married and unmarried (and younger) women. Here too there was a real age norm. It was the contribution of married women, of mothers, to society that was emphasised. It was a struggle of bourgeois women for equal political rights and status, demanding an appreciation of the contribution of married women to society. It was thus also a class issue as the unmarried working women in the cities were not a part of that group but were mostly seen as a social liability.

It is worth noting, however, that a higher voting age for women was never implemented, as it had been in Iceland and Britain. In Iceland the voting age for men was 25 and for women 40 when female suffrage was introduced. In Britain the reason stated for the higher voting age for women was that they outnumbered men in the population after the First World War. In 1906 when Finland passed its universal suffrage legislation which granted women voting rights "a high age limit of twenty-four was utilised to exclude young voters, particularly women deemed more susceptible to political unrest."[6] The Swedish politicians must no doubt have been aware of such arguments in the neighbouring nation. Conservative women in Sweden viewed the higher voting age as a protection against the many new voters that would come with the extension of suffrage, and they feared the influence of the left among politically inexperienced women.[7] The use of a higher voting age to counteract the demographic surplus of women does not seem to have had many advocates in the Swedish debate but such arguments were presented to motivate the 27-year limit for voting to county assemblies and the First Chamber.[8] When universal and equal suffrage was introduced in Sweden, men and women had the same voting age, although it was considerably higher than before.

It took the Liberals until 1915 to change their minds about the 40-grade scale, which was based on an implicit age norm, and it was not until December 1918 that they accepted universal suffrage for all citizens—not just taxpayers. Until then, they argued that married women should only be able to vote if their husbands had paid all his taxes. With the decisions of 1918–1921, the voting age was set at 23 in elections to municipal councils and the Second Chamber for both men and women, and at 27 in elections to county councils and the First Chamber. Ironically, married women were declared legally competent in the same year, 1921, that the reform was finally passed. They were thus not granted the right to vote at the same time as they became full citizens on a par with men. Furthermore, this also meant that men and women between the age of majority, 21, and the new voting ages, now lost (or were not granted) the right to vote. Before 1921, then, women's citizenship, in the sense of the right to vote, was conditional on their marital status (and economy), whereas men were legally competent at the age of 21, but from 1909 their

Fig. 8.1 The photographer Anna Larsson was born in 1900 and was 21 when the photograph of these timber raftsmen in Dalarna was taken in 1921. As a young adult woman, she documents an adult working life but is not trusted to vote. Some of the workers in the picture appear to be the same age. (Source: Foto Anna Larsson. Nordiska museets arkiv)

full citizenship (voting right) was delayed by a higher age limit. From the age of 21, both men's and women's citizenship were conditional on age limits higher than the age of majority. Unmarried women with an income and paid taxes between the ages of 21 and 23 lost their right to vote, while married women were no longer assessed in relation to their husbands' income and tax payment, but in relation to their age, as in the case of men (Fig. 8.1).

Family and Youth as Sources of Conflict

The subordination of women was questioned in the changes to marriage legislation that were discussed during the 1910s and implemented in 1915 and 1921. This breakthrough for a more individualistic view of relations within the family and of women's rights was of great importance for the development of society as a whole. The new law reflects a changed outlook on these issues in broader political camps, with implications for other issues as well, such as family policy, although it also emphasises the distinctive character of women and their specific contributions to society.[9]

With a high voting age and women's suffrage, the family gained more gravity. The suffrage reform proposed in 1918, based on a voting age of 21, had risked giving greater influence to "immature" interests in society. This was the justification for demands from the Right to raise the ages of voting and eligibility in order to strengthen the influence of the responsible family. Granting married women the right to vote could also serve to reinforce the stable and slightly older part of the population. An argument along these lines is included, for example, in the explanatory statement of the government's suffrage proposal in the autumn of 1918 and in the third select committee's proposal for a compromise on the suffrage issue in December 1918. Women's suffrage also meant that the family now got two votes, without men being given an extra vote. Ironically, women's suffrage reinforced the family norm under these new conditions. It supported both modernity and tradition, as Christina Carlsson Wetterberg has pointed out, with regard to the changes made to the legal status of women in 1915 and 1920.[10]

The Liberals shared the opinion of the Right about the higher voting age and indeed the legitimacy of many of the suffrage thresholds introduced in 1909, albeit with some modifications on which they could agree with Social Democrats. The Liberals' demand for women's suffrage from the age of 25 therefore did not come into conflict with the National Association for Women's Suffrage (LKPR), which demanded the right to vote on the same terms as men. The demand meant, however, that women under the age of 24 would not have the conditional suffrage that the Liberals demanded for women, and for whom the National Association also fought, regardless of whether they paid taxes or not. Once again, in this matter too, the class conflict is visible because these women were predominantly unmarried and/or wage earners.

The Liberals' alliance with the Social Democrats on the issue of women's suffrage was thus considerably impaired because the Social Democrats demanded women's suffrage also for married women from the age of 21, in fact for all women. Moreover, the Liberals' conception of suffrage was tied to citizens who paid taxes, which might not include all women (nor crofters, unmarried men and women still living with their parents, and so on). According to the Liberal proposal in the spring of 1918, however, married women whose husbands paid taxes would gain the right to vote in elections to the Second Chamber. On the question of the voting age, the Liberals and the Right were much closer because they also shared the same fundamental view on the importance of the First Chamber as an institution representing the older, more mature elements of society, although the Liberals wanted to reduce the significance of the First Chamber. The Social Democrats demanded a voting age of 21 and equal and universal suffrage with all thresholds abolished, and some also called for the abolition of the First Chamber and the monarchy. The left-wing socialists also made firm demands for a unicameral parliament and for the abolition of the monarchy. These demands were radically opposed to the platform of the Liberals and the Right.

In the final stages of the political agreement on suffrage, in the shadow of international and national unrest, the discussion boiled down to its central elements: various aspects of tax payment as the basis for voting, combined with an age of eligibility that could favour stable groups in society, those who were married and settled. Introducing women's suffrage was the obvious thing to do at this time. It would benefit the family and the stable elements of society if it went hand in hand with a high voting age.

But the November 1918 bill with a voting age of 21 risked eliminating the guarantee of stability demanded by the Right. This was what Lindman so emphatically objected to in the final debate on 17 December 1918. Jeopardising the position of the mature elements of society—married people—in the municipalities would have negative consequences for the composition of the First Chamber. This was what the 40-grade scale had prevented when it was introduced—it allowed power in the municipalities to be concentrated in the older population, according to Lindman. There was a similar risk if the right to vote became universal for all citizens from the age of 21 without being restricted to taxpayers. The realisation that the 40-grade voting scale was about to be abolished had put the spotlight on the voting age as a key to the political compromise, together with payment of taxes.

A high age for voting and eligibility made it possible, as I have shown, to introduce universal suffrage. The idea was that the right to vote would be limited to include only citizens of both sexes with family responsibilities. The compromise of 1918–1921 must be understood as a temporary victory for Conservative and Liberal forces that were dubious of the influence of the "immature". Democracy was still conditional. The value of a higher voting age was not obvious to everyone, however. It was a price the Social Democrats accepted in order to have the decision passed.

An argument that made it possible to raise the voting age was that it affected everyone equally. This was heard often during the debates of 1917–1918, and it has also been repeated in earlier research.[11] Perhaps this is because age is not permanent or difficult to change, unlike characteristics such as gender or class. It is something that everyone passes through. But it was actually, as I have shown, a class issue and also reflected the gender composition of the potential electorate and where they lived.

It was perceived as such at the time, implicitly and often explicitly, among both critics and advocates of the higher voting age. Previous scholars have not problematised this aspect and thus the central role of age limits in the political process has not been noticed. Those who argued that it was the same for everybody deliberately chose to ignore that it affected a permanent social category, all those of a certain age, essentially non-settled young workers in the towns and cities. Quite obviously, that was also the intention. Data from various statistical surveys could be invoked, but it was really a struggle against the influence of the cities, a struggle concerning gender, marriage, and settled status.

At the same time, the high age limits were crucial in resolving the difficult negotiating situation. The Social Democrats, who had consistently argued that it was a class issue, changed their rhetoric in the final debate. They toned down their critique of the exclusion of the young workers in the cities and joined the Liberals and the Right in portraying it as a transient problem. Youth was just a brief period in life.

However, we can speculate as to why the Social Democrats so willingly accepted the proposals for higher age limits in the last minute. Did this reflect the old conflict between the youth association and the party that had beset the Social Democrats since the 1890s? Was it a matter of the difficulty of reconciling the perspectives of youth and class? Did it mean that they distanced themselves from the groups that voted for the Social Democratic Left Party, as the latter hinted? Did the Social Democrats also share the belief that democracy was grounded in the family, as expressed by the Right and the Liberals? Or was it a tactical move? To these questions I have no answer. The Social Democrats obviously thought that the risk of playing into the hands of the Social Democratic Left Party was worth the advantages of compromising, so that they played down the significance of the decision to raise the age limits.

Long-Term and Short-Term Processes of Change

At the same time, the analysis shows that the political crisis over democracy was not just about the forms and content of democracy. It was also a reflection of a deeper economic transformation that in turn affected the short-term economic development, the nation's institutions, and the demographic development. These observations are fairly well established in previous research, but my study shows that the discussion of suffrage in the parliamentary debates was also fundamentally a question of age categorisation in society. Class, gender, town, and country were basically concepts that were also coded with age-related meanings, some of them explicitly voiced in the discussion and some implicit. Age was coded both by place and by social relations, the meanings of which were transformed around the turn of the century. A truly intersectional phenomenon.

A central issue for the suffrage struggle was the demographic consequences of urbanisation and rural industrialisation. These were a part of the demographic transition that in Sweden was initiated with the decline in mortality 1810–1830 which had fundamental political consequences for the organisation of poor relief and the education as well as a push factor behind emigration. It also accounted for the demographic character of the growing cities and rural industrial communities during the latter part of the nineteenth and early twentieth century with a large proportion of young and unmarried working-class people, which was reinforced when emigration declined. The conflicts about the political competence of the working class, their right to vote in municipal and parliamentary elections, were waged against this background, and the meanings were clear in the debate about marriage and the family as a basic social institution to be represented in politics. Demographics were also a subset in the urban-rural conflict and likewise served as a framework for legislation on children and families, and also, of course, in the discussions about the political influence of the young generation of urban workers. The debates in Parliament reflect the politicians' attempts to understand, interpret, and control social development.

Age limits were the key to democracy with guarantees. When Parliament agreed on the high voting and eligibility ages for municipalities and county councils, it was also possible to preserve the position of the First Chamber.

The Swedish path to a more democratic social order was just as complicated and contradictory as suggested in the research that I discussed at the start of this book. A need was identified to conduct more detailed investigations of democratisation processes in view of the fact that these can reflect different contemporary processes. This study has drawn attention to different logics for the suffrage struggle in the municipalities and in Parliament, along with the long-term demographic consequences and the conflict between town and country as interacting factors in the discussion of the voting age.

But as recent researchers have also underscored, the struggle for and against the forms and content of democracy has no end point—it is still going on. The continuing debates about the people excluded in the 1918–1921 decisions are a good demonstration of this. Democracy was not fully accomplished. The struggle to include the excluded (those dependent on poor relief, those with unpaid taxes), the issue of voting and eligibility ages in the twentieth century, and the slow dismantling of the First Chamber, all this was rooted in the processes described in this book. These processes created the institutional and political conditions for the development of democracy after 1921, but also its limitations and deadlocks. People wondered whether it was reasonable that some groups, such as the young, those in long-term dependence on poor relief, or those who could not put away money to pay their taxes, were denied a vote (Fig. 8.2). The various thresholds were gradually abolished, military training being the first. But the suffrage struggle had taken on a different meaning and form; there was no longer just one suffrage issue but several distinct issues. The restrictions imposed on people's citizenship were no longer dealt with collectively in the political discourse, but separately. The issues were: the right of young people to vote; suffrage for those who did not pay taxes; completion of military training as a prerequisite for voting; granting suffrage to people declared legally incompetent or sentenced for criminal offences. The demands for reforms were now driven by various organisations, individuals, or groups, and new issues now became relevant, such as the right of immigrants to vote in municipal elections and the right of Swedes living abroad to vote in parliamentary elections. It was not until the 1970s that the position of the First Chamber was resolved and the unicameral Riksdag was established. At the same time, the voting age was lowered to 18. Those under the age of 18 still lack the right to vote.[12]

Fig. 8.2 First of May demonstration on Kungsgatan, Stockholm in 1934. The young generation's voting rights issue was not resolved with the reforms of 1918–21. Their suffrage struggle also characterised politics during the 1920s and 1930s. (Source: Foto, Axel Malmström. Arbetarrörelsens arkiv och bibliotek)

Notes

1. Ebba Berling Åselius, *Rösträtt med förhinder: Rösträttsstrecken i svensk politik 1900–1920* (Stockholm: Acta Universitatis Stockholmiensis, 2005), pp. 212–214.
2. Ibid., pp. 181–188.
3. Riksdagstrycket, *Bihang till samtlige riks-ståndens Protokoll vid Lagtima Riksdagen i Stockholm Åren 1859 och 1860. Bilagor till första samlingen. 1sta Afdelningen. Tillförordnade Kommitterades afgifna och genom Kongl. Maj:ts Nådiga Propositioner eller Skrifvelser till Rikets Ständer öfverlemnade Betänkanden*, ed. Christian Nauman (Stockholm: P. A. Norstedt & Söner, 1866), p. 306.
4. Inclusion can also be said to have been based on ideas about what the individual contributed to the community. See Jonas Hultin Rosenberg och Fia Sundevall, "Contributivist views on democratic inclusion: On economic contribution as a condition for the right to vote", *Critical Review of International Social and Political Philosophy* 31 juli, 2022, s. 1–25.
5. Ibid.
6. Erla Hulda Halldórsdóttir and Ragnheiður Kristjánsdóttir, "Genomförandet: Politiken, institutionerna, valdeltagandet på Island", *Nordisk tidskrift för vetenskap, konst och industri* 2022:3; Berling Åselius (2005, pp. 188–189); Minna, Harjula, "The Poor and Deservingness for Political and Social Citizenship: 'Universal suffrage' in Finland Since 1906", *Suffrage, Capital and Welfare: Conditional Citizenship in Historical Perspective*, Eds. Fia Cottrell-Sundevall, and Ragnheiður Kristjánsdóttir (Palgrave, 2024), pp. 225–250.
7. Berling Åselius (2005, p. 189, 230).
8. According to a statement in the debate by the minister Lövgren, it was at the age of 27 that men and women voters were equal in number in the population. He commented on the discussion about the possibility of different voting ages for men and women and argued that the difference in their number did not affect the development of society. See Riksdagstrycket, *Protokoll FK 1918:27*, p. 26.
9. Niclas Stenlås, "Demokratins vedersakare? Högerns kamp för och emot demokratin", i Christer Jönsson (red.), *Rösträtten 80 år: Forskarantologi* (Stockholm: Justitiedepartementet, 2001), pp. 64–67.
10. Carlsson Wetterberg, Christina, "Kvinnans rätt och nationens väl: Debatten kring 1920 års giftermålsbalk", i Lars M. Andersson (red.), *Rätten: En festskrift till Bengt Ankarloo* (Lund: Nordic Academic Press, 2000), p. 63.
11. See, e.g., Stenlås (2001, p. 66); Berling Åselius (2005).
12. Sandin and Josefsson 2022; Berg and Ericsson (eds.), 2021; Fia Sundevall, Annika Berg, and Bengt Sandin, "An Unfinished Suffrage Reform: Voting Rights in Sweden after the 'Democratic Breakthrough'", *Scandinavian Journal of History* 2024. 2024 vol. 49. No 3, 376–396.

Sources and Literature

Unpublished Sources

Stadsarkivet i Norrköping

Släkten Swartz i Norrköping Arkiv

Arbetarrörelsens arkiv och bibliotek

Hjalmar Brantings arkiv 1889–1922
Socialdemokratiska riksdagsgruppen, Protokoll 1918–1923, vol. A 2:2 1918–1920
Socialdemokratiska riksdagsgruppen, Förtroenderådets protokoll 1918–1920

Uppsala universitetsbibliotek

Edéns arkiv
Gunnar Gerdners papper
Handskriftssamlingen

Riksarkivet

Andrakammarriksdagens arkiv
Lindmanska samlingen
Värner Rydéns arkiv

B. Sandin, *Voting and Eligibility Age in Sweden, 1866–1921*,
https://doi.org/10.1007/978-3-031-95276-0

Baroniet Adelswärds gårdsarkiv

Theodors Adelswärds tal

Internet

historia.se/löner och inflation., http://historicalstatistics.org/Jamforelsepris.htm. Accessed 17 October 2022.

https://www.riksdagen.se/sv/dokument-lagar; https://stockholmskallan.stockholm.se

Newspapers

Dagens Nyheter
Dagny: Tidning för svenska kvinnorörelsen
FRAM: Socialdemokratiska Ungdomsförbundets Organ
Frihet: Organ för Sveriges socialdemokratiska ungdomsförbund
Morgonbris: Tidning för den socialdemokratiska kvinnorörelsen
Post-och Inrikes Tidningar
Social-Demokraten
Svenska Dagbladet

Primary Sources

Betänkande och förslag angående minderåriga förbrytares behandling. 1899. Stockholm: K. L. Beckmans Boktryckeri.

Bihang till Riksdagens Protokoll 1862–1863, 3 Saml. *Konstitutionsutskottets Memorial* no. 7.

Bihang till samtlige riks-ståndens Protokoll vid Lagtima Riksdagen i Stockholm Åren 1859 och 1860. Bilagor till första samlingen. 1sta Afdelningen. Tillförordnade Kommitterades afgifna och genom Kongl. Maj:ts Nådiga Propositioner eller Skrifvelser till Rikets Ständer öfverlemnade Betänkanden, ed. Christian Nauman. 1866. Stockholm: P. A. Norstedt & Söner.

Branting, Hjalmar. 1893. Motion nr 32 Hj. Branting, med förslag till principuttalanden dels emot planerna inom första kammaren om ny utredning av rösträttsfrågan och af rösträttens s. k. garantier, dels emot andra kammarens förslag om 500-kr streck. *Folkriksdagen: Tryckta handlingar vid 1893 års folkriksdag*. Uppsala.

Branting, Hjalmar. 1900. Rösträtt och värnplikt: Kätterska strötankar. *SocialDemokraten*, July 1.

Branting, Hjalmar. 1927. *Tal och skrifter* 3: *Kampen för demokratin* 1. Stockholm: Tiden.

Clason, Sam. 1902. *Hvad gäller rösträttsfrågan: Statistik och anmärkningar*. Stockholm: Nordiska bokhandeln.

De Geer, Louis. 1865. Ännu ett ord om representationsförslaget. *Post-och Inrikes Tidningar*, September 23.

De Geer, Louis. 1906. *Minnen* (2 vols.). Stockholm: P. A. Norstedt & Söner.

Folkriksdagen 1893, 1896: Samling Tryckta handlingar. n.d. n.p.

Folkriksdagen: Tryckta handlingar vid 1893 års folkriksdag. 1893. Uppsala.

Hagman, Konrad. 1911. *Sveriges kommunallagar: Förordningarna den 21 mars 1862 jämte en mängd andra till kommunallagstiftningen hörande författningar*. Stockholm: Fröléen.

Hamilton, Hugo E. G. 1956. In *Dagböcker 1917–1919*, ed. Gunnar Gerdner and Carl-Gustaf Thomasson. Stockholm: Norstedt.

Hansson, Per Albin. 1908. Ungdomens medborgrätt. *Fram: Socialdemokratiska Ungdomsförbundets Organ*, 1, p. 2.

Justitiestatsministern ämbetsberättelse. 1900. *BiSOS B, Rättsväsendet: Ny följd XLII:2 1899*. Stockholm.

Kungl. Kommerskollegii Afdelning för Arbetsstatistik. 1911. *Arbetsstatistik L:1: Till belysning af Landtarbetarnas arbets- och löneförhållanden i Sverige år 1910*. Stockholm: P. A. Norstedt & Söner.

Kungl. Statistiska centralbyrån. 1871. *BiSOS 1870 A, Befolkningen: Tredje avdelningen*. Stockholm: P. A. Norstedt & Söner.

Kungl. Statistiska centralbyrån. 1881. *BiSOS, BiSOS 1880 A, Befolkningen: Tredje avdelningen*. Stockholm.

Kungl. Statistiska centralbyrån. 1892. *BiSOS 1890 A, Befolkningen: Tredje avdelningen*. Stockholm.

Kungl. Statistiska centralbyrån. 1901. *BiSOS 1900 A, Befolkningen: Tredje avdelningen*. Stockholm.

Kungl. Statistiska centralbyrån. 1903a. *BiSOS G, Fångvården: Ny följd XLIII 1901*. Stockholm.

Kungl. Statistiska centralbyrån. 1903b. *BiSOS R, Valstatistik XV: Riksdagsmannavalen 1900–1902*. Stockholm.

Kungl. Statistiska centralbyrån. 1904. *BiSOS R, Valstatistik XIV:3: Valrätt till riksdagens andra kammare 1900*. Stockholm.

Kungl. Statistiska centralbyrån. 1907. *BiSOS B, Rättsväsendet: Ny följd XLVIII:2 1905*. Stockholm.

Kungl. Statistiska centralbyrån. 1908. BiSOS R, Valstatistik XIV:4: Valrätt till riksdagens andra kammare år 1900. Kvinnor över 24 år. Stockholm.

Kungl. Statistiska centralbyrån. 1913. *Folkräkningen den 31 december 1910: II. Folkmängdens fördelning efter kön, ålder och civilstånd*. Stockholm.

Kungl. Statistiska centralbyrån. 1915. *SOS, Allmänna val: Landstingsmannavalen år 1914.* Stockholm.

Kungl. Statistiska centralbyrån. 1916. *Statistiska meddelanden*, Serie A, Band 1:5, *Utom äktenskapet födda barn.* Stockholm.

Kungl. Statistiska centralbyrån. 1920. *SOS, Allmänna val: Kommunala valen år 1919.* Stockholm: P. A. Norstedt & Söner.

Kungl. Statistiska centralbyrån. 1921. *SOS, Allmänna val: Kommunala valen år 1920.* Stockholm: P. A. Norstedt & Söner.

Kungl. Statistiska centralbyrån. 1926. *Folkräkningen den 31 december 1920: III. Folkmängden efter ålder, kön, civilstånd och födelseort. Äktenskapen efter varaktighet och efter makarnas ålder.* Stockholm.

Möller, Gustav. 1918. Studier i valstatistiken. *Tiden*: 5.

Nilsson, August. 1908. *Rapport över den Socialdemokratiska riksdagsgruppens verksamhet under treårsperioden 1906–1908.* Stockholm.

Palmstierna, Erik. 1953. *Orostid: Politiska dagboksanteckningar 2, 1917–1919.* Stockholm: Tiden.

Statistisk årsbok för Stockholms stad 1920. 1921. Stockholm.

Statistisk tidskrift 1898. 1900. Stockholm: P. A. Norstedt & Söner.

Statistisk tidskrift 1903:2. 1905. Stockholm: P. A. Norstedt & Söner.

Statistisk tidskrift 1912. 1913. Stockholm: P. A. Norstedt & Söner.

Stéenhoff, Frida. 1904. *Den reglementerade prostitutionen ur feministisk synpunkt.* Stockholm: Björck & Börjesson.

Sundbärg, Gustav. 1903. Rikets folkmängd åren 1750–1900. *Statistisk tidskrift* 2:169–170.

Sundbärg, Gustav. 1913. *Emigrationsutredningen: Betänkande i utvandringsfrågan och därmed sammanhängande spörsmål.* Stockholm: Nordiska bokhandeln.

Wägner, Elin. 1908. *Norrtullsligan: Elisabeths krönika.* Stockholm: Ljus.

Wägner, Elin, and Helena Forsås-Scott. 2003. *Pennskaftet.* Stockholm: Svenska Akademien i samverkan med Atlantis.

Wicksell, Anna. 1910. De gifta kvinnorna och kommunallagarna. *Dagny: Tidning för svenska kvinnorörelsen* 3:28–30.

Winroth, A. O. 1913. Myndighetsålder. In *Nordisk Familjebok.* Stockholm: Nordisk Familjeboks förlag.

Literature

Ahlbeck, Anders, and Fia Sundevall. 2021. Värnplikt, rösträtt och kön: Värnpliktsstrecket i debatt och praktik. In *Allmän rösträtt? Rösträttens begränsningar i Sverige efter 1921*, ed. Annika Berg and Martin Ericsson. Göteborg and Stockholm: Makadam.

Åmark, Klas. 2002. Familj, försörjning och livslopp under 1900-talet. In *Familjeangelägenheter: Modern historisk forskning om välfärdsstat, genus och politik*, ed. Helena Bergman and Peter Johansson. Eslöv: Brutus Östlings bokförlag Symposion.

Ambjörnsson, Ronny. 1988. *Den skötsamme arbetaren: Idéer och ideal i ett norrländskt sågverkssamhälle 1880–1930*. Stockholm: Carlsson.

Andræ, Carl Göran. 1998. *Revolt eller reform: Sverige inför revolutionerna i Europa 1917–1918*. Stockholm: Carlsson.

Andrén, Georg. 1933. *De ekonomiska valbarhetsvillkoren till första kammaren i 1866 RO: Deras tillkomst och motivering*. Göteborg: Wettergren och Kerbers förlag.

Andrén, Georg. 1937. *Sveriges riksdag: Historisk och statsvetenskaplig framställning*, vol. 9, *Tvåkammarsystemets tillkomst och utveckling*. Stockholm.

Arias, Santa. 2010. Rethinking Space: An Outsider's View of the Spatial Turn. *GeoJournal* 75.

Aronsson, Peter. 1992. *Bönder gör politik: Det lokala självstyret som social arena i tre Smålandssocknar, 1680–1850*. Diss., Lund University Press, Lund.

Arvidsson, Malin. 2022a. Malmös Förening för Kvinnans Politiska Rösträtt. *Ale*. 3:1–18.

Arvidsson, Malin. 2022b. Samarbete med förhinder: socialdemokratiska kvinnors relation till LKPR 1907–1921. *Arbetarhistoria*. 3–4:60–69.

Arvidsson, Malin, and Nelly Thüring. 2024. teosof, feminist, socialist. Makadam förlag.

Bagge, Gösta. 1933. *Wages, Cost of Living and National Income in Sweden 1860–1930, Vol. 2, Wages in Sweden 1860–1930*. London: P. S. King.

Beckman, Ludvig. 2018. Rösträttsåldern och demokratins avgränsningsproblem. In *Demokratins framtid*, ed. Katarina Barrling and Sören Holmberg. Stockholm: Sveriges riksdag.

Bengtsson, Erik. 2020. *Världens jämlikaste land?* Lund: Arkiv förlag.

Berg, Annika, and Martin Ericsson, eds. 2021. *Allmän rösträtt? Rösträttens begränsningar i Sverige efter 1921*. Göteborg & Stockholm: Makadam.

Berggren, Henrik. 1995. *Seklets ungdom: Retorik, politik och modernitet 1900–1939*. Diss., Tiden, Stockholm.

Berggren, Lars, and Kjell Östberg. 2018. Reformism eller revolution: Arbetarrörelsen inför rösträttsbeslutet 1918–19. In *Rösträttens århundrade: Kampen, utvecklingen och framtiden för demokratin i Sverige*, ed. Ulrika Holgersson and Lena Wängnerud. Göteborg and Stockholm: Makadam.

Bergman, Helena, and Peter Johansson. 2002. *Familjeangelägenheter: Modern historisk forskning om välfärdsstat, genus och politik*. Eslöv: Brutus Östlings bokförlag Symposion.

Berling, Åselius Ebba. 2005. *Rösträtt med förhinder: Rösträttsstrecken i svensk politik 1900–1920*. Stockholm: Acta Universitatis Stockholmiensis.

Bersbo, Zara. 2011. *"Rätt för kvinnan att blifva människa – fullt och helt": Svenska kvinnors ekonomiska medborgarskap 1921–1971*. Växjö: Linnaeus University Press.
Björk, Gunnela. 1999. *Att förhandla sitt medborgarskap: kvinnor som kollektiva politiska aktörer i Örebro 1900–1950*. Arkiv, Diss. Stockholm; Lund.
Björk, Gunnela. 2017. *Kata Dalström: agitatorn som gick sin egen väg*. Lund: Historiska Media.
Braudel, Fernand. 1981. *Civilization and Capitalism: 15th–18th Century, Vol. 1, The Structures of Everyday Life*. London: Collins.
Braudel, Fernand, and Siân Reynolds. 1985. *The Structures of Everyday Life: The Limits of the Possible*. London: Fontana.
Capoccia, Giovanni, and Daniel Ziblatt. 2010. The Historical Turn in Democratization Studies: A New Research Agenda for Europe and Beyond. *Comparative Political Studies* 43 (8–9): 931–968.
Carlsson, Sten. 1953. *Lantmannapolitiken och industrialismen: Partigruppering och opinionsförskjutningar i svensk politik 1890–1902*. Stockholm: Lantbruksförbundets Tidskrifts AB.
Carlsson Wetterberg, Christina. 1986. *Kvinnosyn och kvinnopolitik: En studie av svensk socialdemokrati 1880–1910*. Diss., Lund: Arkiv.
Carlsson Wetterberg, Christina. 2000. Kvinnans rätt och nationens väl. In *Rätten: En festskrift till Bengt Ankarloo*, ed. Lars M. Andersson. Lund: Nordic Academic Press.
Carlsson Wetterberg, Christina. 2010. *– bara ett öfverskott af lif –: En biografi om Frida Stéenhoff (1865–1945)*. Stockholm: Atlantis.
Carlsson Wetterberg, Christina. 2020. *Jag saknar fruntimmer här: En biografi över Anna Bugge Wicksell*. Stockholm: Natur & Kultur.
Collier, Ruth Berins. 1999. *Paths toward Democracy: The Working Class and Elites in Western Europe and South America*. Cambridge: Cambridge University Press.
Collier, Ruth Berins, and David Collier. 2002. *Shaping the Political Arena: Critical Junctures, the Labor Movement, and Regime Dynamics in Latin America*. Notre Dame, IN: University of Notre Dame Press.
Cottrell-Sundevall, Fia. 2024. Money and the Vote: Economic Suffrage Restrictions in Sweden, Before and After the Introduction of 'Universal Suffrage' in 1921. In *Suffrage, Capital and Welfare: Conditional Citizenship in Historical Perspective*, ed. Fia Cottrell-Sundevall and Ragnheiður Kristjánsdóttir. Palgrave.
Cottrell-Sundevall, Fia, and Ragnheiður Kristjánsdóttir, eds. 2024. *Suffrage, Capital and Welfare: Conditional Citizenship in Historical Perspective*. Palgrave.
Dahl, Robert. 1989. *Democracy and Its Critics*. New Haven: Yale University Press.
Daun, Johannes. 2016. *Vägen till den moderna familjen: Fruktsamhet i den växande industristaden Borås cirka 1830–1930*. Diss. Göteborgs universitet, Göteborg.

Edgren, Monika. 1994. *Tradition och förändring: Könsrelationer, omsorgsarbete och försörjning inom Norrköpings underklass under 1800-talet.* Diss. Lund University Press, Lund.

Ekman, Stig. 1966. *Slutstriden om representationsreformen.* Diss., Appelberg, Uppsala.

Engerman, Stanley L., and Kenneth L. Sokoloff. 2005. The Evolution of Suffrage Institutions in the New World. *Journal of Economic History* 65 (4): 891–921.

Engwall, Kristina. 2008. Barns röst och rätt. In *Att göra historia: Vänbok till Christina Florin*, ed. Maria Sjöberg and Yvonne Svanström. Stockholm: Institutet för framtidsstudier.

Engwall, Kristina, and Ingrid Söderlind. 2001. Barn och demokrati i ett historiskt perspektiv. In *Rösträtten 80 år: Forskarantologi*, ed. Christer Jönsson. Stockholm: Justitiedepartementet.

Fairclough, Isabela, and Norman Fairclough. 2013. *Political Discourse Analysis: A Method for Advanced Students.* Abingdon: Taylor & Francis.

Florin, Christina. 2006. *Kvinnor får röst: Kön, känslor och politisk kultur i kvinnornas rösträttsrörelse.* Stockholm: Atlas.

Förhammar, Staffan. 1975. *Reformvilja eller riksdagstaktik: Junkrarna och representationsfrågan 1847–54.* Stockholm: Almqvist & Wiksell.

Fraser, Nancy, and Axel Honneth. 2003. *Redistribution or Recognition? A Political-Philosophical Exchange.* London: Verso Books.

Fridholm, Rolf. 1927. Folkriksdagarna 1893 och 1896. *Statsvetenskaplig tidskrift* 30 (5): 411–440.

Geijerstam, Gustaf. 1894. *Anteckningar om arbetarförhållanden i Stockholm.* Stockholm: Samson & Wallin.

Gerdner, Gunnar. 1944. Ministären Edén och författningsrevisionen 1918. In *Statsvetenskapliga studier till Statsvetenskapliga föreningens i Uppsala tjugofemårsdag 7/11 1944*, ed. Axel Brusewitz. Uppsala: Almqvist & Wiksell.

Gerdner, Gunnar. 1960. *Krigsslut, vänsterseger och reformer: Axel Schottes "regeringsrapporter" till David Bergström 1918–1920.* Uppsala.

Gogman, Lars. 2019. Material om rösträttsfrågan i ARABs samlingar. *Arbetarhistoria*73–90.

Gröning, Lotta. 1988. *Vägen till makten: SAP:s organisation och dess betydelse för den politiska verksamheten 1900–1933.* Diss., Uppsala universitet, Uppsala.

Grönlund, Otto. 1924. Den allmänna politiska rösträtten och valen till riksdagens andra kammare åren 1911–1921 i statistisk belysning. *Statsvetenskaplig tidskrift* 27 (3): 214–267.

Gustavsson, Gunnel. 2001. Rösträtten och barnen. In *Rösträtten 80 år: Forskarantologi*, ed. Christer Jönsson. Stockholm: Justitiedepartementet.

Gustavsson, Gunnel. 2009. *Rösträtt för barn: En demokratisk framtidsfråga?* Umeå: Statsvetenskapliga institutionen.

Hägglund, Josefin. 2023. *Demokratins stridslinjer: Carl Lindhagen och politikens omvandling, 1896–1923, diss.* Huddinge: Södertörns högskola.

Halldórsdóttir, Hulda Erla, and Ragnheiður Kristjánsdóttir. 2022. Genomförandet: Politiken, institutionerna, valdeltagandet på Island. *Nordisk tidskrift för vetenskap, konst och industri* 3:287–294.

Harjula, Minna. 2024. The Poor and Deservingness for Political and Social Citizenship: "Universal suffrage" in Finland Since 1906. In *Suffrage, Capital and Welfare: Conditional Citizenship in Historical Perspective*, ed. Fia Cottrell-Sundevall and Ragnheiður Kristjánsdóttir, 225–250. Palgrave.

Hinnemo, Elin. 2016. *Inför högsta instans: Samspelet mellan kvinnors handlingsutrymme och rättslig reglering i Justitierevisionen 1760–1860*. Uppsala: Acta Universitatis Upsaliensis.

Hjärne, Harald. 1892. *Rösträtt och värneplikt: Föredrag vid ett den 9 oktober 1892 av Uppsala rösträttsförening anordnat möte mot urtima riksdagen*. Stockholm: Bibliografiska institutet.

von Hofer, Hanns. 2011. *Brott och straff i Sverige: Historisk kriminalstatistik 1750–2010, diagram, tabeller och kommentarer*. Stockholm: Kriminologiska institutionen, Stockholms universitet.

Holmbäck, Åke. 1966. Karl Staaff: Anteckningar kring en biografi. *Svensk Juristtidning* 42:42–44.

Horgby, Björn. 1993. *Egensinne och skötsamhet: Arbetarkulturen i Norrköping 1850–1940*. Stockholm: Carlsson.

Hultin Rosenberg, Jonas, and Fia Sundevall. 2022. Contributivist Views on Democratic Inclusion: On Economic Contribution as a Condition for the Right to Vote. *Critical Review of International Social and Political Philosophy*1–25.

Ihalainen, Pasi. 2017. *Springs of Democracy*. Finnish Literature Society / SKS.

Isacson, Maths, and Mats Morell. 2002. *Industrialismens tid: Ekonomisk-historiska perspektiv på svensk industriell omvandling under 200 år*. Stockholm: SNS förlag.

Jansson, Torkel. 1985. *Adertonhundratalets associationer: Forskning och problem kring ett sprängfullt tomrum eller sammanslutningsprinciper och föreningsformer mellan två samhällsformationer c:a 1800–1870*. Uppsala: Uppsala universitet.

Josefsson, Jonathan, and Bengt Sandin. 2021. Ålder som måttstock för politiskt medborgarskap: Rösträtts- och valbarhetsålder i Sverige under 1900-talet. In *Allmän rösträtt? Rösträttens begränsningar i Sverige efter 1921*, ed. Annika Berg and Martin Ericsson. Göteborg and Stockholm: Makadam.

Karlsson Sjögren, Åsa. 2006. *Männen, kvinnorna och rösträtten: Medborgarskap och representation 1723–1866*. Stockholm: Carlsson.

Karlsson Sjögren, Åsa. 2008. Kvinnors röst i sekelskiftets städer: Kommunalt valdeltagande före den allmänna rösträtten. In *Att göra historia: Vänbok till*

Christina Florin, ed. Maria Sjöberg and Yvonne Svanström. Stockholm: Institutet för framtidsstudier.

Katz, Richard S. 1997. *Democracy and Elections*. New York: Oxford University Press.

Keyssar, Alexander. 2000. *The Right to Vote: The Contested History of Democracy in the United States*. New York: Basic Books.

Knutsen, Carl Henrik, Jan Teorell, Tore Wig, Agnes Cornell, John Gerring, Haakon Gjerløw, Svend-Erik Skaaning, Daniel Ziblatt, Kyle L. Marquardt, Daniel Pemstein, and BrigitteSeim. 2019. Introducing the Historical Varieties of Democracy Dataset: Political Institutions in the Long 19th Century. *Journal of Peace Research* 3:440–451.

Knutson, Ulrika. 2020. *Den besvärliga Elin Wägner*. Lund: Historiska Media.

Koblik, Steven. 1976. Between Reform and Revolution. *Scandia* 42 (1): 115–132.

Kohl, Gerald. 2008. Alter und Wahlrecht: Zum Verhältnis bürgerlicher und politischer Rechts- und Handlungsfähigkeit seit der Mitte des 19. Jahrhunderts. *Parliaments, Estates and Representation* 28 (1): 151–163.

Krekula, Clary, Anna-Liisa Närvänen, and Elisabet Näsman. 2005. Ålder i intersektionell analys. *Kvinnovetenskaplig tidskrift* 26 (2): 81–94.

Kristjánsdóttir, Ragnheiður. 2024. The Politics, Practices, and Emotions of Suffrage Exclusion in Iceland, 1915–1934. In *Suffrage, Capital and Welfare: Conditional Citizenship in Historical Perspective*, ed. Fia Cottrell-Sundevall and Ragnheiður Kristjánsdóttir, 175–198. Palgrave.

Kronborg, Bo, and Thomas Nilsson. 1975. *Stadsflyttare: Industrialisering, migration och social mobilitet med utgångspunkt från Halmstad 1870–1910, diss.* Uppsala: Uppsala universitet.

Langkjaer, Jenny. 2011. *Övervakning för rikets säkerhet: Svensk säkerhetspolisiär övervakning av utländska personer och inhemsk politisk aktivitet, 1885–1922.* Stockholm: Acta Universitatis Stockholmiensis.

Lefebvre, Henri. 1991. *The Production of Space*. Oxford: Basil Blackwell.

Lennartsson, Rebecka. 2002. *Malaria urbana: om byråflickan Anna Johannesdotter och prostitutionen i Stockholm kring 1900*. Diss., Uppsala University, Uppsala.

Lennartsson, Rebecka. 2007. *Den sköna synderskan: sekelskiftets Stockholm : betraktelser från undersidan*. Stockholm: Norstedt.

Lewin, Leif. 1978. *Det politiska spelet: En simulering av beslutsfattandet i svensk inrikespolitik*. Stockholm.

Lewin, Leif. 2017. *Ideologi och strategi: Svensk politik under 100 år*. Stockholm: Carlsson Bokförlag.

Lewin, Leif. 2020. *Konsten att bilda regering när ingen har majoritet*. Göteborg: Daidalos.

Lindberg, Staffan, and Jan Teorell. 2018. Demokratins utveckling i världen: Tendenser under och efter rösträttens århundrade. In *Rösträttens århundrade: Kampen, utvecklingen och framtiden för demokratin i Sverige*, ed. Ulrika

Holgersson and Lena Wängnerud. Göteborg and Stockholm: Makadam i samarbete med Riksbankens jubileumsfond.

Lindgren, Cecilia. 2006. *En riktig familj: Adoption, föräldraskap och barnets bästa 1917–1975*. Stockholm: Carlsson.

Lindgren, Mattias. 2021. Hur många drabbades? Kvantitativa effekter av rösträttsbegränsningarna. In *Allmän rösträtt? Rösträttens begränsningar i Sverige efter 1921*, ed. Annika Berg and Martin Ericsson, 249–260. Göteborg and Stockholm: Makadam.

Lundberg, Victor. 2007. *Folket, yxan och orättvisans rot: Betydelsebildning kring demokrati i den svenska rösträttsrörelsens diskursgemenskap 1887–1902*. Umeå: h:ström – Text & kultur.

Lundkvist, Sven. 1977. *Folkrörelserna i det svenska samhället 1850–1920*. Stockholm: Sober.

Lundquist, Tommie. 1982. *Den disciplinerade dubbelmoralen: Studier i den reglementerade prostitutionens historia i Sverige 1859–1918*. Diss., Göteborgs universitet, Göteborg.

Manns, Ulla. 2000. Den gifta kvinnans frigörelse: Reflexioner kring rösträtt och myndighet i svensk kvinnorörelse. In *The Nordic Model of Marriage and the Welfare State*, ed. Kari Melby. Copenhagen: Nordiska Ministerrådet.

Markkola, Pirjo, Seija-Leena Nevala-Nurmi, and Irma Sulkunen. 2009. *Suffrage, Gender and Citizenship: International Perspectives on Parliamentary Reforms*. Newcastle: Cambridge Scholars Publishing.

Matović, Margareta. 1984. *Stockholmsäktenskap: Familjebildning och partnerval i Stockholm 1850–1890*. Stockholm: LiberFörlag.

Melby, Kari, Anu Pylkkänen, Bente Rosenbeck, and Christina Carlsson Wetterberg, *The Nordic Model of Marriage and the Welfare State* (Copenhagen: Nordic Council of Ministers, 2000).

Mellquist, Einar D. 1974. *Rösträtt efter förtjänst? Riksdagsdebatten om den kommunala rösträtten i Sverige 1862–1900*. Stockholm: Stadshistoriska institutet.

Montgomery, Arthur. 1947. *Industrialismens genombrott i Sverige*. Stockholm: Skoglunds bokförlag.

Nilsson, Göran B. 1964. Folkval och fyrkval 1863–1909. *Scandia* 30 (1): 89–137.

Nilsson, Göran B. 1967. *Självstyrelsens problematik: Undersökningar i svensk landstingshistoria 1839–1928*. Uppsala: Acta Universitatis Upsaliensis.

Nilsson, Göran B. 1969. Den samhällsbevarande representationsreformen. *Scandia* 35:2.

Nilsson, Torbjörn. 1994. *Elitens svängrum: Första kammaren, staten och moderniseringen 1867–1886*. Stockholm: Almqvist & Wiksell International.

Nilsson, Torbjörn. 2001. Högern 1900–1940: En historisk vandring mot demokrati. In *Rösträtten 80 år: Forskarantologi*, ed. Christer Jönsson. Stockholm: Justitiedepartementet.

Nilsson, Hans, and Lars-Göran Tedebrand. 2005. *Familjer i växande städer: Strukturer och strategier vid familjebildning i Sverige 1840–1940*. Umeå: Demografiska databasen.

Norburg, Ulrika. 2015. *Fängelse, skola, uppfostringsanstalt eller skyddshem? Åkerbrukskolonien Hall för pojkar år 1876–1940, diss*. Linköping: Linköpings universitet.

Norrlid, Ingemar. 1970. Kommunen som bolag? En studie i liberal rösträttspolitik före första världskriget. *Scandia* 36:1.

Norrlid, Ingemar. 1983. *Demokrati, skatterättvisa och ideologisk förändring: Den kommunala självstyrelsen och demokratins genombrott i Sverige*. Lund: Liber/ Gleerup.

North, Douglass C. 1990. *Institutions, Institutional Change and Economic Performance*. Cambridge: Cambridge University Press.

Ohlsson, Per T. 2017. *1918: Året då Sverige blev Sverige*. Stockholm: Albert Bonniers förlag.

Olson, Hans-Erik. 1982. *Från hemgård till ungdomsgård: En studie i den svenska hemgårdsrörelsens historia*. Stockholm: Riksförb. Sveriges fritids- och hemgårdar (RSFH).

Olsson, Lars. 1984. Barns arbete och arbetets barn. In *Barn i tid och rum*, ed. Karin Aronsson. Malmö: Liber.

Olsson, Stefan. 2003. *Den svenska högerns anpassning till demokratin*. Enskede: TPB.

Oredsson, Sverker, and Nils Edén. 2017. *Demokratins statsminister*. Stockholm: Ekerlid.

Östberg, Kjell. 1996. *Kommunerna och den svenska modellen: Socialdemokratin och kommunalpolitiken fram till andra världskriget*. Eslöv: Brutus Östlings bokförlag Symposion.

Przeworski, Adam. 2009. Conquered or Granted? A History of Suffrage Extensions. *British Journal of Political Science* 39 (2): 291–321.

Qvist, Gunnar. 1960. *Kvinnofrågan i Sverige 1809–1846: Studier rörande kvinnans näringsfrihet inom de borgerliga yrkena*. Diss., Göteborgs universitet, Göteborg.

Rasmussen Leonora Lottrup. 2024. Constitutional rights in conflict. The evolution of political and social rights in Denmark, 1849–1961. In *Suffrage, Capital and Welfare: Conditional Citizenship in Historical Perspective*, ed. Fia Cottrell-Sundevall and Ragnheiður Kristjánsdóttir, 107–128. Palgrave.

Rönblom, Hans-Krister. 1929. *Frisinnade landsföreningen 1902–1927: Skildringar ur den liberala organisationsrörelsens historia i vårt land*. Stockholm: Saxon & Lindström.

Rönnbäck, Josefin. 2004. *Politikens genusgränser: Den kvinnliga rösträttsrörelsen och kampen för kvinnors politiska medborgarskap 1902–1921*. Stockholm: Atlas.

Rönnbäck, Josefin. 2008. För förändringarnas skull: Om kvinnor, politik och kampen för medbestämmande. In *Att göra historia: Vänbok till Christina Florin*, ed. Maria Sjöberg and Yvonne Svanström. Stockholm: Institutet för framtidsstudier.

Rosenbeck, Bente, and Hanne Sanders. 2010. *Det politiska äktenskapet: 400 års historia om familj och reproduktion*. Göteborg and Stockholm: Makadam i samarbete med Centrum för Danmarksstudier vid Lunds universitet.

Runestam, Staffan. 1966. *Förstakammarhögern och rösträttsfrågan 1900–1907*. Uppsala: Acta Universitatis Upsaliensis.

Sandin, Bengt. 1986. *Hemmet, gatan, fabriken eller skolan: Folkundervisning och barnuppfostran i svenska städer 1600–1850*. Lund: Arkiv.

Sandin, Bengt. 2012. Children and the Swedish Welfare State: From Different to Similar. In *Reinventing Childhood After World War II*, ed. Paula S. Fass and Michael Grossberg, 110–138. Philadelphia: University of Pennsylvania Press.

Sandin, Bengt. 2014. History of Children's Well-Being. In *Handbook of Child Well-Being: Theories, Methods and Policies in Global Perspective*, ed. Asher Ben-Arieh, Ferran Casas, Ivar Frønes, and Jill E. Korbin. New York and London: Springer.

Sandin, Bengt. 2017. The Parent – A Cultural Invention: The Politics of Parenting. *European Journal of Developmental Psychology* 14 (6): 733–746.

Sandin, Bengt, and Jonathan Josefsson. 2022. Age as a Yardstick for Political Citizenship: Voting Age and Eligibility Age in Sweden During the Twentieth Century. *Continuity and Change* 2:257–280.

Sandin, Bengt, Johanna Sköld, and Johanna Schiratzki. 2022. Var går gränserna för statens ansvar? *Statsvetenskaplig tidskrift* 2:349–378.

Schrag, Francis. 1975. The Child's Status in the Democratic State. *Political Theory* 3 (4): 441–457.

Skottsberg, Brita. 1934. Den svenska diskussionen om parlamentarismen i samband med rösträttsfrågan 1904–1907. *Statsvetenskaplig tidskrift* 2:130–152.

Söderpalm, Sven Anders. 1969. *Storföretagarna och det demokratiska genombrottet: Ett perspektiv på första världskrigets svenska historia*. Lund: Gleerup.

Stenlås, Niclas. 2001. Demokratins vedersakare? Högerns kamp för och emot demokratin. In *Rösträtten 80 år: Forskarantologi*, ed. Christer Jönsson. Stockholm: Justitiedepartementet.

Stjernquist, Nils. 1996. *Tvåkammartiden: Sveriges riksdag 1867–1970*. Stockholm: Sveriges riksdag.

Sundevall, Fia. 2017. Military Education for Non-Military Purposes. *History of Education Review* 1:58–71.

Sundevall, Fia. 2021. Ekonomi och rösträtt: Skatteskulder, konkurs och fattigvård som rösträttshinder. In *Allmän rösträtt? Rösträttens begränsningar i Sverige efter 1921*, ed. Annika Berg and Martin Ericsson. Göteborg and Stockholm: Makadam.

Sundevall, Fia, Annika Berg, and Bengt Sandin. 2024. An Unfinished Suffrage Reform: Voting Rights in Sweden After the 'Democratic Breakthrough'. *Scandinavian Journal of History* 49 (3, 99): 376–396.

Sundkvist, Maria. 1994. *De vanartade barnen: Mötet mellan barn, föräldrar och Norrköpings barnavårdsnämnd 1903–1925.* Uppsala: Hjelm.

Svanström, Yvonne. 2006. *Offentliga kvinnor: prostitution i Sverige 1812–1918.* Stockholm: Ordfront.

Teorell, Jan, Michael Coppedge, Staffan Lindberg, and Svend-Erik Skaaning. 2019. Measuring Polyarchy Across the Globe, 1900–2017. *Studies in Comparative International Development* 54 (1): 71–95.

Thyselius, Erik. 1902. *Kampen för allmän rösträtt: En fullständig historik och förklaring öfver rösträttsfrågan från början till närvarande tid.* Stockholm: Fröléen.

Tidman, Yngve. 1998. *Spräng Amalthea! Arbete, facklig kamp och strejkbryteri i nordvästeuropeiska hamnar 1870–1914.* Lund: Lund University Press.

Tolvhed, Helena. 2010. Intersektionalitet och historievetenskap. *Scandia* 76 (1): 59–72.

Uppenberg, Carolina, and Mats Olsson. 2022. Under the Landlord's Thumb: Municipalities and Local Elites in Sweden 1862–1900. *Social History* 47 (3): 265–289.

Vallinder, Torbjörn. 1962. *I kamp för demokratin: Rösträttsrörelsen i Sverige 1866–1900.* Stockholm: Natur & Kultur.

V-Dem: Varieties of Democracy, Codebook, version 11.1. 2021, March.

Wåhlstrand, Arne. 1947. *Regeringsskiftena 1900 och 1902.* Uppsala: Almqvist & Wiksell.

Wall, John. 2012. Can Democracy Represent Children? Towards a Politics of Difference. *Childhood* 19 (1): 86–100.

Weiner, Gena. 1995. *De räddade barnen: Om fattiga barn, mödrar och fäder och deras möte med filantropin i Hagalund 1900–1940.* Uppsala: Hjelm.

Ziblatt, Daniel. 2006. How Did Europe Democratize? *World Politics* 2:311–338.

Index[1]

NUMBERS AND SYMBOLS

[1] Note: Page numbers followed by 'n' refer to notes.

B. Sandin, *Voting and Eligibility Age in Sweden, 1866–1921*,
https://doi.org/10.1007/978-3-031-95276-0

FSC
www.fsc.org
MIX
Papier | Fördert gute Waldnutzung
FSC® C083411

Kolibri 360 GmbH
Ferdinand-Jühlke-Straße 7
99095 Erfurt, Deutschland
produktsicherheit@kolibri360.de